A

DISSERTATION

ON

THE MYSTERIES

OF

THE CABIRI.

A

DISSERTATION

ON

THE MYSTERIES

OF

THE CABIRI;

OR THE

GREAT GODS OF PHENICIA, SAMOTHRACE, EGYPT, TROAS, GREECE, ITALY, AND CRETE;

BEING

An Attempt to deduce the ſeveral Orgies of

ISIS, CERES, MITHRAS, BACCHUS, RHEA, ADONIS, AND HECATE,

FROM AN

Union of the Rites commemorative of the DELUGE with the Adoration of the HOST of HEAVEN.

BY GEORGE STANLEY FABER, A. M.

FELLOW OF LINCOLN COLLEGE.

Η γαρ τον ϐρανον προσαραξειν, η τα κρυπτα της Ισιδος εκφανειν, η το εν αβυσσω απορρητον δειξειν, η στησειν την Βαριν, η τα μελη τϐ Οσιριδος διασκεδασειν τῳ Τυφωνι, η αλλο τι τοιουτον απειλει ποιησειν. Jamb. de Myſt. ſect. vi. cap. 51.

VOL. I.

OXFORD:

AT THE UNIVERSITY PRESS FOR THE AUTHOR:

And ſold by F. and C. RIVINGTON, London; and W. HANWELL and J. PARKER, Oxford.

1803

TO THE

RIGHT REVEREND FATHER IN GOD

SAMUEL

LORD BISHOP OF ST. ASAPH.

THIS WORK,

AS A SMALL TRIBUTE OF VENERATION

JUSTLY DUE

TO SPLENDID TALENTS AND PROFOUND ERUDITION

UNIFORMLY AND SUCCESSFULLY DEVOTED

TO THE

CAUSE OF GENUINE RELIGION,

IS,

WITH PERMISSION,

RESPECTFULLY INSCRIBED,

BY

HIS LORDSHIP'S MUCH OBLIGED

HUMBLE SERVANT,

GEORGE STANLEY FABER.

PREFACE.

THE object of the following Diſſertation is to ſhew, that the Myſteries of the Cabiri, which I conceive to have been the very ſame as thoſe of Iſis, Ceres, Mithras, Bacchus, Rhea, and Adonis, were principally founded upon certain mutilated traditions of the Deluge. Pagan records abound with corrupted accounts of that cataſtrophè, and even frequently enter into the minutiæ of its hiſtory with a moſt ſurpriſing degree of accuracy; inſomuch that the moſt careleſs obſerver cannot but be ſtruck with their reſemblance, in this point, to the Moſaical narrative. All *ſuch* traditions may be conſidered as the *direct* atteſtations, which the Mythology of the Gentiles bears to the exiſtence of a general flood. In addition to them, it is replete alſo with *alluſions* to it. Theſe latter indeed are neceſſarily leſs obvious than the former, and are therefore more eaſily overlooked; but yet, when combined together, when viewed in all their different bearings, and when connected with a variety of kindred circumſtances, they will be found to afford, if not ſo palpable, yet certainly a more curious proof of the authenticity of the Book of Geneſis.

With reſpect to the Titans, whom the reader will find to make a very prominent figure in the enſuing pages, it is proper to obſerve, that in elucidating their Hiſtory I have been obliged to diſſent entirely from the ſyſtem adopted in that eminently learned work, *the Analyſis of ancient Mythology.* I have long ſuſpected, that the Titanic war, ſo celebrated in Grecian ſtory, relates to the events of the deluge, and not to the miraculous overthrow of Nimrod and his followers in the plains of Shinar. This I intimated in a former publication [a]; but was at that time prevented, by the extenſiveneſs of my ſubject, from purſuing the ſuppoſition in the manner which I could have wiſhed to have

[a] Horæ Moſaicæ, vol. i. p. 122, 209.

done.

done. Upon communicating my ſentiments to Mr. Bryant, I had the pleaſure of finding, that his opinion was at preſent *nearly* the ſame as my own; and I doubt not, but that the permiſſion, which he has given me, to ſanction my hypotheſis with the weight of ſuch an authority as his, will have its due influence upon the minds of my readers. "You "make an excuſe," ſays he, "for differing "from me in reſpect to the Titans and gi"ants of antiquity. There is no occaſion for "apology at any rate: but more particularly "as I am of the ſame opinion; and have "been ſo for many years.—I was of a differ"ent opinion once, as you very properly in"timate; but I was obliged to alter my "notions."

In the ſyſtem, which forms the baſis of the preſent work, it is ſuppoſed, that the word *Titan* is derived from Tit (טיט), *the colluvies of the deluge*; and conſequently, that it ſignifies *a diluvian*. It is further conjectured, that the appellation *Titans* was a general name of all the perſons, who were living at the

the era of the deluge, both thoſe who were ſaved in the Ark, and thoſe who periſhed beneath the waves. Hence it will follow, that the Titans of ancient Mythology ought to be divided into two diſtinct claſſes: the former of which, conſiſting of Cronus and his ſeven children, mentioned by Sanchoniatho, and enumerated by the Orphic poet, is the arkite Ogdoad; while the latter, conſiſting of the other Titans, who are feigned to have fought againſt Jupiter, and to have been overthrown by that deity, comprehends all the perſons who were deſtroyed by the flood. To this diviſion of the Titans I have been obliged to have recourſe, in order to account for the ſeeming contrariety of their being ſometimes deſcribed as the impious opponents of heaven, and sometimes as the great gods of the Gentiles: nor do I ſee how it can be accounted for on any other principles, though upon this point I differ apparently, though I believe not really, from Mr. Bryant. In his laſt letter to me he ſays, "There "ſeems to me to be no occaſion to make "any diviſion of the Titans, eight of whom "were

" were ſaved in the deluge, when all the reſt " of that name periſhed [b]. What you men- " tion concerning the Cabiri appears to me " very juſt: every point is confirmed by hiſ- " tory.—I have written a great deal upon " the gods of Greece and Rome, and upon " the principal female deities, which may " poſſibly be publiſhed after my death. It " is of large amount, and aims at the ſame " ſcope, to which you direct your preſent " labours. I have alſo written concerning " the ſeveral parts of the world, to which " thoſe of the diſperſion betook themſelves, " which were widely ſeparated and far diſ- " tant: yet the identity of the original peo- " ple may be plainly in all parts perceived." I need ſcarcely obſerve, how great an acquiſition to every ſerious believer in the truth of the Jewiſh Scriptures this promiſed work of Mr. Bryant will be.

[b] This in reality is the whole that I contend for: namely, that *all* the diluvians were called *Titans*; that *eight* of thoſe Titans were ſaved; and that *the reſt* of mankind, namely *the other* Titans, miſerably periſhed.

In

In the following attempt to elucidate the Myſteries of the Cabiri, I have ventured to diſſent from *the Analyſis of ancient Mythology*, in various matters, beſides my account of the Titanic war [c]. I have alſo differed conſiderably from many other very learned and valuable works; but I truſt, that, whenever I have found it neceſſary to expreſs my diſſent, I have always done it in that reſpectful language, to which the worth and talents of their authors ſo juſtly intitle them. The field of inquiry is open to all; nor ought any man to be cenſured on the ſcore of preſumption, merely becauſe he diſagrees with his predeceſſors. Fully conſcious at the ſame time of the deep obſcurity, which involves the hiſtory of the Cabiri, as I have made objections to the ſyſtems of others, I am prepared to expect, that objections may alſo be made to various parts of my own

[c] I feel a great pleaſure however in finding, that the ſentiments of Mr. Bryant reſpecting the Cabiri of Sanchoniatho perfectly accord with my own. See a ſhort chapter upon this ſubject in Anal. vol. ii. p. 461.

ſyſtem.

ſyſtem. Upon this point however I can with the utmoſt ſincerity adopt the ſentiment of Tully; *Refellere ſine pertinacia, et refelli ſine iracundia, parati ſumus.*

OXFORD, *Oct.* 22, 1802.

CONTENTS.

VOL. I.

CHAP.

VOL. II.

A DISSERTATION ON THE MYSTERIES OF THE CABIRI.

CHAP. I.

PRELIMINARY OBSERVATIONS.

THE fictions of ancient poetry, however wild and extravagant, will generally be found to comprehend ſome portion of hiſtorical truth. Hence, the claſſical mythology of paganiſm, although it be now happily ſuperſeded by a purer religion, may yet give riſe to inveſtigations, not totally devoid of utility. Impious and abſurd as it was, much valuable information may nevertheleſs be extracted from it; and it is pleaſing to find, that, while the idols of the Gentiles bow down before the God of Chriſtianity, their fabulous legends alſo are conſtrained to bear teſtimony to the truth of Scripture.

Perhaps no part of heathen mythology is involved in a greater degree of obſcurity, than the Myſteries of the Cabiri. The rites of theſe highly venerated perſonages were carefully concealed from the vulgar eye; the authors, who occaſionally mention them, ſeem to ſhudder with ſuperſtitious dread at the thought of revealing their ſecrets to the profane;

fane; the ſcattered fragments of their hiſtory are full of apparent contradictions; and, in addition to theſe difficulties, their officiating prieſts were not unfrequently confounded with the gods whom they worſhipped, and both called by the common name of *Cabiri*[a].

Many different attempts have been made to throw light upon the obſcure hiſtory of the deities in queſtion; but theſe, might I venture to obſerve it without the imputation of invidiouſneſs, appear for the moſt part to have failed, from taking only a *partial* view of the ſubject. In the framing of each hypotheſis, ſome ſtriking *particulars* indeed have been ſelected, and thoſe diſcuſſed with much learning and ingenuity; but, at the ſame time, other circumſtances have been totally omitted, which, if examined, would have

[a] Θεραπευτας των ἱερων εκαλουν Καβειρους, και Κορυβαντας, και Πανας, και Σατυρους, και Τιτυρους, και τον θεον Βακχον, και την Ῥεαν Κυβελην, και Κυβηνη, και Δινδυμηνην. Strab. Geog. lib. x. p 469. Ετι δ' αν τις και ταυτα εὑροι περι των δαιμονων,—'τι ου προσπολοι θεων μονον, αλλα και αυτοι θεοι προσηγορευθησαν. Ibid. The prieſts of the Cabiri were ſometimes alſo ſtyled *Camilli*, or *Mercurii*. This interchange of names between the deities and their prieſts ſeems to have very frequently taken place. Thus, in addition to the inſtance of the Cabiric gods and their miniſters, we find, that one of the Roman emperors of infamous memory aſſumed the title of *Egh-Baal*, which the Greeks expreſſed *Heliogabalus*, in honour of עגל–בעל *the helio-arkite ox Baal*, whoſe prieſt he had formerly been.

been

been found utterly irreconcileable with the system, thus too hastily adopted.

Bp. Horsley[b], Dr. Cudworth[c], Mr. Cooke[d], and Mr. Maurice[e], are of opinion, that in the Cabiric Triad we may discover a remote allusion to the doctrine of the Trinity; a doctrine, which, however degraded, they imagine to have been in some measure known to the Gentile world: while Mr. Parkhurst[f] conjectures, that this Triad relates to a certain material Trinity of the heavens, consisting of Fire, Light, and Air, which he affirms to have been worshipped by the Phenicians.

Both these suppositions evidently originate from the oriental etymology of the word *Cabiri*[g], and from the circumstance of those

[b] Horsley's Tracts, p. 44 edit 1789

[c] Cudworth's Intell System, p 451, 547.

[d] Cooke's Inquiry into the Patriarchal and Druidical Religion, p. 37, 53. I fully agree with Mr Cooke, that the Abiri, who seem to have been worshipped at Abury, were the same as the Cabiri: but I cannot think, that they had even the remotest connection with the doctrine of the Trinity. That the worship of the Samothracian deities was established in Britain, appears from the testimony both of Artemidorus and Dionysius. Artem. apud Strab. Geog. lib. iv p 198. Dion Perieg v. 565. But concerning these matters more shall be said hereafter. Vide infra chap iv.

[e] Indian Ant. vol. iv. p. 707.

[f] Heb. Lex. Voc. אבר, כבר.

[g] כבירים Cabirim, *the mighty ones*.

 dei-

deities being occaſionally deſcribed as *three:* but, unleſs their number be uniformly the ſame, and their hiſtory unincumbered with matters directly hoſtile to ſuch opinions, the ſyſtems at preſent under conſideration will ſcarcely be found tenable. In the ſequel however it will appear, that their number is by no means limited to *three*; and that their hiſtory comprehends ſuch a ſingular combination of events, that we are almoſt compelled to refer their Myſteries to a totally different origin.

Reland[g] ſuppoſes the Cabiri to be gods of the infernal regions, on account of their connection with Mercury, Ceres, Pluto, and Proſerpine.

This hypotheſis ſpeaks the truth, but not the whole truth; for it muſt neceſſarily be deemed imperfect, becauſe the principal matter is totally omitted, no reaſon being aſſigned *why* ſuch a connection ſhould have ſubſiſted[h].

Dr. Shuckford[i] thinks, that the Cabiri were the ſons of Mizraim; but deſpairs of reducing their hiſtory to any tolerable conſiſtency, becauſe, as he imagines, moſt of the

[g] Diſſert. de Cab apud Ugol Theſ. ant. ſacr. v. 23.

[h] This ſubject will be conſidered at large hereafter. Vide infra chap v.

[i] Connect. vol. 1. p. 213.

various

various fables, which are related concerning them, were the inventions of a comparatively modern period.

That the primitive traditions were corrupted, I am very ready to allow; but I can by no means grant, that the bulk of their hiſtory is a mere poetical legend, or a recent Hellenic fabrication.

Col. Vallancey adopts the opinion of M. Court de Gebelin concerning pagan mythology in general; and aſſerts, that the "names and "explanations of the Cabiri appear to be all al-"legorical, and to have ſignified no more than "an almanack of the viciſſitudes of the ſea-"ſons, calculated for the operations of agricul-"ture." Hence he makes the *Uranus* of Sanchoniatho to be a corruption of the Iriſh word Aoran, *a ploughman*; his eldeſt ſon Ilus to be *weeds*, or *ſtones*; his ſecond ſon Betylus to be Biadhtal, *food*; his third ſon Dagon to be Dagh, *great crops of wheat*; and his fourth ſon Atlas to be Athlus, *fallow*. In a ſimilar manner, Cronus, whom Sanchoniatho declares to be the ſame as Ilus, he ſuppoſes to be Crainn, *a ploughman*; Ceres to be Ceara, *a flail*; and her daughter Proſerpine to be Por-Saibhean, *the ſeed of oats*. Such is the firſt part of his ſyſtem. Afterwards he maintains, that Eon, Cronus, Saturn, and Dagon, are all one perſon, and all equally the patriarch Adam: and concludes at length, that the Myſteries of the Cabiri were founded upon the arkite worſhip[k].

The hypotheſis of Bp. Cumberland varies widely from thoſe of Horſley, Cudworth, Cooke, Maurice, Parkhurſt, Reland, Shuckford, and Vallancey; being founded partly upon the account of the Cabiri given by Mnaſeas in *the ſcholia upon Apollonius Rhodius*, and partly upon the narrative of Sanchoniatho preſerved by Euſebius in his *Præparatio Evangelica*. He ſuppoſes, that there were two diſtinct races of Cabiri, the firſt conſiſting of Ham and Mizraim, whom he conceives to be the *Jupiter* and *Dionuſus* of Mnaſeas[l]; the ſecond, of the children of Shem, who are the *Cabiri* of Sanchoniatho, while their father Sydyk is conſequently the ſcriptural *Shem*[m].

It is ſuperfluous to point out the inconſiſtency of theſe two genealogies[n]; the Biſhop himſelf is perfectly aware of it, and the reaſon, which he aſſigns for the ſuppoſed irregularity, is, that the prieſts carefully concealed the names of the Cabiri, in order that they

[k] Collect. de Reb Hibern. No 13 Præf Sect 5

[l] Append de Cabiris ap. Orig Gent. p. 364, 376

[m] Ibid p 357.

[n] The conſideration of Bp. Cumberland's ſyſtem ſhall be reſumed more at large hereafter Vide infra chap ii. It may not be improper to obſerve, that Montfaucon, and Banier, do not attempt to decide who the Cabiri were. Ant explain. b. ii. c. 7 and Suppl. b. v. c. 4. Mythol. b. vii. c. 8.

might

might occaſionally enroll among them any eminent perſons although of another family, and thus have it in their power to increaſe or diminiſh the number of their gods at pleaſure.

I ſhall now, previous to a more particular inquiry into the nature of the Cabiric Myſteries, proceed to give a brief ſtatement of the plan of the enſuing diſquiſition.

We have no reaſon to think, that the idolatry of the Gentile world was of a merely arbitrary contrivance; on the contrary, it ſeems to have been built, almoſt univerſally, upon a traditional remembrance of certain real events. *Theſe events I apprehend to be the deſtruction of the firſt race of mankind by the waters of the deluge, and the introduction of the Sabian ſuperſtition by Nimrod.*

It is ſcarcely poſſible, that all recollection of the flood could have been very ſoon eraſed from the minds of the Noachidæ; hence it is natural to ſuppoſe, that the anniverſary either of its commencement, or of its termination, would be duly commemorated by a ſolemn religious feſtival. Such a commemoration, in its primitive ſimplicity, would doubtleſs be not only innocent, but even ſerviceable to the cauſe of piety and morality; but at the ſame time it would be liable to groſs abuſe, which in the reſult proved unhappily

happily to be the cafe. The commemorative feftival, however irreprehenfible it might originally have been, was but too foon corrupted; Noah and his family were elevated to the rank of demons or hero-gods; and at length unblufhing obfcenity ufurped the name and garb of religion.

The antediluvian worfhip appears to have been of a totally different fort. "In the days "of Enos the fon of Seth," fays Maimonides, "men fell into grievous errors, and even "Enos himfelf partook of their infatuation. "Their language was, that *fince God had "placed on high the heavenly bodies, and ufed "them as his minifters, it was evidently his "will, that they fhould receive from men the "fame veneration, as the fervants of a great "prince juftly claim from the fubject multitude.* "Impreffed with this notion, they began to "build temples to the Stars, to facrifice to "them, and to worfhip them, in the vain "expectation, that they fhould thus pleafe "the Creator of all things. At firft indeed, "they did not fuppofe the Stars to be the "only deities, but adored in conjunction with "them the Lord God Omnipotent. In pro"cefs of time however that great and vene"rable name was totally forgotten; and the "whole human race retained no other reli-

"gion,

"gion, than the idolatrous worſhip of the "hoſt of heaven [n]."

With this ſuperſtition the patriarch Ham ſeems to have been tainted, and to have conveyed the knowledge of it to his own particular deſcendants. Although he had been mercifully preſerved in the ark, along with the other members of his family, yet his ſubſequent conduct plainly ſhewed, that he was not only ignorant of the ſanctifying influence of pure religion, but that he was a ſtranger to the laws even of common decency. This leaven of the ancient idolatry lay ſecretly working in the boſoms of his poſterity, during the ſpace of near four hundred years [o];

[n] בימי אנוש טעו בני האדם טעות גדול—ואנוש עצמו מן הטועים היה וזו היתה טעותם: אמרו הואיל והאל ברא כוכבים אלו וגלגלים להנהיג את העולם ונתנם במרום וחלק להם כבוד והם שמישים המשמשים לפניו ראויים הם ולפארם ולחלוק להם כבוד וזהו רצון האל ברוך הוא לגדל ולכבד העומדים לפניו וזהו כבודו של מלך: כיון שעלה דבר זה על לבם התחילו לבנות לכוכבים היכלות ולהקריב להן קרבנות ולשבחן—ולהשתחוות למולן—היה עיקר עבודת כ״ום וכך היו אומרים עובדיה היודעים עיקרה לא שהן אומרים שאין שם אלוה אלא כוכב;—וכיון שארכו הימים נשתקע השם הנכבד והנורא מפי כל היקום כמדעתם ולא הוירוהו; Maimon. de Idololatria. See alſo Sanchon apud Euſeb Præp. Evan. l. 1. c. 10.

[o] It is not eaſy to fix the preciſe era of the building of the Babylonic tower, becauſe the ſacred hiſtorian does not connect it with any of the various dates that he ſpecifies. I cannot think however, that this ſtupendous work was undertaken at ſuch

but was prevented from openly ſhewing itſelf by the dread of Noah, who was ſtill living.

ſuch a *very* early period after the deluge, as the birth of Peleg, which, according to the chronology of the Hebrew Pentateuch at leaſt, was at the cloſe of the firſt poſtdiluvian century, becauſe it appears to be phyſically impoſſible, that mankind ſhould have ſufficiently multiplied in ſo ſhort a ſpace of time. (See various calculations in Anc. Univ. Hiſt. vol 1 p. 361.) But, however this may be, there is perhaps no juſt ground for ſuppoſing, that the birth of Peleg, and the building of the tower, were contemporary; notwithſtanding they are uſually placed at the ſame era, and notwithſtanding the name of *Peleg* is thought to allude to the diſperſion from the plains of Shinar. *Two* entirely different events, ſubſequent to each other in point of time, appear in fact to be ſpoken of. The *firſt* was the *orderly* and *regular diviſion* of the world among all the children of Noah, (ſee Gen x.) the *ſecond* was the *diſorderly* and *miraculous diſperſion* of the Cuthites, *poſterior* to their having violated the primitive arrangement, by invading the territories of Aſhur. (See Gen xi) In memory of *the firſt* of theſe events, Peleg received his deſcriptive appellation, whence it will follow, that *the ſecond* certainly took place *after* the birth of that patriarch, but how long after it is difficult to determine. The general opinion ſeems always to have been, and indeed Scripture apparently intimates it, (Gen. x 10 and xi. 9.) that Nimrod was principally concerned in the building of the tower. (Syncel Chronog. p. 42. Cedren Hiſt. Compend. p 11) Nimrod however was the grandſon of Ham, and, from the peculiar manner in which he is mentioned, (Gen. x. 7, 8) he appears to have been the youngeſt of the ſons of Cuſh, whence perhaps we may be allowed to conjecture, that he was born about 120 years after the deluge. and, ſince the great influence, which he poſſeſſed over his followers, could ſcarcely have been acquired in his youth, and during the lives of his elder brothers, we may alſo infer, that he muſt have been near 250 years old, before

At length that venerable patriarch was removed by the hand of death; and the mighty hunter of men, the tyrannical Nimrod, rose, like a baleful comet, above the political horizon. He was the grandson of Ham, and the son of Cush; and he appears to have been the first avowed postdiluvian apostate. We are informed by the sacred historian, that "the beginning of his kingdom was Babel, "and Erech, and Accad, and Calneh in the "land of Shinar [p]." Here he attempted to

before he attempted to build the tower, and found the empire of Babel. If this mode of computation be allowable, every chronological difficulty will be removed: for Noah will then have died previous to the events of Shinar, and the world will have become sufficiently populous to remove all doubts respecting the possibility of such events. This computation moreover will perfectly accord, in point of time, with the ancient tradition, that Abraham was cast into a furnace by Nimrod, for refusing to worship his grand deity Fire. See Fabric. Codex Pseudepig vol. 1 p. 344.

The preceding calculation however is offered with great diffidence, for I am aware that it is liable to some objections. If therefore it should be maintained, that the birth of Peleg and the building of the tower were contemporary, instead of successive events, the adoption of the Samaritan chronology, which places the birth of Peleg 401 years after the deluge, would equally with the foregoing hypothesis allow a sufficient period of time for the repeopling of the earth: but, whether it be allowable to set aside the Hebrew computation in favour of the Samaritan, I leave to abler judges than myself to determine.

[p] Gen. x. 10.

esta-

eſtabliſh an univerſal monarchy, and an univerſal religion; which produced a ſtruggle between him, and the deſcendants of Aſhur, whoſe dominions he had invaded. The reſult of the conteſt was, that Aſhur was compelled to quit his territory, and to provide for himſelf elſewhere. "Out of that land went "forth Aſhur, and builded Nineveh, and the "city Rehoboth, and Calah, and Reſen, be-"tween Nineveh and Calah[q]."

The very name indeed of *Nimrod*, which apparently ſignifies *a rebellious panther*[r], points out the nature of his offence; and we are juſtified in concluding, that the *firſt* poſtdiluvian idolatry was openly eſtabliſhed at his metropolis Babylon, becauſe that city, when its name is myſtically applied to papal Rome, is ſtyled *the* MOTHER *of harlots and abominations of the earth*[s]. The analogy is obvious: as the pure worſhip of the patriarchs was firſt authoritatively corrupted at Babel, ſo was the divine religion of Chriſt at Rome.

Previous to the building of the tower then, I conceive, that all mankind were accuſtomed ſolemnly to commemorate the cataſtrophè of the deluge; but, at the ſame time, I think

[q] Gen x 11.

[r] נמרד is probably a contraction of נמר-מרד.

[s] Rev. xvii. 5.

it

it probable, that they had now begun to entertain too exceſſive a veneration for their arkite anceſtors. This veneration was by the degenerate Nimrod ſoon perverted into groſs idolatry, and blended with the antediluvian worſhip of the hoſt of heaven. Noah and the Sun were henceforth regarded as one divine object; and the Ark, in which he was preſerved, was profanely reverenced in conjunction with the Moon. The Chaldèans ſoon became famous throughout the world for their aſtronomical reſearches; and, while they marſhalled the ſtars in a variety of diſtinct conſtellations, they contrived to depict upon their ſphere the principal events, which are narrated in the hiſtory of the deluge.

Noah however was not the only patriarch worſhipped along with the Sun; in ſubſequent ages Ham not unfrequently obtained the ſame honour. I may here therefore with propriety notice a ſingular ſort of confuſion, which will be found very generally to pervade the mythology of the heathens. Noah and his triple offspring are continually repreſented to us under the character of an ancient deity and his three ſons; and yet every one of theſe three ſons is, upon various occaſions, confounded with his father. Thus Saturn, Jupiter, Neptune, and Pluto, taken

con-

conjointly, are evidently Noah, Ham, Japhet, and Shem; neverthelefs, as will hereafter fufficiently appear, Saturn, Jupiter, and Pluto, when confidered feparately, are all equally the folar Noah, while Neptune very frequently feems to be the fame patriarch adored as a diluvian god. This remark will equally apply to the *Cronus* of Sanchoniatho, and his three fons, Cronus the younger, Jupiter-Belus, and Apollo; to the *Brahmè* of Hindoftan, and his children Brahma, Vifhnou, and Seeva; and to the *Bore* of Scandinavia, and his triple offspring Odin, Vile, and Ve. Many obfervations, in the courfe of the prefent work will be built upon this curious, though to my own conviction at leaft undoubted, circumftance.

That the Moon and the Ark were worfhipped together will abundantly appear in the fequel. It is not improbable, that this peculiar kind of idolatry might have originated from the following circumftance. When the two great fuperftitions were united, and when Noah began to be adored along with the Sun, the Chaldèan aftronomers, having obferved the refemblance of a crefcent to a boat, thought that the waning Moon was no unapt fymbol of the Ark. Hence they were reverenced conjointly; and hence we find, that

that the very ſame goddeſs was ſometimes a perſonification of the one, and ſometimes of the other. Varro accordingly aſſerts, that the Moon, when in the form of a creſcent, was called *Jana* [t]; but Janus is the ſcriptural Noah, conſequently Jana is the Noetic ark or creſcent.

This I apprehend to be the only key, that can unlock the hidden meaning of the myſterious polytheiſm of the ancients. Oſiris, Bacchus, Cronus, Pluto, Adonis, and Hercules, taken in one point of view, as will be ſhewn at large hereafter, are all equally the Sun; but, if we examine their reſpective hiſtories, and attentively conſider the actions, which are aſcribed to them, we ſhall be convinced, that, in their human capacity, they can each be no other than the great patriarch. In a ſimilar manner, the various goddeſſes of paganiſm ſeem to be all one and the ſame mythological character; though they ſometimes repreſent the Moon, ſometimes the Ark, and ſometimes the globe of the Earth emerging from the waters of the deluge [u].

[t] Varr. de Re Ruſt. lib. i. c. 37.

[u] Juno and Minerva are perhaps the only exceptions to this rule.

From

From this union of the two primitive ſuperſtitions originated the cuſtom of beſtowing the names of the hero-gods upon the celeſtial cataſteriſms. Modern aſtronomy ſtill continues to retain the ſame titles; and Nimrod himſelf, the founder of this compound idolatry, ſtill holds a conſpicuous place in the ſphere, and ſtill overlooks the affairs of mortals, from the brilliant conſtellation of Orion [x]. The ſervile flattery of more recent times tranſlated the deified ſpirit of the firſt Ceſar into the Julium Sidus; and a great aſtronomer of the preſent day, adopting the claſſical compliment without the claſſical impiety, has given the appellation of *the Georgium Sidus* to his newly diſcovered planet.

The attempt of Nimrod, to force his abominations upon the reluctant conſciences of mankind, produced a war between his followers, and thoſe, who ſtill perſevered in commemorating the event of the deluge, and who rejected with horror the profane reveries of Sabianiſm. The iſſue of it was ſuch as I have mentioned; the arkite feſtival was perverted

[x] It is a curious circumſtance, that he is repreſented upon the celeſtial globe, encountering the arkite bull, which, as we ſhall hereafter ſee, was the bull of Europa. His followers ſeem to have taken this method of deſcribing his attack upon the anti-ſabian votaries of the commemorative rites of the ark.

verted into a ſuperſtitious idolatry, and was for ever united with the worſhip of the heavenly bodies. *The Myſteries of the Cabiri are in fact nothing more than a mythological account of theſe events; and they will be found throughout to refer at once to the cataſtrophè of the deluge, and to the impious rites of that Sabianiſm, which was united by Nimrod with the arkite ſuperſtition* [y].

The preſent attempt to analyſe the hiſtory of the Cabiri is built upon the following principles.

1. Allegory and perſonification were peculiarly agreeable to the genius of antiquity; and the ſimplicity of truth was perpetually ſacrificed at the ſhrine of poetical decoration. Hence we find, that the old mythologiſts invented a variety of ſacred emblems, expreſſive of the helio-arkite objects of worſhip, which

[y] Some few broken traditions alſo of antediluvian events ſeem to be blended with the general helio-arkite worſhip of the Pagans. Thus the garden of the Heſperides may poſſibly allude to the garden of Paradiſe; and thus Euſebius thinks, that the cry of *Evoè*, uſed by the Bacchanalians, relates to the name of *Eve*. All theſe fables, however, are ſtrangely intermingled with the hiſtory of the arkite hero-gods. Many of them have been noticed by me in a former publication. See Horæ Moſaicæ, book i.

 I ſhall

I ſhall very frequently have occaſion to notice in the enſuing pages. The moſt uſual ſymbols of the Sun were a lion, and a ſerpent; thoſe of Noah, a bull, a horſe, and a fiſh united with a man; thoſe of the Ark, a heifer, a mare, a fiſh united with a woman, a ram, a boar, a cup, a ſea-monſter, and a beautiful female, who was ſometimes deſcribed as a virgin, and ſometimes repreſented as the mother of the gods, and as the conſort, the daughter, the parent, or the ſiſter, of the principal arkite deity. That ſuch emblems were really uſed, will be ſhewn hereafter; at preſent therefore I merely notice them.

2. The obſcurity, neceſſarily attendant upon allegorical perſonifications, was heightened by the vanity, which prompted each nation to adapt, to their own peculiar mythology, facts equally connected with the whole race of mankind. Commemorative ordinances were eſtabliſhed, and remarkable events were exhibited in a kind of ſcenical repreſentation. In moſt caſes their origin, and their import, ſeem to have been equally forgotten; and thus would for ever have remained, had not the page of Scripture afforded that explanation, which had long been

been obliterated from the annals of the Gentiles [z].

3. A confiderable portion of ancient hiftory has been handed down to us, through the medium of the literature of Greece, and in its paffage has received a very great degree of corruption. The religion of that celebrated peninfula is confeffedly of foreign extraction [a]. Egypt and the Eaft were the fources, from which, in a great meafure, the Greeks equally derived their origin, and their mythology: but the faftidious delicacy of claffical ears, and the vain affectation of remote antiquity, induced them to corrupt various oriental words, and to feek for the radicals of them in their own language. This vanity has been productive of many abfurd mifreprefentations, and has fuperinduced much obfcurity over feveral very remarkable traditions. It will be neceffary therefore, in the elucidation of Greek antiquity, frequently to have recourfe to the oriental tongues: for Diodorus Siculus informs us, that the Samothracians had a peculiar dialect of their own,

[z] The treatifes of Jamblichus *upon the Myfteries*, and of Porphyry *upon the cave of the nymphs*, are remarkable inftances of this

[a] Herod. lib. ii. cap. 4, 43, &c.

 which

which prevailed in their ſacred rites[b]; and Jamblichus plainly declares, that the language, uſed in the Myſteries, was not that of Greece, but of Egypt and Aſſyria[c]. Accordingly, he highly cenſures the folly of thoſe, who imagined that barbarous words poſſeſſed no inherent ſignification; and tells us, that the language of the Myſteries was the language of the gods, the firſt and moſt ancient language which was ſpoken upon earth[d]. Hence we may learn the meaning of that conſtant and curious diſtinction, made by Homer, between the dialect of the gods, and the dialect of men. Theſe gods were the famous arkite ogdoad, and their language was Chaldee or Hebrew; while that of mortals was the more modern dialect of Greece. The derivation indeed of the very alphabet, uſed by that polite and ingenious nation, of-

[b] Εσχηκασι δε παλαιαν ιδιαν διαλεκτον οἱ αυτοχθονες (Σαμοθρᾳκες), ἡς πολλα εν ταις θυσιαις μεχρι τȣ νυν τηρειται. Diod. Bibl. lib. v. p. 322.

[c] It is remarkable, that he ſtyles theſe nations *ſacred:* των ἱερων εθνων, ὡσπερ Αιγυπτιων τε και Ασσυριων.

[d] Jamb de Myſt. ſect. vii. cap. 4. The whole chapter is extremely intereſting, but too long to be inſerted. The reader will alſo find ſome curious particulars reſpecting the introduction of the Phenician letters into Greece, in Herod. lib. v. cap. 58. The hiſtorian mentions, that he himſelf ſaw at Thebes ſome very ancient tripods inſcribed with Cadmèan characters.

fers

fers itſelf as a clue to direct us in our reſearches. It leads us obviouſly to that wide-ſpreading language, which once extended itſelf over ſo many of the weſtern regions of Aſia; and which ſtill prevails, in the ſhape of one of its dialects, through ſo large a portion both of Africa, and of the Eaſt. The ſame radicals equally ſerve to form the baſis of the kindred tongues of Chaldèa, Syria, Paleſtine, Phenicia, and Arabia; by the commerce of Tyre, and by the early coloniſts from Aſia, it was diffuſed round the coaſts of the Mediterranean; and the adventurous navigators of Carthage have left ſome traces of it even upon the remote ſhores of Britain. The ſecluded deſcendants of Iſrael occupied but an inconſiderable diviſion of that immenſe tract, over which this ancient tongue had extended itſelf; nor does it appear probable, that the Greeks borrowed many oriental radicals *immediately* from that people. It is more likely, that they were adopted from ſome of the collateral dialects of thoſe eaſtern nations, which were leſs averſe than the Jews to an unreſtrained intercourſe with mankind.

4. As the Greeks have borrowed moſt of their ſacred terms from the oriental dialects, ſo we ſhall find, that the names of their an-

cient kings and heroes are, for the moſt part, mere variations either of the word *Noah*, or of the titles of the ſolar deity. Hence it will follow, that the long genealogies of theſe imaginary perſonages, which occur ſo frequently in the writings of the Greek mythologiſts, are purely fabulous, and can never be eſteemed any part of genuine and authentic hiſtory. When carefully examined, they will be found to be nothing more than a ſeries of repetitions; inſomuch that a grandfather, a father, and a ſon, though apparently diſtinct characters, prove, in reality, to be only one and the ſame perſon, Noah worſhipped in conjunction with the Sun. Thus, to give a ſingle inſtance, Minyas was ſometimes eſteemed the offspring, and ſometimes the father of Orchomenus, who was deſcended from Pelaſgus, Phoroneus, Inachus, and Oceanus. All theſe however, excepting the laſt, are merely different appellations of the great patriarch.

I ſhall conclude this chapter with a liſt of ancient radicals, which ſeem to enter into the compoſition of moſt of the ſacred terms of Hellenic mythology [e]. The greateſt part

[e] In Mr. Bryant's catalogue of radicals, ſeveral occur, which I ſhall find no occaſion to uſe; while ſome, which to me will prove of eſſential ſervice, are omitted by that excellent writer. Hence

of them are either Punic or Chaldee: ſome few do not occur in thoſe dialects, which are probably fragments of the old language of the Mizraim; and one or two are Sanſcreet, from which they have paſſed into ſeveral different tongues both ancient and modern. I am aware of the prejudice entertained againſt remote etymologies, and am perfectly ſenſible, that the derivation of words ought to be admitted with very great caution. Hence, generally ſpeaking, I ſhall endeavour, not to deduce an imaginary hiſtory from a derivation equally imaginary; but, on the contrary, to deduce the derivation from the circumſtances of an actually exiſting hiſtory[f]. I am aware alſo of the objection made by Sir William Jones to the ſyſtem adopted throughout the principal work of Mr. Bryant, that "he, who profeſſes to derive the words of "any one language from thoſe of another, "muſt expoſe himſelf to the dangers of per-

Hence the ſubjoined liſt will be found to vary, in many particulars, from that of Mr. Bryant.

[f] For inſtance, when I meet with a curious legend of a great deluge, which happened in the days of an ancient king, denominated *Nuctimus*, and am thence led to derive the name from Nuch-Tam, *Noah the perfect man*, I cannot diſcover, why ſuch an etymology ſhould be deemed either abſurd or improbable.

"petual

" petual errors, unlefs he be perfectly ac-
" quainted with both[g]." This objection however, I truft, will in a great meafure be found inapplicable to the following remarks on the Cabiric Myfteries: for, fince the theology of Greece is allowedly of Chaldèan, Phenician, and Egyptian extraction; fince Diodorus Siculus afferts, that the Samothracians ufed the remains of a very ancient dialect, which was not Greek, in their facred rites; and fince Jamblichus declares, that the language of the Myfteries was that of Egypt and Affyria: I cannot fee, why the derivation of Hellenic mythological terms from the Punic, or the Coptic, fhould be thought juftly deferving of cenfure[h]. I purpofe therefore almoft exclufively to confine my etymological refearches to Greek, Latin, Phenician, or Ilienfian names; and, whenever I venture to extend them beyond thefe limits, the reader will judge for himfelf, how far I am au-

[g] Sir Wm. Jones's ninth Anniv. Difc. Afiat. Ref. vol. iii. p. 430.

[h] I have derived fome of thefe terms alfo from the Sanfcreet, for which I have the authority of Sir William Jones himfelf, who has declared, that there is fuch a refemblance between that language and the Greek and Latin, " that no philologer could " examine them all three without believing them to have " fprung from fome common fource, which perhaps no longer " exifts." Third Anniv. Difc. Afiat. Ref. vol. i. p. 423.

thorized

thorized to do ſo by the particular combination of circumſtances.

The following are the radicals, which I ſhall principally uſe.

Ain [i], *A fountain.*
Ag, Og, Ac, Oc, Onc, Ong [k], *The Ocean.*
Al, El [l], *God, or the ſolar God.*
Ai, Aia [m], *A country.*
Aph [n], *Heat.*
Adar, contractedly Dar [o], *Illuſtrious.*
Ani [p], *A ſhip.*
Aran [q], *An Ark.*
Ar, Aur, Ur, Or [r], *Light.*
Ar [s], *A mountain.*
Arc, Arg, Org, Erech, Arech [t], *A long ſhip, or ark.*
Ares, Eres [u], *The Sun.*

[i] Heb. עין.

[k] Heb. אגם; Gr. ΩΚεανος, ΩΓην (Heſych); Goth. Oggur.

[l] Heb. אל, Gr. Ἡλιος.

[m] Heb. אי; Gr. Αια.

[n] Heb. אף; Gr. ανΑΠτω, *to kindle a fire*; φΕΨαλος, *a ſpark.* the φ in φεψαλος is merely the common prefix.

[o] Heb. אדר.

[p] Heb. אני.

[q] Heb. ארן; Gr. λΑΡΝαξ.

[r] Heb. אור; whence, from its brightneſs, Lat. Aurum, *gold*; Gr. π' υρ; Eng. Burn, Lat. uro.

[s] Heb. הר; Gr. Ορος.

[t] Heb. ארכה ספינה, *a long ſhip*; Eng. Bark, from the compound P'Arca, or B'Arca.

[u] Heb. חרם.

As,

As, Ath, Ait, Es [x], *Fire.*
Bal, Bel, Bol, Baal [y], *Lord.*
Bu, Bo, Boi, Bo [z], *An ox.*
Car, Cur, Cor, Sar, Sir [a], *The Sun.*
Chan, Chon, Chen [b], *A Prieſt.*
Cal, Cul, Col [c], *Hollow, an epithet of the ark.*
Da [d], *The.*
Dac, Dag [e], *A fiſh.*
Du, Dus, Thu, Thus [f], *God.*
Ga, Gai [g], *Illuſtrious.*
Ham, Om [h], *Heat, Fire.*
Hipha, Siphina, Hiph, Siph [i], *A decked, or covered ſhip.*
Luc [k], *The Sun.*

[x] Heb אש; Chald ארת, Gr. Αιθω; Eng. Aſhes, Heat; Corn. Etau, a *fire-brand.*

[y] Heb. בעל; Iriſh. Bealtine, *fires in honour of Belus.*

[z] Heb. בוקר; Gr. Βȣς; Lat. Bos, Bucellus; Eng. Bull, Bugle; Corn. Bouin, Bu; Iriſh. Bo, Armor. Byuh.

[a] Heb. צהר, זהר, חרה, שער; Perſic. Curos (Heſych.); Sanſ Surya; Gr. Σειρος, Σειριος.

[b] Heb. כהן; and, from the union of the regal with the ſacerdotal character, Tart Khan; Germ. Koning; Eng. King.

[c] Heb. כול; Gr. Κοιλος, Κοιλια, Κωλον; Eng. Gully, Galley.

[d] Chald. דא; Eng The, pronounced *Dhe.*

[e] Heb. דוג; Dutch. Dogger, *a fiſhing-boat.*

[f] Sanſ Dew, Deo, Deva: Lat. Deus, Divus; Gr. Θεος; Celt. Du, Dia, Deu.

[g] Heb. גאה; Gr. Γαιω; Lat. Gaudium, Eng Gay, Gaudy.

[h] Heb. חם; Lat. Amo; Sanſ. Cama, *the god of love.*

[i] Heb. חפה, ספינה; Eng. Ship; Dutch. Skipper, Gr. Σκαφη, Σκεπω, Σκυφος, Ἱππος; Eng. Skiff.

[k] Hence Gr. Λυκαβας, *a year* or *a* [illegible] ειςς, an

Ma, Mai, M' [l], *Great.*

Menu, Manes, Menes [m], *Noah.*

Menah, Men, Monah, Mon [n], *Any thing Noetic, the Ark, the Moon.*

Nuh, Nuch, Nuach, Nus, Nau [o], *Noah.*

Ob, Op, Aub [p], *A ſerpent.*

On, Aun [q], *the Sun.*

an epithet of Apollo, Λυκαβηττος, *a name of mount Parnaſſus*, equivalent to Luca-Bet, *the temple of the Sun*; Λυκοφως, *the morning light*; (Suid. Lex) Λυχνος, *a lantern*, Λευκος, *white* or *ſhining*; Λυκος, *a wolf* from its being ſacred to Luc or Apollo: Lat. Lux, *light*, Lucus, a *grove* from its being uſually planted round the high places of Luc; Lucerna, *a lantern*, Luceo, *to ſhine*; Eng Luck, from the uſual metaphor of proſperity being repreſented by light, and adverſity by darkneſs. The ſame idea cauſed the ancients to mark lucky days with chalk, and unlucky ones with coal;

Illa prius *creta,* mox hæc *carbone* notâſti.

Perſ. Sat. v. ver. 108.

Creſſa ne careat pulchra dies *nota.*

Horat Od lib. i. Od. 36 ver. 10.

Look, from the circumſtance of light being neceſſary for the exerciſe of the organs of viſion.

[l] Heb מאד; Sanſ Maha, Mah, Mai (Heſych Lex Vox Μαι), Lat. Magnus; Gr. Μεγα, from the feminine of which Μεγαλη, old Eng Mickle.

[m] Heb. מנוח, the name of Noah with the addition of the prefix מ, or the particle *Ma:* thus Ma-Nuh will ſignify *the great Noah*

[n] Heb מנידה, Gr. Μην; Lat. Menſis, Eng Moon.

[o] Heb. נוח.

[p] Heb. אוב, Gr Οφις; Span. Cobra.

[q] Heb. און. See Bp. Horſley's very valuable and curious remarks upon this radical. (Tranſlat. of Hoſea, p. 102) The

word

Patar, Petar [q], *to dismiss, to open, to let out.*
Ph', P', Pu' [r], *The.*
Phree, Phri, Phra, Pherah [s], *The Sun.*
Phi [t], *A mouth, an oracle.*
Phont [u], *A priest.*
S' [x], *A common prefix to an aspirated vowel.*
San, Son, Azan, Azon [y], *The Sun.*
Tal, Ital, Aital [z], *the Sun.*

word *On* was used by the Egyptians as a name of the Sun; and it seems moreover to be nearly connected with the sacred Hindoo triliteral *Aum*, or *Om*. See *Instit of Menu*, p 26.

[q] Heb. פטר.

[r] Pu vel Pi articulus omnibus nominibus propriis olim præfigebatur, non tantum a vetustioribus Hebræis, sed et ab Ægyptiis, Arabibus, Chaldæis, cæterisque Orientis populis. Voss. de LXX. p. 409.

[s] This Coptic word (see Jablon. Panth. Ægypt. lib. iii. cap. 1.) is perhaps ultimately derived from the Hebrew פרה Phree, *to be fruitful*; the Sun being the great material cause of fructification.

[t] Heb. פי.

[u] Phont is also a Coptic word Jablon. Panth. Ægypt. Pars I. p. 139.

[x] Thus *Hindus*, and *Sindus*; *Hipba*, and *Sipba*; Ἁλς, and *Sal*; Ἅλλομαι, and *Salio*; Sans *Naga*, and Eng. *Snake*; Ἄλσος, and *Saltus*; Ἅρπω, and *Sarpo*; Ἕδεω (2 Fut Ion. ab Ἕζω), and *Sedeo*, Ἡμισυς, and *Semi* (used in composition); Ἑπτα, and *Septem*, Ἑξ, and *Sex*, Ἕρπω, and *Serpo*; Ὑπο, and *Sub*; Ὑπερ, (Eng. *Upper*) and *Super*; Ὑπερβιος, and *Superbus*.

[y] Azan or Azon appears to be compounded of As-On, *the fiery Sun*. San is the contracted form of the one, and Son of the other. Gr. Ζην; Eng. Sun.

[z] Ταλος, ὁ ἡλιος. (Hesych.) Ital, or Aital, is compounded of Ait-Al, *the god of heat*. Tal is the contracted form.

The-

Theba[a], *An ark.*
Tin, Tinin[b], *A ſea-monſter.*
Tit[c], *The diluvian chaos.*
Tor[d], *A bull.*
Yuneh, Yoneh, Juneh, Jonah[e], *A dove.*
Za[f], *Greatly.*

[a] Heb. תבר.

[b] Heb. תני, Gr Θυννος; Lat. Thynnus, Eng. Tunny.

[c] Heb טיט.

[d] Chald. תור; Gr Ταυρος; Lat. Taurus, Torvus; Celt. Tarw

[e] Heb. יונה; Sanſ. Yoni. Vocula hæc Indica valet *natura muliebris*. Brachmanni fingunt, το *Yoni* inter diluvium formam columbæ induiſſe. Fabula procul dubio ad nefanda phalli pertinet myſteria.

[f] Gr. Ζα.

CHAP.

CHAP. II.

AN ANALYSIS OF THE PHENICIAN HISTORY OF SANCHONIATHO.

THE moſt detailed account of the Cabiric deities is given in *the Phenician hiſtory* of Sanchoniatho, which Euſebius has happily preſerved in his *Præparatio Evangelica*[a]. This hiſtory has been largely commented upon by Bp. Cumberland; and the reſult of his inveſtigation is, that Sydyk is the patriarch Shem, and that the Cabiri, whom the Phenician mythologiſt deſcribes as the ſons of Sydyk, are the children of Shem, and the brethren of Arphaxad. Mnaſeas however, according to the ſcholiaſt upon Apollonius Rhodius, having pronounced, that Jupiter and his ſon Dionuſus were the moſt ancient Cabiri[b], the Biſhop thinks, that the former of theſe was Ham, and the latter Mizraim; whence he concludes, that there were two entirely diſtinct races of Cabiri, the firſt con-

[a] Euſeb. Præp Evan lib i cap 10.
[b] Schol. in Apoll. Argon. lib. i. ver. 917.

ſiſting

ſiſting of Ham and his ſon Mizraim, the latter of the children of Shem.

The objections, to which the ſyſtem of Bp. Cumberland is liable, will beſt appear from an attentive examination of the Phenician narrative itſelf. This curious fragment, like many other pagan traditions, is by no means perfectly accurate; nor can it be ſatisfactorily explained, if we ſtrictly abide by every gradation in the Cabiric genealogy. The obvious import of names, and the peculiar hiſtory of each moſt remarkable deſcent, muſt be carefully noticed, or it will be impoſſible to avoid falling into a variety of errors: for we ſhall find, that the ſame perſon frequently recurs, under different appellations, in the courſe even of the ſame genealogy; and that of the two antediluvian families of Seth and Cain the former is entirely omitted. Nor will this confuſion be thought wonderful, when we recollect, that the patriarch Noah is evidently deified in the mythology of the heathen world under ſeveral diſtinct characters, alluſive to the various actions and circumſtances recorded in his hiſtory. *Deucalion*, *Ogyges*, *Saturn*, and *Janus*, are only different names of the ſame perſon; and what is obſervable in the fables of Greece

 and

and Rome applies with equal force to the narrative of Sanchoniatho.

In order that the following obſervations may be more clearly underſtood, I ſhall begin with ſtating the ſubſtance of the Phenician hiſtory, as detailed by that writer.

Sanchoniatho, after his account of the coſmogony, proceeds to inform us, that all mankind were produced from two perſons, denominated by Philo his tranſlator *Protogonus* and *Eon*, the *latter* of whom firſt gathered fruit from trees [c]. Their children were called *Genus* and *Genea*. Theſe, in a ſeaſon of great drought, began to adore the Sun, ſtyling him *Beel-Samen*, or *Lord of the Heavens*. The offspring of Genus was *Phos*, *Pyr*, and *Phlox*; who invented the mode of procuring fire by rubbing dry ſticks againſt each other. Theſe begot ſons of a gigantic ſtature, who bore the names of *Caſſius*, and *Libanus* [d]. The next generation conſiſted of *Memrumus*, *Hypſuranius*, and *Uſous*; who were born dur-

[c] "And when the *woman* ſaw, that the tree was good for "food, and that it was pleaſant to the eyes, and a tree to be "deſired to make one wiſe, *ſhe* took of the fruit thereof and did "eat, and gave *alſo* unto her huſband *with her*; and he did "eat." Gen iii 6

[d] "There were giants in the earth in thoſe days" Gen. vi. 4.

ing

ing a period of extreme depravity, their mothers living in a ſtate of open proſtitution[e]. Uſoüs conſtructed the firſt rude boat from the trunk of a tree, and conſecrated two pillars to Wind and Fire. Next ſucceeded *Agreus* and *Halieus*, the inventors of hunting and fiſhing; one of whom was the father of *Chryſor* or *Vulcan*[f]. From Chryſor were born two brothers, *Technites* and *Geinus*; who were the parents of *Agruerus* and *Agrus*. Agruerus was highly venerated by the Phenicians, and his ſhrine was drawn about from place to place by a yoke of oxen; while among the Byblians he was eſteemed, in an eſpecial manner, even the greateſt of Gods. The perſons, of whom this generation was compoſed, were known by the general name of *Aletæ* or *Titans*; and their children were *Amynus* and *Magus*. From theſe were born

[e] "And God ſaw that the wickedneſs of man was great in "the earth, and that every imagination of the thoughts of his "heart was only evil continually—The earth alſo was corrupt "before God, and the earth was filled with violence And "God looked upon the earth, and, behold, it was corrupt; for "all fleſh had corrupted his way upon the earth." Gen. vi 5, 11, 12.

[f] This Vulcan was a totally different character from the Egyptian Vulcan, who is ſaid by Herodotus and Pherecydes to have been the father of the Cabiri. His hiſtory will be conſidered hereafter.

Miſor and *Sydyk.* Miſor was the father of Taautus, the inventor of letters, who is called by the Egyptians *Thoör,* by the Alexandrians *Thoyth,* and by the Greeks *Hermes:* but Sydyk begot the *Dioſcori* or *Cabiri,* who are likewiſe denominated *Corybantes* and *Samothraces.* Theſe were the builders of the firſt complete ſhip; and from them was deſcended *another generation,* who diſcovered the uſe of medicinal herbs. Sydyk, in addition to the ſeven Cabiri, had, by one of the Titanides, a ſon named *Aſclepius.* He was afterwards added to the number of the Cabiri, and was then ſtyled *Eſmunus*[g] from the circumſtance of his being the eighth brother.

In the age of theſe men lived *Eliun the moſt high,* and his wife *Beruth,* who dwelt in the neighbourhood of Byblus. Their ſon was *Epigèus* or *Autochthon,* who was afterwards called *Uranus* or *Heaven;* and their daughter was *Ge* or *Earth.* Uranus, eſpouſing his ſiſter Ge, had by her four ſons, *Betylus, Atlas, Ilus* or *Cronus,* and *Dagon* who is alſo called *Siton.* He was moreover the inventor of Betylia, or ſtones that moved as if endowed with animation. His ſon Cronus

[g] Heb. השמוני, *octavus.* See alſo Damaſ. vit. Iſid. apud Phot Bibl. p. 1073.

begot

begot *Proſerpine* and *Minerva*; and was likewiſe the father of the ſeven *Titanides* by his ſiſter *Aſtartè*, and of the ſeven *Titans* by his ſiſter *Rhea*. He had alſo three other ſons born to him in Perèa, *Cronus the younger*, *Jupiter-Belus*, and *Apollo*[h].

Contemporary with theſe were *Pontus*, and *Typhon*, and *Nereus* the father of *Pontus*. The children of Pontus were *Sidon* and *Neptune*.

Between Uranus and his ſon Cronus a ſevere war broke out, in the courſe of which a pregnant concubine of Uranus was taken priſoner. Cronus gave her in marriage to Dagon, who is alſo intitled *Jupiter Arotrius* from his being the patron of agriculture; ſoon after which ſhe brought forth the child, that ſhe had conceived by Uranus, and called his name *Demaroön*. Subſequent to theſe matters Cronus founded Byblus, and threw his brother Atlas, upon a ſuſpicion of treaſon, into a deep pit.

[h] He is alſo ſaid to have had daughters by his ſiſter Dionè, but Sanchoniatho does not mention their names. The author of the works aſcribed to Orpheus enumerates Dionè among the ſeven Titanides, (Orph. apud Proc. in Tim. lib. v p. 295.) and Euripides makes her the mother of Bacchus, or Noah. (Eurip. apud ſchol in Pind Pyth iii. ver. 177.) Dionè is merely a contraction of Da-Ionah, *the dove*.

Uranus next made war upon Pontus, and leagued himſelf with Demaroon: upon which Demaroön forthwith invaded Pontus; but Pontus ſpeedily put him to flight, and Demaroön vowed to offer up a ſacrifice in caſe he ſhould eſcape. Cronus meanwhile, having laid an ambuſcade for his father Uranus, caſtrated him in a certain place in the centre of the earth, in the neighbourhood of rivers and fountains. Then Aſtartè, and Jupiter-Demaroön, and Adod the king of the gods, reigned over the country of Phenicia, with the conſent of Cronus; and Aſtartè placed upon her head, as an enſign of authority, the horns of a bull[i]. This is ſhe, whom the Greeks call *Aphroditè*, or *Venus*[k]: but to Demaroön was born *Hercules-Melicarthus*.

[i] The city of Aſhteroth-Carnaim, near which Chedorlaomer defeated the Rephaim, is evidently ſo denominated from this goddeſs, a circumſtance, which ſhews the high antiquity of her worſhip. *Aſteroth Carnaim* is equivalent to *Aſtartè the horned*.

[k] Sanchoniatho adds, that Cronus was by the Phenicians called *Iſrael*, that he and all his followers were circumciſed, and that he ſacrificed upon an altar, to his father Uranus, his only ſon by the nymph Anobret. The whole of this is evidently a corrupted interpolation, which relates entirely to the hiſtory of Abraham and Iſaac, and which has not the ſlighteſt connection with that of Cronus, Sydyk, and the Cabiri. The ſame remark may be applied to another tradition reſpecting Cronus, which

After theſe things Cronus gave the city Byblus to the goddeſs Baaltis or Dionè, and the city Berytus to Neptune and the Cabiri, who there conſecrated the relics of the Ocean. Cronus then, proceeding ſouthward, inveſted Taautus with the ſovereignty of Egypt. All theſe matters, according to Sanchoniatho, were recorded by the Cabiri the ſeven ſons of Sydyk, and their eighth brother Aſclepius, at the command of the god Taautus[1].

In the preceding narrative three diſtinct genealogies are detailed, the firſt of which commences with Protogonus, the ſecond with Eliun Hypſiſtus, and the third with Nereus.

TABLE I.

The Line of Protogonus.

1. Protogonus, Eon.
2. Genus, Genea.
3. Phos, Pyr, Phlox.
4. Caſſius, Libanus.
5. Memrumus, Uſous.
6. Agreus, Halieus.
7. Chryſor or Vulcan.
8. Technites, Genus.
9. Agruerus, Agrus.
10. Amynus, Magus.
11. Sydyk, Miſor.
12. The Cabiri, Aſclepius, Taautus.
13. The ſons of the Cabiri, inventors of medicinal preparations from herbs.

which has been alſo preſerved by Sanchoniatho: he is ſaid to have ſlain with his ſword his own ſon Sadid.

[1] Euſeb. Præp. Evan. lib. i. cap. 10.

TABLE II.

The Line of Eliun, contemporary with Sydyk and the Cabiri.

- Eliun — Beruth
  - Ge — Uranus — A concubine
    - (Ge and Uranus): Betylus. Dagon. Cronus. Atlas.
      - (Cronus): Minerva. Proserpine. The 7 Titanides.
        - The 7 Titans. Cronus. Jupiter-Belus. Apollo.
    - (Uranus and a concubine): Demaroön.
      - Melicarthus.

TABLE III.

The Line of Nereus, contemporary with Cronus and his children, and consequently with Sydyk and the Cabiri.

- Nereus.
  - Pontus.
    - Sidon. Neptune.
- Typhon.

The first of these genealogical tables is adjusted by Bp. Cumberland to the Mosaical account of the line of Cain, in the following manner.

1. Proto-

1. Protogonus.	1. Adam.
2. Genus.	2. Cain.
3. Phos.	3. Enoch.
4. Caffius.	4. } *Omitted by Mofes.*
5. Memrumus.	5. }
6. Agreus.	6. Irad
7. Chryfor.	7. Mehujael.
8. Technites	8 Methufael.
9. Agruerus.	9. Lamech
10. Amynus, Magus.	10. Jabal, Jubal.
The flood ends Cain's Line.	
11. Sydyk.	11. Shem.
12. The Cabiri.	12. Children of Shem.
13. The fons of the Cabiri.	13. Grandchildren of Shem.

From the preceding table it appears, that Bp. Cumberland commences his analyfis with pronouncing Protogonus to be Adam, and Genus Cain[m]; whence it will neceffarily follow, that the defcendants of Genus, as detailed by Sanchoniatho, are the children of Cain, and not thofe of Seth. To this *general* pofition I fully affent; but I cannot venture to adopt the Bifhop's opinion refpecting the Mofaical account of the genealogy of Cain. From Adam to Noah, in the line of Seth, the facred hiftorian enumerates *ten* generations; but from Adam to Jabal, in the line of Cain, he fpecifies only *eight*. The

[m] *Genus* is formed from *Cain* merely by fuffixing the Greek termination.

Bifhop,

Bishop, observing this difference in the number of generations, which respectively compose the lines of Seth and Cain, boldly declares, that two patriarchs have been omitted by Moses in the genealogy of Cain between Enoch and Irad; as if it were necessary, that the line of Cain, and the line of Seth, should both equally consist of ten persons[n]. Hence he supposes Agreus to be Irad; Chrysor, Mehujael; Technites, Methusael; Agruerus, Lamech the Cainite[o]; and Amynus, Jabal:

[n] "It seems more credible to me," says the Bishop, "that "Moses passed over two generations of Cainites, as not worth "the mentioning, than that eight generations in this line "should live as long as ten in Seth's line." Cumb. Sanchon. p. 228.

Upon this it may be observed, that it by no means follows, that the individuals, who composed the *eight* Cainite generations, should have severally attained to a greater age than the descendants of Seth, notwithstanding there were *ten* descents in the line of that Patriarch The reason is obvious—the number of generations, extending through any given period, depends upon the time when each individual became a father, and not upon his longevity alone. Hence, if we suppose, (what is certainly not improbable) that the pious Sethites married earlier in life than the debauched Cainites, who preferred the free gratification of their lusts to the restraint of matrimony; the difference between the number of their *legitimate* generations, (for such only we may reasonably suppose to have been recorded by Moses,) will be very satisfactorily accounted for, without there being any necessity for imagining the latter more long-lived than the former.

[o] Gen. iv. 18.

not-

notwithſtanding Agreus, Chryſor, Technites, Agruerus, and Amynus, are ſeverally the ſixth, ſeventh, eighth, ninth, and tenth in deſcent from Protogonus; while Irad, Mehujael, Methuſael, Lamech, and Jabal, are only the fourth, fifth, ſixth, ſeventh, and eighth from Adam.

Granting however for a moment, that the line of Cain did really, at the cataſtrophè of the deluge, end with Amynus, we might naturally expect the latter part of the firſt genealogical table to commence with Noah; inſtead of which we are informed, that Sydyk is Shem. Noah therefore, upon the hypotheſis of Bp. Cumberland, is entirely omitted in the principal line, and appears only in the ſecond table, under the denomination of *Uranus*; while his father Lamech is conjectured to bear the ſingular title of *Eliun Hypſiſtus*, or *God the moſt high* [p].

With regard to Agruerus, whom the Biſhop ſuppoſes to be the other Lamech the deſcendant of Cain, Sanchoniatho informs us, that his ſtatue was greatly revered by the Phenicians, that his ſhrine was drawn from place to place by a yoke of oxen, and that among the Byblians he was eſteemed even

[p] Cumb. Sanchon. Table oppoſite p. 41.

the

the greateſt of gods. He further adds, that he was of the race of thoſe, who were known by the names of *Aletæ* or *fire-worſhippers*, and *Titans*, or *diluvians* [q], and that he was the father of Amynus the magician [r]. Since Agruerus then was venerated by the country-men of Sanchoniatho as the firſt of deities, it is only reaſonable to ſuppoſe, that he muſt have ſignalized himſelf in ſome very particular manner to obtain ſo proud a diſtinction. But, if Agruerus be merely the Cainite Lamech, we are left utterly at a loſs to conceive why *he* ſhould be thus preeminently honoured. Almoſt the only circumſtance recorded of this patriarch is, that he was guilty of homicide, apparently in ſelf-defence [s]; after which his name is diſmiſſed for ever from the ſacred page. Can we then think it probable, that *he*, by an *eſpecial ſelection* [t], ſhould be venerated by the Phenicians as the greateſt of their gods?

Agruerus or Agrotes moreover ſignifies *a*

[q] *Aletes* is derived from Al-Ait, *the god of fire*, and *Titan*, from Tit, *the colluvies of the deluge*

[r] I doubt whether Amynus and Magus are two diſtinct perſons; Magus ſeems rather to be only a deſcriptive title of Amynus.

[s] Gen. iv. 23 Vide Lowth de ſacra Poeſi Hebræor. Præl. iv. p. 53

[t] Gr. εξαιρετως.

huſ-

husbandman; we may therefore reasonably conclude the name to have been bestowed descriptively: but upon examination we shall find, that not the slightest hint is given by the inspired historian respecting the particular occupation of Lamech.

On these grounds, we could scarcely admit the identity of Lamech and Agruerus, even if Lamech were *really* the ninth in descent from Adam; for it would be more easy to believe, that some error had crept into the narrative of Sanchoniatho, than to erect Lamech into the greatest god of the Phenicians, and to esteem him the peculiar patron of agriculture. But when, upon recurring to Scripture, we find Lamech, not the *ninth*, but the *seventh* from Adam, we can surely require nothing more to convince us, that Agruerus is a totally different person from that patriarch.

Who then, it may be asked, is the *Agruerus* of Sanchoniatho, the great God of Phenicia, and the patron of husbandry? Let us only compare the genealogy of Cain recorded by Moses, with the same genealogy as preserved by Sanchoniatho, and we shall immediately be led to a satisfactory and consistent answer.

The generations of Cain enumerated in Scrip-

Scripture amount to eight: Adam, Cain, Enoch, Irad, Mehujael, Methusael, Lamech, and Tubal-Cain. If these be connected with the Phenician genealogy, the table of descents will stand as follows.

1 Protogonus, Eon.	1. Adam, and Eve.
2. Genus, Genea.	2. Cain, and his wife.
3. Phos, Pyr, Phlox.	3 Enoch, and his brethren.
4 Cassius, Libanus.	4 Irad, and his brethren.
5. Memrumus, Usoüs.	5 Mehujael, and his brethren.
6. Agreus, Halieus.	6. Methusael, and his brethren.
7. Chrysor.	7 Lamech
8. Technites.	8. Tubal-Cain [u].

The Phenician historian, having now reckoned up the line of Cain, which terminated with the deluge, will naturally proceed to the head of a new family, from which the whole postdiluvian world was peopled. Agruerus therefore or Noah, considered with reference to the line of Cain, will necessarily stand in the *ninth* place of descent; although, with respect to his own line, he be the *tenth* from Adam. And this supposition may be adopted with perfect propriety: for, although

[u] The word *Technites* signifies *an artizan*, and Tubal-Cain, as we learn from the inspired historian, was "an instructor of "every artificer in brass and iron." Gen. iv 22 This Tubal-Cain had two brothers, Jabal and Jubal. Sanchoniatho only mentions one brother of Technites, whom he styles *Genus*.

Bp.

Bp. Cumberland ſeparates the ten firſt generations of Sanchoniatho from thoſe which follow, and places them before the flood; yet this diviſion is entirely arbitrary, the Phenician mythologiſt never making any direct mention of that cataſtrophè.

In the perſon of Agruerus then we may conceive the ſecond part of the firſt genealogical table to commence, the eight generations which precede him being antediluvian, and correſponding with the eight generations of the family of Cain. Accordingly we ſhall find, that the character of Agruerus or Agrotes preciſely agrees in every particular with that of the great Patriarch. Agruerus, as the name imports, was a huſbandman; ſuch alſo was the occupation of Noah[x]. Agruerus was venerated by the Phenicians as the greateſt of gods; ſuch likewiſe were the honours univerſally paid to the ſecond progenitor of mankind. Agruerus is ſaid to have been the father of Amynus the magician; Noah was the father of Ham, who is generally ſuppoſed to have been addicted to ſorcery, and to have inſtructed his ſon Mizraim in the ſame nefarious practices[y]. The very name *Amynus*

[x] Gen. ix. 20.

[y] Chamum eundem eſſe volunt cum Zoroaſtre Mago. Hujus ſententiæ primus author, quod quidem ſciam, eſt Pſeudo-Clemens,

indeed ſufficiently eſtabliſhes the truth of this ſuppoſition: it is evidently the *Am-on* of the Egyptians, under which title the ſcriptural *Ham* ſeems to have been uſually worſhipped.

The children of Amynus, according to Sanchoniatho, were Miſor and Sydyk; and the ſon of Miſor was Taautus. This Taautus was the inventor of the alphabetic mode of writing; and was called by the Egyptians *Thoër*, by the Alexandrians *Thöyth*, and by the

Clemens, qui libro quarto Recognitionum Magiam ſcribit, hominibus ante diluvium a mulierofis illis angelis traditam, Ægyptiorum conditorem Meſraimum didiciſſe a Chamo patre, et Chamum a poſteris, hujus artis admiratoribus, Zoroaſtrem, ſeu vivum aſtrum, propterea fuiſſe dictum, et pro deo habitum. Id ſequutus Caſſianus collationis 8væ cap. 21mo. Quantum, inquit, antiquæ traditiones ferunt, Cham filius Noæ, qui ſuperſtitionibus iſtis et ſacrilegis fuit artibus ac profanis infectus, ſciens nullum ſe poſſe ſuper his memorialem librum in Arcam prorſus inferre, in quam erat cum patre juſto ac ſanctis fratribus ingreſſurus, ſceleſta ac profana commenta diverſorum metallorum laminis, quæ ſcilicet aquarum inundatione corrumpi non poſſent, et duriſſimis lapidibus inſculpſit. Quæ diluvio peracto eadem qua celaverit curioſitate perquirens, ſacrilegiorum ac perpetuæ nequitiæ ſeminarium tranſmiſit in poſteros. Inde invaluit hæc opinio Chamum fuiſſe Magum, et carmine magico patrem, dum dormiebat nudus, ita devotâſſe et obligâſſe, ut deinceps ad mulierem non potuerit affectari, et magicos libros ſcripſiſſe, quorum partem combuſſerit Ninus, altera ſuperſtite Nam hodieque extat impium opus continens elementa et praxim artis necromanticæ ſub titulo *Scripturæ Chami fili Noæ*. Bochar. Phaleg lib. iv. cap. 1.

the

the Greeks *Hermes*. Hence it manifeſtly appears, that Miſor is the *Mizraim* of Scripture, the father of the Egyptians; a circumſtance, which affords an additional proof of the identity of Amynus and Ham, and conſequently of Agruerus and Noah.

Hitherto the narrative of Sanchoniatho has been equally clear and accurate; but the genealogy of Sydyk, whatever patriarch be deſignated by that name, is certainly erroneous. He is ſaid to be the ſon of Amynus, and the father of the Cabiri, who were likewiſe ſtyled *Dioſcori, Corybantes,* and *Samothraces.* Theſe Cabiri were the builders of the firſt ſhip; and were contemporary with a myſterious perſon denominated *Eliun the Moſt High*, and with a female, who bore the name of *Beruth*[z]. Eliun and Beruth dwelt in the neighbourhood of Byblus; and from them ſprung Epigèus or Autochthon, who was afterwards intitled *Uranus*, and a daughter, who was called *Ge*. In proceſs of time, Uranus eſpouſed his ſiſter Ge, and became the father of Ilus or Cronus, Betylus, Dagon, and Atlas.

Bp. Cumberland, as I have already obſerved, pronounces Sydyk to be Shem, and

[z] With Eliun and Beruth the ſecond genealogical table of Sanchoniatho commences. Vide ſupra p. 40.

 the

the Cabiri to be his children. He is ſenſible however of the genealogical difficulties, which attach to this ſuppoſition; difficulties, which, I readily allow, cannot be entirely avoided, whatever ſyſtem be adopted.

"We will begin with Sydyk," ſays the Biſhop, "whom Philo well tranſlates δικαιος, "*the Juſt*. This was, I conceive, his title "that he was known by; and I believe he "deſerved this title well, for I take him to "be no other than Shem, the beſt Son of "his good father Noah, the man, in whoſe "tabernacle, mentioned Gen. ix. 27. was "the church of the true God, the ſchool of "piety and juſtice; and he dwelt at Salem "in Canaan, to whoſe princes our Sanchoni-"atho, being a Canaanite, hath a conſtant "eye; and he was in the eleventh genera-"tion, counted from the firſt man, as our "author placeth him: and no other man "can be named in that generation, which "conſiſted wholly of the children iſſuing from "Noah, who can claim this title ſo juſtly as "Shem.

"And I am glad, that I can cite Grotius, "to abet my opinion in this thus far, that he "ſaith in his notes on *Heb.* vii. 1. Melchiſe-"dec is the man meant by Sydyk in *Philo* "*Byblius:* and that Shem had this title of

"*Mel-*

" *Melchisedec*, or *the just king*, as Pompey " was ordinarily called *Magnus*, and Octavius " called *Augustus*, is the judgment of the eldest " and learnedest Jews, and of many modern " learned men in Jewish antiquity, to whose " judgment herein I subscribe with great sa- " tisfaction [a]."

Having thus stated his opinion, the Bishop proceeds to consider the difficulty of reconciling this system with the genealogical table of Sanchoniatho.

" I am in an especial manner concerned to " answer an objection rising out of Sancho- " niatho my author: for he tells us, that Sy- " dyk and Misor were the sons of Magus and " Amynus; which consists not with Sydyk's " being Shem, because he was the son of " Noah, who is Uranus in our writer, and is " in a line distinct from that wherein Amy- " nus and Magus stand.

" The best kindness, that I can shew to " our author in this case, is to acknowledge, " that I believe he honestly wrote this out of " those Cabiric records which he searched, " (which yet perhaps might be somewhat al- " tered between his time and the time of " those Cabiri, that were Sydyk's children)

[a] Cumb. Sanchon. p. 173.

" which contained the greateſt antiquities, " that their prieſts would communicate: but " yet I believe, that in this link of their " line, or genealogy, their books were cor- " rupted; and that it was thought neceſſary " to the intereſt of their falſe religion, or " idolatry, to miſrepreſent this part of its hiſ- " tory in later times, when none alive could " contradict by their own teſtimony from " their ſenſes, and few or no records were " likely to be compared, that might atteſt " the contrary [b]."

I have given the Biſhop's ſtatement at large, both that it may be conſidered how far the hiſtory of Shem, and his children, correſponds with that of Sydyk and the Cabiri; and alſo on account of the difficulty, which, as he obſerves very juſtly, attends this part of the Phenician genealogy.

As for the two hiſtories, I cannot diſcover the ſlighteſt reſemblance between them. We have no reaſon to ſuppoſe, that the children of Shem were either ſeven, or eight, in number; that they had any particular connection with Berytus, and Neptune; that they, in an *eſpecial* manner, recorded the circumſtances of their times, or that they were the firſt in-

[b] Cumb. Sanchon. p. 176.

ventors

ventors of the art of navigation. *Five* only of his ſons are recorded in Scripture; Elam, Aſhur, Arphaxad, Lud, and Aram[c]. Theſe appear plainly to have been the reſpective anceſtors of the Perſians[d], the Aſſyrians, the Hebrews, the Lydians, and the Syrians[e]; all which nations, with the ſolitary and ſlight exception of the Lydians[f], totally abſtained from maritime affairs. Their very ſituation indeed upon the vaſt continent of Aſia compelled them to exert their ſtrength by land, rather than by ſea. Accordingly, while we are told by Moſes, that the dwelling of the children of Shem "was from Meſha as thou "goeſt unto Sephar, a mount of the Eaſt[g]," words by which their inland ſettlements are plainly deſcribed; the maritime diſpoſition of the ſons of Japhet is pointed out with equal accuracy in the paſſage, which aſſigns to them "the iſles of the Gentiles[h]." Hence it per-

[c] Gen. x 22.

[d] Or Elamites

[e] Or Araměans.

[f] See Herod lib i cap 94. in which, part of the Lydians are ſaid to have emigrated into Tuſcany, through mere ſtreſs of famine; but, how very little this nation was habitually addicted to maritime affairs, appears in a ſtriking manner from a ſtory related of Creſus and Bias See Herod lib i. cap. 27

[g] Gen x 30.

[h] Gen. x 5

haps is impoſſible to diſcover a reaſon, why the moſt mediterranean of all the deſcendants of Noah ſhould be excluſively mentioned by Sanchoniatho as the builders of the firſt ſhip, and as conſecrating at Berytus the relics of the Ocean.

The Biſhop lays a great ſtreſs upon the propriety of applying the name of *Sydyk*, or *The juſt man*, to Shem; and upon the coincidence of that appellation with the ſcriptural *Melchiſedec*. The *peculiar* integrity of Shem however is never extolled by the ſacred hiſtorian, above that of Japhet; and the only definite inſtance of his piety, which has been recorded, redounds equally to the honour of his elder brother[1]. Shem accordingly is never once ſtyled *The juſt man*; and even if his identity with Melchiſedec could be proved, it would not be ſufficient to eſtabliſh the Biſhop's poſition, unleſs there was *ſome* reſemblance at leaſt between the hiſtories of Shem and Sydyk.

The circumſtance of Shem being the eleventh in deſcent from Adam, as Sydyk is from Protogonus, is alſo inſiſted upon. But ſurely very little importance can be annexed to it, when we recollect, that the Biſhop himſelf

[1] Gen. ix 23.

allows

allows the direct line to be broken; and when moreover we consider, that the *eight* descents in the family of Cain, not the *ten* in the family of Seth, are enumerated by Sanchoniatho.

Having thus endeavoured to prove, that Sydyk and Shem cannot be the same person, I may now proceed to state and establish the system, which appears to me the most consonant with truth. This system then supposes, that both Agruerus and Sydyk are only two different descriptive names of one patriarch; of him, who beheld the ruin of a desolated world, and became the father of the second great race of mankind.

If we consult the sacred records, we shall be informed, that Noah was saved from the destruction occasioned by the deluge, because he was "*a just man*, and perfect in his generations[k]:" hence it is manifest, that the title of *Sydyk*, or *The just man*, is peculiarly applicable to him; and thus far therefore the mutual resemblance of the scriptural Noah, and the Phenician Sydyk, is perfectly exact. Nor is the correspondence between their respective families less singularly accurate. The

[k] Gen vi. 9. Moses indeed expressly applies the very name of *Sydyk* or *Sadik* to Noah. נח איש צדיק.

Cabiri, whom Sanchoniatho deſcribes as the children of Sydyk, are ſaid to be ſeven in number[l]; the family of Noah, preſerved along with him in the Ark, were alſo preciſely ſeven in number. The Cabiri are further ſaid to have built the firſt ſhip that was ever navigated; and to have received, in conjunction with the marine deity Neptune, a grant from Cronus of the city Berytus, where they ſolemnly conſecrated the relics of the Ocean. The former of theſe traditions exactly agrees with the conſtruction of the firſt recorded veſſel, the Ark; and the latter is nearly unintelligible, unleſs it be ſuppoſed to have a reference to the events of the deluge[m].

[l] It may perhaps be thought, that the ſeven Cabiri, being deſcribed by Sanchoniatho as *males*, do not perfectly correſpond with the Noetic family. To this it might be anſwered, that we are not to expect undeviating accuracy in the annals of paganiſm, at the ſame time however it is very remarkable, that Pherecydes has preſerved a tradition of the Cabiri, which *exactly* agrees with the ſcriptural account of the arkite ogdoad. According to this writer, Vulcan (that is Noah worſhipped in conjunction with the ſolar fire) eſpouſed Cabira, the daughter of the marine deity Proteus, and by her became the father of the three Cabiri, and the three Cabiræ Pherec. apud Strab. Geog lib. x. p. 472.

[m] That it actually has ſuch a reference will appear more evidently when the hiſtory of Cronus and Beruth ſhall have been examined, and when the curious legend of Beroë ſhall have been analyſed. Nonnus informs us, that Beroè and Berith

Here it may perhaps be objected, that ſince, even according to my own opinion, Amynus is Ham, how is it poſſible, that Sydyk, whom Sanchoniatho repreſents as the ſon of Amynus, can be the *Noah* of Scripture?

While I readily allow the full force of this difficulty, I may be permitted to obſerve, that it no leſs affects the ſyſtem of Bp. Cumberland, than that which is here advanced. Whether Amynus be Jabal, as the Biſhop ſuppoſes, or Ham, as I have attempted to prove him to be; in either caſe, he aſſuredly is not the father of Shem. Hence the Biſhop, as we have already ſeen, maintains, that ſome great diſlocation muſt have taken place in this part of the Phenician narrative. Upon ſuch a ſuppoſition then, the preſent hypotheſis will, at any rate, be liable to no *greater* objection than that of the Biſhop; but if a plauſible reaſon can be aſſigned for this error of Sanchoniatho, the objection will of courſe be proportionably diminiſhed.

The confuſion in this part of Sanchoniatho's account might poſſibly ariſe in the fol-

rith are the ſame, and that the city Berytus received its appellation from this ancient allegorical goddeſs. Dionyſ. lib xli. Cronus, who made the grant of Berytus to the Cabiri, was the ſame perſon, as we ſhall hereafter ſee, as Sydyk or Noah.

lowing

lowing manner. Having ſtated the *eight* generations in the line of Cain, he next mentions Noah and Ham, under the names of *Agruerus* and *Amynus*. Finding, however, that there were *ten* generations in the line of Seth previous to the deluge, and that the firſt man after that event was an eminently juſt and pious character, he attempts to compriſe all theſe accounts in one genealogy. For this purpoſe, at the end of ten generations, he makes a freſh ſeries to commence with Noah; who may at once be eſteemed the *laſt* or *tenth* in deſcent before the flood, and the *firſt* after it. Hence, as he had already made Agruerus or Noah to be the ſon of Technites or Tubal-Cain, in order that he might preſerve his genealogical line unbroken; ſo he now, for the ſame reaſon, makes Sydyk, or Noah under another appellation, to be the ſon of Amynus or Ham. In the midſt of this confuſion, he ſtill keeps his eye upon the real ſon of Ham, whom, from records more authentic than his own, he had learned to be Mizraim. Accordingly, while Noah, under the name of Sydyk, occupies the *firſt* place after the *ten* primary generations, Mizraim, under that of *Miſor*, is with perfect accuracy ſaid to be the ſon of Ham or Amynus: and though, agreeably to this arrangement, Noah, as Sydyk, muſt neceſſarily ſtand in the falſe relationſhip of *brother* to Miſor or Mizraim, yet, as Agruerus, he ſtill preſerves his true relationſhip of *grandfather* to him. In ſhort, the whole confuſion appears to have ariſen from three ſources: Sanchoniatho's conſciouſneſs that *ten* generations had actually flouriſhed before the deluge; his perceiving that the line of Cain conſiſted of only *eight* deſcents; and his certainty that Noah was the *firſt* poſtdiluvian. The following table may perhaps throw additional light upon a ſuppoſition, which it is more eaſy to conceive in the mind, than to expreſs clearly in words.

San-

Sanchoniatho's first genealogical table compared with and adapted to Scripture.

The ten generations of the line of Seth, not specified by Sanchoniatho.	*The eight generations of the line of Cain, specified by Sanchoniatho, with the addition of Noah and Ham.*	
1. Adam.	1. Protogonus.	1. Adam.
2. Seth.	2. Genus.	2. Cain.
3. Enos.	3. Phos.	3. Enoch.
4. Cainan.	4. Cassius.	4. Irad.
5. Mahalaleel.	5. Memrumus.	5. Mehujael.
6. Jared.	6. Agreus.	6. Methusael.
7. Enoch.	7. Chrysor.	7. Lamech.
8. Methuselah.	8. Technites.	8. Tubal-Cain.
9. Lamech.	9. Agruerus.	9. Noah.
10. Noah.	10. Amynus.	10. Ham.
	The deluge.	
9. Agruerus.	11. Sydyk.	9. or 11. Noah[u].
10. Amynus-Magus.	12. Cabiri.	10. or 12. Ham, and the rest of the family of Noah.
11. Misor.	13. Sons of the Cabiri.	11. or 13. Mizraim, and the other grandchildren of Noah.

[u] Noah, or Agruerus, is the *ninth*, when considered with a reference to the *eight* generations of Cain; but Noah, or Sydyk, is the *eleventh* when considered as the *first* postdiluvian, the *ten* generations of Seth having preceded the flood. Noah therefore, as Sydyk, reckons both as the *tenth* or *last* man before that catastrophè, and as the *eleventh* or *first* after it.

I have

I have obſerved, that Sanchoniatho cloſely connects Miſor or Mizraim, and Taautus or Thoth, with Sydyk and the Cabiri; and that he ſuppoſes Cronus to have proceeded ſouthward to the land of Egypt[o]. From this circumſtance I have little doubt but that the eight primitive great gods of that country were no other than the arkite Cabiric Ogdoad. Herodotus mentions a deep and broad lake near Buto, in which, according to the Egyptians, there was a floating iſland. On this iſland was a large temple, dedicated to Apollo, and furniſhed with three altars. It was not ſuppoſed however to have been always in a floating ſtate, but to have loſt its original firmneſs in conſequence of the following circumſtance. When Typhon, or the Ocean[p], was roaming through the world in queſt of Horus, or Apollo, the mythological ſon of Oſiris, Latona, who was one of the primitive eight gods, and who dwelt in the city Buto, having received him in truſt from Iſis, concealed him from the rage of that deſtructive monſter in this ſacred iſland, which then firſt began to float[q]. Theſe eight gods

[o] Vide ſupra p. 39.

[p] Plutarch expreſsly aſſerts the identity of Typhon and the ſea. Plut. de Iſid. et Oſir. p. 363.

[q] Herod. lib. ii. cap. 156.

the

the Egyptians conceived to be prior to the twelve, whoſe names and worſhip were adopted by the Greeks[q] and, in alluſion to the origin of the adoration, which was paid to them, they were accuſtomed to repreſent them, not ſtanding upon dry ground, but ſailing together in a ſhip[r].

As for the floating iſland mentioned by Herodotus, it was probably only a large raft conſtructed in imitation of the Ark[s]; while Horus, whoſe temple was built upon it, was the ſame perſon as his ſuppoſed father Oſiris[t], or Noah worſhipped in conjunction with the Sun. The three altars, I apprehend, were dedicated to the triple offspring of that patriarch; and the word *Buto* is obviouſly deducible from Bu-Do, the divine heifer, which was one of the moſt uſual ſymbols of the Ark[u], whence the city *Buto* will ſignify *the city of the arkite heifer.* The word occurs very frequently both in the mythology and

[q] Ibid. cap. 46.

[r] Τȣς δε Αιγυπτιȣς τȣς δαιμονας ἁπαντας ȣκ ἑϛαναι επι ϛερεȣ, αλλα παντας επι πλοιου. Porphyr. apud Cudworth's Intell. Syſt. p. 249.

[s] See Bryant's Anal. vol ii. p. 329.

[t] Adonim, Attinem, Oſirim, et Horum, aliud nihil eſſe quam Solem. Macrob. Saturn. lib. i. cap 21.

[u] I cannot think with Mr. Bryant, that the word *Buto* ſignifies *the ark,* any further than as it primarily ſignifies *an ox.*

geo-

geography of the ancients. Thus we read of a hero denominated *Butes*, who, according to Nonnus, was no other than Argus, or the god of the Ark [x].

——————ϗκ επι Βϗτης
Αργος ακοιμητοισι πολυσπερεεσσιν οπωπαις
Κλεψιγαμϗ Κρονιδαο νεωτερα λεκτρα φυλασσει[y].

There was a city called *Buta* in Achaia [z]; a ſeaport intitled *Butua* in Dalmatia [a]; and a town, which bore the name of *Buthos*, in Egypt [b]. There was likewiſe a city of Illyricum, upon which Cadmus, as we are informed by Stephanus of Byzantium, beſtowed the appellation of *Buthoè* from the Egyptian *Buto* [c]; and another town in Ionia, or *the land of the arkite dove*, which was called *Buthia* [d]. Perhaps alſo the Scottiſh iſle of *Bute* may once have been the ſeat of the ſame ſuperſtition, and may once, together with its ſiſter iſland *Arran*, have beheld the wild rites, which were celebrated in honour of

[x] Butes was the ſame as Buddha, or Mercury, whoſe character ſhall be conſidered at large hereafter. Vide infra chap. v.
[y] Dionyſ. lib. viii. p. 146.
[z] Diod. Bibl. lib. xx. p 828.
[a] Plin. Nat. Hiſt lib. iii. cap. 22.
[b] Ibid lib v. cap. 10.
[c] Steph.-Byzant. de Urb. p. 236.
[d] Ibid.

Aran,

Aran, or *the ark*[e]. The very ſtrong reſemblance at leaſt, diſcoverable between the religion and inſtitutes of the Druids, the Egyptians, and the Hindoos, gives ſome reaſon to ſuppoſe, that they all originated from one common ſource[f].

The mode of repreſenting the Ark by a floating iſland was not excluſively confined to Egypt. As Latona and Apollo were two of the great gods worſhipped at Buto; ſo we find the ſame traditions prevalent at Delos, both with reſpect to its once having been a floating iſland, and to the various dangers by which Latona was aſſailed.

——Σε δ' ȣκ εθλιψεν αναγκη,
Αλλ' αφετος πελαγεσσιν επεπλεες—[g].

Thou, Delos, unconſtrain'd,
Through the wide Ocean's trackleſs paths didſt roam.

Illa ſuam vocat hanc, cui quondam regia Juno
Orbe interdixit; quam vix erratica Delos
Orantem accepit, cum tum levis inſula nabat.

[e] This ſuppoſition will appear the more probable, when we find, as ſhall be ſhewn hereafter, that the myſteries of the Samothracian or Cabiric Ceres, Proſerpine, and Bacchus, were eſtabliſhed in the Britiſh iſles.

[f] See Maurice's Ind. Ant. vol. vi.

[g] Callim. Hymn. ad Del. ver. 35.

Illic

Illic incumbens cum Palladis arbore palmæ,
Edidit invita geminos Latona noverca[h].

From earth excluded by the furious hate
Of Juno, wandering Delos ſcarce receiv'd
Fair-hair'd Latona; there her double offspring
Firſt ſaw the light beneath a ſpreading palm.

The iſland was afterwards rendered ſtable by Apollo, in gratitude for the preſervation, which he owed to it.

——εισοκεν αυτην
Αςατον ιππολυουσαν αμοιβαδι συνδρομον αυρη,
Κυμασιν αςυφελικτον ενερριζωσεν Απολλων[i].

As for the various wanderings of Latona, detailed at ſome length by Callimachus[k], they allude, like thoſe of Iſis and Ceres, to the erratic courſe of the Ark over the diluvian waters.

There was another of theſe ſacred floating iſlands, in the midſt of a lake of immenſe depth, at Cotylè in Italy, to which the Pelaſgi are ſaid to have been directed by the following oracle.

Στειχετε μαιομενοι Σικελων Σατορνιαν αιαν,
Ηδ' Αβοριγινεων Κοτυλην, ου νασος οχειται[l].

[h] Ovid Metam. lib. vi. ver. 332

[i] Nonni Dionyſ. lib. xxxiii p 552 See alſo Callim. Hymn. ad Del. ver. 51. For ſome further remarks on the hiſtory of Delos vide infra chap. viii.

[k] Ibid. ver. 70. et infra.

[l] Dion Halic. Ant. Rom. lib. i. cap. 15, 19.

Haſte, to the realms of Saturn ſhape your courſe,
Where Cotylè's fam'd iſland wandering floats
On the broad ſurface of a ſacred lake.

The ſame iſland is mentioned by Pliny, who adds, upon the authority of Varro, that it was eſteemed the navel of Italy[m]. The Greeks had a ſimilar notion of Delphi being the navel of the world. The idea originated in both caſes from a miſconception of the ſacred term Om-Phi-Al, *the oracle of the ſolar god*, which the Greeks perverted into *Omphalus*, and the Latins into *Umbilicus*. Delphi is a word of the very ſame import, being compounded of Tel-Phi, *the oracle of the ſun*[n]. I doubt not, but that Cotylè was, like the iſland near Buto, dedicated to Apollo and the Cabiri: accordingly we find, that the Pelaſgi, in a time of great dearth, with which their

[m] Plin. Nat. Hiſt. lib. iii. cap. 12.

[n] The connection of Delphi with the diluvian, as well as with the ſolar worſhip, appears from a tradition preſerved by Tzetzes, that this oracular city derived its name from Delphus, who was ſuppoſed to have been the ſon of Neptune by Melantho, the daughter of Deucalion. Αλλοι δε φασι Δελφες κληθηναι απο Δελφε υἱε Ποσειδωνος και Μελανθες της Δευκαλιωνος θυγατρος. Tzet. in Lycoph. ver. 208. Deucalion is ſaid by the Greeks to have firſt landed after the deluge upon the ſummit of mount Parnaſſus, at the foot of which Delphi was built. Apollod. Bibl. lib. i. cap. 7.

new

new ſettlements were afflicted, vowed tenths to Jupiter, the Cabiri, and Apollo [o].

Having thus attempted to arrange the firſt genealogical table of Sanchoniatho, which conſiſts of the deſcendants of Protogonus, I ſhall proceed to conſider the ſecond, of which Eliun-Hypſiſtus is the head.

I can by no means aſſent to Bp. Cumberland's ſuppoſition, that Eliun is the Sethite Lamech, Uranus his ſon Noah, and Cronus Ham. *Eliun* is evidently a mere variation of the Hebrew word *Eloah*; conſequently, when connected with *Hypſiſtus*, it will ſignify *God the Moſt High*. A title, like this, can ſurely never be applied with any propriety to a *man*; I ſhould rather apprehend, that it means no other, than the Almighty Lord and Creator of the whole world. As for Uranus and Ge, according to the moſt natural and obvious interpretation, they are the material heaven and earth; their allegorical children, Cronus, Atlas, and Dagon, are, like Agruerus and Sydyk, only different names of the ſame great patriarch; while Betylus is not a man, but a term expreſſive of a peculiar mode of adoration [p].

[o] Dion Halic. Ant. Rom lib. i. cap 23.

[p] This mode of worſhip ſhall be conſidered towards the cloſe of the preſent chapter.

 The

The ſecond table therefore, when connected with the firſt, will ſtand as follows.

Sanchoniatho's ſecond genealogical table.

1. Eliun-Hypſiſtus	1. God the Moſt High.
2. Uranus, Ge.	2. Heaven, Earth.
3. Cronus, Atlas, or Dagon.	3. Noah.
4. Cronus the younger, Jupiter-Belus, Apollo.	4. Shem, Ham, Japhet [q].

The latter part of Table II. connected with the latter part of Table I. and adapted to Scripture.

1. Agruerus. — 2. Amynus, or Ham. — 3. Miſor, or Mizraim.

1. Sydyk. — 2. The 7 Cabiri. — 3. The ſons of the Cabiri.

1. Cronus. — 2. Cronus. Jupiter-Belus. | Apollo. — 2. The 7 Titans.

1. Noah. — 2. Shem. Ham. | Japhet. — 2. The 7 perſons, of whom the arkite family was compoſed, excluſive of Noah.

[q] In this inſtance, Belus, Apollo, and the younger Cronus, from the circumſtance of their being deſcribed as the three ſons of the elder Cronus, are evidently Shem, Ham, and Japhet; but nevertheleſs we ſhall frequently find the great patriarch himſelf deſignated by the name of *Baal* or *Apollo*. Vide ſupra p. 16.

Eliun-

Eliun-Hypſiſtus being the true God, Sanchoniatho does not attempt to enumerate his progenitors, but ſimply obſerves, that a perſonage, known by that appellation, who was the father of heaven and earth, flouriſhed in the days of Sydyk and the Cabiri. This mode of ſpeaking is evidently metaphorical, implying only, that he was the Creator of the Univerſe; and the reaſon, why he is ſo particularly ſaid by Sanchoniatho to have been contemporary with Sydyk, ſeems to be on account of his having exerted his power, in a more tremendous and peculiar manner at that period, than at any other.

To Eliun the Phenician mythologiſt aſſigns a conſort, whom he calls *Beruth*. For a ſatisfactory explanation of this part of the tradition, little more is neceſſary than barely to refer to the Hebrew ſcriptures.

"God ſpake to Noah, and to his ſons with "him, ſaying,—I will eſtabliſh *my covenant* "(in the Hebrew *Berithi*) with you; neither "ſhall all fleſh be cut off any more by the "waters of a flood to deſtroy the earth [r]."

Hence it appears, that, in the uſual ſtrain of oriental allegory, the ſolemn covenant, the

[r] Gen ix. 8, 11.

inviolable *Berith* of God, is perſonified by a female, who is deſcribed as his conſort [s].

From this union of Eliun and Beruth ſprung Uranus and Ge; or, in the unadorned language of hiſtorical narration, the Almighty, after the confuſion of the deluge, created anew the heaven and the earth, and covenanted with man, that he would never more deſtroy the world by water [t].

The offspring of Uranus and Ge were Cronus, Dagon, Atlas, and Betylus. With regard to Cronus, he is evidently the ſame perſon as the claſſical Cronus or Saturn: accordingly both the Phenician and the Grecian deity of that name are equally deſcribed as the ſon of Heaven and Earth [u]. Such a deſcent is doubtleſs allegorical. The traditions

[s] This Berith is the ſame as the Beroë of Nonnus, whoſe mythological hiſtory ſhall be conſidered hereafter The Hindoo chronology mentions a pious prince named *Prithu*, who was the tenth in deſcent from the firſt created pair Adim and Iva, and who is deſcribed as the inventor of agriculture. Captain Wilford, and I think very juſtly, ſuppoſes Prithu to be Noah. (Aſiat Ref vol v. p. 254) The word *Prithu* may poſſibly be compounded of Berith-Thu, *the god of the covenant*.

[t] The proceſs of the renovation of the world after the deluge ſeems nearly to have reſembled that of the primeval creation. See Catcott's Treatiſe on the Deluge.

[u] Heſiod Theog ver. 126, 137.

of

of the pagans rarely extended beyond the epoch of the deluge; they were obliged therefore to aſcribe to the firſt poſtdiluvian a mythological, rather than a natural origin. Hence Cronus, or Noah, ſuſpended as it were between heaven and earth upon the face of the great deep, is ſaid in the metaphorical language of poetry to be their *ſon*.

One circumſtance indeed is mentioned in his hiſtory, the unworthy treatment, that his father Uranus, or the Heavens, experienced from him, which perhaps it may not be quite ſo eaſy to reconcile with the ſcriptural account of Noah [x]. Nevertheleſs, if it be taken in an allegorical ſenſe, the awful event of the deluge may perhaps ſufficiently explain it. Obedient to the command of the Almighty, the waters, gradually riſing from the central abyſs, encroached upon the ancient limits of the material heaven, or the atmoſphere, and thus curtailed it of its former extent [y]. Hence we are informed by He-

[x] ——— Φιλȣ δ' απο μηδεα πατρος
Εσσυμενως ημησε ——— Heſiod Theog ver. 180

[y] I venture to ſay, curtailed it, in the ſtrict philoſophical ſenſe of the word, as will ſufficiently appear to any one, who has conſulted Catcott's theory reſpecting the cauſes of the deluge, one of the principal of which he ſuppoſes to be, a portion of the atmoſphere forced into the central abyſs, and expelling its waters to the ſurface of the globe.

ſiod[z], that it was the earth, which brought this calamity upon the heavens.

The war between Cronus and Uranus, and between Uranús and Pontus, as detailed by Sanchoniatho, blended as it is with the wildeſt fictions, comprehends ſeveral very curious particulars, which remarkably confirm the preceding ſuppoſition. The heaven is ſaid to make war upon the ſea: in other words, the atmoſphere, ruſhing violently into the central abyſs, forces it to diſgorge its waters, which, in conjunction with thoſe of the Ocean, ſpeedily overflow the habitable globe. Demaroön, who is deſcribed as the ſon of Uranus by a concubine, but who, like his brother Cronus, ſeems to be merely Da-Ma-Aron, *the great arkite patriarch*, is repreſented as having leagued himſelf with his father in his attack upon Pontus, or the ſea; but, unable to reſiſt the impetuoſity of the waters, and trembling with the apprehenſion of impending danger, he vows to offer up a ſacrifice, provided he ſhould eſcape. Cronus meanwhile, in ſingular conformity with the preceding ſuppoſition, caſtrates his father Uranus, *in a certain place in the centre of the earth, in the neighbourhood of fountains*

[z] Heſiod. Theog. ver. 159. e .inceps.

and rivers[a]. It is remarkable, that Cronus, in his war againſt Uranus, is ſaid to have been aſſiſted by Elohim. This word is the Hebrew name of God: whence it is manifeſt, that the tradition ſignifies nothing more, than that the Almighty lent his divine aid to Noah during the perils of the deluge.

The Phenician Cronus is ſuppoſed to have had three ſons, Cronus the younger, Jupiter-Belus, and Apollo. This triple offspring manifeſtly correſponds with the ſcriptural Shem, Ham, and Japhet. Contemporary with them, according to Sanchoniatho, were the ſea, and Typhon, and Nereus the father of the ſea; a declaration very remarkable, inaſmuch as it naturally refers us to that awful period, when

[a] Should the reader diſlike this mode of interpreting the fable of Uranus and Cronus, which indeed is principally founded upon the expreſſion of Sanchoniatho, εν τοπῳ τινι μεσογαιῳ, he may adopt inſtead of it another ſuppoſition: namely, that Uranus has been confounded with Cronus or Noah, and Cronus himſelf with the younger Cronus or Ham. Hence, as Porphyry juſtly obſerves, Jupiter or the younger Cronus is ſaid to have committed the very ſame crime againſt the elder Cronus, as the elder Cronus had previouſly done againſt Uranus. (Porph. de ant. Nymph. p. 260.) I am bound moreover to mention, that Uranus, though properly the material Heaven, is ſometimes undoubtedly Noah. (Vide infra chap. ix. in init.) It is in fact a vain labour to attempt to reduce the mythology of paganiſm to a [illegible] of perfect acc[illegible]racy.

the Ocean, ſwollen beyond its uſual limits, overwhelmed a guilty world beneath its waves. The various names of *Pontus*, *Typhon*, and *Nereus*, are only different titles of the ſame element, for we are plainly informed by Plutarch, that the Egyptian deity Typhon was a perſonification of the ſea, no leſs than Nereus and Pontus [b].

[b] Τυφωνα δε την θαλασσαν. Plut. de Iſid et Oſir. p. 363 It is worthy of obſervation, that the Arabs ſtill expreſs *the general deluge* by the term *al Tufan* Anc Univ Hiſt vol. i p. 200. note E. Nereus may perhaps be derived either from the Sanſcreet Nara, or from the Hebrew Ner, *to flow or run as water.* " Hence," ſays Mr. Parkhurſt, " the Greeks and Romans had " their Nereus, which originally ſignified *the great abyſs*, or " *the ſea conſidered as communicating with it.* Thus Nereus is " addreſſed in the Orphic hymn:

Poſſeſſor of the Ocean's gloomy depth,
Ground of the ſea, earth's bourn and ſource of all!
Shaking prolific Ceres' ſacred ſeat,
When in the deep receſſes of thy reign,
The madding blaſts are by thy power confin'd:
But oh! the earthquake's dreadful force forefend!

" The reader will make his own reflections on theſe lines, " while I proceed to obſerve, that the Roman poets uſed Ne- " reus for the ſea or ocean, even ſo late as the time of Ovid, " who has this expreſſion:

——qua totum Nereus circumtonat orbem.

" Old Nereus was, according to the Greek and Roman mytho- " logy, conſtantly attended by fifty daughters, called *Nereids*, " who repreſented the numerous rivers, that proceed from the " ocean, and run into it again." Heb. Lex. Vox נהר.

If Nereus then be allowed to ſignify *the great central abyſs*, as contradiſtinguiſhed

A general notion ſeems to have prevailed, that Saturn or Janus, for they are in fact one deity, the ſame as the Phenician Cronus or Noah [c], viſited Italy [d]: hence, as I ſhall here-

contradiſtinguiſhed from *the viſible ſea*, we ſhall immediately perceive the propriety with which Sanchoniatho deſcribes him as the *father* of Pontus.

[c] Thus Cato directly aſſerts, that the Italian Saturn was a Phenician deity. Italiæ ſplendidiſſima origo fuit, tum tempore, tum origine gentis. Cœpit enim aureo ſæculo ſub principibus diis Jano, Cameſe, Saturno gente Phœnica, et Saga, quæ poſt inundationem terrarum per orbem prima colonias miſit. M Caton. Fragm. de Orig Fol. 160. Saga was the ancient name of Armenia, the country where the Ark landed; and it is remarkable, that the epithet *Araxea*, or *arkite*, was beſtowed upon this territory. Omnes hiſtorici Græci, Latini, et Barbari, qui de priſcis ante Ninum antiquitatibus conſcripſerunt, unanimi conſenſu affirmant in priſca Armenia Araxea cœpiſſe genus humanum quacunque via cœperit Eadem regio prius *Aramea Scythia Saga* dicta fuit. Ann. Viterb. Comment. in Beroſ Antiq. lib ii. fol. 12. Saga ſeems to be Z-Ag-Ai, *the land of the mighty waters*.

The ſymbolical mode of repreſenting the pagan deities is aſcribed by Sanchoniatho to Taautus or Thoth, who is ſaid to have deſignated the Phenician Saturn, in a manner preciſely reſembling the ſtatues of the Roman Janus. The poſition of his four eyes was ſuch, as enabled him to look both proſpectively and retroſpectively, alluſive to the double view of Noah into the old and new worlds. Euſeb. Præp Evan lib i. cap 10.

[d] Cauſſa ratis ſupereſt, Thuſcum rate venit in amnem
Ante pererrato falcifer orbe deus.
Ovid Faſt lib i. ver. 233

after

after take occaſion to ſhew[e], the Cabiric worſhip was introduced at an early period into that country. Saturn is uſually deſcribed as a very ancient deity: Macrobius accordingly ſtyles him *the firſt of the gods*[f]; and Salluſt, in reference perhaps to the connection of Noah with the watery element, affirms, that Cronus is water[g]. He is repreſented in the Latin, no leſs than in the Phenician theology, as the parent of three ſons, and as the conſort of Rhea or Opis, by whom he became the father of the ſeven Titans. Rhea however is ſimply a perſonification of the lunar Ark: whence, as we learn from Damaſcius, the commencement of a new order of things, or a kind of new creation, was aſcribed to Saturn and Rhea[h]; and the number *eight*, the number equally of the perſons preſerved in the Ark, of Cronus and the Titans, and of Sydyk and the Cabiri, was conſecrated in a peculiar manner to that goddeſs[i].

As for Janus, he was depicted holding a

[e] Vide infra chap. vi.

[f] Saturn. lib i. cap. 7.

[g] Κρονον μεν ὑδωρ. Sall. de Diis et Mundo, cap. 4. Thus alſo Stobèus; Δακρυ μεν εςι Κρονος. Eclog. Phyſ. lib. i. cap. 9.

[h] Ἡ Ῥεα του Κρονȣ εις αλλην διακοσμησιν προαγει τα γεννηματα. Damaſ. apud Annot. in Phorn. Theor ſect. 6.

[i] Τη Ῥεᾳ ἡ Ογδοας προσηκει. Ibid.

staff

ſtaff in his left hand, with which he appears to ſtrike a rock, and to cauſe water to flow from it[k]. He was eſteemed the peculiar deity of gates; and many ſuperſtitious rites were obſerved, in opening and ſhutting the doors of his temple. This notion ſeems to have originated from the circumſtance of Noah having made a door in the ſide of the Ark, which was opened during his ingreſs and egreſs, and which was ſhut during the continuance of the deluge: hence alſo the goddeſs of the Ark was ſometimes ſtyled *Prothyrèa*. Macrobius informs us, that Janus and Jana were the ſame as Apollo and Diana[l], or in other words, the ſolar Noah, and the lunar Ark: and he adds that Janus-Apollo was worſhipped by the Greeks under the name of *Thyrèus*, or *the god of doors*, and was eſteemed the preſident of ingreſs and egreſs[l]. His original appellation was not *Janus* but *Eanus*[l], which I apprehend to be only a variation of the Babylonic *Oan*, or *Oannes*. In his ſacred rites, Janus was intitled *the double god*, from his having beheld two worlds; *Junonius* from Juneh *the dove*, the *Juno* of claſſi-

[k] In ſiniſtra habebat (Janus) baculum, quo ſaxum percutere, et ex illo aquam producere videbatur. Albrici Philoſ. de Deor. Imag. cap. 14.

[l] Macrob. Saturn. lib. i. cap. 9.

cal

cal mythology; *Consivius*, from his being a husbandman; *Quirinus*, from Cur, *the Sun*; and *Patulcius*, and *Clusivius*, from the opening and shutting of his gates[m]. The Phenicians represented him under the usual solar emblem the dragon[m]: and Plutarch, in consequence of his being the diluvian patriarch no less than the Sun, speaks of an ancient medal of the doublefaced Janus, which had the head or the stern of a ship on the reverse; but he was unable to assign any very satisfactory reason for it[n]. Lastly, Inghiramius, if his authority can be depended upon, notices an Etruscan fragment, in which the identity of Janus and Noah is absolutely asserted. According to this curious relic of antiquity, Vandimon, known by the Latins under the name of *Janus*, and by the Syrians under that of *Noah*, came into Hetruria with his son *Japhet* and his children; where he founded a city, upon which he bestowed the appellation of *Cethem*[o]. Vandimon, or Oandimon,

[m] Macrob. Saturn. lib. i. cap 9.

[n] Quæst. Rom p 274.

[o] Magnus pater Vandimon, qui a Latinis *Janus*, a Syris *Noa* vocatur, advenit in hanc regionem (scil Hetruriam) cum secundo filio Iapeto, et illius filiis; et cum venissent super hunc montem sibi commodum, posteris jucundum putavit. Quare in superiori parte, quæ salubrior esset, civitatem ædificavit, et *Cethem* appellavit. Inghir. apud Annot. ad Lact. de Fal. Rel. lib.

ſeems to be Oan-da-Mon, *the Oannes* [p] or *Noah of the Ark*; and he was worſhipped by the ancient Tyrrhenians in conjunction with Veſta, whom they denominated *Horchia*, or *the goddeſs of the Ark* [q]. Titèa, who is mentioned by Pſeudo-Beroſus, as the wife of Noah, bore the ſame title of *Horchia*, and for the very ſame reaſon; the Ark being frequently deſcribed as the allegorical conſort of the principal arkite deity [r].

As Cronus then is ſaid by Sanchoniatho to

lib. i cap. 13. Pſeudo-Beroſus alſo aſſerts, that Janus was the patriarch Noah, and that he derived his name from Jain יין, *wine*. Ob beneficium inventæ vitis et vini dignatus eſt (ſcil. Noe) cognomento *Jano*, quod Arameis ſonat *vitifer* et *vinifer*. Beroſ. Ant. lib. iii. fol. 25. It may be proper here to obſerve, that the writings of this Beroſus, which I ſhall frequently have occaſion to cite, were publiſhed by Annius of Viterbo, and are certainly not thoſe of the real Beroſus. We are informed by Pliny, (Nat Hiſt. lib vi. cap. 55) that the genuine hiſtory of Beroſus contained the events of 480 years; but of that work there now only remain a few fragments, cited by Joſephus in his *Writings againſt Apion*, and by Alexander Polyhiſtor in *the Chronographia* of Syncellus.

[p] The hiſtory of Oannes or Dagon ſhall be conſidered at the latter end of the preſent chapter.

[q] Soli Turreni colunt Janum et Veſtam, quos lingua ſua vocant *Jamb Vadimona* et *Labith Horchiam*. Myrſil. de bello Pelaſg. cap. 6. Labith ſeems to be a contraction of Labeneth, (לבנת) *the moon*; whence Labith Horchia will ſignify *the arkite creſcent*.

[r] Beroſ. Ant. lib. v. fol. 64.

have

have had three ſons, Cronus the younger, Jupiter-Belus, and Apollo, in alluſion to the triple offspring of Noah; ſo, in reference to the number of the arkite family excluſive of their head, he is alſo deſcribed, like Sydyk, as being the father of ſeven ſons by Rhea, and of ſeven daughters by Aſtartè. Theſe laſt of his children were called *Titans*, and *Titanides*; whence it will follow, that the war of the Titans, ſo celebrated in Grecian ſtory, relates to the deluge, and not to the events which took place at Babel. The traditional hiſtory indeed of the Titans is involved in ſome degree of confuſion, becauſe the name is equally applied to all, who lived at the era of the deluge, both thoſe who were deſtroyed by that cataſtrophè, and thoſe who were ſaved; but the genealogy, aſcribed to them, by Sanchoniatho, along with various matters which ſhall hereafter be adduced, abundantly proves the truth of the foregoing aſſertion. The legend however of the ſeven Titans muſt be reſerved for future conſideration[s]; at preſent

[s] Vide infra chap. ix. Since Cronus is the ſame perſon as Sydyk, the ſeven Titans will of courſe be the ſame as the ſeven Cabiri; and ſince Agruerus is alſo the ſame perſon as Cronus or Sydyk, we ſhall ſee the exact propriety of Sanchoniatho's aſſertion, that Agruerus and his family were known by the general name of *Titans* or *Alotæ*.

there-

therefore I ſhall only notice that of Aſtartè, and her children the Titanides.

Aſtartè, the mythological conſort of Cronus, or Noah, is the ſame deity as Venus[t], who was uſually repreſented by the poets riſing in youthful beauty from the waves of the troubled ocean, and ſurrounded by fiſhes and other aquatic animals. She is in ſhort the Noëtic Ark, which by the allegorizing ſpirit of antiquity was perſonified in the character of a graceful female[u]. Accordingly we find, that the dove is always ſaid to be the peculiar favourite of Venus; an opinion, which will eaſily be accounted for, when we recollect, that that bird brought the firſt tidings of the waters having retired from off the ſurface of the earth. Hyginus has preſerved a curious tradition reſpecting the Aſſyrian Venus, in which the arkite dove, and the mundane egg, make a very conſpicuous

[t] *Την δε Αςαρτην Φοινικες την Αφροδιτην ειναι λεγουσι.* Euſ Præp. Evan lib. 1 cap. 10. Aſtartè is alſo in fact the ſame as Rhea. The identity of the heathen goddeſſes will be ſhewn in the following chapter.

[u] Venus, like Ceres, was ſometimes alſo eſteemed the earth, and ſometimes the moon Aſſyriorum, apud quos Veneris Architidis—maxima olim veneratio viguit, quam nunc Phœnices tenent · nam Phyſici terræ ſuperius hemiſphærium, cujus partem incolimus, Veneris appellatione coluerunt. Macrob. Saturn. lib. 1. cap. 21.

 ap-

appearance. An egg of wonderful magnitude was reported to have fallen from heaven into the river Euphrates, and to have been rolled by fishes to the bank. Upon it sat doves[x]; and out of it was at length produced that Venus, who was afterwards styled the *Syrian goddess*[y]. The same writer, upon the authority of Diogenetes Erythrèus, mentions the peril to which Venus was exposed by the attack of the monster Typhon, or the sea[z].

[x] Ampelius is more exact in this particular than Hyginus; for, in relating the same fable, he speaks of only *one* dove. Amp cap 2

[y] In Euphratem de cœlo ovum mira magnitudine cecidisse dicitur, quod pisces ad ripam evolverunt: super quod columbæ consederunt, et excalfactum exclusisse Venerem, quæ postea *dea Syria* est appellata. Hyg Fab. 197.

[z] Mr Whiston supposes, that the deluge was occasioned by the too near approach of a comet; and he calculates, that it was that comet, which appeared in the year 1680. Many parts of his theory may perhaps be thought objectionable; but at the same time it is not impossible, that the power of attraction, exerted by a comet, might force the waters of the great abyss to rush forth in a tremendous torrent, and thus produce the catastrophè of the deluge It is foreign however to my present subject to examine into the merits of Mr Whiston's system; I mention it only for the purpose of introducing some very singular coincidences with his opinion respecting a comet's being the natural cause of the flood. Sanchoniatho asserts, that while Astartè was travelling about the world, (or in other words, while the Ark floated in an erratic state upon the surface of the waters,) she found a star falling from the sky, which she afterwards consecrated at Tyre: Pliny affirms, that a comet appeared

Closely pursued by her irresistible enemy, she assumed the shape of a fish, and thus avoided the threatened danger[a].

Venus then, or Astartè, being a personification of the Ark emerging from the waters of the deluge, and being uniformly attended by the Noëtic dove, we shall see the propriety with which the Laconians consecrated a temple to Venus-Juno, on account of a flood supposed to have been occasioned by the river Eurotas[b]. Juno is Juneh, *the dove*; whence Venus-Juno will be equivalent to Venus attended by her dove. To this deluge of the Eurotas, and to such other traditions

peared during the reign of Typhon or the deluge, the effects of which were extremely detrimental and tremendous · and Hyginus mentions, that, when Phaëthon the son of Apollo had set the whole world on fire by mismanaging the chariot of his father, Jupiter, to quench the flames, caused a general inundation, from which Pyrrha and Deucalion alone escaped. Sanch. apud Eus. Præp. Evan. lib i. cap. 10 —Plin. Nat. Hist lib ii. cap 25 —Hyg Fab 152.

[a] Diogenetes Erythræus ait, quodam tempore Venerem cum Cupidine filio in Syriam ad flumen Euphratem venisse, et eodem loco repente Typhona giganta apparuisse Venerem autem cum filio in flumen se projecisse, et ibi figuram piscium forma mutasse: quo facto periculo esse liberatos. Hyg. Poet. Astron. lib ii. cap. 30.

[b] Ἡρας δε ἱερον ὑπερχειριας κατα μαντειαν εποιηθη, τε Ευρωτα πολυ της γης σφισιν επικλυζοντος ξοανον δε αρχαιον καλουσιν Αφροδιτης-Ἡρας. Paus. Lacon. p. 239

of a deluge, as may hereafter be mentioned, I ſhall apply the judicious obſervation of Voſſius, that from the general flood of Noah were derived all the heathen ſtories of local and particular inundations[c].

In conſequence of Venus being a perſonification of the Ark, we find her denominated *Arſinoè*[d], or Baris-Noè, *the Ark of Noah*; *Hippodamia*[e], or Hippa-da-Maia, *the arkite mother*; and *Arenta*, or Aran-Thea, *the goddeſs of the Ark*.

> Και τον θεᾳ κλαυσθεντα Γαυαντος ταφον,
> Σχοινιδι μυσοφθαρτον, ΑΡΕΝΤᾼ, ξενῃ,
> Κρανταιει λοῦκῳ τον ποτ' εκτανε πλεκας[f].

She was not however *merely* the Ark, but the Ark worſhipped in conjunction with the Moon; hence the author of the Orphic hymns invokes her in terms, partly applicable to her diluvian and partly to her aſtronomical character. He ſtyles her *the goddeſs ſprung from the ſea, the ruler of the three diviſions*[g], *the*

[c] Voſſ. de Idol. lib. i. cap. 18.

[d] Strab. Geog. lib. xvii. p. 800.

[e] Heſych.

[f] Lycoph. Caſſan. ver. 831.

[g] This I apprehend to be an alluſion to the triple diviſion of the world among the ſons of Noah. Theſe three diviſions are ſaid by the poets to be heaven, earth, and hell; hence Diana upon earth is Luna in heaven, and Hecatè in the infernal regions. If we ſurvey the ſame fable in a different point of view, as relating to the three ſons of Cronus, heaven is aſſigned

nurse of Bacchus or Noah[h], *the visible and the invisible*[i], *the tutelary deity of Syria and of Egypt.*

——————Αφροδιτη,
Ποντογενης, γενετειρα θεα, φιλοπαννυχε σεμνη,
Νυκτερια·—
Και κρατεεις τρισσων μοιρων·—
——Σεμνη Βακχοιο παρεδρε,
Φαινομενη τ' αφανης—
——Ειτ' εν Ολυμπω
Ει συ θεα βασιλεια καλω γηθεσα προσωπω,
Ειτε και ευλιβανε Συριης εδος αμφιπολευεις,
Ειτε συ γ' εν πεδιοισι συν αρμασι χρυσεοτευκτοις
Αιγυπτε κατεχεις[k].——

In the East Venus was worshipped under the appellation of the *Syrian goddess*. Lucian indeed considers it as doubtful whether this goddess was Juno or Derceto[l]; but it matters little which opinion be adopted, for Juno is the dove, and Derceto, or Atargatis, was the same as Astartè[m], who is declared both by

signed to Jupiter, hell to Pluto, and the sea comprehending the earth to Neptune, whence his frequent Homeric title Ενοσιχθων.

[h] In her character of the Ark. She was the same as Hippa, who is also described as the nurse of Bacchus.

[i] In her character of the Moon.

[k] Orph. Hymn. 54.

[l] Αλλοι δε Σεμιραμιν την Βαβυλωνιην, της ηδη πολλα εργα εν τη Ασια εστι, ταυτην και τοδε το εδος εισασθαι νομιζεσι, ουκ Ηρη δε εισασθαι, αλλα μητρι εωυτης, της Δερκετω ουνομα. Luc de Dea Syra, sect 14.

[m] Artemid. Oniroc. lib. i. cap 9. Hence it is evident, that the Syrian goddess is the same as the *Venus-Juno* of Laconia.

Sanchoniatho and Glycas[n] to be Venus. Derceto however, or Venus, aſſumed the form of a fiſh; and it is remarkable, that her daughter Semiramis was ſuppoſed to have been changed into a dove.

——Dubia eſt, de te, Babylonia narret,
Derceti, quam verſa ſquamis velantibus artus
Stagna Palæſtinæ credunt celebrâſſe figura:
An magis ut ſumtis illius filia pennis
Extremos albis in turribus egerit annos[o].

Venus and Juno therefore I apprehend to be the ſame as Derceto and Semiramis. The ſcholiaſt upon Aratus indeed ſuppoſes Dercè, or Derceto, to be the daughter of Venus, rather than Venus herſelf; but, ſince he aſſerts, that they were changed into the two fiſhes, which were afterwards placed in the zodiac, and ſince he particularly mentions Derceto as the Syrian goddeſs, it evidently appears to be only a variation of the preceding fable[p]. The conſtellations of Aquarius and the great fiſh appear to be connected in a ſimilar manner with the hiſtory of the de-

[n] Euſeb. Præp. Evan. lib. i. cap. 10.—Glyc. Annal. p. 184.

[o] Ovid. Metam. lib. iv. ver. 44. See alſo Athen. Legat. p. 33.

[p] Οὗτοι τε εισιν οἱ τȣ μεγαλȣ ιχθυος εκγονοι, περι ὧ εν τοις ἑξης ερει, οἵτινες Δερκην την Αφροδιτης θυγατερα εμπεσȣσαν εις θαλασσαν εσωσαν· ὅθεν εις τιμην της θεας ὁ Συριοι ιχθυων απεχονται. Schol. in Arat. Phœnom. p. 32.

luge.

luge. The fiſh, which was one of the moſt uſual ſymbols of the Ark, is repreſented ſwallowing the water, which flows from the urn of Aquarius; and it was firſt ſeen, according to Cteſias, in a lake near Bambycè. Derceto, or Venus, the Syrian goddeſs, falling into the lake, was by this fiſh ſafely conveyed to the ſhore [q]. According to Xanthus the Lydian, Derceto had a ſon, who was denominated *Ichthus*, or *the fiſh*. This Ichthus, I doubt not, was the Dagon, or fiſh-god of the Philiſtines, under which name they worſhipped the patriarch Noah [r].

With regard to the ſeven Titanides, the mythological daughters of Derceto, or Aſtartè, we learn from the author of the works aſcribed to Orpheus, that their names were *Themis*, *Tethys*, *Mnemoſynè*, *Thea*, *Dionè*, *Phebè*, and *Rhea*:

[q] Ουτος εϛιν ὁ μεγας καλϐμενος ιχθυς, ὁν και πιειν λεγϐσι το ὑδωρ της ὑδροχοϐ εκχυσεως. Ἱϛορειται δε περι τϐτϐ, ὡς φησι Κτησιας, ειναι προτερον εν λιμνη τινι κατα την Βαμϐυκην· εμπεσϐσης δε της Δερκητϐς νυκτος, σωσαι αυτην, ἡν οἱ περι τϐς τοπϐς οικϐντες Συριας θεον ωνομασαι. Erat. Cataſt. Ιχθυς.

[r] See Athen. Deipnoſ. lib. viii. p. 346. where the reader will find a truly Greek derivation of the word *Atargatis*. It is remarkable, that a particular kind of fiſh was denominated *Bacchus* from the deity of that name, who was no other than Noah. Athen. Deipnoſ. lib. viii p 356.

῾Επτα μεν ευειδεις κουρας, ἑπτα δε παιδας ανακτας.
Θυγατερας μεν Θεμιν, και ευφρονα Τηθυν,
Μνημοσυνην τε βαθυπλοκαμον, Θειαν τε μακαιραν,
῾Η τε Διωνην τικτεν αριπρεπες ειδος εχουσαν,
Φοιβην τε, ῾Ρειην τε Διος γενετειραν ανακτος [s].

Of these Titanides, Rhea, Phebè, Tethys, and Dionè, are the most remarkable characters.

Rhea is the same as Cybelè, a mere personification of the lunar Ark [t]; and Dionè is a contraction of Da-Ionah, *the dove*. Hence we find, that the mysteries of Rhea were immediately connected with those of Bacchus, or Noah, and that Dionè was sometimes esteemed his mother [u].

Phebè, or Diana, is usually described by the poets as a huntress; but, since she is declared by Orpheus to be a Titanis, we are led to conclude, that her real character is that of

[s] Orph. apud Proclum in Timæum, lib. v. p. 295.

[t] Consequently she is the same as her supposed mother Venus, or Astartè, as shall be shewn at large hereafter, when I treat of the identity of the heathen goddesses. Sanchoniatho, as we have seen, makes Rhea the sister of Astartè, and the consort of Cronus. This variation however is more apparent than real, for the Ark was indifferently represented as the wife, the daughter, the sister, or the mother, of Noah.

[u] Ω παι Διωνης, ὁς εφυς μεγας θεος, Διονυσε. Eurip. apud Schol. in Pind. Pyth. iii. ver. 177. She is said by Sanchoniatho to have been one of the wives of Cronus.

a dia diluvian goddeſs [x]. Accordingly Artemidorus [y], Pauſanias [z], and Strabo [a], all concur in beſtowing upon her the title of *Limnatis*, or the *maritime deity* [b]; and, in an ancient inſcription preſerved by Gruter, ſhe is called Regina undarum, *the queen of the waves* [c]. Hence Apollonius, with the utmoſt propriety, repreſents Orpheus as invoking her under the appellation of *the preſerver of ſhips*.

Τοισι δε φορμιζων ευθημονι μελπεν αοιδη
Οιαγροιο παις ΝΗΟΣΣΟΟΝ, ευπατερειαν
Αρτεμιν [d].——

Diana then being one of the ſeven Titanides, and thus connected with the hiſtory of the deluge, we ſhall be able to account for a ſingular ſuperſtitious notion reſpecting her

[x] Diana is the Moon worſhipped along with the Ark.

[y] Oniroc. lib. ii. cap. 42.

[z] Της δε αγορης αντικρυς κατα ταυτην εξοδον τεμενος εστιν Αρτεμιδος και ναον Λιμναλιδος. Achaic. p 575. Αρτεμιδος ἱερον εστιν εν τη Επιδαυριων Λιμνατιδος. Lacon. p. 271.

[a] Geog lib. viii p. 361.

[b] The word Λιμνη is applied to the ſea by Homer, which, I apprehend, juſtifies this tranſlation of *Limnatis*.

——Ενθα δε οἱ κλυτα δωματα βενθεσι ΛΙΜΝΗΣ,
Χρυσεα, μαρμαιροντα, τετευχαται——

Iliad. xiii 21. See alſo Odyſſ. iii. 1. The ſimilar title of *Limnæus* was beſtowed upon Bacchus, and for the ſame reaſon: Λιμναιον κληθηναι τον Διονυσον. Athen. Deipnoſ. lib xi. p. 465.

[c] Grut. p. 37.

[d] Argon. lib. i. ver. 569.

tem-

temple at Bargylia in Caria. According to Strabo and Polybius, while the rain fell in torrents around it, the ſacred edifice, protected by a ſupernatural influence, remained perfectly dry[e]. This temple, like that of Buto, ſeems to have been deſigned as an emblem of the Ark, the interior of which was unaffected by the ſtorm, while its exterior was plunged in the midſt of ſurrounding waters[f].

The fabulous hiſtory of the Titanis Tethys will equally ſerve to ſhew *her* relation alſo to the cataſtrophè of the deluge. We learn from Tzetzes, that ſhe was the mother of Inachus by Oceanus[g]; and that Inachus was the father of Phoroneus and Egialeus[h], by Melia

[e] Πλησιον δε εστι των Βαργυλιων το της Αρτεμιδος ἱερον της Μινδυαδος, ὁπερ πεπιστευκασι περιϋεσθαι. Strab. Geog. lib. xiv. p. 658. Πεπιστευται παρα μεν τοις Βαργυλιηταις, διοτι το της Κινδυαδος Αρτεμιδος αγαλμα καιπερ εν ὑπαιθριον ουτε νιφεται το παραπαν, ουτε βρεχεται. Polyb. lib. xvi.

The appellation of *Mindyas*, applied by theſe writers to Diana, ſeems to be compounded of Mena-Du, *the divine Noetic Ark*; as Bargylia is of P'Arg-El-Aia, *the land of the divine Ark*.

[f] In alluſion perhaps to the ſhip of Noah, the Greek appellatives for *a ſhip* and *a temple* are nearly the ſame.

[g] Oceanus and Tethys were alſo the parents of Beroè, whoſe hiſtory ſhall be conſidered hereafter. Vide infra chap. ix.

[h] Egialeus ſignifies *a fiſherman dwelling upon the ſea-ſhore*. The circumſtance of his dying childleſs may poſſibly allude to the deſtruction of the antediluvians, the poſterity of Inachus, or Phoroneus, being alone preſerved in the Ark.

daugh-

daughter of Oceanus. Egialeus was childiſh; but Phoroneus, eſpouſing the nymph Telodicè [i], begot Apis and Niobè. Apis reigned in a very tyrannical manner, and was ſlain by Thelxion and Telchin; but from his ſiſter Niobè and Jupiter were born Argus and Pelaſgus [k]. In the days of Inachus happened the fabulous conteſt of Neptune and Juno for the ſovereignty of Argos; in other words the allegorical conteſt of the ſea, and the Noëtic dove, for the poſſeſſion of the Ark. The matter in diſpute was referred to Inachus, who decided in favour of Juno; upon which Neptune immediately deluged the whole country. Juno however at length perſuaded him to cauſe the ſea to retire; and the Argives, in gratitude, built a temple to Neptune the Inundator, at the place where the waters firſt began to abate [l]. Near this

[i] Telodicè is Telo-Daga, *the arkite fiſh of the Sun.* The whole of the genealogy of Inachus is entirely mythological, relating partly to the ſolar, and partly to the arkite worſhip.

[k] Ωκεανȣ και Τηθυος Ιναχος. Ιναχȣ και Μελιας της Ωκεανȣ Φορωνευς, και Αιγιαλευς απαις—Φορωνευς δυναϛευων Πελοποννησȣ εκ Τηλοδικης νυμφης γεννᾳ Απιν και Νιοϐην. Απις ȣν τυραννικως ζων αναιρειται ὑπο Θελξιονος και Τελχινος—Νιοϐης της Απιδος αδελφης και Διος Αργος, αφ' ȣ ἡ χωρα, καλα δε Αχȣσιλαον, και Πελασγος συν Αργῳ. Schol. in Lycoph. ver. 177. See alſo Apollod. Bibl. lib. ii. cap. 1.

[l] Ενταυθα Ποσειδωνος εϛιν ἱερον επικλησιν Προσκλυϛιȣ· της γαρ χωρας

was the Taphos, or high place of the arkite god Argus, and the temple of the Dioſcori, who, according to Sanchoniatho, were the ſame as the Cabiri [m].

Both Inachus, and his imaginary ſon Phoroneus, as well as his grandſon Argus, are equally the ſcriptural *Noah*. Inachus is a corruption of the Hebrew word *Nuach* or *Nach*; and Phoroneus is compounded of Ph' Aron-Nus, *the arkite Noah*. Hence Pauſanias mentions, that Inachus was ſuppoſed to have ſacrificed to Juno, or the dove [n], who was ever eſteemed the peculiar guardian of Argos. He aſſerts moreover, that Phoroneus firſt brought men together into one place, a circumſtance, which accurately correſponds with the aſſembling of the Noachidæ in the Ark [o]; and ſuppoſes him, notwithſtanding he was the reputed ſon of Inachus, to have

ρας τον Ποσειδωνα επικλυσαι την πολλην, ὁτι Ἡρας ειναι και ου αὐτου την γην Ιναχος, και οἱ συνδικασαντες, εγνωσαν Ἡρα μεν δη παρα Ποσειδωνος εὑρε το απελθειν οπισω την θαλασσαν. Αργειοι δε ὁθεν το κυμα ανεχωρησεν, ἱερον Ποσειδωνι εποιησαν Προσκλυστιω. Pauſ. Corinth. p. 161.

[m] Προελθοντι δε ου πολυ ταφος εστιν Αργου, Διος ειναι δοκουντος και της Φορωνεως Νιοβης. Μετα δε ταυτα, Διοσκουρων ναος. Ibid.

[n] Corinth p. 144.

[o] Φορωνευς δε ὁ Ιναχου τους ανθρωπους συνηγαγε πρωτον εις κοινον, σποραδας τεως, και εφ' ἑαυτων ἑκαστοτε οικουντας. Ibid. p. 145.

been

been the firſt, who exiſted in that country [p]. The reaſon of this is obvious; the whole of the preceding genealogy is a ſeries of repetitions, and both *Phoroneus* and *Inachus* are equally appellatives of Noah.

The concluſion of the genealogy of Inachus mentions, that Argus and Pelaſgus were brethren: Apollodorus however aſſerts, that they were one and the ſame perſon [q], and that with great propriety; for, as Argus is the god of the Ark, ſo I apprehend, that, under the title of *Pelaſgus*, we again diſcover the great diluvian patriarch [r].

The Arcadians, ſo called from their devotion to the arkite myſteries, were wont to aſſert, that Pelaſgus flouriſhed firſt in their country [s], and accordingly the citadel of Argos was named *Lariſſa* from his daughter, as well as two cities in Theſſaly, one upon the ſea-coaſt, and another near the river Peneus [t].

[p] Φορωνεα εν τῃ γῃ ταυτῃ γενεσθαι πρωτον. Pauſ. Corinth. p. 144.

[q] Apollod Bibl. lib ii. cap. 1

[r] Pelaſgus was the reputed anceſtor of the Pelaſgi, whoſe hiſtory, as connected with the Cabiri, ſhall be conſidered hereafter. Vide infra chap vi.

[s] Φασι δε Αρκαδες, ὡς Πελασγος γενοιτο εν τῃ γῃ ταυτῃ πρωτος. Pauſ. Arcad. p. 598.

[t] Την δε ακροπολιν Λαρισσαν μεν καλουσιν απο της Πελασγου θυγατρος· απο ταυτης δε και δυο ταις εν Θεσσαλιᾳ πολεων, η τε επι θαλασσῃ,

When Ceres, in the course of her wanderings, came to Argos, she is said to have been received by this Pelasgus[u]. Hence the name *Pelasgis* was given to her[x]; and it is observable, that Isis, who according to Herodotus is the same as Ceres[y], bore the similar title of *Pelagia*[z]. The rites of this deity related immediately to the deluge[a]; which will account for her being thus connected with Pelasgus.

The Scholiast upon Apollonius Rhodius mentions, that Pelasgus was esteemed by some the offspring of Inachus, by others of Neptune and Larissa, and by others of Jupiter and Niobe; a variation, which is alone suffi-

σα, και η παρα τον Πηνειον, ωνομασθησαν. Pauf Corinth. p. 165. Larissa is Lares-Ai, *the land of the Lares*, or *solar Cabiri*. Concerning the Lares more will be said hereafter. Vide infra chap. iii.

[u] Λεγεται ουν, ως Δημητρα ες Αργος ελθουσαν Πελασγος δεξαιτο οικω. Pauf. Attic p. 34.

[x] Δημητρος εστιν ιερον επικλησιν Πελασγιδος, απο τε ιδρυσαμενε Πελασγε. Pauf. Corinth. p. 160.

[y] Ισις δε εστι κατα την Ελληνων γλωσσαν Δημητηρ. Herod. lib. ii. cap. 59

[z] Ες δε τον ακροκορινθον τουτον ανιουσιν, εστιν Ισιδος τεμενη· ων την μεν Πελαγιαν, την δε Αιγυπτιαν αυτων επονομαζουσιν Pauf. Corinth. p 121. Pelasgus, Pelasgis, and Pelagia, are all equally derived from Pelagim, *streams of water*; whence also the Greek and Latin word Pelagus, *the sea*.

[a] Vide infra chap x.

cient

cient to prove, that he is a mythological character. Staphylus accordingly asserts, that he was an Argive, or arkite; and his reputed children the Pelasgi were reckoned a *barbarous* nation, who formerly inhabited Thessaly and Argos[b].

Pelasgus is said by Apollodorus to have espoused Melibèa, the daughter of Oceanus. Their son Lycaon was king of Arcadia; and his extreme wickedness, according to Ovid, was one principal cause of the catastrophè of the deluge[c]. Lycaon was the father of Titanas, and Orchomenus[d], whose son was the famous Minyas, the ancestor of the Argonauts[e].

Here we have another series of genealogical repetitions; for Minyas is simply Menu, or *Noah*, while Orchomenus is Orca-Menu, *the arkite Noah*. The Greeks indeed pretended, that he was a native of their country; but Nonnus informs us, that he was a Pheni-

[b] Πελασγων, των Θεσσαλων, απο Πελασγȣ τȣ Ιναχȣ· η απο Πελασγων, εθνȣς βαρβαρικȣ οικησαντος την Θεσσαλιαν και το Αργος· η απο Πελασγȣ τȣ Ποσειδωνος υἱȣ και Λαρισσης. Σταφυλος δε ὁ Ναυκρατιτης Πελασγον φησιν Αργειον το γενος. Schol Apoll. Argon. lib. 1 ver. 580.

[c] The word *Lycaon* seems to be derived from Luca-On, *the orb of the Sun*, in reference to the solar worship.

[d] Apollod Bibl. lib. III. cap 8.

[e] Anton. Liber. Metam cap x

cian

cian deity, coëval with Oceanus and Tethys, and worſhipped in conjunction with a ſtar[f]. Conſidered then as the great patriarch, he is joined with Titanas; deſcribed as the ſon of an Arcadian; repreſented as flouriſhing at the era of the deluge; and ſuppoſed to be deſcended from Pelaſgus, Oceanus, Inachus, Tethys, and Phoroneus. Several different cities were named after him. There was an Orchomenus near Caryſtium[g]; another in Arcadia[h]; a third in Beotia; and a fourth in Theſſaly[i]. It is remarkable, that the moſt ancient Orchomenus, along with ſome other cities, was believed to have been deſtroyed by a flood; and a chaſm was ſhewn near the more modern town of the ſame name, in which the waters were ſaid to have been ſwallowed up, and into which the river Melas ſtill continued to empty itſelf[k].

[f] Dionyſ lib xli p. 698. I ſhall reſume the conſideration of the hiſtory of Orchomenus, when the fable of Beroë is analyſed, with whom he is cloſely connected.

[g] Περι Καρυστον δ' ην τις Ορχομενος. Strab. Geog lib. ix. p. 416.

[h] Strab Geog. lib. x. p. 338

[i] Plin. Nat Hiſt. lib iv cap 8.

[k] — εν οἷς οἱ μεν τον Ορχομενον οικεισθαι τον αρχαιον ὑπελαμβανον· οἱ δ' Ελευσινα, και Αθηνας παρα τον Τριτωνα ποταμον. Λεγεται και κατα Κεκροπα, ἡνικα της Βοιωτιας ὑπηρξε καλουμενης τοτε Ωγυγιης, αφανισθηναι δε ταυτας επικλυσθεισας ὑστερον· γενεσθαι δε φασι και κατα Ορχομενον χασμα, και δεξασθαι τον Μελανα ποταμον. Strab. Geog. lib.

From the preceding obſervations upon the mythological character of the arkite Venus, the Aſtartè of Sanchoniatho, and the parent of the ſeven Titanides, we ſhall not be ſurpriſed to find her eſteemed a Cabira. Thus we are informed by Euthymius Zegabenus, that the idolatrous Saracens, previous to the age of the Emperor Heraclius, worſhipped her under the name of *Cabar*[l].

As Venus was called *Cabira*, ſo we find, that Pliny makes mention of the fountain *Cabura* in Meſopotamia, in which Juno was ſaid to have bathed herſelf[m]. The fact is, that, although Noah and his three ſons, or Noah and the ſeven perſons who were preſerved along with him in the Ark, be the original Cabiri, or great Gods of the Pagans;

lib ix p 407 Lucian mentions a ſimilar tradition reſpecting a chaſm in the midſt of the temple of the Syrian goddeſs, which was ſuppoſed to have ſwallowed up the waters of the flood of Deucalion Luc de Dea Syra

[l] Οἱ Σαρακηνοι μεχρι του Ἡρακλειυ τυ βασιλεως χρονον ειδωλολατρυν, προσκυνυντες τῳ Ἑωσφορῳ αστρῳ, και τη Αφροδιτη, ἡν και Χαβαρ τη ἑαυτων επονομαζυσι γλωττη· δηλοι δε ἡ λεξις αυτη την Μεγαλην. Euthym Zegab Panop ap Seld de Diis Syr. p. 211. In a ſimilar manner Cedrenus Τον Αφροδιτης αστερα τον Ἑωσφορον ειναι μυθολογυσιν ἡν δε και Κυβαρ τη ἑαυτων κακεμφατῳ επωνομασαντο γλωσσῃ, ὁπερ εστι Μεγαλη. Cedren. Chronog.

[m] Unus in toto orbe traditur fons aquæ jucundè olentis in Meſopotamia Caburæ Fabulæ rationem afferunt, quoniam eo Juno perfuſa ſit. Plin Nat. Hiſt. lib. xxxi. cap 3

 yet,

yet, as it will abundantly appear in the courſe of the preſent diſquiſition, they applied the name to every deified object, which bore any reference to the deluge. The Ocean, the Ark, and the Dove, participated in the honours beſtowed upon the ſacred Ogdoad; and, in conſequence of the adoption of the ſolar worſhip, the Sun, the Moon, and the hoſt of heaven, were admitted to the ſame dignity.

It remains only, before I conclude the analyſis of the hiſtory of Aſtartè, to offer a few obſervations on the mythological character of Eſculapius, or Aſclepius; who is ſaid by Sanchoniatho to have been the ſon of Sydyk by one of the Titanides, and to have been afterwards added to the ſeven Cabiri under the title of *Eſmuni*. This deity connects together the firſt and ſecond tables of the Phenician genealogies, his father Sydyk occupying a conſpicuous place in the one, while his mother the Titanis is enumerated among the daughters of Cronus in the other. I am much inclined to think, that the imaginary god of health is, in reality, the very ſame perſon as his reputed father Sydyk, both of them being equally the patriarch Noah worſhipped in conjunction with the Sun. Macrobius accordingly informs us, that *Eſculapius* was one of of the many names of the ſolar deity, and that he was uſually adored along with Salus, or the Moon[n]. Salus however was no leſs a perſonification of the Ark, than of the Moon; thoſe two great objects of idolatrous veneration being nearly allied to each other, in conſequence of the union of the arkite and Sabian ſuperſtitions. Thus, while Noah was reverenced as the god of health, and as one of the eight Cabiri, the veſſel, in which he was preſerved, was honoured with the title of *Salus*, or *Safety*[o].

Captain Wilford ſuppoſes, that the *Eſculapius* of claſſical mythology is the Hindoo *Aſwiculapa*, or *the chief of the race of the horſe*; and he further intimates, that Aſwiculapa was very nearly related to two hero-gods, who are evidently the ſame as Caſtor and Pollux[p]. Theſe were believed to be the children of the Sun, and the goddeſs Devi; the Sun, at the time of their intercourſe, having aſſumed the form of a horſe, and Devi that of a mare[q].

[n] Macrob. Saturn lib i cap. 20.

[o] It is not eaſy to conceive, why the Moon ſhould be diſtinguiſhed by the name of *health* or *ſafety*, except from the circumſtance of its being worſhipped in conjunction with the Ark.

[p] Aſiat. Reſearch. vol iii. p. 168.

[q] Ibid

 Hence

Hence it appears, how very widely the helio-arkite ſuperſtition had extended itſelf. A horſe was one of the moſt uſual ſymbols of Noah, and a mare, of the Ark [r]: the Sun therefore, united with the horſe, is no other than the great ſolar patriarch, while his conſort is merely the Hippa, or Ark [s]. Conſequently, the children of Aſwi, or the horſe, at the head of whom was placed Aſwiculapa, are the allegorical offſpring of the Ark, whoſe chief was Noah, conſidered in his double character of both a ſolar and a diluvian deity.

We find Eſculapius connected with the Dioſcori or Cabiri, no leſs in the mythology of Greece than in that of Hindoſtan. Pauſanias mentions a temple of this deity at Braſiæ in Laconia, built near a promontory projecting into the ſea, upon which were placed three ſmall ſtatues of the Dioſcori or Corybantes, and a fourth of Minerva [t]. I make

[r] Vide infra chap vii.

[s] Noah, united with a horſe, while his ſuppoſed conſort is deſcribed as a mare, is the very ſame mode of repreſentation as that adopted in the figures of Dagon and Derceto: the only difference between them is, that in the one caſe the ſymbolical horſe, and in the other the ſymbolical fiſh, is introduced.

[t] After giving an account of this temple of Eſculapius, Pauſanias adds · Ακρα δε εϛιν εν ταις Βρασιαις μικρα, προεχοντα ηρεμα ες την θαλασσαι, και επ' αυτη χαλκοι ποδιαιων εϛηκασιν ου μειζονες πιλους

no doubt, but that Efculapius and the three Diofcori are the very fame mythological characters, as Cronus and his three fons; in other words, they are Noah and his triple offspring.

The genealogy of Efculapius, as detailed by the Greeks, although it varies from that given by Sanchoniatho, ferves equally to fhew his relationfhip to the Cabiric Diofcori. He was faid by fome to be the fon of Apollo, and Arfinoè the daughter of Leucippus; and by others of Apollo, and Coronis the daughter of Phlegyas. The mother of Arfinoè was Philodicè, and the father of Philodicè was Inachus. The two fifters of Arfinoè were efpoufed to Caftor and Pollux. As for Coronis, who was alfo reputed to be the mother of Efculapius, fhe was flain by Apollo himfelf in a fit of jealoufy, the raven having falfely accufed her of infidelity to his bed; for which crime, having afterwards difcovered his error, he changed the colour of that bird from white to black [u]. Both thefe genealogies are equally mythological; and the firft of them is replete with thofe repetitions,

πιλους επι ταις κεφαλαις εχοντες· ουκ οιδα η Διοσκουρους σφας, η Κορυβαντας νομιζουσι· τρεις δ' ουν εισι τεταρτον δε Αθηνας αγαλμα. Lacon. p. 272.

[u] Apollod Bibl. lib. iii cap. 10.

which are so common in the fables of the poets. Inachus and his descendant Esculapius are the same great patriarch; Leucippus is Luc-Hiph, *the solar God of the Ark*; Arsinoè is a variation of Baris-Noè, *the Ark of Noah*[x]; Philodicè is Bala-Daga, *the lordly fish*; and Coronis seems to have derived her name from Cor-On, *the Sun*. With regard to the fable of the raven, it appears to be an allusion to that, which was sent by Noah out of the Ark. It did not answer the end of its mission, and was therefore esteemed by the heathens an ill-omened, though sacred bird; while the dove, on the contrary, was always reckoned highly propitious. The raven however was believed to be peculiarly sacred to Apollo; and accordingly we learn from Myrsilus, that two ravens were kept tame in the temple of that god, on mount Lepetymnus[y]. The raven, in short, gave his name to the priests of Mithras, the Persian *Apollo*, who were denominated, from that bird, *Coraces*, or *Hierocoraces*[z].

[x] Arsinoè is the same as Venus. Vide supra p. 84.

[y] Antig, Caryst Mirab. Hist. cap. 17 There were two more of these birds at Cranon in Thessaly, and likewise a brazen chariot, which the inhabitants, in time of drought, were accustomed to strike upon, in order that they might obtain water from their deity. Antig. Caryst Mirab. Hist. cap. 15.

[z] Banier's Mythol. vol i. p. 289

Al-

Although Esculapius was thus venerated by the Greeks, yet the Berytian Esculapius [a], as we are informed by Damascius, was neither a Greek, nor an Egyptian, but a Phenician deity. He was beloved, like Attis or Bacchus [b], by the mother of the gods, whom the Phenicians called *Astronoè*; and, like Attis also, he was reported to have mutilated himself [c]. *Astronoè* is clearly a variation of *Ashtaroth*, or Astartè, which I apprehend to be the compound term As-Tora, *the heifer of the Sun* [d]; while Astronoè seems to be

[a] Or *the chief of the Hippian family, who entered into covenant.* The first part of this title, as I have before observed, relates to the arkite Hippa, or mare, the latter to the covenant of God with Noah.

[b] The history of this deity shall be considered hereafter.

[c] Ὁ εν Βηρυτῳ Ασκληπιος ουκ εστιν Ἑλλην, ουδε Αιγυπτιος, αλλα τις επιχωριος Φοινιξ. Σαδυκῳ γαρ εγενοντο παιδες, ους Διοσκουρους ἑρμηνευουσι και Καβειρους· ογδοος δε εγενετο επι τουτοις ὁ Εσμουνος, ὁν Ασκληπιον ἑρμηνευουσιν. Οὑτος καλλιστος ων θεαν, και νεανιας ιδειν αξιαγαστος, ερωμενος γεγονεν, ὡς φησιν ὁ μυθος, Αστρονοης θεου Φοινισσης, μητρος θεων· ειωθως τε κυνηγετειν εν ταις δε ταις ναπαις, επειδη εθεασατο την θεον αυτον εκκυνηγετουσαν, και φευγοντα επιδιωκουσαν, και ηδη καταληψομενην, αποτεμνει πελεκει την αυτος αὑτου παιδοσπορον φυσιν. Damasc. vit. Isid. ap. Phot Bibl. p 1073

[d] I cannot think, that *Astartè* is derived from After, *a star*, because it is manifestly the same word as the Hebrew *Ashtaroth*; and I am the more confirmed in the etymology which I have given of it, because Asterius, the masculine form of Astartè or Asteria, concerning whom more shall be said hereafter, is

As-Tora-Noè, *the heifer of Noah the Sun.* This etymology will perfectly accord with the narrative of Sanchoniatho, who teaches us, that Aſtartè was repreſented with the horns of a bull [d]. The Phenician mother of the gods in fine was merely the Noëtic Ark, repreſented, in the perſon of Aſtartè, under its uſual emblem,

declared by Tzetzes to be the ſame as Minotaurus, Taurus, Talus, or Italus.

[d] I am fully aware, that *Aſhtaroth* is written in the Hebrew עשתרות, and not אשתרות, and alſo that עשתרית ſignifies *ſheep* in that language, but, as the teſtimony of Sanchoniatho is ſo expreſs, and as there does not appear to be any connection between Aſtartè and a flock of ſheep, I feel myſelf obliged to conclude, that the Iſraelites, in expreſſing the name of this idol, regarded rather the ſound than the letters, and thus entirely deſtroyed the ſenſe. This caſe is by no means an unuſual one. Thus, in a ſimilar manner, inſtead of Beth-Zan, *the temple of the Sun*, they wrote בית-שן, *the temple of the tooth*; inſtead of Beth-Aron, *the temple of the Ark*, בית-חורן, *the temple of anger*; and inſtead of Air-Ares, *the city of the Sun*, עיר-הרם, *the city of deſtruction.* The LXX render this laſt name Πολις Ασεδὲν, *the city of righteouſneſs*, but why, I will not pretend to determine; Aquila and Theodotion, *the city Ares*; Symmachus, *the city of the Sun*; and the Chaldee paraphraſt, *the city of the Sun doomed to deſtruction*, which is an evident attempt to retain both the readings, הרם and חרם. Bochart was conſcious, that the hiſtory of Aſtartè accorded much better with her being repreſented under the form of a heifer, than under that of a ſheep · hence he conjectures, that the Hebrew word עשתרות ſignifies *oxen* as well as *ſheep*. Boch. Canaan. p 709. The whole difficulty however is removed by ſimply ſuppoſing, that the Iſraelites wrote עשתרות inſtead of אש-תורת'

Hem, the heifer; while her lover Eſculapius was the ſolar Noah. Hence he had a temple in Achaia, denominated *Curos*, which was a name of the Sun[e]; and at the ſame time, in alluſion to his diluvian character, was intitled *Archagetes* or Archa-Ga-Theus, *the illuſtrious god of the ark*[f].

In addition to the ſeven Titanides, whoſe hiſtory has been laſt conſidered, Cronus had alſo two other daughters, Proſerpine, and Minerva. Proſerpine is ſaid by Mnaſeas[g] to be one of the Cabiri; and, as I ſhall hereafter attempt to ſhew, is, like her mother Ceres or Iſis, a perſonification of the Ark worſhipped in conjunction with the Moon. Minerva appears to be a ſimilar perſonification of the divine wiſdom, by which the Ark was ſaved from deſtruction; and, as ſuch, ſhe is very frequently joined with the Cabiric gods. Thus, in the citadel of Epidaurus, there was a temple of Venus, a ſtatue of Eſculapius,

[e] Απωτερω δε ȣ πολυ απο τȣ Μυσαιου ἱερον εστιν Ασκληπιου καλουμενον Κυρος. Pauſ Achaic. p. 236 I am much inclined to think, that the proper reading in this paſſage is καλουμενȣ Κυρȣ, for *Curos* is, in reality, not the name of the temple, but of the deity.

[f] Ναος εστιν Ασκληπιου καλειται δε Αρχαγετας. Pauſ. Phoc. p. 879

[g] Schol. in Apoll. Argon. lib. i. ver. 917.

and

and a temple of Minerva: that of Jupiter the Preserver stood at the entrance of the harbour, and near it was a promontory called *Minoa*[h]. With a reference to the arkite worship, Minerva was surnamed *Erganè* from Ereg or Erech, *the ark*; under which title she was venerated both in Laconia[i], and in Beotia. She had in this last country a temple conjointly with Plutus, or Pluto[k]; who was one of the *Cabiri* of Mnaseas, and the same person as Adonis and Osiris, titles, under which the scriptural *Noah* received idolatrous honours from his posterity. She was likewise called *Taurobolos*, or Toro-Bolah, *the sovereign mistress of the tauriform Ark*[l]; *Budèa*, or Bu-Dea, the goddess *of the heifer*; and *Ethyia*, or *the sea-gull.*

[h] Pauf. Lacon. p. 271. There were many other places, which bore the same name of *Minoa*, an appellation seemingly derived from Minos, who is usually celebrated as one of the earliest kings of Crete, but who appears to be the same as the scriptural *Noah*. Minos is Menus, or Menu. his history will be resumed hereafter, when the solar worship of Crete is taken into consideration. Vide infra chap. vi.

[i] Pauf Lacon. p. 251.

[k] Την δε Αθηνην την Εργανην, και αυτην και Πλουτον οἱ παρεστηκοτα εποιησε. Pauf Bœot p 761.

[l] Ταυροβολος, ἡ Αθηνα Suid Lexic. Hence likewise the pagan ceremony of regeneration was called *Taurobolium*. For an account of this, vide infra chap. x.

Η πολλα

Η πολλα δη Βυδειαν, Αιθυιαν, Κορην,
Αρωγον αυδαξασα[m]—

Tzetzes informs us, that her title *Budèa* alluded to her having yoked oxen together in the plow; while her other name *Ethyia* was given to her, becaufe fhe firft taught men the art of navigation[n]. In confequence of the introduction of the Sabian fuperftition, Minerva was no lefs celebrated under folar than under arkite appellatives. Thus Minerva *Coria* had a temple in Arcadia[o]; Minerva *Coryphafia*, another at Pylos[p]; and Minerva *Larifsèa*, a third on the river Larifus between Achaia and Elis[q].

According to Clemens Alexandrinus, there were five Minervas: but I apprehend, that, notwithftanding this apparent variety, they are are all in reality one and the fame mythological character. The firft Minerva was

[m] Lycoph. Caffan ver. 359.

[n] Tzet. in loc. Αιθυια is *a fpecies of fea-bird*, which dives beneath the waves, and the name feems to have been metaphorically applied to Minerva, from the circumftance of her being a diluvian goddefs.

[o] Ναος και αγαλμα Αθηνας Κοριας. Pauf. Arcad. p. 639.

[p] Ενθαυθα ἱερον εςιν Αθηνας επικλησιν Κορυφασιας. Pauf. Meffen. p. 371.

[q] Αχαιοις δε ὁροι και Ηλειοις της χωρας ποταμος τε Λαρισος, και Αθηνας επι τῳ ποταμῳ ναος εςι Λαρισσαιος. Pauf. Achaic. p. 564.

the daughter of Vulcan; the second, of the Nile; the third, of Cronus; the fourth, of Jupiter, whom the Messenians denominated *Coryphasia* from her mother; while the fifth was the offspring of Pallas, and Titanis daughter of Oceanus[r]. The descent of this last deity is very remarkable: her father Pallas is P'Al-As, *the God of fire*; and, from what has been already said respecting the Titanides, it is evident, that, in the maternal part of her genealogy, she is immediately connected with the deluge, and consequently with the Cabiri. Such I conceive to be the reason, why she was represented, in her temple at Priene, sailing in a ship, like the Egyptian Isis; a mode of imagery, which originated, according to Pausanias, from the following curious legend. The goddess, choosing to leave the city of Tyre where she had previously been worshipped, entered into a ship. The vessel, as if conscious of the presence of the deity, forthwith set sail, and at length concluded its

[r] Εισι δε οι πεντε Αθηνας ὑποτιθενται· την μεν, Ἡφαιστου, την Αθηναιαν· την δε Νειλου, την Αιγυπτιαν· τριτην, του Κρονου, την πολεμου εὑρετιν· τεταρτην, την Διος, ἡν Μεσσηνιοι Κορυφασιαν απο της μητρος επικεκληκασιν· επι πασι, την Παλλαντος και Τιτανιδος της Ωκεανου. Clem Alex. Cohort ad Gent. p 24. See also Jul. Firm de Err. Prof. Rel. p. 32. et Cic de Nat. Deor. lib. iii. cap 23

course

courſe in the bay of Priene, at the temple of Juno, ſurnamed *the Mediatrix*[s]. The ſingular termination of this mythological voyage ſeems to intimate, that, when the Ark guided by the divine wiſdom ceaſed to float upon the ſurface of the waters, Juno or the dove was employed by Noah to bring him tidings how far the earth was habitable.

The tradition of Minerva's having ſailed

[s] Ἡδεις δ' αν και τω εν Ερυθραις Ἡρακλειω, και Αθηνας τω εν Πριηνη ναω· τουτω μεν του αγαλματος εἱνεκα, Ἡρακλειω δε τω εν Ερυθραις κατα αρχαιοτητα. Το δε αγαλμα ουτε τοις καλουμενοις Αιγιναιοις, ουτε των Αττικων τοις αρχαιοτατοις εμφερες· ειδε τι και αλλο, ακριβως εστιν Αιγυπτιον. Σχεδια γαρ ξυλων, και επ' αυτης θεος εκ Τυρου της Φοινικης εξεπλευσε· καθ' ἡντινα δε αιτιαν, ουδε αυτοι τουτο οἱ Ερυθραιοι λεγουσιν. Ὡς δε ες την θαλασσαν αφικετο ἡ σχεδια την Ιωνων, φασιν αυτην ὁρμισασθαι προς Ἡρα καλουμενη Μεσατη Pauſ. Achaic. p 533 It is proper however to remark, that this tradition may poſſibly relate to Hercules, and not to Minerva The Greek is unfortunately ſo ambiguous, that, at the beginning of the paſſage, Pauſanias appears to be ſpeaking of the ſtatue of Minerva, but at the concluſion of it, he ſeems rather to mean Hercules. Και ἑτως οἱ Ερυθραιοι την σχεδιαν καθελκουσιν· εσοδος δε ταις Θρῃσσαις ες το Ἡρακλειον εστι γυναικων μοναις. The Latin tranſlation annexed to the edition of Kuhnius makes the ſtatue to be that of Minerva, and not of Hercules. Erythris præterea Herculis, et Priene Minervæ delubra magna cum voluptate viſas; hoc certe propter *deæ* ſignum, illud ob vetuſtatem Ipſum ſane ſimulacrum, non iis quæ Æginæa vocantur—But whether Hercules or Minerva be the deity ſailing in the ſhip, the import of the tradition will remain unaltered; for Hercules, as ſhall be ſhewn hereafter, was equally a marine or arkite god.

from

from *Tyre* perfectly accords with Sanchoniatho's narrative. That writer, as I have just observed, speaks of her as the daughter of Cronus, the Phenician Noah, and as the sister of Persephonè or Proserpine. Hence Ulysses, who conveyed away the sacred statue of Minerva from the citadel of Troy, is styled by Lycophron, *the stealer of the Phenician Goddess:*

Δελφινοσημον κλωπα Φοινικης θεας [t].

Having now sufficiently considered the history of Cronus and his children, I shall proceed to investigate that of his collateral relations.

As for Betylus, who is said by Sanchoniatho to be the brother of Cronus, he is certainly a mere allegorical personification. The word is precisely the same as the Hebrew Beth-El, *the house of God*; and it alludes to the altar erected by Noah, for the purpose of sacrificing to the Lord of Heaven and Earth, after his miraculous escape from the perils of the deluge. If we turn to the page of Scrip-

[t] Lyc Cass. ver 658. The history of the Palladium and Dardanus will be considered in a future page more at large. The Greek Athenè seems to have derived her name from Ath-Ain, *the fountain of fire*, while the Latin Minerva is Menah-Rabah, *the great Noetic deity*, *B* and *V* being letters of the same organ.

ture,

ture, we ſhall find that *Beth-El* is the uſual patriarchal name for ſacred ſtructures of this nature.

"And Jacob roſe up early in the morn-
"ing, and took the ſtone that he had put
"for his pillows, and ſet it up for a pillar,
"and poured oil upon the top of it. And
"he called the name of that place *Beth-El:*
"but the name of that city was called *Luz*
"at the firſt. And Jacob vowed a vow, ſay-
"ing, If God will be with me, and will keep
"me in this way that I go, and will give me
"bread to eat, and raiment to put on; ſo
"that I come again to my father's houſe in
"peace: then ſhall the Lord be my God:
"and *this ſtone, which I have ſet for a pillar,*
"*ſhall be God's houſe*[u]."

With a ſimilar alluſion, no doubt, to the ſcriptural *Beth-El,* Sanchoniatho mentions, that Uranus, or Heaven, contrived ſtones called *Betulia,* which poſſeſſed the power of motion, as if they were inſtinct with life[x]. Theſe were,

[u] Gen. xxviii. 18.

[x] The Greeks retained ſome knowledge of theſe Betulia, as connected with Saturn or Noah, though they have ſtrangely perverted the original tradition. They feigned, that, when Saturn was about to devour his ſon Jupiter, Rhea gave him, inſtead of the infant, a ſtone named *Betylus.* Βαιτυλος, ὅτως εκαλειτο ὁ δοθεις λιθος τῳ Κρονῳ αντι Διος Heſych.

were, in all probability, ſacred rocking ſtones; numbers of which, erected by the Druids, are to be found in various parts of our own iſland [y].

Betylus then, the imaginary brother of Cronus, ſeems to be a mere perſonification of the patriarchal mode of worſhip; and is therefore a character of a very different nature from the two remaining ſons of Uranus, whom Sanchoniatho denominates *Atlas* and *Dagon*. Theſe, no leſs than Cronus, Demaroön, Agruerus, and Sydyk, I take to be ſeverally the patriarch Noah; who was celebrated by the ancient heathens under a great variety

[y] For an account of the connection between the Druids and the ancient Patriarchs ſee Stukeley's Abury and Stonehenge; Cooke's Inquiry into the Patriarchal and Druidical Religions; and Borlaſe's Antiq. of Cornwall, book iii. chap. 2. and 4. This laſt author gives the following account of a very remarkable ſtone of the Betulian kind on the iſland of St. Agnes in Scilly. "The under rock is ten feet ſix high, and 47 feet in "circumference round the middle, and touches the ground "with no more than half its baſe. The upper rock reſts on "one point only, ſo nice, that two or three men with a pole "can move it; it is eight feet ſix high, and 47 in girt. On "the top is a large baſon, three feet eleven in diameter, (at a "medium) at the brim wider, and three feet deep by the "globular ſhape of this upper ſtone, I gueſs that it has been "rounded by art at leaſt, if it was not placed on the hollow "ſurface of the rock it reſts upon by human force, which to "me appears not unlikely."

of

of names, allusive to various parts of his history. The astronomical solar superstition, as I have already observed, was very soon ingrafted upon the commemorative rites of the Ark: hence Atlas is described, as supporting the heavens upon his shoulders; a circumstance, which, when stripped of its poetical dress, points out to us the attention paid by the early postdiluvians to the motions of the heavenly bodies. Thus, we are informed by Heraclitus, that Atlas was the first astronomer, and that the fiction of his sustaining the heavens arose from his predicting the rising and setting of the stars[z].

The genealogy of Atlas is variously detailed by the Greeks. The scholiast upon Aratus assigns to him two brothers, Prometheus and Epimetheus; and makes him the son of Uranus by Clymenè daughter of Oceanus[a]; Apollodorus represents him, as the offspring of Iapetus and Asia, another of the daughters of

[z] Ατλας ανηρ σοφος ων τα κατα αστρολογιαν πρωτος κατωπτευσε, προλεγων δε χειμωνας και μεταβολας αστρων και δυσεις, εμυθευθη φερειν επ᾽ ωμων τον κοσμον. Herac. de Incred. cap. 4. See also Diod. Sic. lib. iii. p. 193. Albric. Philos. de Deor. Imag. cap. 22. and Serv. in Æneid. lib. iv. ver. 745.

[a] Ὁ δε Ατλας, μεθ᾽ ου και ὁ Προμηθευς και ὁ Επιμηθευς, εγεννηθησαν εκ του Ουρανου και Κλυμενης της του Ωκεανου θυγατρος. Schol. in Arat. Phænom. p. 35.

Oceanus[b]; and Proclus deſcribes him, and his two brothers, as the children of Iapetus, either by Aſopè, or Clymenè, or Themis[c]. With regard to Prometheus, and Epimetheus, they each ſeem to be the ſame perſon as Atlas, or the helio-arkite Noah[d]; Prometheus being Phra-Ma-Theus, *the great ſolar deity*[e], and Epimetheus, Ippa-Ma-Theus, *the*

[b] Ιαπετȣ δε και Ασιας της Ωκεανȣ, Ατλας, ὁς εχει τοις ωμοις τον Ουρανον. Apoll. Bibl. lib. i. cap. 2. Hyginus agrees with Apollodorus in making Atlas the ſon of Iapetus, excepting only that he aſſigns Clymenè to him as a mother inſtead of Aſia. Hyg Præf. Fab.

[c] Ὁ δε Προμηθευς ην παις Ιαπετȣ και Ασωπης, η Κλυμενης, η Θεμιδος. Proc. in Heſiod. p. 23.

[d] Hence Prometheus is ſaid to have been a Cabirèan, and a prieſt of Ceres, or the Ark. Pauſ. Bœot. p. 758.

[e] Prometheus is plainly ſaid by the author of the Orphic hymns to be the ſame perſon as Cronus, or Noah.

Αιωνος Κρονε παγγενετωρ, Κρονε ποικιλομυθε·
Γαιης τε βλαστημα και ȣρανȣ αστεροεντος·
Γεννα, φυη μειωσι, Ῥεας ποσι, σεμνε Προμηθευ.

Orph. Hymn xii.

" *Praw*, in the Birman tongue, imports *Lord*, and is always " annexed to the name of a ſacred building; it is likewiſe a " ſovereign and a ſacerdotal title, and is frequently uſed by an " inferior, when addreſſing his ſuperior. The analogy between " the Birmans and ancient Egyptians, in the application of " this term, as alſo in many other particulars, is highly de- " ſerving of notice. *Phra* was the proper name, under which " the Egyptians firſt adored the Sun, before it received the al- " legorical appellation of *Oſiris*, or *author of time*; they like-
wiſe

great deity of the Ark: the deſcent however of Atlas from Iapetus is a preciſe inverſion of his real genealogy; for Iapetus, or Japhet, was the ſon, not the father, of Noah.

The mother of Atlas, as we have juſt ſeen, is ſometimes ſaid to be Clymenè, ſometimes Themis, ſometimes Aſopè, and ſometimes Aſia. Clymenè is a contraction of Cula-Menah, *the Noëtic Ark*; Themis was one of the ſeven Titanides; and Aſopè appears to have borrowed her name from the worſhip of As-Op, *the ſolar ſerpent.* In a ſimilar manner, both Aſia the allegorical parent of Atlas, and Aſia the continent, ſeem alike to have derived their reſpective appellations from As, *fire,* in alluſion to the propenſity of the oriental world

" wiſe conferred the ſame title on their kings, and on their " prieſts. In the firſt book of Moſes, Pharaoh gives Joſeph to " wife the daughter of *Potiphcrah,* prieſt of On. In the book " of Jeremiah a king of Egypt is ſtyled Pharaoh-*Hophra*; and " it is not a very improbable conjecture, that the title of *Pharaoh,* given to ſucceſſive kings of Egypt, is a corruption of " the word *Phraw,* or *Praw,* in its original ſenſe ſignifying " *the Sun,* and applied to the ſovereign and prieſthood, as the " repreſentatives on earth of that ſplendid luminary." Aſiat. Reſ vol. v. p. 115.

The words *prieſt of On* ſeem to have been added by the ſacred hiſtorian as explanatory of the title *Potipherah. A prieſt of On* is *a prieſt of the Sun*; and Potipherah is Petah-Phrah, which ſignifies likewiſe *a prieſt of the Sun.*

to bestow idolatrous honours upon the solar Noah[f]. Hence we find, that, in the language of the Mysteries, all things were said to have sprung from one fire[g]; by which nothing more was meant, than that Noah, who was worshipped in conjunction with the Sun, was the universal father of mankind.

When the rites of the east were imported into Greece, a strong charge was given, that barbaric names should never be changed[h]: concerning which injunction it is observed by Psellus, that there are sacred names of ineffable import, preserved in the mysteries of every nation, and delivered to them immediately by the gods; a circumstance, which makes it unlawful to translate them into the Greek language[i]. The word *Atlas* I apprehend to

[f] The Lydians, according to Herodotus, asserted, that the great eastern continent borrowed its title from Asieus, the son of Cotys, the son of Manes —Λυδοι, φαμενοι απο Ασιεω, τευ Κοτυος, τȣ Μανεω, κεκλησθαι την Ασιαν. Herod. lib. iv. cap. 45. This Asieus I take to be Nimrod, so called from his having introduced the worship of fire. His father Cotys is Cush, or, as the Babylonians styled him, Cuth; and Manes is Menus, the *Noah* of Scripture. In this genealogy Ham has been omitted between Manes and Cotys.

[g] Εισιν παντα πυρος ἑνος εγγεγαωτα. Orac. Magic. p. 22.

[h] Ονοματα βαρβαρα μη ποτ' αλλαξης. Ibid. p. 70.

[i] Τȣτεστιν, εισιν ονοματα παρ' ἑκαστοις εθνεσι θεοπαραδοτα, δυναμιν εν ταις τελεταις αῤῥητον εχοντα. Μη ȣν μητ' αλλαξης αυτα εις την Ἑλ-

be one of theſe ſacred names, being compounded of At-Al-As, *the fiery god of heat*, or *the Sun*, in the conjunction with which the patriarch Noah was idolatrouſly reverenced.

According to Sanchoniatho, the aſtronomical Atlas was thrown by his brother Cronus into a deep pit. I am much inclined to think, that this wild legend relates only to a mode of contemplating the heavenly bodies, which, we are informed, was uſual among the ancient aſtronomers. They are ſaid to have cauſed themſelves to be let down to the bottom of pits, in order that they might be able to ſee the ſtars in the day time; by means of which contrivance, they prevented the picture on the retina of the eye from being confuſed or diſturbed by adventitious rays of light[k].

As Atlas, conſidered in one point of view, is the Sun, ſo, if we examine his character in

Ἑλληνικην διαλεκτον. Pſel Schol in Orac Magic. p. 70. Plato ſpeaks to the ſame purpoſe in his *Cratylus* Εννοω γαρ, ὅτι πολλα οἱ Ἑλληνες ονοματα, αλλως τε και οἱ ὑπο τοις βαρβαροις οικουντες, παρα των βαρβαρων ειληφασι.—Ει τις ζητοι ταυτα κατα την Ἑλληνικην φωνην, ὡς εοικοτως κειται, αλλα μη κατ᾽ εκεινην, εξ ἡς το ονομα τυγχανει ον, οισθα ὁτι αποροι αν. See alſo Jamblichus cited in the preceding chapter. Theſe extracts will ſufficiently ſhew the propriety of deriving the terms of Greek mythology from the oriental dialects.

k Adams's Lect. on Nat Philoſ vol. ii. p. 317.

another point, we ſhall have ſufficient reaſon to conclude, that he is alſo a diluvian god. Thus, as it appears from the preceding account of his genealogy, he is repreſented as a deſcendant of the Ocean; and thus Nonnus beſtows upon him the title of *Titanius*, or *diluvian*, from his connection with the hiſtory of the deluge.

—— Ει ποτε Μαιη
Συζυγον Ηλεκτρην Τιτηνιος ηροσεν Ατλας [l].

He is further ſaid to have been the firſt king of Arcadia, or *the land of the divine Ark* [m]; the huſband of Pleionè, or Bala-Ionah, *the lordly dove* [n]; and the father of the ſeven Pleiades [o], whoſe hiſtory plainly ſhews them to be the ſame as the ſeven Cabirides, or Titanides. At preſent however I muſt deſiſt from a more particular analyſis of the curious legend of the diluvian Atlas, reſerving it for that portion of my work, which treats of the various countries devoted to the Cabiric ſuperſtition [p].

With regard to Dagon, which I apprehend to be another of the many titles, under which

[l] Dionyſ. lib. iv. p. 72.
[m] Dionyſ. Halic. Ant. Rom. lib. i. cap. 61.
[n] Dict. Cret. de Bel. Troj. lib. 1. cap. 9.
[o] Schol in Arat. Phœn. p. 35.
[p] Vide infra chap. vi.

Noah was worſhipped, he was repreſented, like Derceto the Aſſyrian Venus, as having a human body terminating in the tail of a fiſh. Derceto however, or Atargatis, was a mere perſonification of the lunar Ark; whence, as we learn from Simplicius, ſhe was ſtyled by her votaries *the receptacle of the gods*[q]. Accordingly, we are informed by Xanthus the Lydian, that Ichthus, or Dagon, was ſuppoſed to be her ſon[r]; becauſe the Ark was the allegorical parent of Noah.

The names both of *Dagon* and *Atargatis* are purely deſcriptive, the former being Dag-On, *the ſolar fiſh-god*, in other words *Noah worſhipped in conjunction with the Sun*; and the latter being a corruption of Adar-Daga, *the illuſtrious fiſh*[s]. In alluſion to this ſymbo-

[q] Την Συριαν Αταργατιν τοπον θεων καλουσιν. Simp. in Ariſt Auſc Phyſ lib iv

[r] Athen Deipnoſ. lib. viii. p. 346.

[s] This deity had a temple in one of the iſlands of the Delta, called *Atarbechis*, or Adar-Beth, *the houſe of Adar*; the *Th* in *Beth* being changed into *C*, as in the ſimilar reading of Bal-Bec for Bal-Beth, *the houſe of Baal*. Ουνομα τη πολει Αταρβηχις· εν δ' αυτη Αφροδιτης ἱρον ἁγιον. Herod. lib. ii. cap. 41. She ſeems to have given her name *Adar* or *Athyr* to the ſecond of the Egyptian months; the very month, in ſhort, on the ſeventeenth day of which Oſiris was incloſed in the Ark, when purſued by the fury of Typhon, or the Ocean. "In the ſix hundredth "year of Noah's life, in the *ſecond month, the ſeventeenth day of "the month*, the ſame day were all the fountains of the great

lical mode of repreſentation, Rabbi Kimchi, commenting upon the paſſage in Scripture, which relates the overthrow of Dagon before the ark of God, obſerves, that, after his head and his hands had been broken off, nothing was left but the figure of a fiſh [t].

There is indeed every reaſon to believe, that Dagon is no other, than the *Oannes* of the Chaldèans, and the *Viſhnou* of the Hindoos.

Oannes is ſaid by Alexander Polyhiſtor to have been compounded of a man and a fiſh. By day he aſcended from the waters of the Red ſea, and conveyed his inſtructions in a human voice to the aſſembled multitudes; but at night he retired from the land, and concealed himſelf within the receſſes of the Ocean [u]. From him the Chaldèans derived their knowledge of the creation of the world; a knowledge, which they could only have received from that great patriarch, who, on account of his ſingular preſervation in the midſt of the waters, would naturally be repreſented in the ſhape of a mer-man by his allegorizing poſterity.

" deep broken up—*In the ſelf-ſame day entered Noah—into the* " *Ark.*"

[t] Seld. de Diis Syr. Synt. ii cap 3.

[u] Alex. Polyhiſt. apud Syncelli Chronog. p. 29.

As

As for the *Vishnou* of Hindostan, he is said to have assumed, in the first of the *Avatars*, precisely the same form as that, in which Dagon and Derceto are ordinarily depicted; and, from the conspicuous part, which he bears in the Hindoo account of the deluge, there can be little reason to doubt of the connection of Dagon also with the same event [x].

This deity however was not always represented as being absolutely, and literally, *compounded* of a man and a sea-monster. In the *Matsya Avatar*, which has just been noticed, Vishnou appears to issue out of the mouth of a fish, which elevates itself above the surface of the water; and Oannes is described by Berosus as having a human head and human feet, as well as a fish's head and a fish's tail [y]. Such probably was the most ancient mode of representing Noah, in allusion to his proceeding out of the Ark, which was symbolized not unaptly by the image of a huge sea-monster [z].

[x] See Asiat. Research. vol. i. p. 230. and a print of this *Avatar* in Maur. Hist. of Hind. vol. i.

[y] Το μεν αλλο σωμα ειχε ιχθυος, ὑπο δε την κεφαλην παραπεφυκυιαν αλλην κεφαλην ὑποκατω της τυ ιχθυος κεφαλης, και ποδας ὁμοιως ανθρωπυ, παραπεφυκοτας δε εκ της ὑρας τυ ιχθυος. Ειναι δε αυτῳ φωνην ανθρωπυ· την δε εικονα αυτυ ετι και νυν διαφυλασσεσθαι. Beros. apud Seld de Diis Syris, Synt. ii. cap 3.

[z] Hence Cetenè, one of the derivatives of Cetus, *a sea-monster*,

The love of augmenting the number of their gods, ſo prevalent among the ancient mythologiſts, occaſioned them to feign four different Oannes, who ſucceſſively made their appearance out of the Red ſea [a]. One of theſe was called *Odacon*, which is a manifeſt corruption of *Dagon*, ariſing, as it ſeems, from the inadvertence of ſome careleſs Greek tranſcriber [b]. Dagon was the peculiar god of the Philiſtines, who are ſuppoſed by Captain Wilford to have been a very ancient colony of the Indian Palli [c]. If the opinion of this learned and ingenious writer be well founded, the reaſon of the ſimilarity between Viſhnou and Dagon will appear in a yet more ſtriking point of view.

The account, which Sanchoniatho gives of Dagon, exactly agrees with the hiſtorical character of Noah. He is ſaid to have been the inventor of bread, from which circumſtance he was called *Siton*; and the firſt contriver

ſter, ſignifies *a large ſhip*. Κητηνη, πλοιον μεγα ως κητος. Heſych.

[a] It is poſſible indeed, that theſe four Oannes may be Noah, Shem, Ham, and Japhet. The Red ſea, as we ſhall hereafter find, is repreſented by the poets, as the principal ſcene of the exploits of Bacchus, or Noah.

[b] Inſtead of ὁ Δαγων he wrote Ωδακων. Vide Seld. de Diis Syris, Synt. ii. cap 3.

[c] Wilford on Egypt in Aſiat. Reſearch. vol. iii.

of

of the plow, which procured him the title of *Jupiter-Arotrius*. In fact, like Agruerus, whose history has been already considered, he was one of the many deities, in whom the great diluvian and agricultural patriarch was adored by his infatuated posterity.

The author of *the Etymologicon Magnum* removes all possibility of doubt upon the subject, by plainly asserting, that *Betagon* is the Phenician name of Cronus, or Noah [d]. He confounds indeed the temple with the deity, to whom it was consecrated, Betagon being evidently a compound of Beth-Dagon; but, when this slight inaccuracy has been rectified, his assertion will no less tend to prove the identity of Dagon and Cronus, and consequently of Dagon and Noah.

Dagon was sometimes worshipped under the appellations of *Nebo* and *Nisroch*. Hence we find, that the LXX. in translating the passage of Isaiah, which describes the bowing down of Bel, and the stooping of Nebo, substitute *Dagon* for *Nebo*; and that, in a similar manner, the *Hebrew* of *Tobit*, published by Munster, calls Nisroch *Dagon* [e]. Nebo or Nabo seems to be Nah-Bo, *the tauric Noah*;

[d] Βηταγων, ὁ Κρονος ὑπο Φοινικων.

[e] See Calmet's Dict. Vox Nisroch.

and

and Nifroch to be Nus-Aroch, *the arkite Noah.* Kircher thinks, that Nifroch was reprefented as a man failing in a fhip; and obferves, that the Rabbins derived the word from Nefra-Noacha (נסרא-נוחא) *the plank of Noah*[f]. I prefer however the former etymology, which appears to me more eafy and natural. The LXX. in one part of their tranflation, exprefs *Nifroch* by *Meforach*; and, in another, by *Afarach*[g]. I think it probable, that that deity was indifferently called by all thefe various names, the feveral fignifications of which however are virtually the fame: for, as Nifroch is Nus-Aroch, *the arkite Noah,* fo Afarach is As-Arach, *the arkite folar deity,* and Meforach is M'Es-Orach, *the great arkite folar deity.* I am perfuaded, that this Nifroch or Afarach is the very fame mythological character as the Trojan Affaracus, who is defcribed as the brother of Ilus, the fon of Tros, the grandfon of Erichthonius, and the great-grandfon of Dardanus. The whole of this famous genealogy is a mere feries of repetitions, as I fhall hereafter fhew at large[h]. At prefent therefore I fhall content myfelf

[f] Kirch. Panth. apud Beyer. Addit ad Seld. de Dis Syris, p. 323.

[g] See Seld de Dis Syris, Synt. ii. cap. 10.

[h] Vide infra chap. vi.

with

with observing, upon the authority of Sanchoniatho, that *Ilus* was only another name of Cronus.

Hercules-Melicarthus also, and *Posidon* or *Neptune*[i], seem, as will appear in the sequel, to be, no less than *Cronus* or *Dagon*, titles of Noah. The former of these deities is said to be the son of Demaroön, or Da-Ma-Aron, *the great arkite*; and the latter, of Pontus, or *the sea*. Hercules accordingly, when considered in one point of view, is the Sun, but, when considered in another, is the god of the Ark; while Neptune is allegorically represented as the offspring of the ocean, and as enjoying a grant of Berytus in conjunction with the Cabiri. The Latin title of *Neptune* is perhaps compounded of Nu-Hiph-Tanin, *the Hippian Fish-god Noah*; and his Greek name *Posidon* seems to be Bos-Adon, *the lordly bull*. In perfect conformity with these appellations, he is supposed to have assumed, at different times, the several forms of a horse[k], a dolphin[l], and a bull[m]; all which animals were used as symbols of the principal god of the Ark. Hence he is deno-

[i] Vide supra p. 16.
[k] Ovid. Metam. lib. vi. ver. 118.
[l] Ibid ver. 120.
[m] Ibid. ver. 115.

minated

minated by Hesiod *the tauric god*; and is celebrated by him as the defender of Thebah, or *the Ark.*

——Ταυρεος Εννοσιγαιος,
'Ος Θηβης κρηδεμνον εχει, ρυεται τε πολημα[n].

Upon which Tzetzes observes, that the tauric Neptune was highly venerated in Beotia, or *the land of the heifer*, and particularly at Onchestus, or *the city of the Ocean*[o].

Sanchoniatho concludes his narrative with informing us, that the circumstances detailed in it were recorded by the seven Cabiri, and their eighth brother Esculapius, at the command of the God Taautus. As for this Taautus or Thoth, there is every reason to think, that he is the same mythological character as the *Hermes* of the Greeks, the *Mercury* of the Latins, the *Buddha* of the Hindoos, the *Fohi* of the Chinese, and the *Wodin* of the Scandinavians; in other words, as I shall hereafter attempt to shew at large[p], all these ancient personages are equally the patriarch Noah. Hence Taautus, although Sanchoniatho very erroneously describes him as the son of Misor or Mizraim, is nevertheless said by that wri-

[n] Hes Scut. Herc. ver. 104.
[o] Tzet Schol. in loc.
[p] Vide infra chap. v.

ter to have exercifed a fort of authority over the Cabiri, commanding them to write thofe memoirs, from which the Phenician mythologift profeffes to have copied his narrative.

The following tables contain a fummary of the remarks, which have been made, in the prefent chapter, upon the Phenician Hiftory of Sanchoniatho.

TABLE I.

REAL PERSONS.

Eliun-Hypfiftus.	God the Moft High.

Antediluvian Line of Cain.

1. Protogonus.	1. Adam.
2. Genus.	2. Cain.
3. Phos.	3 Enoch.
4. Caffius.	4. Irad.
5. Memrumus.	5. Mehujael.
6 Agreus.	6. Methufael.
7. Chryfor.	7. Lamech.
8. Technites.	8. Jabal.

Poftdiluvian Line of Noah.

First generation.	Agruerus. Sydyk. Afclepius. Taautus. Cronus. Dagon. Atlas. Demaroon. Melicarthus. Neptune	Noah.

Second

Second generation.	Amynus-Magus.	Ham.
	Cronus Junior, Jupiter-Belus, Apollo.	Shem. Ham. Japhet.
	The seven Cabiri. The seven Titans.	The family of Noah.
Third generation.	Misor	Mizraim.
	Sons of Cabiri.	Grandchildren of Noah.

TABLE II.

ALLEGORICAL PERSONS.

Beruth.	The divine covenant.
Uranus.	Heaven.
Ge.	Earth
Betylus.	Beth-El.
Minerva.	The divine wisdom.
Dionè.	The dove.
Astartè. Proserpine. Rhea	The Ark worshipped in conjunction with the Moon.
Nereus. Pontus. Typhon.	The diluvian ocean.

To avoid confusion, I have noticed in these tables no persons, excepting those who are mentioned by Sanchoniatho. Hence Venus, Derceto, Semiramis, Juno, and several other mythological characters, whose history has been discussed in the course of the present chapter, are purposely omitted in the tables.

CHAP. III.

THE IDENTITY OF THE CABIRI, CORYBANTES, CURETES, DIOSCORI, ANACTES, DII MAGNI, IDEI DACTYLI, TELCHINES, LARES, PENATES, MANES, TITANS, AND ALETÆ, AND THE MYTHOLOGICAL CHARACTER OF THE HEATHEN GODDESSES.

SANCHONIATHO closes the account, which he gives of Agruerus the great god of Phenicia, by asserting, that he and his contemporaries were the persons known by the names of *Aletæ*, or *fire-worshippers*, and *Titans*, or *diluvians* [a]. He observes moreover, that the Titans were the children of Cronus, and that they were seven in number; accordingly, with their parent Agruerus or Cronus at their head, their number is exactly the same as that of the persons preserved in the Ark. In a more extended signification indeed, all the diluvians were called *Titans*, which will account for the apparent inconsistency observ-

[a] *Aletes*, as I have already observed, is derived from Al-Ait, *the god of fire*, and *Titan*, from Tit, *the colluvies of the deluge*.

 able

able in their hiſtory; for, while the wickedneſs, and conſequent deſtruction, of the old world is poetically deſcribed by the war of the Titans againſt Jupiter[b], the *arkite* Titans are repreſented as the great gods of the Gentiles, and as the offspring of Cronus and Rhea[c]. Cronus however, as we have ſeen, was the ſame perſon as Sydyk and Agruerus; whence it will follow, that, ſince the ſeven Titans were the children of Cronus, and the ſeven Cabiri the children of Sydyk, we can have very little reaſon to doubt their identity. The truth of this ſuppoſition is yet further proved by the remarkable circumſtance of the ſcriptural name of *Japhet* being accurately preſerved in the liſt of the Titans[d].

[b] This will be ſhewn at large in a ſubſequent chapter.

[c] In other words, the children of Noah and the Ark. It is highly neceſſary, in an analyſis of the Titanic hiſtory, to recollect this diſtinction between the *impious* and the *arkite* Titans.

[d] According to the author of the works aſcribed to Orpheus, the names of the ſeven arkite Titans were Cèus, Crèus, Phorcys, Cronus, Oceanus, Hyperion, and *Iapetus*.

Κοιον τε, Κρειον τε μεγαν, Φορκυν τε κραταιον,
Και Κρονον, Ωκεανον θ', Ὑπεριονα τ', Ιαπετον τε.

Orph. apud Proc. in Tim lib. v. p 295.

I have no doubt of the ſeven Titans or Cabiri being the ſame alſo as the ſeven Riſhis of the Hindoo mythology, who are ſaid to have eſcaped in a boat along with Menu the head of their family. The Hindoos, in their wild legends, have variouſly

per-

The Cabiri were alſo worſhipped under the various titles of *Dioſcori, Corybantes, Curetes, Idæi Dactyli, Anactes*, and *Telchines*. Sanchoniatho himſelf aſcribes to them the two firſt of theſe appellations; and his authority is corroborated by the teſtimony of Strabo[e], and Clemens Alexandrinus[f]. Julius Firmicus, ſpeaking of the murder of one of the Corybantes by his two brethren[g], aſſerts, that he was a *Cabirus*[h]; and Suidas mentions it as the prevailing opinion, that the term *Curetes* was only another name of the Corybantes[i].

perverted the hiſtory of the Noachidæ, yet it is remarkable, that they ſeem religiouſly to have adhered to the number *ſeven*. hence Captain Wilford very judiciouſly obſerves, that "perhaps the ſeven Menus, the ſeven Brahmadicas, and the "ſeven Riſhis, are the ſame, and make only ſeven individual "perſons. The ſeven Brahmadicas were prajapatis, or lords of "the prajas, or creatures. From them mankind were born, "and they are probably the ſame with the ſeven Menus— "Theſe ſeven grand anceſtors of the human race were—created "for the purpoſe of repleniſhing the earth with inhabitants" Aſiat Reſ. vol. v. p. 246. The mutual reſemblance of the Cabiri, the Titans, the Riſhis, and the Noëtic family, is too ſtriking to be the effect of mere accident.

e Τȣς Κορυϐαντας οἱ μεν τȣ Διος και Καλλιοπης φασι, τȣς αυτους τοις Καϐειροις. Strab. Geog. lib. x. p. 472.

f Καϐειρȣς δε τȣς Κορυϐαντας καλȣντες, και τελετην Καϐειρικην καταγγελλȣσιν. Clem. Alex. Cohort. ad Gent. p. 16.

g More ſhall be ſaid of this murder hereafter.

h Jul. Firm. de Error. Prof. Rel p 23.

i They were reckoned the guards of Jupiter, and, like the Titans,

Pausanias informs us, that the inhabitants of Amphissa in Phocis celebrated mysteries in honour of the Anactes, who were supposed to be the Dioscori, the Curetes, or the Cabiri [k]; the ancient Scholiast upon Aratus declares the Curetes, the Corybantes, and the Idèi Dactyli, to be the same [l]; and Nonnus joins together the Corybantes, the Cabiri, the Idèi Dactyli, and the Telchines.

Πρωτα μεν εκ Ληµνοιο πυρεγλωχινος ερπνης
Φημη αελληεσσα Σαμου παρα μυσιδι πευκη,
Υἱεας Ἡφαιστοιο δυω θωρηξε Καβειρους,
Ουνομα μητρος εχοντας ὁμογνιον· ους πυρος αμφω
Ουρανιῳ χαλκηϊ τεκε Θρηϊσσα Καβειρω,
Αλκων, Ευρυμεδων τε δαιμονες εσχαρεωνος.
Και βλοσυροι Κρητηθεν αολλιζοντο μαχηται,
Δακτυλοι Ιδαιοι Κραναης ναετηρες ερπνης,
Γηγενεες Κορυβαντες ὁμηλυδες· ὡν ποτε Ῥειη
Εκ χθονος αυτοτελεστον ανεβλαστησε γενεθλην.

\- - - - - - - - - - - - -

Και προμος ἡγεμονευε χοροπλεκεων Κορυβαντων

Titans, were the children of Rhea. Ενιοι τους Κουρητας, και τους Κορυβαντας τους αυτους ὑπειληφασιν ειναι· ησαν δε Διος τραφεις οὑτοι και φυλακες· τινες δε αυτους δεκα φασιν· αλλοι δε εννεα ησαν δε της Ῥεας παιδες. Suid Lex. Vox. Κορυβαντες.

k Αγουσι δε και την τελετην οἱ Αμφισσεις Ανακτων καλουμενων παιδων. Οἱτινες δε θεων εισιν οἱ Ανακτες παιδες, ου κατα ταυτα εστιν ειρημενον, αλλα οἱ μεν ειναι Διοσκουρους, οἱ δε Κουρητας, οἱ δε πλεον τι επισταθαι νομιζοντες, Καβειρους λεγουσι. Phoc p 896.

l Κουρητες δε, και Κορυβαντες, και Ιδαιοι Δακτυλοι, οἱ αυτοι εισιν. Schol, in Arat. Phœn. p. 9.

Πυρῥικος,

Πυῤῥικος, Ιδαιος τε σακεσπαλος, οἱς ἁμα βαινων
Κνωσσιος αιολα φυλα παρωνυμος ὡπλισε Κυρϐας,
Και φθονεροι Τελχινες επηλυδες ες μοθον Ινδων
Εκ βυθεε κενεωνος αολλιζοντο θαλασσης·
Και δολιχη παλαμη δονεων πεπαμηκετον αιχμην
Ηλθε Λικος· και Κελμις εφεσσετο Δαμναμενηϊ,
Πατρωιον ιθυνων Ποσιδηϊον αρμα θαλασσης [m].

To theſe authorities may be added the inſcription, preſerved in the palace *Grimani* at Venice, to which place it was carried from Aquileia. Γαιος Γαιου Αχαρνευς ἱερευς γενομενος Θεων Μεγαλων Διοσκερων Καϐειρων των επι Διονυσιε τε μετα Λικισκον αρχοντος ενιαυτῳ ιδρυσατο [n]. "Gaius, the ſon of Gaius, an Acarnanian, "the prieſt of the Dii Magni, Dioſcori, Cabiri [o], erected this monument, during the "archonſhip of Dionyſius, the ſucceſſor of "Lyciſcus."

The Cabiri were likewiſe denominated *Lares* [p], and *Penates*. Hence Theodoret affirms, that the Dioſcori were the ſame, as the Epheſtii, and Anactes [q]; while Hyginus main-

[m] Nonni Dionyſ. lib. xiv. p 251.

[n] Montfaucon's Suppl. vol. i. book..v. chap. 4.

[o] Similar to this is an ancient inſcription mentioned by Gruter, p. 319. Θεοι μεγαλοι, Διοσκεροι, Καϐειροι.

[p] Lar is a contraction of El-Ar, *the ſolar deity*, whence the term *Lares* is equivalent to *the ſolar Cabiri*.

[q] Και μεν τοι, και Τυνδαριδας θεες εκαλεσαν Ἑλληνες, και Διοσκε-

 ρες

tains the identity of the Corybantes, the Curetes, and the Lares[r]. Hence alſo Virgil unites the Penates, with the Dii Magni, or Cabiri;

—— Feror exul in altum,
Cum ſociis, natoque, Penatibus, et Magnis Dîs[s].

and deſcribes Auguſtus as bringing them into the naval battle of Actium.

Hinc Auguſtus agens Italos in prælia Cæſar,
Cum patribus, populoque, Penatibus, et Magnis Dîs,
Stans celſa in puppi[t].——

Another title, by which the Cabiri were known, was that of *the Manes*; while their mother was ſuppoſed to have been called *Mania*.

Poſſumus, ſi videtur, ſays Arnobius, ſummatim aliquid et de Laribus dicere, quos arbitratur vulgus vicorum atque itinerum Deos eſſe. In diverſis Nigidius ſcriptis modo tectorum domuumque cuſtodes; modo Curetas illos, qui occultâſſe perhibentur Jovis æribus aliquando vagitum; modo Digitos Samothracios,

ρυς ωνομασαν, και Εφεςιυς, και Ανακας. Theod. Græcan. Affect. lib. viii

[r] Græce *Curetes* ſunt appellati; alii *Corybantes* dicuntur; hi autem *Lares* appellantur. Hyg. Fab. 139.

[s] Æneid lib. iii. ver 11.

[t] Ibid. lib. viii. ver. 678.

thracios, quos quinque indicant Græci Idæos Dactylos nuncupari. Varro ſimiliter hæſitans, nunc eſſe illos Manes, et ideo Maniam matrem eſſe cognominatam Larum;—nunc antiquorum ſententias ſequens larvas eſſe dicit Lares, quaſi quoſdam genios, et functorum animas mortuorum [u].

The term *Manes* indeed is uſually applied to the ſouls of the deceaſed; but the reaſon of ſuch an application will plainly appear, when the fabulous hiſtory of the infernal regions is taken into conſideration [x]. At preſent therefore I ſhall only obſerve, that the *Hades* of the Myſteries was not, like the *Hades* of the popular belief, the imaginary reſidence of departed ſpirits; but that the whole of its terrific machinery relates partly to the Sabian idolatry, and partly to the events of the deluge, when the fountains of the vaſt deep, where Plato fixes Tartarus and the four rivers of hell [y], were broken up, when the ſtreams of Styx or hatred overflowed the habitable globe, and when a deathlike gloom brooded over the ſurface of the mighty waters. The maſculine name *Manes*, and the

[u] Arnob. adv. Gent. lib. iii. p. 124.

[x] Vide infra chap. v.

[y] Phæd. ſect. 60, 61, 62.

feminine *Maria*, like the *Menu* of Hindoſtan, the *Minos* of Crete, the *Mneuis* and *Menes* of Egypt, the *Mannus* of Germany, and the *Menes* of Lydia, are equally derived from the ſcriptural appellative *Nuh* or *Noah*. Mania in ſhort is the Noëtic Ark; and her allegorical children, the Manes, however their hiſtory may have been corrupted, are no other than the patriarch and his family.

With regard to the genealogies of the Cabiric gods, Nonnus repreſents the Corybantes as the ſons of Mercury [z], the Telchines as the children of Neptune, and the Cabiri as the ſons of Vulcan [a]; Tzetzes deſcribes the Curetes as the offspring of Apollo and Danais [b]; Apollodorus makes the Corybantes the children of Apollo and Thalia [c]; Heſiod aſſerts, that the Curetes and the Satyrs were deſcended from Hecatèus, and a daughter of Phoroneus [d]; and Sanchoniatho informs us, that the Titans were the ſons of Cronus, and the Cabiri of Sydyk. Some deduced the origin of the

[z] Nonni Dionyſ. lib. xiii. p. 233.

[a] Nonni Dionyſ. lib. xiv. p. 251. See the whole paſſage cited above, p 132.

[b] Κυρητες, Δαναιδος νυμφης Κρηστης και Απολλωνος παιδες. Schol. in Lycoph. ver. 78.

[c] Θαλειας δε και Απολλωνος εγενοντο Κορυβαντες. Apollod. Bibl. lib 1 cap 3.

[d] Heſiod. apud Strab. Geog lib. x. p. 471.

the Corybantes from the Sun and Minerva; others, from Cronus, or Saturn; and others from Jupiter and Calliopè: all however agreed in esteeming them the same as the Samothracian Cabiri; and many, with great propriety, supposed them to be the servants of Hecatè, or the Ark. Acusilaus the Argive affirms, that Camilus, or Mercury, was the son of Vulcan and Cabira, and the father of the three Cabiri, from whom were born the three Cabirides: and lastly Pherecydes mentions, that the Corybantes were the children of Apollo and Rhytia, and that they inhabited Samothrace; while the three Cabiri and the three Cabirides were the offspring of Vulcan, by Cabira the daughter of Proteus [e].

It has been observed, that the seven Titans are the same as the seven Cabiri, and that Cronus is said to be the father of the seven Titanides; we may therefore naturally expect,

[e] Κορυβαντες δαιμονες τινες Αθηνας και Ἡλιου παιδες. Ετι δε Κρονου τινες τους Κορυβαντας· οἱ δε του Διος και Καλλιοπης φασι, τους αυτους τοις Καβειροις οντας· απελθειν δε τουτους εις Σαμοθρακην καλουμενην προτερον Μελιτην, τας δε πραξεις αυτων μυστικας ειναι —Οἱ δε Ἑκατης προσπολους νομιζουσι τους Κουρητας τους αυτους τοις Κορυβασιν οντας —Ακουσιλαος δε ὁ Αργειος εκ Καβειρης και Ἡφαιστου Καμιλον λεγει τους δε τρεις Καβειρους, ὡν νυμφας Καβειριδας. Φερεκυδης δ' εξ Απολλωνος και Ῥυτιας Κορυβαντας εννεα· οικησαι δ' αυτους εν Σαμοθρακη· εκ δε Καβειρης της Πρωτεως και Ἡφαιστου, Καβειρους τρεις, και νυμφας τρεις Καβειριδας. Strab. Geog. lib. x. p. 472.

pect, that these last would be esteemed Cabiræ. Accordingly we learn from an inscription of Methapus the Athenian, who was supposed to have instructed the Thebans in the arkite Mysteries, that some of the Cabiric deities were reckoned goddesses.

> Ηγνισα δε Ἑρμειο δομους τε κελευθα
> Πατρος και πρωτογονου κουρας· ὁθι Φασι
> Μεσσηνην θειναι μεγαλαισι θεαισιν αγωνα [f].

Hence, as we have already seen, upon the authority of Euthymius Zegabenus, Venus was esteemed a *Cabira*; hence likewise the fountain *Cabura* was sacred to Juno; hence Ceres is called by Pausanias *Cabiria* [g]; and hence both Ceres and Proserpine are enumerated by *Mnaseas* in his list of the Cabiri [h]. Most indeed of the ancient goddesses are so

[f] Pauf. Messen. p. 282. The *Pater Protogonus*, here mentioned, is Noah; who was called *Protogonus*, in allusion to his being the first-born of his allegorical mother the Ark, and *Pater*, or more properly *Patur*, (פטור) as having come forth from the womb of the Ark. For some further observations on the word *Patar*, vide infra chap. viii. and x. *Protogonus* seems to have been introduced into this passage, as explanatory of the oriental term *Patur*, with which it is nearly synonymous.

[g] Δημητρος Καβειριας και Κορης εστιν αλσος—Pauf. Bœot. p. 758. Ceres is, in reality, the same as her daughter Proserpine, who is said by Sanchoniatho to be the offspring of Cronus, and the sister of Minerva.

[h] Mnaf. apud Schol. in Apoll. Argon. lib. i. ver. 917.

far

far the same, that their several mythological histories appear, almost universally, to relate partly to the catastrophè of the deluge, and partly to the worship of the heavenly bodies. The World rising from the midst of the waters, the Ark wandering over their surface, and, upon the introduction of Sabianism, the lunar Crescent, seem to be alike described in the diversified characters of all and each of them. Their names moreover are perpetually interchanged; so that one goddess is not uniformly a personification of the Ark, another of the Moon, and a third of the Earth; but, on the contrary, all these various objects of worship are frequently symbolized, upon different occasions, by one and the same deity. Thus, Venus, Derceto, Isis, Ceres, Proserpine, and Latona, are severally and equally the Moon, the renovated Globe, and the Ark of Noah. I know not of any exceptions to this general rule, except perhaps Juno, and Minerva; the former of whom *usually*, though not *always*, signifies *the dove*, and the latter *the divine wisdom*.

The adoption of such an opinion, however visionary it may at first appear, will alone satisfactorily remove our astonishment at finding the identity of these goddesses so repeatedly maintained by mythological writers. Herodorodotus asserts, that Isis and Ceres are the same[i]; Lactantius remarks the similarity between their respective mysteries, observing, that, as Osiris is the object of search in those of Egypt, so is Proserpine in those of Eleusis[k]; and Pausanias mentions, that in the neighbourhood of Hermionè was a temple of Serapis and Isis, within the sacred inclosure of which the mysteries of Ceres were celebrated[l]. According to Heliodorus, Isis was a personification of the Earth[m]; according to Plutarch she was Minerva, and Proserpine[n]; and according to Apuleius, she was Venus, Diana, the Moon, and Proserpine[o]. In a similar manner Servius affirms, that Diana,

[i] Ισις δε ετι κατα την Ἑλληνων γλωσσαν Δημητηρ. Herod lib. ii. cap. 59.

[k] Sacra vero Cereris Eleusinæ non sunt his dissimilia. Nam sicut ibi Osiris puer planctu matris inquiritur: ita hic ad incestum patrui matrimonium rapta Proserpina. Lact. de Fal. Rel lib i cap. 21.

[l] Ὁ δε Σεραπιδι ῳκοδομηται και Ισιδι, και περιβολοι μεγαλων λιθων λογαδων εισιν εντος δε αυτων, ἱερα δρωσιν αποῤῥητα Δημητρι. Paus. Corinth. p. 193. Hermionè seems to have been so called in honour of Armi-Ionah, *the dove of Armenia*, in which country the Ark landed.

[m] Προς τους μυςας Ισιν την γην. Heliod. Æthiop. lib. ix. p. 424.

[n] Plut. de Isid. et Osir. p. 354, 361.

[o] Regina Cœli, sive tu Ceres Alma frugum parens originalis,—seu tu cœlestis Venus,—seu Phœbi soror,—seu nocturnis ululatibus horrenda Proserpina. Apul. Metam. lib. ii.

Ceres,

Ceres, Juno, and Proserpine, were only different names of the Moon [p]; Lucian says the same with respect to Astartè and Rhea [q]; Varro observes, that the Moon was called *Jana* [r]; Austin mentions, that Juno was indifferently denominated both *Mena* and *Levana* [s]; and Macrobius declares, that the Moon was worshipped under the appellation of *Juno* [t].

As for the Syrian Atargatis, or Derceto, while she is called by Simplicius *the receptacle of the gods*, in allusion to the Ark having contained within her womb the hero-gods of the Gentiles; she is declared also by him to be no other than Isis, to whom the same remarkable title was ascribed by the Egyp-

[p] Lunam, eandem Dianam, eandem Cererem, eandem Junonem, eandem Proserpinam dicunt. Serv. in Virg Georg. lib. i. ver. 5.

[q] Luc. de Dea Syra.

[r] Tremellius, Nunquam rure audisti, inquit, octavo Janam lunam et crescentem, et contra senescentem. Varr. de Re Rust. lib. i. cap. 37. From this passage it appears, that the Moon was only called *Jana*, when it bore the form of a crescent or boat. The reason of which is obvious as Janus is Noah, so Jana will be the Noëtic Ark, or crescent Diana, or the moon, is Di-Jana, *the divine Jana*

[s] Aug. de Civ. Dei, lib. iv. cap. 11. et lib vii cap. 2. Mena is Menah, *the Noetic Moon* or *Ark*, and Levana is evidently the Hebrew Lebanah (לבנה), *the Moon*

[t] Jure Junoni addixerunt Calendas, lunam ac Junonem eandem

tians[u]. Plutarch mentions, that ſome believed her to be Juno, and others Venus[x]; Lucian aſſerts, that ſhe was likewiſe eſteemed the ſame as Rhea[y]; and the author of *the Chronicon Paſchale* maintains the identity of this laſt deity and Semiramis[z]. Hence we perceive the reaſon, why Semiramis is ſaid by Hyginus to be daughter of Derceto[a], and why ſhe is reported to have been changed into a dove. Hence alſo there is reaſon to believe that Semiramis is the ſame as Juno; or, in other words, that they are both equally the dove of Noah. The arkite Venus, or Atargatis, the *Dea Cabira* of the Saracens, was alſo called *Urania*, and *Mylitta*, or, as the Arabs inflected the word, *Alitta*[b]. *Urania* however is ſaid by Olympiodorus to have

dem putantes. Mac. Saturn. lib. i. cap. 15.

[u] Την Συριαν Αταργατιν τοπον θεων καλουσιν, και την Ισιν οἱ Αιγυπτιοι, ὡς πολλων θεων ιδιοτητας περιεχουσας. Simp. in Ariſt. Auſc. Phyſ lib. iv.

[x] Plut. in Vit. Craſſi, p. 553.

[y] Luc. de Dea Syra.

[z] —Σεμιραμιν, και την Ῥεαν καλȣμενην παρα Ασσυριοις. Chron. Paſc. p. 36.

[a] Semiramis Dercetis filia in Syria (condidit) Babylonem. Hyg. Fab. 275

[b] Επιμεμαθηκασι δε τῃ Ουρανιῃ θυειν (οἱ Περσαι) παρα τε Ασσυριων μαθοντες και Αραβιων· καλεȣσι δε Ασσυριοι την Αφροδιτην Μυλιττα, Αραβιοι δε Αλιττα. Herod. lib. i. cap. 131.

been

been likewiſe the name of the ſtar of the Dioſcori, or Cabiri[c]; while *Mylitta* may be plainly traced to the Hebrew root *Ilad*[d]. The Gothic tribes denominated this goddeſs *Frea*, a title, which like that of *Rhea* is moſt probably derived from Phree, *to be fruitful*[e]; and, for the ſame reaſon, the Egyptians were accuſtomed to beſtow the name of *Phree* upon the Sun, as being the great material cauſe of plenty and fertility[f].

The identity of the heathen goddeſſes, which is here contended for, is maintained alſo by Tzetzes. This commentator very juſtly affirms, that *Proſerpine*, *Iſis*, *Terra*, *Rhea*, *Veſta*, *Pandora*, and a thouſand other different appellations, were all titles of one

[c] Περι αστερος τινος τερατολογει, επιδριστεντος τῳ ιστιῳ του πλοιου, μελλειν αυτον βυθιζεσθαι· Ουρανιαν δε το φανεν παρα των ναυτων καλεισθαι. Olymp. ap. Phot. Bibl. p. 193. The Cabiric ſtar, which is uſually repreſented as propitious, but which Olympiodorus deſcribes as wearing a threatening aſpect, ſeems to be the ſame as the ſtar of Aſtartè, or the comet, if the hypotheſis be allowable, which occaſioned the cataſtrophè of the deluge. Urania was worſhipped along with Bacchus, or Noah Διονυσον δε θεον μουνον και την Ουρανιην ἡγεονται ειναι. Herod. lib iii. cap. 8.

[d] ילד *Mylitta* is the Hiphil participle מולידה Mulidah, or the Chaldee inflexion מולדתא Mulidta, *the cauſer of generation*.

[e] פרה. For various derivatives from this root ſee Parkhurſt's Heb Lex.

[f] Jablon. Panth. Ægypt lib. iii. cap 1.

deity.

deity[g]. Hence we find, that the name of *Mater Antèa* was indifferently applied both to Ceres and Rhea.

Ανταια βασιλεια, θεα, πολυωνυμε μητερ
Αθανατων τε θεων ηδε θνητων ανθρωπων,
Ἡ ποτε μαστευουσα πολυπλαγκτῳ ἐν ανιῃ,
Νηστειαν κατεπαυσας Ελευσινος γυαλοισιν,
Ηλθες τ᾽ ες Αϊδην προς αγαυην Περσεφονειαν[h].

Hail queen *Antèa!* parent both of gods
And mortal men; long was thy anxious ſearch
For lovely Proſerpine: nor didſt thou break
Thy mournful faſt, till the far-fam'd Eleuſis
Receiv'd thee wandering.

——————Αμφι δε φυλλοις
Στεψαμενοι δρυϊνοισι θυηπολιης εμελοντο,
Μητερα Δινδυμιην πολυποτνιαν εγκαλεοντες,
Ενναετιν Φρυγιης, Τιτιην θ᾽ ἁμα, Κυλληνον τε.
——————Ενθεν ες αιει
Ῥομβῳ και τυπανῳ Ῥειην Φρυγες ἱλασκονται.
Ἡ δε πυ ευαγεεσσιν επι φρενα θηκε θυηλαις
Ανταιη δαιμων[i].———

On Rhea's guardian power
The heroes call; and with her they invoke
Th' Idèan Dactyls, Titias, and Cyllenus.

[g] Περσεφονη δε, και Ισις, η Γη, και Ῥεα, και Ἑστια, και Πανδωρα, και ἑτερα μυρια ονομαζεται. Schol. in Lycoph. ver. 707.

[h] Orph. Hymn. 40.

[i] Apoll. Argon. lib. i. ver. 1125, 1141.

Hence,

Hence, in ſucceeding years, ſoft Phrygia's ſons,
With ſounding timbrels and revolving wheel,
Their goddeſs honour; while the mighty mother,
Renown'd *Antèa*, pleas'd their zeal beholds[k].

On account of this intercommunion of deities, Ceres is ſaid to have been the parent of Diana, as well as of Proſerpine. Thus, in the Egyptian mythology, Apollo and Diana were the children of Dionuſus and Iſis; from which circumſtance, as Herodotus conjectures, Eſchylus celebrated Diana as the daughter of Ceres[l]. Diana herſelf was worſhipped by the Lydians under the name of *Anaïs*[m]; a title, which appears to be the ſame as the

[k] The word Cybelè is derived from Cy-Bela, *the lordly mother*. Sciendum eſt Cybelem eſſe commune nomen Babylonicum ad matres deorum et Veſtas. *Cy* enim illi *matrem*, *Belum* vero et *Belam deum* et *deam* vocant. Ann. Viterb. Comment. in Beroſ. Ant lib. v fol 92.

[l] Απολλωνα δε και Αρτεμιν, Διονυσε και Ισιος λεγεσι ειναι παιδας·—Αιγυπτιςι δε Απολλων μεν Ωρος· Δημητηρ δε Ισις· Αρτεμις δε Βεβαςις. Εκ τυτε δε του λογε, και ουδενος αλλε, Αισχυλος ὁ Ευφοριωνος ἡρπασε το εγω φρασω, μενος δη ποιητεων των προγενομενων· εποιησε γαρ Αρτεμιν ειναι θυγατερα Δημητρος. Herod. lib ii. cap 156. Hence, in the citadel of Phliaſia there was a temple dedicated to Ceres, Proſerpine, and Diana Εν δε τη ακροπολει και αλλος περιβολος εςιν ἱερος Δημητρος. Εν δε αυτῳ ναος τε και αγαλμα Δημητρος και της παιδος το δε της Αρτεμιδος (εςι γαρ και Αρτεμιδος ενταυθα χαλκεν αγαλμα) εφαινετο αρχαιον ειναι μοι. Pauſan. Corinth. p. 141.

[m] —Λυδων, οἱς εςιν Αρτεμιδος ἱερον Αναιτιδος. Pauſ. Lacon. p 249.

Mater Antèa of Orpheus and Apollonius, and as the *Anèa* or *Nanèa* mentioned by the author of *the hiſtory of the Maccabees*[n], Strabo[o], and Joſephus[p]. All theſe various appellations are probably mere corruptions of Ani-Dea, *the goddeſs of the arkite ſhip*[q].

The Grecian Io likewiſe, however her hiſtory may have been varied, was, as we learn from Lucian[r], and Clemens Alexandrinus[s], the very ſame as Iſis. Accordingly, ſhe was eſteemed the daughter of Inachus or Noah, the imaginary king of Argos, and was feigned to have been metamorphoſed into the emblematical arkite heifer. The opinion of Lucian and Clemens is corroborated by Diodorus Siculus, who expreſsly aſſerts the identity of Io, Iſis, Ceres, Diana, the Moon, and Juno[t];

[n] 1 Macc. vi. 1, 2. 2 Macc. i. 13, 14.

[o] Geog. lib. xvi. p. 738.

[p] Joſeph. Ant. lib. xxii. cap. 13.

[q] Anèa or Nanèa is evidently the ſame as the *Anu*, *Nana*, or *An-Eireann*, of the ancient Iriſh. See Collect. de Reb. Hibern. vol. v. p. 490, 498.

[r] Την δε Ιω δια τε πελαγε εις την Αιγυπτον αναγαγων Ισιν ποιησον, Luc. Dial. Deor. p. 123.

[s] Ισιν δε, την και Ιω, φασιν, δια το ιεναι αυτην δια πασης της γης πλανωμενην. Clem. Alex. Strom. lib. i. p. 382. Io ſeems to be a contraction of Ionah, *the dove*; and Iſis, perhaps originally written *Ioſis*, may be conſidered as a yet further corruption of the ſame radical. Hence the cry of *Io Bacche*.

[t] Diod. Bibl. lib. i. p. 21.

and

and alſo by Statius, who aſſerts, that ſhe, who once ſtabled in the cave of Phoroneus, is now become the queen of Pharos, and the deity of the Eaſt [u].

The preceding remarks on the identity of the heathen goddeſſes are decidedly confirmed by a curious paſſage in *the Metamorphoſes* of Apuleius; in which he pronounces Rhea or Cybelè, Minerva, Venus, Diana [x], Proſerpine, Ceres, Juno, Bellona, Hecatè, Rhamnuſia [y], and Iſis, to be all one and the ſame mythological character.

Me primigenii Phryges *Peſſinuntiam* nominant *Deûm matrem*: hinc autochthones Attici *Cecropiam Minervam*: illinc fluctuantes Cyprii *Paphiam Venerem*: Cretes ſagittiferi *Dictynnan Dianam*: Siculi trilingues *Stygiam Proſerpinam*: Eleuſinii vetuſtam deam *Cererem*: *Junonem* alii: alii *Bellonam*: alii *Hecaten*: *Rhamnuſiam* alii: et qui naſcentis dei Solis inchoantibus radiis illuſtrantur Æthiopes, Ariique, priſcaque doctrina pollentes

[u] Iſi Phoronæis quondam ſtabulata ſub antris,
Nunc regina Phari, numenque Orientis anheli
Stat. Sylv lib. iii. p 49

[x] This Diana was called by the Cretans *Britomartis*. Her mythological hiſtory ſhall be reſumed in a future page. Dictynna is Dag-Tinin, *the arkite fiſh*.

[y] Rhamnuſia is Ram-Nuſa, *the illuſtrious Noetic Ark*.

 Ægyptii,

Ægyptii, ceremoniis me prorſus propriis percolentes, appellant vero nomine reginam *Iſidem*[z].

To this catalogue may be added Latona, who, according to the Greek mythology, was the mother of Apollo and Diana, and, according to that of Egypt, one of the eight great gods. She is evidently the ſame as Iſis or Derceto: whence, as I have already obſerved, ſhe was doomed to wander over the whole earth; while her hiſtory, whether Greek or Egyptian, is uniformly connected with ſome fable of a floating iſland[a].

We may now ſee the reaſon, why the ſtatue of Juno, in the temple of the Syrian goddeſs at Hierapolis, was ſo contrived as to repreſent the various attributes of thoſe deities, whoſe identity I have been attempting to eſtabliſh. Lucian informs us, that in ſome reſpects ſhe reſembled Minerva, in others, Venus, Luna, Rhea, Diana, Nemeſis[b], and the

[z] Apul. Metam. lib. xi.

[a] Latona is ſaid by the ſcholiaſt upon Heſiod to be the ſame as deathlike oblivion, and night. The reaſon of this will plainly appear, when the myſtic Hades is taken into conſideration. Vide infra chap. v. Λητω λεγεται η ληθη, και η νυξ. Schol. in Heſ Theog. ver. 406.

[b] The particular hiſtory of Nemeſis will be reſumed hereafter.

Parcæ.

Parcæ. In her right hand ſhe held a ſceptre, in her left a diſtaff. Her head was encircled with rays of glory, and crowned, like that of Cybelè, with turrets; while her waiſt was girt with the ceſtus, which is uſually given only to Venus Urania [c].

In fine, to adopt the language of Kircher, hoc unum ex omnibus hiſce demonſtratis hactenus collige. Cabar illam Arabum aliam nullam eſſe, quam communem illam Venerem Aſiaticam, Uraniam cœleſtem, quam Ægyptii *Iſidem*; Babylonii *Dagon* [d], *Derceto, Atargatis*; Phœnices *Aſtarten*; Græci nunc *Lunam*, nunc *Hecaten*, *Lucinam*, *Dianam*, *Proſerpinam*; aut, alio nomine, Arabes *Alilath* vocant rem eandem, nominibus diverſitatem effectuum denotantibus diverſam eſſe [e].

[c] Ἡ δε Ἡρη σκοπεοντι τοι πολυειδεα μορφην εκφανεει. Και τα μεν ξυμπαντα ατρεκεει λογῳ Ἡρη εστι· εχει δε τι και Αθηναιης, και Αφροδιτης, και Σεληναιης, και Ῥεης, και Αρτεμιδος, και Νεμεσιος, και Μοιρεων. Χειρι τε τῃ μεν ἑτερῃ σκηπτρον εχει, τῃ ἑτερῃ δε ατρακτον, και επι τῃ κεφαλῃ ακτινας τε φορεει, και πυργον, και κεστον, τῳ μουνην την Ουρανιην κοσμεουσι. Luc. de Dea Syra, ſect 32.

[d] I ſuſpect however, that Kircher is miſtaken when he enumerates Dagon in this liſt, for he was a maſculine idol, ſymbolical not of the Ark, but of Noah the god of the Ark.

[e] Kirch. apud Beyer. Addit. ad Seld. de Dis Syris, p 293.

CHAP. IV.

THE POLYONYMY OF THE SUN; AND THE UNION OF THE ARKITE AND THE SOLAR WORSHIP.

PREVIOUS to any further inquiries into the nature of the Cabiric ſuperſtition, it will be neceſſary to offer ſome obſervations upon the connection, which ſeems almoſt immemorially to have ſubſiſted between the worſhip of the hoſt of heaven, and the adoration of the Noëtic Ogdoad.

The early poſtdiluvians, unawed by the recent judgment of God, ſoon converted the pious remembrance of their anceſtors, into a blind ſuperſtition; and, as error is rarely ſtationary, the idolatrous veneration of the Sun, the Moon, and the Stars, was ere long ſuperadded. Such glorious bodies were eſteemed a fit reſidence for their deified progenitors; and from thoſe lofty ſtations they were thought to overlook and direct the affairs of this ſublunary world. Hence the whole hoſt of heaven was called after the names of different heroes; and hence we ſhall be able to account

count for an apparent confusion in the theology of the Gentiles.

If the several histories of the principal deities, revered by most of the ancient nations, be considered, we shall find them at once allusive to the Sabian idolatry, and to the castrophè of the deluge. Thus, the account, which is given of Osiris and Isis, if taken in one point of view, directs our attention to the Sun and the Moon; but, if in another, it places immediately before our eyes the great patriarch, and the vessel in which he was preserved[a]. Accordingly, we learn from Plutarch, that Osiris was a husbandman, a legislator, and a zealous advocate for the worship of the Gods[b]; that Typhon, or the sea, conspired against him, and compelled him to enter into an ark[c]; and that this event took

[a] Osiris and Isis were sometimes esteemed the children of Cronus, who, as we have seen, was also the father of the Titans and Titanides. Osiris however was in reality the same as Cronus, or Noah; and accordingly both his history, and that of Isis, is immediately connected with the war of the Titans, or in other words the catastrophè of the deluge. Diod Bibl. lib. i. p 23, 24 Cronus was called by the Egyptians the youngest of the gods, as being the son of Uranus and Ge, the allegorical children of Eliun. Ibid.

[b] Plut. de Isid. p 356.

[c] I am aware, that this legend has been applied to the history of Moses, and there are doubtless some circumstances, which favour such an opinion (see Plut. de Isid p. 357.) but

place on the ſeventeenth day of the month Athyr[d], the very day on which Noah is ſaid to have embarked In a ſimilar manner, a ſhip was the peculiar emblem of Iſis[e]; and, while the ſymbolical bull was alike dedicated both to this goddeſs, and to her mythological conſort[f], the hiſtory of her wanderings preſents to us the image of the erratic ſtate of the Ark upon the ſurface of the waters: yet there is no doubt, that the Sun was worſhipped by the Egyptians under the title of *Oſiris*, and the Moon under that of *Iſis*[g], or *Ceres*[h]. This ſingular union of the two

but at the ſame time, though the Egyptians might be acquainted with the fortunes of the Jewiſh legiſlator, it is not eaſy to conceive how other nations ſhould, moſt of which have nevertheleſs a tradition preciſely reſembling this reſpecting Oſiris.

d Plut. de Iſid. p. 356

e Tac de Mor Germ. cap. 9. Pauſ. Phoc p. 866.

f Μνευιν βουν Αιγυπτιοι Ἡλιου φασιν ἱερον· επει τον γε Απιν αναθημα ειναι Σεληνη λεγουσιν. Ælian de Animal lib. xi cap. 11. Τουτον (ſcil Απιν) Αιγυπτιοι τιμωσι Σεληνη, και ἱερος ην ὁδε ὁ βους της Σεληνης, ὡσπερ ὁ Μνευις του Ἡλιου. Suid vox Μεμφις Ὁ δε εν Ἡλιου πολει τρεφομενος βους, ὁν Μνευιν καλουσιν, μελας εστι. Plut. de Iſid. p 364 Τους δε ταυρους τους ἱερους, τον τε ονομαζομενον Απιν, και τον Μνευιν Οσιριδι καθιερωθηναι. Diod. Bibl. lib. i p 19

g Ὑπολαβειν ειναι δυο θεους αιδιους τε και πρωτους, τον τε ἡλιον και την σεληνην, ὡν, τον μεν Οσιριν, τον δε Ισιν ονομασαι Diod. Bibl. lib. i p. 10.

h Iſis, as I have already obſerved, was not only eſteemed the Ark and the Moon, but alſo the Earth; and the ſame remark may

ſuperſtitions will ſatisfactorily explain ſome particulars in the hiſtory of Oſiris, which cannot otherwiſe be very eaſily accounted for. The Egyptians, according to Plutarch, inſtituted two yearly feſtivals in his honour; one of which was deſigned to perpetuate the remembrance of his incloſure within the Ark[i], and the other, that of his entrance into the Moon[k]: and he further adds, that a part of the ceremony, which was commemorative of his myſtic death and burial, conſiſted in incloſing his ſtatue within an ark ſhaped like a lunette[l]. All theſe different rites however allude to one and the ſame event, the entrance of Noah into his veſſel, which was afterwards worſhipped in conjunction with the Moon. The incloſure of the Noëtic family within

may be extended to Venus. Thus, Varro ſuppoſes the Cabiri to be Heaven and Earth, and pronounces them the ſame as Serapis and Iſis, Taautes and Aſtartè, Saturn and Ops. Principes Dei Cœlum et Terra. hi dei iidem qui in Ægypto Serapis et Iſis, qui ſunt Taautes et Aſtartè apud Phœnicas, ut idem principes in Latio Saturnus et Ops. Terra enim et cœlum, ut Samothracum initia docent, ſunt Dei Magni, et hi quos dixi multis nominibus. Varr. de Ling. Lat lib iv p. 17. Thus alſo Macrobius: Nec in occulto eſt neque aliud eſſe Oſirin quam Solem, nec Iſin aliud eſſe quam Terram. Saturn. lib i cap 21.

[i] Plut. de Iſid p. 366.

[k] Ibid p. 368.

[l] Ibid.

the Ark was confidered by the ancient mythologifts as a ftate of death and darknefs; and their quitting it, as a reftoration to life and light[m]. Hence, the death of Ofiris, his confinement within an ark, and his entrance into the Moon, all equally fignified the entrance of Noah into the Ark.

As the Egyptian Ofiris was primarily Noah, and fecondarily the Sun, fuch alfo we fhall find to be the cafe with the other great gods of the heathens; for, notwithftanding their apparent variety, they are in fact mere fynonyms of Ofiris. Thus Damafcius and Suidas affert the identity of Ofiris and Adonis[n]; and Clemens Alexandrinus, that of Dionufus and Attis[o]: while Macrobius informs us, that Adonis, Attis, Ofiris, Horus, and Liber, were all equally the Sun[p]; and Aufonius, that

[m] This fubject fhall be difcuffed at large hereafter. Vide infra chap. v.

[n] Οσιριν οντα και Αδωνιν κατα την μυστικην θεοκρασιαν. Damaf. Vit Ifid apud Phot Bibl p 1049. Αλεξανδρεις ετιμησαντο Οσιριν οντα και Αδωνιν ὁμȣ Suid Lex. vox Ἡραισκος. The ʽμυστικη θεοκρασια, or myftic intercommunion of deities, mentioned by Damafcius, I apprehend to be the fame as that, which I am at prefent attempting to fhew really exifted in the polytheifm of antiquity

[o] Διονυσον τινες Αττιν προσαγορευεσθαι θελȣσιν Clem. Cohort. ad Gent p. 16.

[p] Adonim, Attinem, Ofirim, et Horum, aliud non effe quam Solem.

Bacchus, Osiris, Phanac, Dionusus, Liber, and Adoneus, were one and the same deity.

> Ogygia me Bacchum vocat;
> Osirin Ægyptus putat;
> Mysi Phanacem nominant;
> Dionuson Indi existimant,
> Romana sacia Liberum;
> Arabica gens Adoneum[q].

In a similar manner the author of the works of Orpheus declares, that *Jupiter*[r], *Pluto*, and *Bacchus*, were only different names of the Sun;

> Εἷς Ζεὺς, εἷς Ἀΐδης, εἷς Ἥλιος, εἷς Διονυσος[s].

Virgil makes Bacchus and Ceres to be the Sun and Moon;

> ——Vos, O clarissima mundi
> Lumina, labentem cœlo qui ducitis annum,
> Liber, et alma Ceres[t].——

Solem. Macrob. Saturn lib i cap. 21. In Thracia Solem Liberum haberi. Ibid cap. 18.

[q] Auson. Epig 30 *Adoneus* was a name of Pluto or Hades, and the same title as *Adonis*. They are both Adon-Nus, *the lord Noah*.

[r] Hence the solar Jupiter was called by the Mylassentians *Carius*, from Car, *the Sun* Λεγεται και Καριος· ουτω γαρ ὁ Ζευς παρα Μυλασσευσι τιμαται Steph. Byzant. de Urb. p. 449

[s] Orph Fragm. p. 364. Edit. Gesn

[t] Georg. lib. 1. ver. 6.

And

And Sophocles addreſſes Bacchus as the glorious leader of the fire-breathing ſtars.

Ω πυρ πνεοντων αςρων
Χοραγε, και νυχιων
Φθεγματων επισκοπε,
Παι Διος γενεθλον,
Προφανηθι συν Ναξιαις
Σαις Θυασι προσπολοις,
Αἱ δε σε μαινομεναι
Παννυχοι χορευουσι
Τον ταμιαν Ιακχον[u].

Immortal leader of the ſtarry hoſt[x],
Whoſe torches blaze with unextinguiſhed fire,
Great ſon of Jove, who guid'ſt the tuneful
throng,
Thou, who preſideſt o'er the nightly ſong,
Come with thy Naxian maids, a feſtive train,
Who, wild with joy, and raging o'er the plain,
For thee the dance prepare, to thee devote the
ſtrain. *Francklin.*

Diodorus and Suidas concur with Macrobius

[u] Antig ver. 1162.

[x] This line ſtands in Dr. Francklin's tranſlation;

"Immortal leader of the maddening choir;"

which is certainly very inaccurate; I have therefore taken the liberty to alter it Sophocles deſcribes Bacchus as the leader of "the fire-breathing *ſtars*," not of "a maddening choir" of *mortal followers*.

and

and Aufonius, in maintaining the identity of Ofiris and Bacchus[y]; and yet, notwithftanding both thefe deities have been fo repeatedly pronounced to be the Sun, Tzetzes declares it to be his opinion, that they are equally the *Noah* of the Hebrews.

Αιγυπτιων ανακτος, ὁς κατα Αιγυπτιȣς
Οσιρις ονομαζεται, ητοι των ϖειβλεπτων·
Κατα Ινδȣς δε Διονυσος, Διονυς, και αναξ Νυσσης·
Νωε κατα Ἑβραιȣς δε[z].——

As *Bacchus* then and *Ofiris* were merely titles of the great folar patriarch, fo we find, that another of his appellations was *Ptha* or *Vulcan*; Jamblichus accordingly defcribes this

[y] Τον μεν Οσιριν μεθερμηνευομενον ειναι Διονυσον, την δε Ισιν εγγιστα ϖως Δημητραν. Diod Bibl. lib. i. p. 13. Οσιριν λεγȣσιν ειναι τον Διονυσον. Suid

[z] Chil. v Hift. 26. The fame author, with the utmoft propriety, defcribes Atlas, Hermes Trifmegiftus, Prometheus, Hercules, and Typhon, as all contemporary with Ofiris, or Noah.

Ατλας ὁ Λιβυς, ὡς φασι ϖαιδες των Αιγυπτιων,
Και μαλλον ὁσοι ϖειθονται Σωφιδι χρονογραφῳ,
Εν χρονοις ην Οσιριδος, τȣ Διονυσȣ, Νωε,
Οτ' ην Ἑρμης τρισμεγιστος, ὁς εὑρετης γραμματων,
Ἑρμης ὁμȣ, και Προμηθευς, και Ἡρακλης, Τυφων τε,
Οἱ συμπαντες Αιγυπτιοι· Ἑλληνας νυν μη νοει.

Chil v. Hift. 1.

Hermes and Hercules, as will appear in the courfe of the prefent difquifition, as well as Atlas and Prometheus, are alike the great patriarch; while Typhon is merely a perfonification of the deluge.

deity

deity as being the ſame perſon as Oſiris [a]. Hence, on account of the connection of the arkite and the ſolar worſhip, the Cabiri were ſometimes eſteemed the ſons of Vulcan, and as ſuch received divine honours in Egypt. We learn from Pherecydes, that Vulcan eſpouſed Cabira the daughter of Proteus, who bore to him the three Cabiri, and the three Cabiræ [b]. In this tradition, the union of the two ſuperſtitions is pointed out in a very remarkable manner. The *Vulcan* of Pherecydes and his family exactly complete the number *eight*; he himſelf is Noah adored in conjunction with the Sun; and his conſort is the offspring of a marine deity. Herodotus mentions, that the ſtatues of this Vulcan, and his children the Cabiri, were in form like the Pataici [c]. Theſe were

[a] Ἑλληνες δε, εις Ἡφαιστον μεταλαμβανουσι τον Φθα, τῳ τεχνικῳ μονον προσβαλλοντες· αγαθων δε ποιητικος ων Οσιρις κεκληται. Jamb. de Myſt. ſect viii cap. 3.

[b] Pherec. apud Strab. Geog. lib. x p. 472.

[c] Ες δε δη και Ἡφαιστου το ἱρον ηλθε (Καμβυσης), και πολλα τῳ αγαλματι κατεγελασε· εστι γαρ του Ἡφαιστου τωγαλμα τοισι Φοινικηιοισι Παταικοισι εμφερεστατον, τους οἱ Φοινικες εν τῃσι πρωρῃσι των τριηρεων περιαγουσι. Ὁς δε τουτους μη οπωπεε, εγω δε οἱ σημανεω· πυγμαιου ανδρος μιμησις εστι. Εσηλθε δε και ες των Καβειρων το ἱρον, ες το ου θεμιτον εστι εσιεναι αλλον γε η τον ἱρεα·—εστι δε και ταυτα ὁμοια τοισι του Ἡφαιστου· τουτου δε σφεας παιδας λεγουσι ειναι. Herod lib iii. cap 37. Heſychius agrees with Herodotus in making Vulcan the father of the Cabiri: Καβειροι—πανυ τιμωνται εν Λημνῳ ὡς θεοι, λεγονται δε ειναι Ἡφαιστου παιδες.

ſmall

ſmall figures, which the Phenicians were accuſtomed to place at the heads of their galleys, on account of their ſuppoſed influence over maritime affairs[d], preciſely in the ſame manner as the Greeks did thoſe of the Dioſcori. The Pataici indeed ſeem to have been no other than the Cabiri, who, as it abundantly appears from Sanchoniatho, were originally Phenician deities. The circumſtance of their being the tutelary gods of navigation is noticed by Ariſtophanes;

Ω' νδρες, τι πεισομεθα; νυν αγων μεγας·
Αλλ' ει τις ὑμων εν Σαμοθρᾳκῃ τυγχανει
Μεμυημενος, νυν εϛιν ευξασθαι καλον[e].

Upon which the ſcholiaſt obſerves, that thoſe, who were in great danger, invoked the Samothracian gods, the Corybantes, and Hecatè, from whom the cave Zerinthus acquired its celebrity; and that the initiated in the myſteries of the Cabiri were thought to be ſafe in the midſt of perils, and ſecure from all the violence of tempeſts[f].

[d] Pataicus appears to be compounded of Patah-Oc, *the prieſt of the Ocean.*

[e] Ariſt. Iren. ver 275.

[f] Οἱ εν κινδυνοις γενομενοι, επεκαλουντο τουτους τους δαιμονας τους εν Σαμοθρᾳκῃ, τους τε Κορυβαντας, και την Ἑκατην, εξ ης και διαβοητον τι το Ζηρινθον αντρον, ενθα ταυτῃ ωργιαζον και ελευθερουντο. Μεμυημενος Τα μυϛηρια του Καβειρου. Δοκουσι γαρ οἱ μυημενοι ταυτα δικαιοι

The ſolar patriarch was worſhipped alſo under the name of *Pan*[g]. This deity, however his hiſtory might be afterwards perverted by the mythologizing Greeks, is plainly declared by Herodotus to be one of the eight great gods of Egypt[h], and even the moſt ancient of thoſe eight gods[i]. Hence Diodorus Siculus informs us, that he was the ſame as Serapis, Oſiris, Dionuſus, Pluto, Ammon, and Jupiter[k]. Accordingly, while he is ſtyled by Livy *Lycèus* from Luc, *the Sun*[l]; by Phor-

δικαιοι τε ειναι, και εκ δεινων σωζεσθαι, και εκ χειμωνων. Schol. in loc. Zerinthus ſeems to have derived its name from Z Aran-Thus, *the great god of the Ark*. Hence Venus was worſhipped in this cave, and denominated *Zerinthia*. Εν Θρακῃ αντρον εϛιν, εν ῷ ἡ Ζηρυνθια Αφροδιτη τιμαται. Tzet. in Lycoph. ver 449. With a ſimilar alluſion ſhe was called *Zirenè* by the Macedonians. Ζειρηνη, Αφροδιτη εν Μακεδονιᾳ. Heſych.

[g] Pan ſeems to be an abbreviation of Phanes, whom the author of the Orphic writings celebrates as the Sun Orph. Fragm apud Macrob. Saturn lib. i cap. 18 Phanes or Hanes is compounded of Ph'Ain-Es, *the ſolar fountain of fire*. The author of *the Etymologicon Magnum* accordingly informs us, that the proper name of Pan was *Phan*. Παν, Φαν τις ων. He was the ſame as the Iriſh Fen, *the Sun* Collect de Reb. Hib p 504.

[h] Τον Πανα των οκτω θεων λογιζονται ειναι οἱ Μενδησιοι. Herod. lib. ii. cap 46

[i] Παρ' Αιγυπτιοισι δε, Παν μεν αρχαιοτατος, και των οκτω των πρωτων λεγομενων θεων ειναι Ibid cap 145.

[k] Τον δε Οσιριν οἱ μεν Σαραπιν, οἱ δε Διονυσον, οἱ δε Πλουτωνα, οἱ δε Αμμωνα, τινες δε Δια, πολλοι δε Πανα, νενομικασι. Diod. Bibl. lib. i. p. 22.

[l] Liv Hiſt. lib. i. cap. 5.

nutus,

nutus, *Surtus* from Sur-Thus, *the ſolar deity*[m]; and by Nonnus, *Parrhaſius* from P' Ares, *the Sun*[n]: he is denominated by Livy[o], and Macrobius[p], *Inuus*, or *Junus*, from his connection with Juneh, *the dove*; was worſhipped by the Egyptians under the name of *Mendes*, or Men-Deva, *the divine Noah*[q]; and is deſcribed by Virgil as having gained the affections of the Moon[r]. He is further ſaid by Hyginus to have adviſed the gods to aſſume the forms of different animals, when in danger from the attack of Typhon, or the diluvian Ocean[s]; upon which occaſion he metamorphoſed himſelf into a monſter compounded of a goat and a fiſh[t]. He was alſo brought up along with Jupiter in Crete; and aſſiſted him in his war againſt the Titans, or diluvians, by ſending among them what are termed from him *Panic terrors*[u]. As the Sun, Pan was repreſented with a pipe of ſeven reeds, in alluſion

[m] Phorn. de Nat. Deor. cap. 27.

[n] Πρεσβυγενης φυξηλις εχαζετο Παρρασιος Παν. Dionyſ. lib. xxxii. p. 537.

[o] Liv. Hiſt. lib. i. cap. 5.

[p] Macrob. Saturn. lib. i. cap. 22.

[q] Herod. lib. ii. cap. 46.

[r] Georg. lib. iii. ver. 391.

[s] Hyg Fab. 196.

[t] Hyg. Poet. Aſtron. lib. ii. cap. 28.

[u] Eratoſ. Cataſt. cap 27.

to

to the imaginary muſic of the ſpheres [x]; and, as an arkite god, he was ſaid to be the ſon of Mercury [y], and to have been worſhipped in Daunia [z]. For the ſame reaſon, the word *Pan* was eſteemed ſynonymous with Cetus, *a ſea-monſter* [a].

Another title of Cronus or Noah was *Anubis* [b]; and another was *Horus* [c], an appellation moſt probably derived from Aur, *light*. Horus is deſcribed as the ſon of Oſiris and Iſis; but he is, in fact, like his father, at once the great patriarch, and the ſolar orb. The tawny colour of the lion, his fiery eyes, circular countenance, and ſhaggy mane, rendered him a fit emblem of the Sun; hence the throne of Horus, like that of Cybelè, was ſupported by lions [d]. Horus however was alſo repreſented by the Egyptians

[x] Macrob. Saturn lib. i. cap. 22.

[y] Mercury is M'Erech-Ur, *the great ſolar god of the Ark.* His hiſtory ſhall be conſidered at large hereafter. Vide infra chap. v.

[z] Lactan. Placid Narrat Fab. 11.

[a] Πανα ιχθυν καλειϲθαι κητωδη. Suid. Lex

[b] Plut. de Iſid. et Oſir. p 368.

[c] Macrob. Saturn. lib. i. cap. 21.

[d] Κεφαλην εχει μεγαλην το ζωον, και τας μεν κορας πυρωδεις, το δε προσωπον στρογγυλον, και περι αυτο ακτινοειδεις τριχας, κατα μιμησιν ἡλιου· ὁθεν και ὑπο τον θρονον του Ωρου, λεοντας ὑποτιθεασι, δεικνυντες το προς τον θεον του ζωου συμβολον Horapollinis Hierog. lib. i. ſect. 71.

failing

ſailing in a ſhip[e]; and was ſuppoſed to have encountered Typhon, or the ſea, from whoſe fury he ſaved himſelf, by taking refuge in the floating iſland near Buto[f].

Horus then being Apollo, or Noah worſhipped in conjunction with the Sun, we find him, as ſuch, connected with the Corybantes or Cabiri. Ariſtotle accordingly mentions two deities of that name, the firſt of whom ſprung from Vulcan and Minerva, while the ſecond was the ſon of Corybas, born in Crete[g]. The import of both theſe genealogies is preciſely the ſame; and Vulcan, Corybas, and Horus, are all one perſon. Hence, as Vulcan is deſcribed as the father of the Cabiri[h], ſo Corybas is repreſented as the head of the Corybantes, and as the huſband of Thebah, or the Ark[i].

[e] Ὁ δε δ' επι πλοιου ναυτιλλομενος την διακυβερνωσαν τον κοσμον επικρατειαν παριστησιν. Ὡσπερ ουν ὁ κυβερνητης χωριστος ων της νεως, των πηδαλιων αυτης επιβεβηκεν, ουτω χωριστως ὁ ἡλιος των οιακων του κοσμου παντος επιβεβηκεν Jamblic de Myſt. ſect vii. cap. 2. I have cited this paſſage only to ſhew, that Horus was thus depicted, for I cannot aſſent to the reaſon given by Jamblichus.

[f] Plut. de Iſid. p 371 —Ælian. de Anim lib. x. cap. 21.—Herod lib. ii cap. 156.

[g] Ναι μην Απολλωνα, ὁ μεν Αριστοτελης, πρωτον Ἡφαιστου και Αθηνας, δευτερον εν Κρητη, τον Κορυβαντος. Clem Alex. Cohort p. 24.

[h] Pherec apud Strab Geog lib x. p 472.

[i] Diod Sic. Bibl. lib. v. p. 323.

It will be proper for me here to offer a few obfervations upon the radical fyllable *Car*, *Cur*, *Cor*, or *Sar*, which enters alike into the word *Corybas*, and into a great variety of epithets beftowed upon Apollo. This ancient folar title feems to be originally deducible from the Hebrew *Ser*, *Tzer*, or *Seir*[k]: the Perfians preferved it in the form *Cur*[l]: the Greeks lengthened it into *Sirus*, or *Sirius*[m]; the Celts into *Cearas*, *Croith*, or *Curoith*[n]; and the Hindoos into *Surya*. In our own language we ftill retain the word *Sear* in the fignification of *burning*; while the Hebrews have formed from the fame radical the compound term *Seraph*[o], and the Egyptians, the fimilarly compounded name of their god *Serapis*. With regard to the Grecian Apollo, Paufanias mentions, that at Megara there was a pyramidal ftone, a fhape peculiarly facred to the Sun on

[k] Heb. זהר, צהר, שעיר, or perhaps שור *a prince*.

[l] Κυρος ὁ Ἡλιος παρα Περσαις. Hefych.

[m] Σειριος, ὁ Ἡλιος. Hefych. Σειρ, Σειρος, ὁ Ἡλιος Suid.

[n] Croith or Curoith is Cur-Ath, *the burning Sun*.

[o] Heb. שרף. I ftrongly fufpect, that both Seraph, *to burn*, and Seraph, *a fiery ferpent*, are ultimately deducible from the compound radical Sar-Oph, *the folar ferpent*. The Hebrew Seraph is evidently the prototype of the Latin Serpens, for I am rather inclined to think, that Serpo, *to creep*, was a defcriptive derivation from Serpens, than that Serpens is the participle from Serpo. The ferpent was the principal folar emblem.

ac-

account of its resemblance to the tapering flame, which the inhabitants denominated *Apollo Carinus* [p]. Under the similar name of *Corynthus* this deity was worshipped by the Messenians [q], and under that of *Carnius* by all the Doric tribes [r]; while his festival was styled *Carnia* [s]. Accordingly we find that a grove was consecrated to *Apollo Carnius* near Pharæ [t]; and a cell, at Sicyon [u]. There was

[p] Εστι δε εν τῳ γυμνασιῳ τῳ αρχαιῳ—λιθος παρεχομενος Πυραμιδος σχημα ου μεγαλης· τουτον Απολλωνα ονομαζουσι Καρινον. Pauf. Attic. p. 106. Megara is Ma-Car-Ai, *the land of the great Sun.*

[q] Κορυνθον δε Απολλωνα ονομαζουσι. Pauf Messen. p. 365.

[r] Καρνειον δε Απολλωνα Δωριευσι τοις πασι σεβεσθαι. Pauf. Lacon. p. 238. Pausanias adds, that the Dorians were instructed in this mode of worship by Carnus an Acarnanian. Carnus however appears to be no other than Car-Nus, *the solar Noah*, and the word *Acarnania* is derived from the same radical *Car.* Hence we find, that the Acarnanians were formerly called *Curetes,* one of the titles of the Cabiri, from their devotion to the worship of Cur; while their country bore the name of *Curetis.* Κουρης, ὁ εξ Ακαρνανιας. Steph. Byzan. de Urb. p 474. Φασι δε τινες τους Ακαρνανας πρωτον Κουρητας καλεισθαι Tzet. in Lycoph. ver. 670. Απο του Ακαρνανος τοις εν τῃ ηπειρῳ ταυτῃ το ονομα το νυν γενεσθαι λεγουσι τα προ του Κουρησι καλουμενοις. Pauf. Arcad. p. 646 Acarnaniæ, quæ antea *Curetis* vocabatur. Plin. Nat. Hist. lib. iv. cap 1.

[s] Καρνιος, Απολλων. Καρνια, Απολλωνος ἑορτη παρα Λακεδαιμονιοις. Hesych.

[t] Pauf. Messen. p. 355.

[u] Το ενδοτερω Απολλωνι ανειται Καρνειῳ, και ες αυτο ουκ εστι πλην τοις ἱερευσι εσοδος Pauf. Corinth. p 134. Bacchus, who was the Sun no less than Apollo, was on that account called *Cresius,*

alſo a temple of *Apollo Carnias* at Gytheæ in Laconia [x]; and another, in Arcadia, of *Apollo Cereates* [y]. The ſame title of *Carnius* is applied to Apollo by an ancient oracle;

Ευχεο Καρνιω τελεειν σεβας Απολλωνι [z].

while, in ſtrict conformity with the preceding authorities, he is called by Nonnus *Carnèus.*

Αξομαι εκ Σπαρτης ἑτερϐς κυνας,. ὡς ατιταλλει
Ηιθεων ες ερωτα εμος Καρνειος Απολλων [a].

Car, Cur, or *Ser* then, being a title of the Sun, we find it fabled, that the nymph *Curenè* was beloved by Apollo, and that ſhe bore him a ſon named *Ariſtèus.*

——Αρισαιος,——
Τον ποτε Κυρηνη κεμαδοσσοος Αρτεμις αλλη
Φοιβειη φιλοτητι λεοντοφονος τεκε νυμφη [b].

Ariſtèus is Ares-Thus, *the divine Sun,* and he is reported to have been educated in the cave of Chiron [c]. Curenè herſelf was carried off

or Cur-Es, *the ſolar fire.* —Διονυσου ναος Κρησιου—. Pauf Corinth p. 164

[x] Pauſ. Lacon. p. 265.

[y] Pauſ. Arcad. p. 670.

[z] Orac. Vet. Opſop. p. 41.

[a] Nonni Dionyſ. lib xvi. p. 290.

[b] Ibid lib xiii. p. 240

[c] Apoll. Argon. lib. ii. ver. 512.

by

by Apollo from Aimonia, or Ai-Monah, *the land of the arkite Moon*; whence her son Arisstèus was particularly venerated by the Aimonians [d].

With a similar allusion to the worship of the Sun, Esculapius the eighth Cabir of Sanchoniatho had a temple in Achaia denominated *Curos* [e], and was reckoned in the Grecian mythology, the son of Apollo by Coronis daughter of Phlegyas.

Ω μεγα χαρμα βροτοις βλαστων Ασκληπιε πασιν·
Ὁν Φλεγυηις ετικτεν εμη φιλοτητι μιγεισα
Ιμεροεσσα Κορωνις ενι κραναη Επιδαυρω [f].

Apollo had likewise a son called *Coronus* [g]; which name, as well as that of his mistress

[d] Apoll. Argon. lib ii. ver. 506. Curenè was supposed to have given her name to the city Curenè in Africa, which was deemed peculiarly sacred to Apollo Carnèus Thus Callimachus:

Σπαρτη τοι, Καρνειε, τοδε πρωτιστον εδεθλον,
Δευτερον αυ Θηρη, τριτατον γε μεν αστυ Κυρηνη.

Hymn. ad Apoll. ver 71.

In the same hymn is particularized the fountain Curè, which, according to the scholiast, was at Curenè. Ibid ver. 88. I shall resume the consideration of the history of Aristèus hereafter. Vide infra chap x.

[e] Pauf Achaic. p 236.

[f] Orac. Apoll apud Pauf. Corinth p. 171

[g] Ibid p. 123

Coronis, is derived from the compound, Cor-On, *the ſolar deity*. Hence Eſculapius himſelf was denominated *Curos*; and hence likewiſe may be deduced the etymology of the city *Curtones* in Beotia, where was a temple and grove of Apollo[h].

In conſequence of the ſolar worſhip being ingrafted upon the commemorative rites of the deluge, while Diana, or the lunar Ark, the mythological ſiſter of Apollo, was on the one hand eſteemed a Titanis, ſhe bore alſo on the other hand the ſolar names of *Saronia*[i], *Cora*, and *Coria*[k]. She was alſo called *Peraſia*[l], from P'Ares, *the Sun*; and was ſaid to have been brought by Latona to *Coriſſus*, a city of Epheſus[m]. It is obſervable, that her mother Ceres, in reference to the ſame ſolar worſhip, was by the Cnidians denominated *Curè*[n].

h Pauſ Bæot. p. 757.

i Σαρωνια Αρτεμις. Heſych.

k Η μεν τοι Προιτος γε δυω εκαθισσατο νηυς,
Αλλον μεν Κορινς ——
Callim. Hymn. ad Dian. ver. 233.

l Εν τοις Κασαβαλοις εςι το της Περασιας Αρτεμιδος ἱερον. Strab. Geog. lib xii p. 537.

m Κορισσος πολις της Εφεσιας, δια το την Λητω τεκουσαν, και την Αρτεμιν κομιζουσαν γενομενην κατα τον τοπον. Steph. Byzan. de Urb p. 466.

n Apud Cnidios *Cyre* vocatur Ceres. Cœl Rhodig. Lect. Ant. lib. xvii. cap. 27. Several other inſtances will hereafter

be

The celebrated city of Corinth appears to have derived its name likewiſe from the prevailing worſhip of Cor, *the Sun.* It was ſuppoſed to have been founded by Aletes, one of the Heraclidæ or Heliadæ [o]; whence Pindar calls the Corinthians παιδες Αλατα, *the children of Aletes* [p]. Theſe Heraclidæ [q], Aletæ, or Titans, ſo celebrated throughout the whole world, are ſaid by Sanchoniatho, as we have already obſerved, to be the children of Cronus or Agruerus, the ſcriptural *Noah:* and it is remarkable, that, as the Titans were denominated *Heliadæ* [r], ſo the two great Rajah families in Hindoſtan ſtyled themſelves *Surya-Bans* and *Chandra-Bans,* or *children of the Sun* and

be produced of the Ark being deſignated by titles derived from the ſeveral appellations of the Sun.

[o] Αλητης ἡγησατο της αποικιας των Ἡρακλειδων, ὁτε οἱ Ἡρακλειδαι κατῃσαν εις Πελοποννησον, και αυτος εἱς ων των Ἡρακλειδων—Οὑτος εκρατησε Κορινθου. Schol. in Pind Olymp. xiii. ver 17. Κρατει ὁ Αλητης, και ωνομασεν αυτην Διος Κορινθον. Schol. in Pind. Nem vii. ver. 155. Aletes is merely Al-Ait, *the god of fire,* and he is the ſame mythological character as his ſuppoſed anceſtor Hercules. In reference to the union of the two ſuperſtitions, he is ſaid to have been the ſon of Hippotes, or Hippa-Dus, *the god of the Ark.* Conon. Narrat. 26. Corinthus is Cor-Ain-Thus, *the divine ſolar fountain of heat.*

[p] Pind Olymp. xiii. ver. 17.

[q] Their father Hercules is Erech-El, *the arkite deity*; and he is the ſame perſon as Oſiris, as ſhall be ſhewn hereafter.

[r] Ang. *Children of the Sun.*

Moon.

Moon. The ſame notion prevailed in Peru, the Yncas of which boaſted of their deſcent from the two great luminaries of heaven, or, in other words, from Noah and the Ark, worſhipped in conjunction with the Sun and Moon. Nor ſhall we wonder at this ſimilarity of religious opinion, when we conſider the very remote period, at which the union of the ſolar and arkite worſhip took place; a period ſo remote, that we cannot fix it later, than the age of the tower of Babel, which ſeems in fact to have been erected for the purpoſes of this very idolatry. Such then being the import of the word *Corinth*, we ſhall be at no loſs to underſtand the meaning of the conteſt between Neptune and the Sun, which was reported to have been carried on for the iſthmus of that city[s]. It evidently alludes to the reſiſtance made, in the early ages, to the union of the two primeval ſuperſtitions[t]. Accordingly, as I ſhall take occa-

[s] Λεγουσι δε και οἱ Κορινθιοι Ποσειδωνα ελθειν Ἡλιῳ περι της γης ες αμφισβητησιν. Pauſ. Corinth. p 112.

[t] The ancients had a variety of ſimilar legends reſpecting conteſts between their gods, which I think may be divided into *two* claſſes, as alluſive to *two* entirely different events, *the deluge*, and *the union of the two ſuperſtitions*. I have already noticed the conteſt of Neptune and Juno for the ſovereignty of Argos, and have referred it to the *firſt* of theſe events That of Minerva and Neptune for the territory of Athens has a ſimilar

ſion to ſhew hereafter, we find in the hiſtory of the Corinthians, traces no leſs of the arkite, than of the ſolar worſhip.

From the ſame adoration of Cor or Cur, Crete was formerly called *Curetis* [u], and a

milar alluſion to the hiſtory of the deluge. Hence, in both theſe inſtances, Juno and Minerva are equally deſcribed, not as vanquiſhed, but as having gained the ſuperiority over Neptune. The Trezenians however preſerved a tradition, which ſeems to be a corrupted compound both of the conteſt which relates to the flood, and of that which deſcribes the union of the two ſuperſtitions. They eſteemed Horus the firſt of men; and believed, that a conteſt for their country between Neptune and Minerva took place during the reign of Althepus, the ſon of Neptune, and ſucceſſor of Horus. This is evidently the counterpart of the Athenian legend, and is conſequently to be referred to the hiſtory of the deluge, Minerva being a perſonification of the divine wiſdom, which preſerved the Ark, but, when we find, that the iſſue of the Trezenian conteſt was not a victory gained by Minerva over her adverſary, but an agreement between the parties jointly to poſſeſs the country, this part of the tradition ſeems rather to allude to the junction of the arkite worſhip with that of the Sun. Pauſ. Corinth. p. 181.

[u] Doſiades eam a Creta nympha Heſperidis filia, Anaximander a rege Curetum, Philiſtides Mallotes Crates primum *Æriam* dictam, deinde poſtea *Curetin*. Plin. Nat Hiſt lib. iv. cap. 12. Οἱ μεν φασιν απο τȣ κορης Κορητην, και Κρητην κατα συγκοπην· οἱ δε απο Κρητος τȣ Διος και Ιδαιας νυμφης παιδος· οἱ δ' απο Κρητης μιας των Ἑσπεριδων· οἱ δ' απο τινος γηγενους Κρητος. Steph. Byzant de Urb p. 479 *Crete* is the ſame word in reality as *Curetis*; for, as Stephanus juſtly obſerves, *Crete* is merely the ſyncopated form of *Curete*. The ſame obſervation may be extended to the ſuppoſed earth-born monarch Cres, who

is

diſtrict in Aſia Minor *Caria*. It is remarkable, that the citadel of Megara was likewiſe denominated *Caria*, as it was ſuppoſed from Car the ſon of Phoroneus, in the time of whoſe father Inachus the deluge happened [x]. In a ſimilar manner, and with a ſimilar alluſion to the united ſuperſtitions, a city of Chios, which bore the name of *Carides*, was ſaid to have been built by Macar, and the perſons, who eſcaped from the flood of Deucalion [y].

Another title of the Sun, to return from this digreſſion reſpecting the ſyllable *Cur*, or *Cor*, was *Phaëthon*, or Ph'Aith-On, *the burning ſolar orb*. Thus Sophocles:

Πȣ ποτε κεραυνοι Διος, η
Πȣ Φαεθων Αλιος,
Ει ταυτ' εφορωντες
Κρυπτȣσιν ἑκηλοι [z],

Where is thy lightning, Jove? and where thy
power,

is evidently the ſolar deity Cures. The mythological hiſtory of Crete will be reſumed hereafter, chap. vi.

[x] Εκαλειτο δε και ἡ Μεγαρων ακροπολις Καρια απο Καρος τȣ Φορωνεως. Steph. Byzant. de Urb. p. 449.

[y] Καριδες περι Χιον την νησον. Εφορος εν τη πρωτη ἱςορει, κτισαι φασκων αυτην τȣς διασωθεντας εκ τȣ επι Δευκαλιωνος γενομενου κατακλυσμȣ μετα Μακαρος· και μεχρι νυν τον τοπον καλεισθαι Καριδας. Ibid. p. 451. Macar is Ma-Car, *the great Sun*.

[z] Elect. ver. 825.

All-

All-ſeeing Phaëthon ? if this foul deed
Be unrequited.

Phaëthon indeed is uſually deſcribed as the ſon of Apollo, but this is merely one of the inſtances of genealogical repetition ſo common in the mythology of the ancients. The hiſtory of his birth ſeems to be founded on the junction of the two primitive modes of worſhip: thus, he was ſuppoſed to be the offspring of the Sun by Clymenè the daughter of Oceanus and Tethys; who is ſaid by Nonnus to have been born in the neighbourhood of Nuſa, the ſcene of the fabulous exploits of Bacchus, and who in fact was no other than Cula-Mena, *the hollow Noëtic Ark*[a].

Ωκεανος κελαδων μιτρȣμενος αν τυγα κοσμȣ
Ιχμαλεην περι Νυσαν αγων γαιηοχον ὑδωρ,
Τηθυος αρχεγονοισιν ὁμιλησας ὑμεναιοις
Νυμφιος ὑδατοεις Κλυμενην τεκεν,—
——ἧς επι μορφῃ,——
Καμνε πυρος ποιμνης ἑτερῳ πυρι[b].—

The ſolar Noah was adored likewiſe under the name of *Ares* or *Mars*. Hence the title

[a] Clymenè is alſo ſaid to have been the mother of Atlas, and for the very ſame reaſon Vide ſupra p. 113, 115.

[b] Nonni Dionyſ. lib. xxxvii p. 639.

Ares,

Ares, in the compound form of *Dus-Ares*, was given to Bacchus [c]; and hence, as we learn from Macrobius, Mars was eſteemed the ſame as Bacchus, and the Sun. The Accitani adorned the head of his ſtatue with rays of glory, and denominated him *Neton*, a word poſſibly compounded of Nu-Ait-On, *Noah the burning Sun* [d]: his worſhip however ſeems to have come originally from the Eaſt, for, according to the author of *the Chronicon Paſchale*, Ares was an ancient king of Aſſyria, the ſon of Sames, the brother of Rhea [e]. He was the ſame as the Babylonian Belus or Baal, the word *Ares* ſignifying *the ſolar orb*; and, in a ſimilar manner, his imaginary father Sames was alſo the Sun [f]: hence, in reference to the union of the two ſuperſtitions, he was deſcribed as the brother of Rhea, or the lunar Ark.

[c] Δυσαρην τον Διονυσον. Heſych.

[d] Quæ de Libero patre dicta ſunt, hæc Martem eundem ac Solem eſſe demonſtrant, ſiquidem plerique Liberum cum Marte conjungunt.—Accitani etiam, Hiſpana gens, ſimulacrum Martis radiis ornatum maxima religione celebrant, *Neton* vocantes. Macrob Saturn lib. i. cap. 19. Mars is evidently Ma Ares, *the great Sun*.

[e] Μετα δε Νινον εβασιλευσεν Ασσυριων Θουρας ονοματι, ὁντινα μετωνομασεν ὁ τουτου πατηρ Ζαμης εκ της Ῥεας αδελφης Αρεα. Chron. Paſch. p. 37.

[f] Sames is שמש, and Ares is הרס.

Another

Another title of the ſame import was *Hercules*, who, conſidered in one point of view is Arech-El, *the God of the Ark*, and in another, is a perſonification of the glorious luminary of day. Thus, while Apollodorus deſcribes him as ſailing over the vaſt ocean in a golden cup, which he had received as a gift from Apollo[g]; Macrobius expreſsly aſſerts, that this cup was nothing more than a ſhip, and yet declares, that Hercules was a name of the Sun[h]. Hence, he was worſhipped by the Beotians under the appellation of *Charops*, or Car-Op, *the ſolar ſerpent*[i].

It is remarkable, that although the word *Titan* properly ſignifies *a diluvian*, yet, as we are aſſured by the author of the Orphic hymns, it was likewiſe a title of the Sun.

[g] Ὁ δε (Ἡλιος) την ανδρειαν αυτȣ (Ἡρακλεȣς) θαυμασας, χρυσεον εδωκεν δεπας, εν ᾧ τον Ωκεανον διεπερασε. Apollod. Bibl. lib. ii. cap 5. See alſo Athen. Deipnoſ. lib xi p. 470.

[h] Ego tamen arbitror non poculo Herculem maria tranſvectum, ſed navigio, cui ſcypho nomen fuit. Saturn. lib. v cap. 21. Præterea ſacrorum adminiſtrationes apud Ægyptios multiplici actu multiplicem dei aſſerunt poteſtatem, ſignificantes Herculem hunc eſſe τον εν πασι και δια παντων ἡλιον. Ibid. lib. i. cap. 20. The twelve labours of Hercules moſt probably ſignify nothing more, than the paſſage of the Sun through the twelve ſigns of the zodiac

[i] Ανωτερω δε εςιν Ἡρακλης Χαροψ επικλησιν· ενταυθα δε οἱ Βοιωτοι λεγȣσιν αναβηναι τον Ἡρακλεα αγοντα τον τȣ ᾅδȣ κυνα. Pauſ Bæot. p. 779.

Τιταν

Τιταν χρυσαυγης Ὑπεριων, ουρανιον φως,
Δεξιε μεν γενετωρ ηους, ευωνυμε νυκτος,
- - - - - - - - - - -
Φωσφορε, αιολοδεκτε, φερεσβιε, καρπιμε Παιαν,
Αιεθαλες, αμιαντε, χρονου πατερ, αθανατε Ζευς[k].

The reaſon of ſuch an application of the name *Titan* was evidently the joint adoration of the diluvian Noah and the ſolar orb.

The whole of the preceding obſervations are decidedly confirmed by Nonnus, who pronounces Hercules, Belus, Ammon, Apis, Cronus, Jupiter, Serapis, Phaëthon, Mithras, and Apollo, to be all equally the ſame ſolar deity.

Αστροχιτων Ἡρακλες, αναξ πυρος, ορχαμε κοσμου,
Ἡελιε, βροτεοιο βιου δολιχοσκιε ποιμην,
- - - - - - - - - - -
Βηλος επ᾽ Ευφρηταο, Λιβυς κεκλημενος Αμμων,
Απις εφυς Νειλωος, Αραψ Κρονος, Ασσυριος Ζευς·
- - - - - - - - - - - -
Ειτε Σαραπις εφυς Αιγυπτιος, ανεφελος Ζευς,
Ει Κρονος, ει Φαεθων πολυωνυμος, ειτε συ Μιθρας,
Ἡελιος Βαβυλωνος, εν Ἑλλαδι Δελφος Απολλων[l].

In fine, the Clarian Apollo directly aſſerts his identity with the Sun, with Horus, with Oſiris, and with Bacchus.

[k] Hymn 7.

[l] Nonni Dionyſ. lib. xl. p. 683, 684, 685.

Ἡλιος,

Ἥλιος, Ὧρος, Οσιρις αναξ, Διονυσος, Απολλων,
Ὡρων και καιρων ταμιης, ανεμων τε και ομβρων,
Ηους και νυκτος πολυαστερος ἡνια νωμων,
Ζαφλεγεων αστρων βασιλευς, ηδ' αθανατον πυρ[m].

From theſe remarks on the polyonymy of the ſolar Noah, I ſhall proceed to treat of the union of the two great primitive ſuperſtitions; which event I apprehend to have been the cauſe, why we ſometimes find the principal deity of the Gentiles repreſented as the Sun, and ſometimes deſcribed as having been incloſed within an ark, or having ſailed in a ſhip over the waters of the diluvian Ocean.

Symbolical imagery was very much in uſe among the ancients, and will be found to pervade the whole of their heterogeneous mythology. A heifer ſeems to have been adopted as perhaps the moſt uſual emblem of the Ark, and a ſerpent as that of the Sun; while the great patriarch himſelf was ſometimes worſhipped under the form of a bull, and ſometimes, in conſequence of his union with the Sun, hieroglyphically deſcribed as a ſerpent having the head of a bull[n].

That the heifer was an emblem of the Ark appears from a very curious paſſage in *the*

[m] Orac. Vet. Opſop. p. 6.

[n] Mont. Ant. vol ii p. 204.

Etymologicon Magnum, the author of which informs us, that *Theba*, in the Syrian dialect, signified *a heifer*; and he further observes, that Thebes, the capital of Beotia, owed its name to the circumstance of Cadmus being led by an animal of that species to the place where the city was afterwards built[o]. The import however of *Theba*, in the Hebrew language, is *an ark*; and the only reason, why a heifer was designated by the same appellation, was the circumstance of its being used as an arkite emblem. The whole tradition indeed respecting Cadmus is founded upon the union of the two symbols now under consideration. Europa, who is the very same mythological character as Astartè, Venus, or the lunar Ark, notwithstanding she has borrowed her name from Eur-Op, *the solar serpent*[p], is violently

[o] Θηϐα Συξιςι λεγεται, ἡ βȣς· ὁθεν εκληθησαν αἱ Θηϐαι ὑπο του Καδμȣ κτισθεισαι, ὑτι ζητων την αδελφην, χρησμον ελαϐε κατοικησαι, ὁπȣ ἡ ϐȣς ἑαυτην καταθησει. Etym. Mag. vox Θηϐα. The same observation is made by Tzetzes: Θηϐη γαρ ἡ βȣς κατα Συρȣς. Schol. in Lycoph. ver. 1206.

[p] Lucian informs us, that the priests of Hierapolis assured him, that Astartè and Europa were the same person accordingly, as Europa was feigned to have been carried away by a bull, so Astartè was represented with the horns of that animal The application of the solar epithet *Europa* to the Ark is a species of mythological impropriety by no means uncommon. Thus Ceres, Proserpine, and Venus, were called *Curè*, *Cora*, and *Persithea*, from Cur, and P'Ares, *the Sun*, notwithstanding they

carried away from Phenicia upon *the arkite bull*[q]. Jupiter, her lover, who is said to have assumed the form of that animal, is the Noëtic Sun[r]; whence he is supposed to have conveyed his prize into Crete, the ancient Curetis, or Cur-Ait, *the land sacred to the orb of day*. Cadmus, or Cadm-On, *the oriental solar deity*[s], comes, in search of his sister, to Beotia, *the country of Buto*, or *the tauriform Ark*[t]; where he founds *Theba*, being con-

they were each a personification of the Ark, while Rhea and Diana bore the names of *Ops*, and *Oupis*, words derived, like *Europa*, from Op or Ob, *the solar serpent*. Ουπι αιασσ', ευωπι, φαεσφορε—. Callim. Hymn ad Dian. ver. 204. Ampelius gives the title *Ops* to Diana, as well as to Rhea Tertia, quæ vocatur *Ops*, de Glauco Amp. cap. 9. Persithea seems to be Perazi-Thea, *the goddess of the Perazites*, or *worshippers of the Sun*. *Persitheam* invenio Venerem nuncupatam. Cœl Rhodig. Lect. Ant. lib. xviii. cap 18. Περσιθεα ἡ Αφροδιτη Hesych. With a similar allusion to P'Eres, *the Sun*, the cock, who loudly hails the approach of day, received the appellation of *Persicus*. Περσικος ορνις ὁ αλεκτρυων. Hesych. Περσινος ορνις ὁ αλεκτωρ. Suid.

q Europa is said by Pindar to have been the daughter of Tityus, (Pyth Od 4.) and by Herodotus to have been the mother of Minos. (Herod. lib 1. cap 173) Both these accounts are perfectly accurate, Tityus being only a personification of the deluge, (vide infra chap. v.) and Minos being the patriarch Noah.

r The bull of Europa was the same as the Cretan Talus, Italotus, or Minotaur. Vide infra chap vi

s More will be said of Cadmus hereafter. Vide infra chap vii.

t Buto is Bu-Do, or Bu-Du, *the divine tauriform Ark*

 ducted

ducted by *a heifer*, and having encountered in battle a tremendous *ſerpent* [u].

The traditional hiſtory of Thebes perfectly accords with this interpretation of the fable of Cadmus. Ogyges, the ſuppoſed ſon of Neptune and Aliſtra, was eſteemed its moſt ancient ſovereign [x]; and in his time a great deluge hap-

[u] The continent of Europe derived its name from the worſhip of Eur-Op, *the ſerpent of the Sun,* not from the fabulous Europa. Herodotus juſtly explodes the notion of its being ſo called from the Phenician princeſs, obſerving very naturally, that ſhe never once ſaw the region, which the Greeks denominated *Europe*, but that ſhe was conveyed from Tyre into Crete, and from Crete into Africa. Herod. lib iv. cap 45. Some other fables reſpecting the origin of the word *Europe* may be found in Tzet. in Lycoph. ver. 1283.

[x] Both Ogyges and Cadmus however are reported to have come from Thebes in Egypt Tzet in Lycoph ver. 1206 The fact is, that the Grecian Thebes was a mere tranſcript of the Egyptian Thebes. In both, the rites of the Ark equally prevailed, and both equally derived their reſpective names from *Theba*. The firſt wife of Agenor is ſaid to have been Damno, the daughter of Belus, and the ſecond, Argiopè, the daughter of the river Nile, who was the mother of Cadmus. Pherec. apud Schol in Apoll. Argon. lib iii ver. 1185. Damno and Argiopè are in fact the ſame mythological character, for Damno is Da-Meno, *the Noëtic Ark,* and Argiopè is Arg-Opa, *the ophite Ark.* It is worthy of obſervation, that Ogyges, according to Corinna, was the ſon of Beotus. Beotus, as we ſhall hereafter ſee, was the ſame as Bootes, Arcas, Buddha, or Mercury; in other words, the principal deity of Bu-Do, *the divine ox.* Κοριννα δε τον Ωγυγον Βοιωτου υιον ειπεν Schol. in Apoll. Argon. lib. iii. ver. 1177

pened,

pened, which Varro aſcribes to an inundation of the ſea[y]. After the flood of Deucalion, Jupiter, according to Lycus, became the father of Thebah, by Iodama daughter of Tithonus; but, according to another account, Thebah was the concubine of Jupiter, and the mother of Egyptus, whoſe daughter was named *Carchè*[z]; while a third legend repreſents Thebah as the offspring of Cilix, and the wife of Corybas, who was the father of the Cabiric Corybantes[a]. All theſe variouſly perverted traditions relate equally to one event: Aliſtra is Al-Es-Tora, *the arkite heifer of the Sun*; Iodama is Io-da-Maia, *the great mother Io*, or *Iſis*; Tithonus is Tit-On-Nus, *the helio-diluvian Noah*; and Carchè is G'Archa, *the illuſtrious Ark*. With a ſimilar alluſion to the deluge, Arnè, a town of Beotia, is ſaid to have received its name from Arno, the nurſe of Neptune[b]. Arno however is merely Aran-No, *the Ark of Noah*; and ſhe is the ſame mythological character as Hippa, who was feigned to be the nurſe of Bacchus.

The rape of Europa then ſignifies nothing more than the junction of the two primitive

[y] Varr de Re Ruſt lib iii. cap. 1.
[z] Tzet. in Lycoph ver 1206.
[a] Diod. Sic. Bibl. lib. v. p 323.
[b] Tzet. in Lycoph ver. 644

ſuperſtitions, which appears to have been accompliſhed by violence; and I apprehend, that the fable of Cor'onis being raviſhed by Butes is a legend of preciſely the ſame import [c]. The name of *Coronis*, who is alſo deſcribed as the concubine of Apollo, is derived from Cor-On, *the ſolar orb*, as that of *Europa* is from Eur-Op, *the ſolar ſerpent*; while the appellation of her allegorical lover *Butes* is merely the compound Bu-Dus, *the god of the arkite heifer* [d].

As the ancients were accuſtomed to repreſent the union of the two modes of worſhip under the image of a rape, ſo the circumſtance of the Ark being ſometimes conſidered as the mother, ſometimes as the daughter, and ſometimes as the conſort of its builder, ſeems to have given riſe to ſeveral wild traditions reſpecting inceſtuous connections. A curious legend of this nature has been preſerved by Herodotus, in which the ſymbolical bull makes a very conſpicuous figure. He informs us,

[c] Κορωνιδα δε ἁρπαγεισαν συναναγκασθηναι τῳ Βουτᾳ συνοικισαι. Diod Bibl lib v p. 324.

[d] Butes is the ſame as Buddha or Mercury. He was worſhipped at Athens in conjunction with Vulcan, Neptune, and Erechtheus. His character will be more particularly examined, when I treat of the hiſtory of Mercury. Vide infra chap. v

that

that an ancient king of Egypt, named *Mycerinus*, violently committed inceſt with his own daughter; and afterwards, when ſhe died of grief in conſequence of the crime, incloſed her body in a wooden figure of an ox, which bore between its horns a repreſentation of the Sun [e]. Mr. Bryant is of opinion, that the ox is no other than the ſacred ox of Oſiris, and that Herodotus is totally miſtaken in applying it to the fable of Mycerinus. The firſt of theſe ſuppoſitions I fully admit, but I am much inclined to doubt the propriety of the ſecond. The hiſtory of the early Egyptian princes, like that of the Hindoo ſovereigns, ſeems to be entirely fabulous, conſiſting only of alluſions to the rites of the united Sabian and arkite idolatry. Such I conceive to be the caſe with the ſtory of Mycerinus. This imaginary king is ſimply Ma-Car-Nus, *the great ſolar Noah*; while his daughter, and the wooden image, are the two moſt uſual ſymbols of the Ark, a woman, and an ox [f]. With regard to the figure of the Sun placed

[e] Herod lib ii. cap. 131, 132.

[f] As Theba indifferently ſignifies either *an ark*, or *a heifer*; ſo, in a ſimilar manner, Soros, *a coffin*, is derived from שור Sor, *a bull*, the Ark, as we ſhall hereafter ſee, being conſidered in the Myſteries as the coffin within which the Noetic family was incloſed

between the horns of the animal, it evidently relates to the ſolar worſhip ſo early ingrafted upon the commemorative rites of the Ark [g].

The ſymbol of the ox occurs alſo in the mythological hiſtory of Buſiris, one of the ancient heroes of Egypt [h]. In *the Etymologicon Magnum* his name is derived from the circumſtance of his having yoked oxen together for the purpoſes of agriculture [i]: but I am rather inclined to think it a compound of Bu-Sir, *the helio-arkite bull.* I doubt not, but that this Buſiris was the ſame as Oſiris, or Noah, to whom, as I have already obſerved, the bull was eſteemed peculiarly ſacred.

[g] There are ſeveral other traditions of a ſimilar nature. Thus Procris is ſaid to have borne Aglaurus, or Agl-Aur, (עגל-אור) *the ſolar bull,* to her father Erechtheus, or Erech-Thus, *the god of the Ark* Hyg. Fab. 253 Thus alſo Hippodamia, or Hippa-Da-Maia, *the arkite mother,* is feigned to have committed inceſt with her allegorical father Oinomaus, Ibid and Menephron is reported to have been guilty of the ſame crime with his mother at Cyllenè in Arcadia. Ovid. Metam. lib vii ver 386. The word *Oinomaus* ſignifies *a deſire of wine,* and alludes to the circumſtance of Noah's having planted a vineyard, Menephron is Men-Hiph-Aron, *the arkite Noah*; and Cyllenè was famed for the birth of the diluvian god Mercury. Cyllenè in Arcadia ſeems to have been ſo called in honour of Culah-Nah, *the Ark of Noah.*

[h] Herod. lib. ii cap 61. compared with the preceding citation.

[i] Ειρηται παρα το βες ειρειν. Etym. Mag. vox Βεσιρις.

Hence,

Hence, in reference to the events of the deluge, this animal, the well-known ſymbol of the great patriarch, is repreſented, in the upper compartment of the Bembine table, ſtanding in the ſacred Baris, or ſhip of Iſis, and accompanied by two human figures.

The bull then being emblematical of Noah, and the heifer of the Ark, we ſhall perceive the reaſon, why the Greeks called a particular kind of ſhips by the name of *Taurocercuri*[k]; why *Bubartis* ſignified a *galley*[l]; and why Diana, or the arkite Moon, was denominated *Taurionè*. According to Suidas, ſhe received this title, becauſe ſhe rode upon bulls[m]; but, in reality, Taurionè is a mere compound of Tor-Ionah, *the tauric* or *arkite dove*. In a ſimilar manner, Minerva, another diluvian goddeſs, was ſometimes ſtyled *Taurobolos*, as being Toro-Bolah, *the ſovereign miſtreſs of the Ark*[n]; and ſometimes *Budèa*, and *Ethyia*.

> Η πολλα δη Βυδειαν, Αιθυιαν, Κορην,
> Αρωγον αυδαξασα[o].——

[k] Ταυροκερκυροι, ποταμια πλοια. Suid Lex.

[l] Βυβαρτις, νεως ονομα παρα Φιλιςῳ. Heſych From Bo, *an ox*, the Greek *Cibotus*, and the Engliſh *Boat*, ſeem equally to be derived.

[m] Ταυριωνη,—ἡ αυτη τῃ Σεληνῃ εςι, και εποχειται ταυροις. Suid.

[n] Ταυροβολος, ἡ Αθηνα. Ibid.

[o] Lycoph. Caſſan. ver 359.

The

The former of these two last titles, as we learn from Tzetzes, was thought to allude to her having yoked oxen together in the plow; and the latter to her having first taught men the art of navigation [p]. *Budia* however is a word of the very same import as *Buto*, being the compound term Bu-Dea, *the goddess of the Ark*; and *Ethyia* is the name of a species of sea-bird, applied, as it appears, metaphorically to Minerva, on account of her being a diluvian goddess.

As the heifer was emblematical of the Ark, so was the serpent of the Sun. Hence the Egyptian Osiris, and the Persian Mithras, were alike depicted encompassed in the volumes of a snake. Accordingly we are informed by Macrobius, that a dragon was used as a symbol of the Sun; on which account it was placed at the feet of the statues of Esculapius and Salus, Esculapius being a personification of the Sun, and Salus of the Moon [q]. This declaration is very remarkable; for it is not easy to conceive, why Salus, or

[p] Tzet. in loc.

[q] Simulacris Æsculapii et Salutis draco subjungitur, quod hi ad Solis naturam, Lunæque referuntur.—Virescunt dracones per annos singulos pelle senectutis exuta, propterea et ad ipsum Solem species draconis refertur; quia Sol semper, velut a quadam imæ depressionis senecta in altitudinem suam, ut in robur

ſafety, ſhould be ſuppoſed by the ancient mythologiſts to be deſcriptive of the nature of the Moon, unleſs from the circumſtance of the Ark being adored in conjunction with that planet.

The name, by which the ſolar ſerpent was uſually deſignated, was *Ob* or *Op* [r]; whence the Greeks borrowed their word *Ophis*. This will point out to us the reaſon, why Coropè in Theſſaly, according to Nicander in *Stephanus of Byzantium*, was eſteemed ſacred to Apollo [s]. Coropè is Cor-Op-Ai, *the land of the ſolar ſerpent*; and the ophite ſuperſtition was no doubt eſtabliſhed there. The ſolar title *Corybas* ſeems to have the ſame relation to the emblematical worſhip of the ſnake. I have already obſerved, that the eldeſt Apollo was, like the Cabiri, the ſon of Vulcan; and the ſecond, of Corybas [t]. *Vulcan* however and *Corybas* were both equally names of the

[r] אוב is properly *an oracular ſerpent*, or *a divining ventriloquiſt*.

[s] Κορωπη πολις Θεσσαλιας. Νικανδρος εν Θηριακοις.
——ἠ εν Απολλων
Μαντειας Κοροπαιος εθηκατο, και θεμιν ανδρων.
Steph Byzan. de Urb p. 469.

[t] Apollinum antiquiſſimus is, quem paulo ante a Volcano natum eſſe dixi, cuſtodem Athenarum · alter Corybantis filius, natus in Creta. Cicer. de Nat. Deor. lib. iii. cap 23.

Sun;

Sun; for, as Vulcan is *the ſolar fire,* ſo Corybas, or Curbas, (as the word is written contractedly) is Cor-Ob-As, *the fiery ſolar ſerpent.*

The author of the Orphic hymns accordingly attributes to him the aſſumption of a ſerpentine form, and ſtyles him *the double god, the gloomy Cures* [u].

Κικλησκω χθονος αεναου βασιληα μεγιϛον
Κυρβαντ' ολβιομοιρον, αρηιον, απροσορατον,
Νυκτερινον Κουρητα—
Αιολομορφον ανακτα, θεον διφυη, πολυμορφον,
Φοινιον, αιμαχθεντα κασιγνητων ὑπο δισσων.
Δηους, ὁς γνωμαισιν εναλλαξας δεμας ἁγνον
Θηροτυπου-θεμενος μορφὴν δνοφεροιο δρακοντος [x].

Apollo himſelf is Ab-Baal-On, *father Baal the Sun*; and his title *Phebus,* or, as the Greeks expreſs it, *Phoibos,* ſeems to be compounded of Ph'Ob-As, *the fiery ſerpent:* whence ſome tradition of a ſnake is invariably interwoven with the mythological hiſtory of this deity. Conſidered as the *Baal* of the Eaſt, he is very properly ſaid by Nonnus to be no other than the Aſſyrian *Belus,* who, in alluſion to the union of the two ſuperſtitions, was deſcribed

[u] Theſe expreſſions allude to Noah's having beheld two worlds, and to his having been confined within the gloomy cavity of the Ark.

[x] Orph. Hymn. 38.

as

as the ſon of the diluvian Neptune by Libya daughter of Epaphus; while Epaphus himſelf was ſuppoſed to be the offspring of the arkite heifer Io, the *Iſis* or *Ceres* of Egypt.

——————Αναπλομενοιο δε καρπου
Αιγυπτιης Δημητρος εμης κεραελκεος Ιους
Ευοδμοις ὁμοφοιτος ελισσεται ατμος αηταις·
Ενθ' Επαφον Διι τικτεν ακηρασιων ὑπο κολπων
Ιναχιης δαμαλης επαφησατο θειος ακοιτης
Χερσιν ερωμανεεσσι· θεηγενεος δε τοκηος
Εξ Επαφου Λιβυη, Λιβυης δ' επι πιστον ἑεδνων
Μεμφιδος αχρις ικανε Ποσειδαων μεταναστης,
Παρθενον ιχνευων Επαφηιδα, και τοτε κουρη
Δεξαμενη ναετηρα βυθου χερσαιον ὁδιτην
Ζηνα Λιβυην τεκε Βηλον [y].—

Hence we find, that, although Baal be the Sun, yet he was not unfrequently repreſented under the form of the Noëtic ſymbol, the bull; while the goddeſs Baaltis, or Baalah, bore the figure of a heifer [z]. Baal and Baaltis are the ſame mythological characters as Oſiris and Iſis, whoſe ſymbols were, in a ſimilar manner, a bull and a heifer, and who, as I have already obſerved, were Noah, and the

[y] Nonni Dionyſ. lib. iii. p. 62. See alſo Apollod. Bibl. lib ii cap 1. and Schol. in Pind Pyth. iv. ver. 25.

[z] Τη Βααλ τη δαμαλει. Tobit. i. 5. See alſo Sanchoniatho's account of Aſtartè.

Ark,

Ark, adored in conjunction with the Sun and Moon. The tauriform idol Moloch is another instance of the introduction of the arkite emblem into the worship of the Sun. The image of this deity had the head of a bull; and, in reference partly to the number of the planets, and partly to that of the Cabiri, the hollow space contained within his body was divided into seven partitions, for the purpose of receiving victims of different degrees of dignity [a].

I have observed, that *Bacchus* or *Dionusus* was one of the many titles of the helio-arkite Noah; accordingly in his person the two emblems at present under consideration will be found to be eminently united. The Athenians, as we learn from Arrian, worshipped him as the son of Jupiter and Proserpine [b]; and

[a] Doctissimi Pauli Fagii verba de Moloch, in Chaldæam paraphrasin Levitici scripta, et ex Ebræorum etiam monimentis sumpta, adjungam. Fuit autem Moloch Imago concava habens septem conclavia; unum aperiebant similæ offerendæ, aliud turturibus; tertium ovi, quartum arieti, quintum vitulo, sextum bovi. Qui vero volebat offerre filium, huic aperiebatur septimum cubiculum, et facies hujus idoli erat ut facies vituli. Seld. de Dis Syr. Synt. i. cap. 6.

[b] Αθηναιοι Διονυσον τον Διος και Κορης σεβουσιν. Arrian. de Exped. Alex. lib. ii. cap. 16. This Bacchus, the son of Jupiter and Proserpine, is said by Diodorus Siculus to have been born in Crete or Curetis, and to have been torn in pieces by the Titans. Τουτον δε τοι θεοι γεγονεναι φασιν εκ Διος και Περσεφονης

κατα

the author of *the Etymologicon Magnum* mentions him under the name of *Zagreus*, the terreſtrial or infernal Dionuſus [c]: he is the ſame therefore as Pluto or Hades [d]. Jupiter however accompliſhed the rape of Proſerpine under the figure of a dragon [e]; and Bacchus is univerſally deſcribed as bearing ſome reſemblance to a bull.

Ηδη γαρ μενεαινε νεον Διονυσον αεξειν,
Ταυροφυες μιμημα παλαιγενεος Διονυσε,
Αινομορε Ζαγρηος εχων ποθον υψιμεδων Ζευς·
Ὁν τεκε Περσεφονεια δρακοντειη Διος ευνη [f].

κατα την Κρητην, ὁν Ορφευς κατα τας τελετας παραδιδωσι διεσπωμενον ὑπο των Τιτανων. Diod Bibl lib. v p 342. Bacchus was ſometimes ſuppoſed to be the ſon of Semelè, and it is a curious circumſtance, that the ſcholiaſt upon Heſiod aſſerts, that Semelè was nothing more than a vine. Σεμελη, ἡ αμπελος Schol. in Theog ver 940. The hiſtory of Bacchus indeed is replete with alluſions to the firſt planting of the vineyard by Noah.

[c] Ζαγρευς ὁ Διονυσος παρα τοις ποιηταις· δοκει γαρ ὁ Ζευς μιγηναι τη Περσεφονη, εξ ἡς χθονιος ὁ Διονυσος. See alſo Nonni Dionyſ. paſſim

[d] Ωυτος δε Αιδης και Διονυσος Clem Cohort p 30

[e] Poſtea etiam Proſerpinam filiam ſuam ſub draconis ſpecie violavit, et Dionyſum ex ea genuit. Athenag Legat. pro Chriſt. p. 20 Liberi quinque Primus ex Jove et Proſerpina hic agricola, et inventor vini, cujus ſoror Ceres — Tertius de Cabito, qui regnavit in Aſia Amp cap 9 For *Cabitus*, whom Ampelius deſcribes as the father of Bacchus, we ought undoubtedly to read *Cabirus*

[f] Nonni Dionyſ. lib. v. p 110

Hence

Hence we ſhall ſee the reaſon, why, in the Bacchic Myſteries, the bull was celebrated as the parent of the dragon, and the dragon as the parent of the bull[g].

The whole hiſtory indeed of Bacchus is full of alluſions to the ſymbols of the *bull*, and *the ſerpent*. Thus we learn from Nonnus, that the Corybantes incloſed him, when young, in ox-hides, having received him in charge from Rhea, or the Ark:

Παιδοκομοι Κορυβαντες αεξομενȣ Διονυσȣ·
Οἱ Φρυγα κολπον εχοντες ορεσσιπολῳ παρα Ῥειῃ
Νηπιον εισετι Βακχον εκυκλωσαντο βοειαις[h].

Thus alſo Euripides introduces a chorus of Bacchantes, inviting him to appear in the ſhape of a bull, a dragon, or a lion:

Φανηθι ταυρος, η πολυκρανος γ' ιδειν
Δρακων, η πυριφλεγων
Ορασθαι λεων·
Ιθ' ω Βακχε[i].—

[g] Sequitur adhuc aliud ſymbolum, quod pro magno miſerorum hominum credulis auribus traditur, Ταυρος δρακοντος, και δρακων ταυρȣ πατηρ. Jul. Firm. de Error Prof. Rel. p. 52.

[h] Nonni Dionyſ. lib. xiii. p. 233 Theſe words indeed may perhaps mean, that they danced in a circle round Bacchus, having thongs of ox-hide in their hands; but whichever interpretation be adopted, the alluſion to the emblematical bull will ſtill remain.

[i] Eurip. Bacch. ver. 1015.

And

And thus the author of the Orphic hymns ſtyles him, *the deity with two horns, having the head of a bull, even Mars-Dionuſus, reverenced in a double form, and adored in conjunction with a beautiful ſtar.*

> Κικλησκω Διονυσον, εριβρομον ευαστηρα,
> Πρωτογονον, διφυη, τριγονον, Βακχειον ανακτα,
> Αγριον, αρρητον, κρυφιον, δικερωτα, διμορφον,
> Κισσοβρυον, ταυρωπον, Αρηϊον, ευιον, αγνον [k].

For the ſame reaſon Plutarch inquires, why the women of Elis were accuſtomed to invoke Bacchus in the words of the following hymn. "Come, hero Dionuſus, to thy holy temple "on the ſea-ſhore; come, heifer-footed deity, to thy ſacrifice, and bring the graces in "thy train! hear us, O bull worthy of our "veneration; hear us, O illuſtrious bull [l]!"

After attempting to ſolve this queſtion in a variety of different ways, he concludes with aſking, whether the title of *bull* might not be given to Bacchus, on account of his being the inventor and patron of agriculture [m].

[k] Orph Hymn. 29.

[l] Διοτι τον Διονυσον αἱ των Ηλειων γυναικες ὑμνεσι παρακαλεσι βοεῳ ποδι παραγινεσθαι προς αυτας; Εχει δ' οὑτως ὁ ὑμνος, Ελθειν ἡρω Διονυσε ἁλιον ες ναον ἁγνον, συν χαριτεσσιν ες ναον τῳ βοεῳ ποδι θυων· ειτα δις επαδεσιν, Αξιε Ταυρε Plut Quæſt. Græc. p. 299.

[m] Ὁτι και αροτρε και σπορε πολλοι τον θεον αρχηγον γεγονεναι νομιζεσι.

Bacchus, when confidered as the Sun, is called by the author of the works afcribed to Orpheus, *Phanes*, and *Eubuleus:* the former of which terms is Ph Ain-Es, *the fountain of fire*; and the latter, Ob-El, *the ferpent deity*.

Τηκων αιθερα διον, ακινητον περ εοντα,
Εξανεφηνε θεοις ωραν καλλιςον ιδεσθαι,
Ὁν δη νυν καλεουσι Φανητα τε και Διονυσον,
Ευβουληα τ' ανακτα, και Ανταυγην αριδηλον.
Αλλοι δ' αλλο καλουσιν επιχθονιων ανθρωπων.
Πρωτος δ' ες φαος ηλθε, Διωνυσος τ' επικληθη,
Ουνεκα δινειται κατ' απειρονα μακρον Ολυμπον [n].

Phanes accordingly is defcribed, as producing from himfelf a monfter having the head and hair of a man, and the winding volumes of an immenfe fnake.

Αν δε Φανης αλλην γενεην τεκνωσατο δεινην
Νηδυος εξ ιερης, προσιδειν φοβερωπον εχιδναν,
Ἡς χαιται μεν απο κρατος καλον τε προσωπον
Ην εσιδειν, τα δε λοιπα μερη φοβεροιο δρακοντος
Αυχενος εξ ακρου [o].———

As for Eubuleus, he was one of the moft ancient Diofcori, or Cabiri, who are faid by Cicero, in allufion to the triple offspring of Noah, to be three in number, the children of

n Orph. Frag ap Macrob. Saturn. lib i. cap. 18
o Orph. Frag ap. Athenag. Apol. p. 72

the

the moſt ancient Jupiter and Proſerpine[p]. Hence the Orphic writer celebrates Proſerpine as being the mother of Eubuleus;

Μητερ εριβρεμετȣ πολυμορφȣ Ευβȣληος[q].

and deſcribes his birth as ineffably myſterious.

Ευβȣλ' Ευπολβȣλε, Διος και Περσεφονειης
Αρρητοις λεκτροισι τεκνωθεις[r].——

It is obſervable however, that, in conſequence of Ceres and Proſerpine being both equally the lunar Ark, Eubuleus is ſaid by the author of the Orphic hymns to be the ſon, not only of Proſerpine, but likewiſe of Ceres, who, in her character either of the Earth or of the Ark, is celebrated as the fruitful parent of mortals and of immortals[s].

[p] Primi tres, qui appellantur *Anactes*, Athenis ex Jove rege antiquiſſimo et Proſerpina nati, Tritopatreus, Eubuleus, Dionyſus. Cic. de Nat Deor. lib. iii cap. 21. Noah and Ham are perpetually confounded together in the mythology of the Gentiles. Thus, in the preſent inſtance, Eubuleus, conſidered as one of the three Anactes, ſeems to be Ham, nevertheleſs he is alſo deſcribed as the very ſame perſon as Bacchus or Noah. The ſame remark is equally applicable to Jupiter, who was alſo called *Eubuleus*.

[q] Hymn 28.

[r] Hymn. 29.

[s] Theſe immortals were the arkite ogdoad, or the eight Cabiric gods of Egypt. In alluſion to the two principal ſymbols,

 Ceres

Ανταια βασιλεια, θεα, πολυωνυμε μητερ
Αθανατων τε θεων ηδε θνητων ανθρωπων·
Ἡ ποτε μαστευουσα πολυπλαγκτω εν ανιη,
Νηστειαν κατεπαυσας Ελευσινος γυαλοισιν,
Ηλθες τ' ες Ἀϊδην προς αγαυην Περσεφονειαν,
Δυσαγνος παιδ' ἁγνον ὁδηγητηρα λαχουσα,
Μηνυτηρ' ἁγιων λεκτρων χθονιου Διος ἁγνου,
Ευβουλον τευξασα θεον θνητης απ' αναγκης [t].

It is also observable, that notwithstanding Bacchus and Eubuleus are the very same person, the great patriarch worshipped in conjunction with the Sun; yet Bacchus is sometimes described, even by the Orphic poet himself, as the son of Eubuleus.

Θεσμοφορον καλεω ναρθηκοφορον Διονυσον,
Σπερμα πολυμνηστον πολυωνυμον Ευβουληος [u].

This however is merely an instance of the genealogical repetition so frequent in the mythology of paganism; and is equivalent to the

Ceres herself is represented as having first joined oxen together for the purposes of agriculture, and as riding in a chariot drawn by dragons.

Σεμνη Δημητερ —
\- - - - - - - - - - - - -
Ἡ πρωτη ζευξασα βοων αροτηρα τενοντα,
\- - - - - - - - - - - - - -
Ἁρμα δρακοντειοισιν ὑποζευξασα χαλινοις.
Orph. Hymn. 39.

[t] Hymn. 40.
[u] Hymn 41.

descent

descent of Horus from Osiris, of Esculapius from Apollo, and of Apollo from Jupiter.

The name *Eubuleus* was not confined solely to Bacchus: Jupiter, who was equally the solar Noah, bore the same title[x]. Adonis was likewise called *Eubuleus*; the reason of which was simply his identity with the Cabiric Bacchus. Hence, in allusion to the symbolical ox, the Orphic writer styles him *the deity with two horns*[y]; and describes him as being the lover both of Venus and Proserpine.

Κλυθι μȣ ευχομενȣ πολυωνυμε δαιμον αριϛε,
Ευϐȣλε, πολυμορφε, τροφη παντων αριδηλε.
——— Συ πασιν θαλος αιεν Αδωνι,
Σϐεννυμενε, λαμπων τε καλαις εν κυκλασιν ὡραις,
Αυξιθαλης, δικερως.———
——— Κυπριδος γλυκερον θαλος, ερνος ερωτος.
Φερσεφονης ερασιπλοκαμȣ λεκτροισι λοχευθεις·
Ὁς ποτε μεν ναιεις ὑπο Ταρταρον ηεροεντα,
Ηδε παλιν προς Ολυμπον αϝεις δεμας ὡριοκαρπον[z].

As Bacchus, considered in one point of view, is the Sun; so we find a circumstance recorded in his mythological history, which

[x] Diod Bibl. lib v p 339

[y] Hence also, in allusion to the solar serpent, he was called by the Persians *Abobas*, or Ab-Ob-As, *the great father the fiery serpent* Αϐωϐας, ὁ Αδωνις ὑπο Περσαιων. Hesych.

[z] Orph. Hymn. 55.

plainly ſhews, that, in his human capacity, he is, like Oſiris, no other than the great patriarch. According to Pauſanias, he and his mother Semelè were incloſed by Cadmus in an ark, and were thus thrown into the ſea. They reached the ſhore at Braſiæ near Epidaurus; and Ino, or Iſis, in the courſe of her wanderings, having come to the ſame place, became the nurſe of Bacchus. The cave, where ſhe performed her office, was ſtill ſhewn in the days of Pauſanias[a].

There are ſeveral other fables extant, which preciſely reſemble the preceding tradition re-

[a] Οἱ δε ανθρωποι λεγουσιν ενταυθα,—ὡς Σεμελη τεκοι τον παιδα εκ Διος, και ὑπο του Καδμου φωραθεισα εις λαρνακα αυτη και Διονυσος εμβληθειη· και την λαρνακα ὑπο του κλυδωνος εκπεσειν φασιν εις την σφετεραν.—Βρασιωται δε και ταδε επιλεγουσιν. Ινω σφισιν ες την χωραν αφικεσθαι πλανωμενην· ελθουσαν δε εθελησαι του Διονυσου γενεσθαι τροφον και αποφαινουσιν μεν το αντρον, ενθα τον Διονυσον εθρεψεν Ινω Pauſ. Lacon p. 271. The ancient myſteries were generally connected with ſome ſacred cave, as I ſhall have occaſion to notice in a ſubſequent chapter. The ſame tradition reſpecting Bacchus is preſerved by Diodorus Siculus, excepting only that he ſuppoſes the ark to have landed at Delos. Bibl. lib. v. p 332. The name of this iſland, which was peculiarly ſacred to Apollo, is a mere variation of Talos, one of the titles of the Sun. The reader will recollect the obſervations, which have been already made upon the once floating iſle of Delos. With a ſimilar reference to the rites of the Ark, Bacchus is repreſented by Philoſtratus as ſailing in a ſhip decked with vine-leaves and ivy. Philoſt. Icon. lib. 1. cap. 19.

ſpecting

ſpecting Bacchus, and which I doubt not have the very ſame alluſion to the circumſtance of the ſolar Noah entering into the Ark. The ſubject of one of theſe legends is Perſeus. This hero is deſcribed as the ſon of Danaè by Jupiter; and in the account of his birth, which the ſcholiaſt upon Apollonius gives us from Pherecydes, he repreſents Acriſius as bringing his daughter before the altar of Jupiter Ercius, in order that ſhe might be obliged to acknowledge who was the father of her child [b]. Upon her confeſſion, he placed her along with her ſon in an ark, and caſt them into the ſea; but they were at length thrown upon land in the iſland Seriphus. Acriſius himſelf was king of Argos, from which place he afterwards fled to Lariſſa through fear of Perſeus [c]. The whole of this hiſtory is founded upon the junction of the two great

[b] Δαναην καταγει συν τῳ παιδι επι τον ὑπο του Ερκιυ Διος βωμον Schol. in Apoll. Argon. lib. iv. ver. 1091. See alſo Tzet. in Lycoph. ver. 838

[c] Σεριφος δ' εϛιν, εν ᾗ τα περι τὸν Δικτυν μεμυθευται, τον ανελκυσαντα την λαρνακα τοις δικτυοις, την περιεχυσαν τον Περσεα, και την μητερα Δαναην, καταποντωμενυς ὑπ' Ακρισιυ τυ πατρος Δανανης. Strab. Geog. lib. x. p. 487 In a ſimilar manner Nonnus:

Ου Δαναη λαχεν οικον Ολυμπιον· ὑγροπορυ δε
Λαρνακος ενδον εουσα Διος ναυτιλλετο νυμφη
Μεμφομενη ζυγιαν απατηλιον ομβρον ερωτων.

Dionyſ. lib xxv. p. 425.

 primi-

primitive ſuperſtitions. Perſeus is P'Ares-Zeus, *the Sun*; accordingly Tzetzes plainly informs us, that *Perſeus* was merely a title of the ſolar deity [d]: his allegorical mother Danaè is Da-Nauè, *the Noëtic Ark* [e]: the epithet *Ercius*, applied to Jupiter in the preceding narrative, and the name of the city *Argos*, are both equally derived from Erech, or Arag, *the Ark*: the iſland *Seriphus* owes its appellation to the worſhip of Ser-Oph, *the ſolar ſerpent:* and Lariſſa is Lares-Ai, *the land of the Cabiric Lares.* In alluſion to the ſymbolical ſnake, Perſeus is ſaid to have been

[d] Ὁ γὰρ Περσεὺς, ὁ ἥλιος οὕτω καλούμενος. Schol. in Lycoph. ver 17. Περσευς ὁ ἡλιος εστι. Ibid. Perſeus was ſometimes feigned to have had no father, but to have been born of a virgin Juſt. Mart Dial cum Tryph. p. 297. This virgin is his mythological mother the Ark, from which, in the language of allegory, he was ſaid to have been produced without the co-operation of a father. Preciſely the ſame fable is told of the Chineſe Fohi, and of the Indian Buddha. Mart Hiſt Sin. lib. i p 21 —Ratramn de Nat. Chriſti, cap. 3 Perſes, the imaginary ſon of Perſeus, from whom the Perſians are feigned to have received their appellation, was, like his father, no other than the Sun. Περσην τον ἡλιον λεγει. Schol. in Heſ. Theog. p. 269.

[e] According to Apollodorus, Acriſius confined Danaè in a ſubterraneous brazen vault. Apoll. Bibl lib. ii cap 4. This cavern was one of the ſame nature as that in which the Phigalenſians placed the ſtatue of Ceres-Hippa, or the Ark. Vide infra chap. vii.

armed

armed with the head of Medufa, the hair of which was compofed of ferpents; and as for the deliverance of Andromeda from the fea-monfter, it is only a corrupted tradition of the efcape from the deluge, the fifh being emblematical of the Ark.

A fimilar ftory is told by Strabo refpecting Telephus. He was the fon of Augè, the daughter of Aleus, by the diluvian god Hercules, and was expofed at fea in an ark along with his mother; but, by the providential care of Minerva, the ark reached the mouth of the Caicus in fafety [f]. *Telephus*, like *Perfeus*, is only a title of the folar deity, being compounded of Tel-Oph, *the ferpent of the Sun*; while the name of his allegorical mother Augè is derived from Og, or Aug, *the ocean*. Augè was afterwards married to Teuthras king of the Myfians, who adopted Telephus as his fon. Strabo however mentions another fable, in which Teuthras is faid to have efpoufed the daughter of Arcas, or *the Ark-god* [g]. This tradition is in fact the fame

[f] Ευριπιδης δ' ὑπο Αλεȣ φησι τȣ της Αυγης πατρος εις λάρνακα την Αυγην κατατεθεισαν ἁμα τῳ παιδι Τηλεφῳ καταποντωθηναι, φωρασαντος την εξ Ἡρακλεȣς φθοραν. Αθηνας δε προνοιᾳ την λαρνακα περαιωθεισαν εκπεσειν εις το ϛομα τȣ Καικȣ. Strab. Geog. lib. xiii. p. 615.

[g] Αλλην δε δει γεγονεναι συντυχιαν, δι' ἡν τȣ Αρκαδος θυγατηρ τῳ Μυσων βασιλει συνηλθε. Ibid. In reference to the arkite worfhip,

as the former; for it matters little whether Augè, or the Ark, be the mythological daughter of Aleus, *the ſolar Noah*, or of Arcas, *the great god of the Ark*. It is not improbable, that Teuthras may be the ſame perſon as the *Taautus* of Sanchoniatho, the *Teut* or *Thoth* of Egypt, the *Theutates* of Gaul, and the *Hermes* of Greece. Taautus is ſaid to have been the inventor of ſymbols, and is connected by the Phenician mythologiſt with the Cabiri, as Hermes alſo was by the Samothracians with the ſame deities under the name of *Caſmilus*[h].

The hiſtory of Rheo and Anius is another legend of the ſame import. Staphylus, the ſon of Bacchus, had a daughter called *Rheo*, who became pregnant by Apollo. Her father, having diſcovered the illicit commerce, caſt her into the ſea incloſed within an ark; but ſhe landed ſafely in Eubèa, and entering into

ſhip, Augè is feigned to have come along with her ſon from Arcadia. Ὁ τε Τηλεφος εκ της Αρκαδιας αφιχθαι νομιζοιτ' αν μετα της μητρος. Ibid. lib. xii. p. 572. According to Tzetzes, Arcas ſaved the nymph Chryſopeleia from the fury of a wintery torrent, and afterwards eſpouſed her. Schol. in Lycoph ver 480. Chryſopeleia is literally *the golden dove*. It is perhaps almoſt ſuperfluous to obſerve, that this tradition relates to the preſervation of the dove by the arkite god from the horrors of the yet unabated waters.

[h] Schol in Apoll. Argon. lib. i. ver. 917.

a cave

a cave there brought forth her ſon Anius[i]. Rheo is the ſame as Rhea, a mere perſonification of the Ark; Apollo is the ſolar Noah; and Anius is alſo the great patriarch, under the title of Aniun, *the naval deity*[k]. Rheo is feigned after this event to have married Zarex, the grandſon of Chiron; and it is remarkable, that the daughters of her ſon Anius are ſaid to have been metamorphoſed by Bacchus into doves[l]. Zarex is Z'Arech, *the great arkite*, and his anceſtor Chiron, as ſhall hereafter be ſhewn, is the patriarch Noah.

Upon the union of Sabianiſm with the arkite myſteries, the various emblems of this compound ſuperſtition ſoon occupied diſtinguiſhed places in the ſphere. Hence the conſtellations of *the Fiſhes* and *the ſolar Lion* were placed among the ſigns of the zodiac; and hence the three Hyads were fixed in the

[i] Σταφυλȣ τȣ ϋιȣ Διονυσȣ θυγατηρ γινεται Ῥοιω, ῃ εμιγη Απολλων. Γνȣς δε τȣτο ὁ Σταφυλος, βαλων εις λαρνακα, προς την θαλασσαν αφηκεν. Ἡ δε προσεπελασθη τῃ Ευβοιᾳ, και εξελθȣσα της λαρνακος, παρα τι αντρον γεννᾳ παιδα, και Ανιον καλει. Schol. in Lycoph. ver. 570. Anius is deſcribed by Virgil, according to the ancient patriarchal cuſtom, as being both a king and a prieſt.

Rex Anius, rex idem hominum, Phœbique ſacerdos.

[k] Aniun is אני ן, from אני Ani, *a ſhip* His relationſhip to Apollo is a mere genealogical repetition.

[l] Lycoph Caſſan. ver. 580.—Tzet. Schol. in ibid.—Ovid. Metam. lib. xiii. ver. 674.

head

head of *the ſymbolical Bull.* The Hyads, as we learn from Euripides, were the daughters of Erechtheus, and the nurſes of Bacchus, who was himſelf, according to Euphorion, denominated *Hyas*[m]. Erechtheus and Hyas are equally the patriarch Noah; the former being compounded of Erech-Theus, *the god of the Ark*, and the latter ſignifying *the deity of rain*, a title alluſive to the dreadful torrents of rain, which fell at the time of the deluge. Erechtheus was ſuppoſed to have been an ancient king of Athens; whence we find, that in that city there was a temple called *Erechthium*, within which, in reference to the junction of the two ſuperſtitions, were altars dedicated to Neptune, Butes, and Vulcan. Upon the altar of Neptune they ſacrificed to Erechtheus[n]. At this place there

[m] Φερονται αἱ Ὑαδες εν τῳ μετωπῳ τȣ Ταυρȣ,—ἡ δε προσωνυμια εϛιν, ὁτι τον Διονυσον ανεθρεψαντο. Ὑης δε ὁ Διονυσος. Ευφοριων,

Ὑῃ ταυροκερωτι Διωνυσσῳ κοτεσασα.

Ευριπιδης μεν ȣν εν Ερεχθει, τας Ερεχθεως θυγατερας Ὑαδας φησι γενεσθαι τρεις ȣσας Schol in Arat Phæn. p. 25.

[n] Εϛι δε και οικημα Ερεχθειον καλȣμενον·—εισελθȣσι δε εισι βωμοι Ποσειδωνος, εφ᾽ ȣ και Ερεχθει θυȣσιν εκ του μαντευματος, και ἡρωος Βȣτȣ, τριτος δε Ἡφαιϛȣ Pauſ. Attic p. 62. Erechtheus is ſaid by Tzetzes to be the ſame both as Jupiter and Neptune, or in other words the ſolari-diluvian Noah: Ερεχθευς, ὁ Ποσειδων, η ὁ Ζευς. Schol in Lycoph. ver 158. while Heſychius, and Athenagoras, both agree in making him to be Neptune. Ερεχθευς

Ποσειδων

was alſo a ſacred well, containing ſea-water, and upon the rock the mark of a trident. The conteſt between Neptune and Minerva for the territory of Attica is ſaid to have been here decided; and a tradition of a deluge ſtill continued to prevail in the days of Apollodorus [o]. I have little doubt of Erichtheus being the ſame perſon as Erichthonius, another ancient Athenian ſovereign, whom ſome accounted the ſon of Hepheſtè, daughter of Cranaè, and others of Vulcan, and the Earth [p]. His form is ſaid to have been that of a man terminating in the tail of a ſerpent. Minerva incloſed him in a cheſt or ark, and committed him to the care of one of the daughters of Cecrops. Her ſiſters opened the cheſt, through the impulſe of curioſity; and, ſtruck with terror at the ſight of him, threw themſelves headlong from the top of the citadel. He afterwards eſpouſed a Naiad, and became

Ποσειδων εν Αθηναις. Heſych Ὁ δε Αθηναιος Ερεχθει Ποσειδωνι θυει. Athen. Legat. pro Chriſt. cap 1

[o] Apoſlodorus mentions, that the place, where Neptune ſtruck his trident into the ground, was afterwards called *Erecthèis*, and he adds, that the god, indignant at the preference ſhewn to Minerva, inundated the whole land of Attica. Apoll. Bibl lib. iii. cap. 13.

[p] This happened in conſequence of Vulcan's attempt to raviſh Minerva, the uſual allegory, under which the violent junction of the two modes of worſhip was repreſented.

the

the father of Pandion; in whofe reign Ceres and Bacchus came into Attica [q]. The word *Erichthonius* is compounded of Erech-Ath-On, *the helio-arkite deity*; and accordingly, like Bacchus and Ofiris, he was reported to have been fhut up in an ark. His femi-dragontian form alludes to the folar idolatry, and his marriage with a Naiad to the arkite. His fuppofed anceftrefs Cranaè is G'Arn-Nauè, *the illuftrious Noëtic Ark*; and Cecrops, to the care of whofe daughter he was delivered, is Za-Cur-Op, the illuftrious folar ferpent [r].

As for the celeftial bull, he is fuppofed by fome to be that, which conveyed Europa into Crete, and by others, to be the heifer Io, or Ifis [s]. The import of both thefe different opinions amounts nearly to the fame; for, as the fymbolical heifer is the Ark, fo the fymbolical bull is the god of the Ark. Hence

[q] Apollod. Bibl lib. iii. cap. 13.

[r] The raven, which I have already noticed in confidering the hiftory of Efculapius, is introduced likewife into this legend of Erichthonius. When the three daughters of Cecrops looked into the ark, that contained the dragon form of that fabulous monfter, the raven hafted to carry the intelligence to Minerva; and was, in recompenfe, for ever fhut out of the Athenian citadel. Antig. Caryft. Mirab Hift. cap 12.

[s] Ταυρος λεγεται εν τοις αϛροις τιθεναι, δια το Ευρωπην αγαγειν εκ Φοινικης εις Κρητην—ἑτεροι δε φασι βȣν ειναι της Ιȣς μιμημα, χαριν δε εκεινης ετιμηθη το αϛρον. Eratof. Cataft Ταυρος.

Lyco-

Lycophron informs us in plain terms, that the Curetes, or Cabiri, carried off Europa in a ſhip formed like a bull.

Αυθις γαρ ὑβριν την βαρειαν ἁρπαγης
Κȣρητες αντιποινον Ιδαιοι καπροι[t]
Ζητȣντες, αιχμαλωτον ημπολησαν πορτιν.
Εν ταυρομορφω τραμπιδος τυπωματι
Σαραπτιαν, Δικταιον εις ανακτορον,
Δαμαρτα Κρητης Αςερω ςρατηλατη[u].

The great conſtellation of the dragon is another inſtance of the introduction of the ſacred emblems into the ſphere. We learn from the ſcholiaſt upon Aratus, that the dragon is Jupiter, who, according to a Cretan tradition, aſſumed the form of that reptile, in order to avoid the fury of Saturn; the

[t] I apprehend, that the title *Capri*, which is beſtowed by Lycophron upon the Idèi Dactyli, is preciſely equivalent to *Cabiri* or *Cabiri* The name *Caprus* or *Cabrus* ſeems to have been given to the boar on account of its being an arkite ſymbol. Hence we find, that Viſhnou or Noah was feigned by the Hindoos to have metamorphoſed himſelf into a boar, and in that ſhape to have ſaved the world from the deſtructive ravages of the deluge With the ſame alluſion to the appellation of the Cabiric gods, the goat, into which Bacchus was ſuppoſed to have metamorphoſed himſelf when the deities were attacked by Typhon, was called by the Latins *Caper*, or *Caber*; while the ſhe-goat, which was feigned to have ſuckled Jupiter, was denominated *Capra* or *Cabra*.

[u] Lycoph. Caſſan ver. 1296.

ſame Jupiter in ſhort, who, in the very ſame form, violated his daughter Proſerpine, and by her became the father of Bacchus [x].

The two ſymbols of the bull and the ſerpent were no leſs familiar to the inhabitants of the north of Europe, than to thoſe of Greece, Italy, and Egypt; and there is reaſon to believe, that the theology of the ancient Celts was the ſame in its import, as that of perhaps every other Gentile nation. From the concurrent teſtimony of ſeveral different authors, the Hyperboreans appear to have formerly had a conſiderable intercourſe with the Greeks, and like them to have celebrated the myſterious rites of the arkite and ophite ſuperſtitions. Herodotus has preſerved a curious legend, which it is not very eaſy to underſtand unleſs upon ſuch a ſuppoſition. Two Hyperborean virgins, whoſe names were *Argis* and *Opis*, are ſaid by this hiſtorian to have come, at a very remote period of antiquity, to Delos, bringing offerings to Lucina, in gratitude for the ſafe delivery of the females

[x] Φερεται δε περι τȣ δρακοντος και Κρητικος μυθος, ὡς ἁμα επιοντος ποτε τȣ Κρονȣ ὁ Ζευς ευλαϐηθεις, ἑαυτον μεν εις δρακοντα μετεμορφωσε. Schol in Arati Phænom. p 11 It may not perhaps be improper to remark, that the dragon of ancient mythology was not the imaginary monſter deſcribed by the moderns, but merely a large ſerpent

of

of their country. Nor did these virgins travel unprotected; the gods themselves were their attendants. They never returned to the north, but remained at Delos till the time of their deaths[y]. Although it is difficult to determine the precise import of this tradition, yet I have little doubt that the two virgins borrowed their respective names from Arg and Op, *the Ark* and *the serpent*. As Herodotus brings the two virgins to Delos from the land of the Hyperboreans; so Mnaseas asserts, that this people were formerly called *Delphians*, and Hecatèus mentions, that Apollo was greatly venerated among them[z]. Delphi is Tel-Phi, *the oracle of the Sun*; whence the descriptive title *Delphians* will signify *votaries of the oracular Sun*[a]. We learn from Cicero, that the third Apollo, the son of Jupiter and Latona, was supposed to have come to Delphi from the country of the Hyperboreans[b]; and Diodorus Siculus

[y] Herod. lib. iv. cap. 35

[z] Schol in Apoll. Argon lib ii. ver. 677

[a] I am inclined to suspect, that Elphin, or El-Phi, *the oracle of the solar deity*, was the Delphi of the Irish Hyperboreans; and I think it by no means improbable, that the fantastic pigmy race of Elves, Elfins, or Fairies, so highly celebrated in our northern romances as equally cunning and mischievous, originated from the ancient El-Phi.

[b] Cicer de Nat. Deor. lib. iii.

informs us, that the Hyperboreans were ſeated in Britain, where they worſhipped Apollo in a vaſt circular temple [c]. The title, which they beſtowed upon him, was *Balenus* or *Belis* [d]; and he ſeems to have been the ſame as *Cernunnos*, a deity of the Gauls Belis is manifeſtly the *Baal* of the eaſt; and Cernunnos I take to be Ceren-On-Nus, *the horned Noah the Sun* [e]. Accordingly, as the Druids worſhipped the ſolar orb, ſo we find that they held the ſerpent in peculiar veneration [f], and even built ſome of their temples in the ſhape of that animal. Of theſe the moſt remarkable was that of Abury, which was conſtructed in the form of a ſerpent paſſing through a circle [g]; and I doubt not but that Abury was ſo called, in conſequence of its vaſt temple being dedicated to *the Abiri*, who were the ſame as the Cabiri.

With regard to the devotion of the Hyperboreans to the arkite myſteries, we are plainly informed by Dionyſius, that the rites of

[c] Diod. Bibl. lib. ii. p 130. It is poſſible, that Stone-henge may be the very temple mentioned by Diodorus.

[d] Borlaſe's Cornwall, b. ii. chap. 16

[e] This deity was actually repreſented with horns, like Bacchus. See Borlaſe's Cornwall, b. ii. chap. 15.

[f] Plin lib. xxix. cap. 3.

[g] Stukeley's Abury.

Bac-

Bacchus or Noah were duly celebrated in Britain[h]. Hence arose their veneration for the bull, the constant symbol of the deity of the Ark. "By this God made of brass," says Dr. Borlase, "the Cimbri, Teutones, "and Ambrones, swore to observe the arti-"cles of capitulation granted to the Romans, "who defended the Adige against them. Af-"ter their defeat, Catulus ordered this bull "to be carried to his own house, there to re-"main as the most glorious monument of "his victory. This God is ranked with Ju-"piter, Esus, and Vulcan, being called *Tar-"vos Trigaranus*, from three cranes perching, "one on his head, one on the middle of his "back, and the third on his hinder parts[i]."

The introduction of the diluvian supersti-tion into Britain will account for the preva-

[h] Αλλαι δ' Ωκεανοιο παραι βορεωτιδας ακτας
Δισσαι νησοι εασι Βρετανιδες, αντια Ρηνου·
Κειθι γαρ ύςατιην απερευγεται εις άλα δινην.
Ταων τοι μεγεθος περιωσιον· ουδε τις αλλη
Νησοις εν πασησι Βρετανισιν ισοφαριζει.
Αγχι δε νησιαδων έτερος πορος, ενθα γυναικες
Ανδρων αντιπερηθεν αγαυων Αμνιταων
Ορνυμεναι τελεουσι κατα νομον ίερα Βακχω,
Στεψαμεναι κισσοιο μελαμφυλλοιο' κορυμβοις,
Εννυχιαι παταγης δε λιγυθριος ορνυται ηχη.

Dionys. Perieg. ver 565.

[i] Borlase's Cornwall, book ii. chap. 16.

 lence

lence of arkite names obſervable in theſe dominions. One of our Scottiſh iſles ſtill retains the Egyptian title *Buto,* while its neighbour *Arran* ſeems to have received its appellation in honour of Aran, *the Ark.* In a ſimilar manner, *Mona,* or Angleſey, the grand ſeat of the Druidical worſhip[k], and its frith *Menai,* are probably mere variations of Men-Ai, *the land of Menu.*

Dauntleſs on his native ſands
The *dragon*-ſon[l] of *Mona* ſtands;
In glittering arms and glory dreſt,
High he rears his ruby creſt.
There the thundering ſtrokes begin,
There the preſs, and there the din;
Talymalfra's rocky ſhore
Echoing to the battle's roar.
Check'd by the torrent tide of blood
Backward *Menai* rolls his flood;
While, heap'd his maſter's feet around,
Proſtrate warriors gnaw the ground[m].

[k] See Rowland's Mona Antiqua, and that exquiſitely beautiful drama of Maſon, Caractacus

[l] "The red dragon is the device of Cadwallader, which all "his deſcendants bore on their banners"

[m] Gray's Triumphs of Owen. A variety alſo of ſolar names occur in different parts of Britain. There is a lofty hill in the neighbourhood of Leeds in Yorkſhire, which may perhaps have been one of the high places of the Druidical *Baal.* It ſtill retains the name of *Belin,* or *Billing*; to which, by way of diſ-

As the Druids were accuſtomed to venerate the ſolar ſerpent, ſo we find them equally attached to the myſtic circle, that moſt natural and moſt expreſſive emblem of the Sun [n]. In this ſhape their maſſy temples were univerſally built [o], and their ſacred dances, in honour of the ſolar deity, performed [p]. With ſimilar reverence the Samothracians, whoſe devotion to the Cabiric rites is well known, regarded their magical rings. Theſe were of

diſtinguiſhing it from other *Belins*, the name of *Rawdon*, the village near which it ſtands, is uſually added A few miles higher up the valley is another place of a ſimilar nature A bold natural fortification of rocks, which forcibly remind the mythologiſt of the gloomy worſhip of the Cuthites amidſt the romantic ſcenes of the Thebais, overlooks a village called *Bail-don*, a compound poſſibly of Baal-Don, *the hill of Baal*. However this may be, the Druids at leaſt have certainly frequented that tract of country, as appears from many of their ſtone monuments yet in exiſtence. One of theſe may be ſeen, not far from Byngley; and another, an immenſe Logan ſtone, a few miles from Bolton Abbey. Fewſtone, i e *fire-ſtone*, ſeems to have derived its Norman name from the rites of the ſolar deity celebrated in its vicinity; and above all, Brimham rocks, near Knareſborough, merit the attention of the curious inquirer. For a more particular account of theſe Yorkſhire relics of Druidical antiquity, ſee King's Munimenta Antiqua, vol i

[n] Circus and Circulus are both derived from Cir, or Cur, *the Sun*

[o] Even Abury is no exception, its figure is that of a ſnake paſſing through a circle

[p] Borl. Corn. book ii chap. 17

the nature of amulets, and were believed to have a power of averting danger [q].

In confirmation of the preceding conjectures respecting the theology of the Druids, I shall add, to the testimony of Dionysius concerning the introduction of the Bacchic mysteries into Britain, the authority of Artemidorus concerning those of two other Cabiric deities. "In an island," says he, "close to Britain," (by which in all probability he means Anglesey) "Ceres and Proserpine are venerated "with rites similar to the orgies of Samo-"thrace [r]." This island, the history of which I shall notice more particularly hereafter [s], was dedicated, as we learn from Mnaseas, to the Cabiri; and he further informs us, that Ceres, Proserpine, and Bacchus, were reckoned in the number of those deities [t]. Hence it evidently appears, that the gods of Britain were the same as the Cabiri of Samothrace;

[q] Samothracios hos annulos αλεξιφθονον vim habere credidit antiquitas, ut et Græcorum Φυσικȣς δακτυλιȣς, intus pervios et cassos, quemadmodum scripsit Artemidorus. Annot. ad Plin. Nat. Hist. lib. xxxiii. cap. 1.

[r] Περι δε της Δημητρος και της Κορης, πιστοτερα· ὁτι φησιν (Αρτεμιδωρος) ειναι νησον προς τῃ Βρεττανικῃ, καθ' ἡν ὁμοια τοις εν Σαμοθρακῃ περι την Δημητραν και την Κορην ἱεροποιειται. Strab lib. iv. p. 198.

[s] Vide infra chap vi.

[t] Schol. in Apoll. Argon. lib. i. ver 917.

and

and consequently whatever observations are applicable to the latter, are no less applicable to the former.

If from Britain we pass into Germany, we shall find, that part of the Suevi sacrificed to Isis, a circumstance which Tacitus was unable satisfactorily to account for; though, from a ship's forming the symbolical part of their worship, he was induced to conclude, that the emblem had been adopted, in memory of their having borrowed their superstition from some foreign country [u]. It cannot however be reasonably doubted, but that this ship was merely the sacred Baris, the perpetual concomitant of the worship of Isis or Ceres; and that it was used by the Germans in the same sense as it was by the Egyptians.

In memory of the Ark, the ancients were not only accustomed to carry about small navicular shrines, but sometimes even built their temples in the form of ships. Diodorus Siculus mentions, that Sesostris constructed a ship, which was 280 cubits long: and adds, that it was made of cedar, that it was covered with plates of gold and silver; and that it was dedicated to Osiris or Noah at the city of Theba or the Ark [x]. It is sufficiently

[u] Tac de Mor Germ. cap 9

[x] Diod Bibl. lib 1 p 52

evident both from the preceding deſcription of this ſhip, from its being dedicated to Oſiris, and from its being placed in the *inland* diſtrict of the Thebais, that it never was deſigned for a voyage at ſea. It was in fact an immenſe navicular temple, built in imitation of the Ark, and deſtined for the ſolemn performance of the diluvian Myſteries. Hence the Greeks deſignated a temple and a ſhip by the very ſame word *Naus* or *Naos*; and hence, what is doubtleſs a relic of the primeval arkite idolatry, we ſtill call the body of a church, in contradiſtinction to the chancel, the *nave* or *ſhip*.

As the Hyperboreans then worſhipped Iſis, and introduced into their Myſteries the ſymbolical Baris, we ſhall not be ſurpriſed to find, that they occaſionally conſtructed their temples in the figure of ſhips. The ruins of a very curious temple of this nature are yet remaining in the neighbourhood of Dundalk in Ireland. Its form, even in its preſent mutilated ſtate, is preciſely that of a galley; and its very name ſufficiently points out the idea, which was impreſſed upon the mind of its architect. According to Colonel Vallancey, *Faghs na ain eighe*, the appellation by which it is uſually diſtinguiſhed, is a corruption of *Faghas na heum Naoi*, which may ſignify *the remains*

remains of the only ſhip[y]. I fully agree with Governor Pownall, that this curious temple was a repreſentation of the ſhip Skidbladner; but at the ſame time I am perſuaded that the prototype of Skidbladner was the Ark of Noah. Skidbladner is ſaid to have been built by a race of men called *Nani*, and to have been ſufficiently large to contain all the deities of the Gothic mythology, who are repreſented ſailing in it, preciſely in the ſame manner as the Egyptians deſcribed their gods, not ſtanding upon dry land, but ſailing together in a ſhip[z]. Theſe Nani I apprehend to be the Noachidæ, for Nanus is equivalent to Noah, being indeed the name of that patriarch without any other variation than the reduplication of the firſt letter: accordingly, as the Ark was eſteemed the conſort of Noah, ſo the *magna mater* of the Iriſh, whom I conceive to be the ſame as Cybelè, Antèa, Anèa, or Nanèa, was called, as we learn from Col. Vallancey, *Anu*, *Nana*, or *An-Eireann*[a].

Tacitus mentions alſo another rite preva-

[y] Collect. de Reb. Hiber. vol. iii p 199. et infra.

[z] Edda Fab. 21

[a] Vallan. Vind apud Collect vol v. p. 490, 498 An-Eireann is Ani-Eran, *the arkite ſhip*. The reader will find a very curious account of the introduction of the Cabiric Myſteries into Ireland, in Collect de Reb. Hib vol. iv p 29 Pref 2d

lent

lent among the Germans, in which we behold the great goddeſs connected, as in the myſteries of Egypt, with the ſmall lake, the conſecrated iſland, and the ſymbolical ox.

"In an iſland in the Ocean," ſays he, "is "a ſacred grove, and in it a chariot covered "with a garment, which the prieſt alone can "lawfully touch. At particular ſeaſons, the "goddeſs is ſuppoſed to be preſent in this "ſanctuary; ſhe is then drawn in her car by "heifers with much reverence, and followed "by the prieſt. During this period un-"bounded feſtivity prevails, and all wars are "at an end, till the prieſt reſtores the deity "to the temple, ſatiated with the converſa-"tion of mortals. Immediately the chariot, "the garments, and even the goddeſs herſelf, "are plunged beneath the waters of a ſecret "lake[b]."

This portable ſhrine, drawn by oxen, was one of the ſame nature as that of Agruerus or Noah, mentioned by Sanchoniatho. The reader will recollect, that Agruerus is ſaid to have been venerated by the Byblians as the greateſt of gods, and to have had a ſmall temple, which was drawn about from place to place by a yoke of oxen. It is not improbable, that the mode, which the Philiſtines

[b] Tac de Mor Germ cap 40.

adopt-

adopted of ſending home the ark of God, was borrowed from this very ſuperſtition. Wiſhing to pay it all poſſible honour, they conveyed it, like the ſhrine of the great Phenician deity Agruerus, in a cart drawn by cows.

"Now therefore make a new cart, and "take two milch kine, on which there hath "come no yoke, and tie the kine to the cart, "and bring their calves home from them: "and take the ark of the Lord, and lay it "upon the cart; and put the jewels of gold, "which ye return him for a treſpaſs offering, "in a coffer by the ſide thereof; and ſend it "away that it may go[c]."

It is remarkable, that a portable ſhrine of the ſame ſort as that, in which the ſtatue of Agruerus was drawn about, was uſed by the ancient idolatrous Iriſh. This ſhrine they denominated *Arn-Breith*, which is evidently Arn-Berith, *the Ark of the covenant*[d], and which was the very ſame as the Iſiac ſhip venerated by the Suevi.

We find likewiſe among the Germans the ſame religious veneration for the myſtic ſolar circle, as appears from the following deſcrip-

[c] 1 Sam vi. 7.

[d] Vallancey's Vindication apud Collect. de Reb. Hiber. vol. v p 460.

tion,

tion, given by Verſtigan from Johannes Pomarius, of the Gothic idol Seater, who, like the claſſical Saturn, is manifeſtly the patriarch Noah.

" Firſt, on a pillar was placed *a pearch*, on " the ſharp prickled back whereof ſtood this " idol. He was lean of viſage, having long " hair, and a long beard; and was bare-head- " ed, and bare-footed. In his left hand he " held up *a wheel*, and in his right he car- " ried *a pail of water*, wherein were flowers " and fruits. His long coat was girded unto " him with a towel of white linen [e]."

The conjunction of the fiſh, the wheel, and the water, is a freſh inſtance of the wide prevalence of that idolatry, which originated from an union of the two moſt ancient ſuperſtitions [f].

There is moreover another circumſtance in the mythology of the Germans, which is not unworthy of our attention. Tacitus informs us, that the Eſtyi worſhipped the mother of the gods, and that the ſymbol, which they uſed, was a boar [g]. Rhea, or the mother of

[e] Verſt. Reſtit of decayed Intell. p 64

[f] Moſt of the Hindoo gods are repreſented, holding a circle in one of their numerous hands.

[g] Ergo jam dextro Suevici maris litore Æſtyorum gentes alluuntur—Matrem deum venerantur. Inſigne ſuperſtitionis formas aprorum geſtant. Tac de Mor. Germ. cap 45.

the

the gods, as it has been abundantly ſhewn, was the ſame as Ceres, Venus, Iſis, or Derceto. She was in ſhort the Ark of Noah, from which iſſued all the hero-gods of paganiſm. With regard to the boar, uſed by this German tribe as an emblem, we find it introduced very conſpicuouſly into many of thoſe legendary traditions, which relate to the great event of the deluge. It appears to have been one of the ſymbols of the Ark, although not adopted ſo generally as the mare or the heifer [h]. In the firſt Hindoo *Avatar* Viſhnou aſſumes the form of a fiſh, and in the third that of a boar, when he is repreſented as emerging from the midſt of the Ocean, and ſupporting the world upon his tuſks [i]. Both theſe incarnations, as well as the ſecond, are ſuppoſed by Sir Wm. Jones to allude to the hiſtory of the flood; whence, as we have already ſeen that a fiſh was emblematical of the Ark, it is not unreaſonable to conclude,

[h] Perhaps, if the matter be expreſſed with perfect accuracy, we ought rather to ſay, that a boar was ſymbolical of Noah, and a ſow of the Ark Hence we find, that, as Viſhnou was feigned to have metamorphoſed himſelf into a boar; ſo the nurſe of the arkite Jupiter, or in other words the Noëtic ſhip, is ſaid by Agathocles to have been a ſow Agath. apud Athen. Deipnoſ. lib. ix p. 375.

[i] Maur. Hiſt. of Hind. v. i p. 577.

that

that the boar may be ſo likewiſe. Accordingly, in the account, which Plutarch gives us of the Egyptian Oſiris, he mentions, that Typhon, or the deluge, being in purſuit of one of thoſe animals, found the Ark, which contained the body of Oſiris, and rent it aſunder [k]. In ſtrict analogy with the preceding tradition, Hercules, who was the ſame mythological character as Oſiris, is ſaid alſo, like him, to have been ſlain by Typhon [l]. Hence he is enumerated by Pauſanias and Strabo among the Idèi Dactyli or Cabiri, and connected with the Cabiric goddeſs Ceres [m]. The boar is ſometimes fabled to have been beloved by Typhon [n]; who, in reference to the union of the ſolar and arkite ſuperſtitions, was eſteemed, what is very remarkable, a perſonification of heat, no leſs than of the Ocean [o]. This union of the two modes of worſhip ſeems to have procured for the lake, into which Typhon was ſuppoſed to have been precipitated, the name of *Serbonis* [p]; a word

[k] Ὁ Τυφων ὑν διωκων προς την πανσεληνον εὑρε την ξυλινην σορον, εν ᾗ το σωμα τȣ Οσιριδος εκειτο, και διερριψεν. Plut. de Iſid. p. 354.

[l] Jablonſ Panth Ægypt. lib. ii. cap 3

[m] Pauſ. Bœot p. 763.—Strab. Geog. lib. viii p. 355 and lib. x. p 473.

[n] Plut de Iſid. p. 354, 357.

[o] Ibid. p 364.

[p] Λιμνη δε Σερβωνις, και χωρα, περι ἡν φασι τον Τυφωνα κεκρυφθαι,

πλησιον

derived, like Osiris, from Sir, Cur, or Cor, *the Sun*. For the same reason the bed of that allegorical monster was denominated *Coricus*, which I apprehend signifies nothing more than the great central abyss; accordingly, a tradition prevailed, that fountains had formerly burst forth from it [q]. With a similar allusion to the compound idolatry introduced by Nimrod, while Adonis, or Noah, was called *Ciris* by the Lacedemonians, and *Cirrhis* by the Cyprians; he at the same time conferred his name upon a particular species of fish [r], and was feigned to have been killed by a boar, which called forth the yearly lamentations of the women of Byblos [s]. The death of Adonis, like that of Bacchus, Osiris, and Hercules, is a mere allegory, and relates solely to the mythological death of Noah, his confinement within the Ark; whence it is said to have been occasioned by the symbolical boar. According to Nonnus, Mars himself assumed

πλησιον εσαν τε προς τῳ Πηλεσιῳ Κασιε ορες. Eustath. in Dionys. Perieg. ver 253.

[q] Senec. Quæst. Nat. lib iii cap. 10.

[r] Κιρις, Αδωνις, Λαγωνες. Hesych. Αδωνις, ιχθυς θαλασσιος. Ibid. Κιρρις, ὁ ιχθυς—ὁμοιως δε λεγεται παρα Κυπριοις Κιρρις ὁ Αδωνις. Etym. Mag.

[s] Luc. de Dea Syra.

the

the ſhape of that animal, and under it flew the beautiful ſavourite of Venus.

——Επει συος εικονι μορφης
Αρης καρχαροδων, θανατηφορον ιον ιαλλων,
Ζηλομανης ημελλεν Αδωνιδι ποτμον υφαινειν [t].

The tradition here however appears, in one reſpect, to have been ſomewhat corrupted, for Mars and Adonis are in reality the ſame perſon, both being equally the patriarch adored in conjunction with the Sun.

[t] Dionyſ. lib. xli. p. 700.

CHAP.

CHAP. V.

THE CONNECTION OF THE FABULOUS HADES WITH THE MYSTERIES OF THE CABIRI.

IT has been intimated, that the arkite deity Bacchus, or Adonis, was the ſame as Adoneus, or Pluto [a]. In conſequence of this cir-

[a] Phornutus has preſerved a curious liſt of the titles of Pluto, which he has reſolved, according to the manner of the Greeks, into his own language, but which appear in reality to be oriental appellations. He informs us, that this deity was called *Diallatton*, or Di-Al-At-On, *the divine ſolar fire*; *Clymenus*, or Cula-Menus, *the arkite Noah*, *Polydectes*, or Bol-Dag-Theus, *the lordly fiſh-god*, *Polydegmon*, or Bol-Dagon, *the lord Dagon*, and *Polyarchus*, or Bol-Archa, *the lord of the Ark*. Phorn. de Nat. Deor cap 35 The laſt of theſe titles is ſaid by the ſcholiaſt upon Apollonius to have been beſtowed by the Samothracians upon Dardanus, and Diodorus Siculus declares, that the language, uſed in the Myſteries of thoſe iſlanders, was not Greek. Schol in Apoll Argon lib 1. ver. 916—Diod. Bibl. lib. v. p. 322. Dardanus, as I ſhall hereafter attempt to ſhew, is Dar-da-Nus, *the illuſtrious Noah*. Vide infra chap. vi. To the preceding appellations of Pluto may be added the name *Orcus*, which ſeems to be derived from Orech, *the Ark*. Age porro Jovem et Neptunum deos numeras: ergo etiam Orcus, frater eorum, deus. Cic. de Nat Deor lib. iii cap. 17 Davies, in his note upon this paſſage, cites a variety of authorities to ſhew, that *Orcus* was a title of Pluto.

 cum-

cumſtance, Adonis is ſaid by Clemens Alexandrinus and Theocritus to have been beloved by Proſerpine [b]. The fact is, that *Bacchus*, *Pluto*, *Ceres*, *Proſerpine*, and *Mercury*, were all names, as we are informed by Mnaſeas, of the Cabiric deities [c]. Thus it neceſſarily follows, that the Cabiri were gods of the infernal regions, the cauſe of which was ſimply this: the Ark, that floated upon the ſurface of the mighty waters, was conſidered in the light of a coffin, which contained the relics of univerſal nature; while the *Hades* of the Myſteries was nothing more than the vaſt central cavity of the earth, from which principally iſſued the waters of the deluge, when the fountains of Tartarus or the great abyſs were broken up, and when a death-like obſcurity was diffuſed over the face of the deep [d]. Hence the Phenician word *Aron*, and its Greek derivative *Larnax*, ſignify either *an*

[b] Επι Αδωνιδι Φερεφαττα Clem. Alex Cohort. p 29. Ὁ τριφιλατος Αδωνις, ὁ κεν Αχεροντι φιλειται Theoc. Idyll. xv. ver 86

[c] Schol. in Apoll. Argon lib i. ver. 917.

[d] I cannot think with Mr Bryant, that the *Hades* of the myſteries was the interior of the Ark, becauſe it is repreſented as containing things, which it was impoſſible that the Ark ſhould have contained namely, the four rivers of hell, the Stygian lake, and the Titanic hoſt that periſhed beneath the waves of the deluge.

ark

ark or a *coffin*[e]: and hence the inclosure of the Noetic family within the gloomy inte-

[e] Tzetzes indifferently uses the terms *Larnax* and *Soros* to describe *the ark* or *coffin*, in which the infant Jason was inclosed. (Tzet Chil 7. Hist. 96—Schol. in Lycoph ver. 175) *Larnax* seems to be compounded of El-Arn-Ac, *the divine Ark of the ocean*, and *Soros* to be derived from Sor (שור), *a bull* or *heifer*. With regard to the word *Aron*, it is constantly used in Scripture to denote *the ark of the covenant*, and as such is uniformly rendered by the LXX Cibotus, *a boat* It occurs likewise in the last verse of *Genesis*, where it is properly translated *a coffin*. I am much inclined to think, that the sacred ark or boat of God, overshadowed by the protecting wings of the Cherubim, has the very same commemorative allusion to the Noetic Ark, as the *Baris* of Egypt It is perpetually called *the ark of the covenant*, with a primary reference, I apprehend, to the covenant vouchsafed by God to Noah, though, doubtless, with a secondary reference to that same covenant renewed in a particular manner with the seed of Abraham Hence, in the Jewish tabernacle, it was surmounted by the mercy-seat and the Cherubim, as the mercy of God rested upon the diluvian ark, and as his providence guarded it from surrounding dangers. In all the sacred processions, and in all the marches of Israel through the wilderness, it was borne aloft upon the shoulders of the priests, exactly in the same manner as the Baris of the Egyptian Ogdoad but there was this essential difference between them. the ark was consecrated to the service of the Most High, and served perpetually to remind his chosen people of the most signal instance of divine mercy and justice, while the primitive use of the Baris was miserably perverted to the purposes of a base and degraded idolatry. Nor is the sacred symbol of the ark confined to the mysteries of the Levitical dispensation. St. Peter compares the water, upon which it floated, to the cleansing streams of baptism (1 Pet. iii 20. 21.), and the Anglican Liturgy mentions it, as an expressive

 emblem

rior[f] of their divinely conſtructed veſſel, was repreſented under the image of death and darkneſs; and their quitting it, under that of a reſtoration to life and light[g]. From this

emblem of the church of Chriſt, toſſed about upon the waves of the troubleſome world, yet ſecure beneath the foſtering wings of the Almighty (Office of baptiſm) It is a ſingular circumſtance, that, as the ſtone tables, on which were written the ten commandments, were kept within the ark of the covenant, ſo the Chineſe were accuſtomed to preſerve in a ſacred ark their books of divination. (Mart Hiſt Sin lib. iv p. 105)

[f] It is evident from the ſcriptural account, that the interior of the Ark could have had no light, excepting that of lamps or torches; for in the whole of that immenſe veſſel there was only a ſingle window, and that no more than a cubit ſquare.

[g] This idea is ſo natural and obvious, that it occurred to the excellent Abp. Leighton, even when conſidering the Ark ſolely in a theological point of view, and without the moſt remote deſign of eſtabliſhing a ſyſtem. "Noah," ſays he, "ſeemed to "have rather entered into a grave, as dead, than into a ſafe-"guard of life, in going into the Ark, yet, being buried there, "he roſe again, as it were, in his coming forth to begin a new "world" Comment on 1 Peter iii 21. The ſame thought, as far as the deep gloom attendant upon the deluge is concerned, is beautifully expreſſed by Mr. Giſborne

———One morn the heavens
Grew dark with wings, earth with unnumber'd ſteps
Sounded, bird, beaſt, in long proceſſion ſought
Their deſtin'd refuge. With his kindred train
The builder next aſcended From the gloom
Of congregating clouds put forth, a Hand
The entrance clos'd. Then darkneſs cover'd all,
Deathlike, unſunn'd, as though primeval night
Return'd her empire——— *Walks in a Foreſt*, p. 125.

In

notion originated the feveral myfteries of Bacchus, Adonis, Ofiris, Ceres, Rhea, and the Cabiri; in which we uniformly find, that fome ancient perfonage was firft bewailed as being dead, or as having defcended into Hell, and that afterwards his fuppofed revivification was celebrated with the moft violent and frantic expreffions of joy [h]. It further appears from Jamblichus, that the Myfteries profeffed to difclofe certain curious fecrets, which treated of the burfting afunder of the heavens, the bringing to light the hidden things of Ifis, the difplaying the ineffable wonders of the great abyfs, the refting of the facred Baris, and the fcattering of the limbs of Ofiris to the rage of the monfter Typhon [i]. If then

In a fimilar manner, Milton:

Meanwhile the fouth wind rofe, and with black wings
Wide hovering, all the clouds together drove
From under heaven; the hills to their fupply
Vapour and exhalation, dufk and moift,
Sent up amain; and now the thicken'd fky
Like a dark ceiling ftood, down rufh'd the rain
Impetuous, and continued till the earth
No more was feen——— *Paradife Loft*, b. xi.

[h] For a more particular account of thefe myfteries, vide infra chap x.

[i] Η γαρ τον ουρανον προσαραξειν, η τα κρυπτα της Ισιδος εκφανειν, η το εν αβυσσῳ αποῤῥητον δειξειν, η στησειν την Βαριν, η τα μελη του Οσι-

Osiris be Noah, Typhon the Ocean, and Isis the Ark, these particulars, mentioned by Jamblichus, will evidently relate to the events of the deluge.

It may perhaps however be said, that, although the entrance of Noah into the Ark might possibly be described under the image of death, and his quitting it, under that of a restoration to life; yet the circumstance of the principal deity of the Gentiles having descended into Hell does not precisely accord with the supposition. that the *Hades* of the Mysteries was the central abyss, because Noah never descended into that abyss.

This no doubt is literally true; but the answer to such an objection is sufficiently obvious. Since the streams of Tartarus, as I am about to attempt to shew, were merely the deluge, it was evidently impossible for the ancient mythologists to represent the Ark as floating upon their surface, without at the same time placing it, and consequently the persons whom it contained, in their fabulous Hell; although the infernal rivers had then by a supernatural impulse quitted their gloomy station, and had overflowed the whole ha-

ριδος διασκεδασειν τῳ Τυφωνι, η αλλο τι τοιουτον απειλει ποιησειν. Jamb. de Myst sect. vi. cap 5.

bitable

bitable globe. If we conſider moreover what muſt have been the ſtate of the Ark during ſo dreadful a convulſion as the flood, when the waves were breaking over it in all directions, and when ever and anon it was "carried down to the deep[k]," we may without impropriety put into the mouth of the great patriarch the prayer of the prophet Jonah.

"I cried by reaſon of mine affliction unto "the Lord, and he heard me: out of the "belly of Hell cried I, and thou heardeſt my "voice. For thou hadſt caſt me into the "deep, in the midſt of the ſeas, and the "floods compaſſed me about: all thy billows "and thy waves paſſed over me—The wa- "ters compaſſed me about even to the ſoul, "the depth cloſed me round about, the weeds "were wrapped about my head. I went "down to the bottoms of the mountains: "the earth with her bars was about me for "ever: yet haſt thou brought up my life "from corruption, O Lord my God[l]."

[k] Pſalm cvii. 26.

[l] Jonah ii 2. It is remarkable, that our Lord himſelf makes the hiſtory of Jonah a type of his own ſepulture and reſurrection, and that baptiſm, which is conſidered by St. Peter as having ſome analogy to the deluge, is directly compared by St. Paul to the burial of the body. "Buried with him in bap- "tiſm, wherein alſo ye are riſen with him through the faith

I do not mean however to aſſert, that ſuch was the *general* opinion reſpecting the infernal regions; the vulgar, I believe, really ſuppoſed, that they were the abode of the ſouls of the deceaſed. At preſent therefore, let it be underſtood, I am ſpeaking only of the *Hades* of the Myſteries, the *Hades* deſcribed by Virgil in the 6th book of his Eneid, which Bp. Warburton ſuppoſes to contain a deſcription of the orgies of the Eleuſinian Ceres. To this ſuppoſition I very fully aſſent in the abſtract, though at the ſame time I can in no wiſe adopt the ſyſtem, which he has built upon it; namely, that *the* ſole *end of the myſteries was to expoſe the abſurdity of the prevailing polytheiſm, and to declare to a few ſelect epoptæ the unity of the godhead*[m]. The queſ-

"of the operation of God, who hath raiſed him from the dead." Coloſſ ii. 12. See alſo Rom vi 4

[m] Div Leg book ii. ſect iv. p. 149 Thus far I agree with Bp. Warburton, that the mere humanity of the hero-gods was doubtleſs revealed in the Myſteries, as indeed it neceſſarily muſt be, upon the ſuppoſition, that thoſe Myſteries treated of the events of the deluge; but I cannot believe, that ſuch a diſcloſure was made with any *particular* view of depreciating the eſtabliſhed religion It is evident however, that this diſcloſure *alone*, with *whatever* view it might be made, will ſufficiently account for the following remarkable language of Cicero, without obliging us to adopt the hypotheſis of Bp. Warburton.

Quid? totum propè cœlum, ne plures perſequar, nonne humano genere completum eſt? Si vero ſcrutari vetera, et ex his

ea,

tion is, what was the import of the ancient Myſteries? If they relate to the helio-arkite ſuperſtition, whatever they are connected with muſt likewiſe neceſſarily relate to the ſame helio-arkite ſuperſtition; conſequently, if they be connected with the 6th book of the Eneid, that mythological epiſode muſt of courſe alſo relate to the ſame helio-arkite ſuperſtition. We have already ſeen, that the great god of the Gentiles, whether denominated *Bacchus*, *Pluto*, *Oſiris*, *Hercules*, *Mars* [n], or *Adonis*; and that the great goddeſs of the Gentiles, whether intitled *Ceres*, *Proſerpine*, *Iſis*, *Venus*, *Rhea*, *Latona*, *Diana*, or *Hecatè* [o]; were partly diluvian, and partly aſtronomical deities: that they were alſo the Cabiri, and the gods of the infernal regions, is evident

ea, quæ ſcriptores Græciæ prodiderunt, eruere coner; ipſi illi, majorum gentium Dii qui habentur, hinc a nobis profecti in cœlum reperientur. Quære, quorum demonſtrantur ſepulchra in Græcia: *reminiſcere, quoniam es initiatus, quæ tradantur myſteriis, tum denique, quam hoc late pateat, intelliges.* Cic Tuſc. Diſp. lib i cap 12, 13. cited by Bp. Warburton.

[n] Although Mnaſeas does not enumerate Mars among the Cabiri, yet Nonnus repreſents Samothrace, the principal ſeat of the Cabiric ſuperſtition, as being ſacred to him.

Ημαθιην Θρηισσαν εχων Σαμος Αρεος εδρην

Dionyſ. lib. iii. p. 58.

[o] The cave Zerinthus in Samothrace was ſacred to Hecatè. Suid. Lex.

both

both from the teſtimony of Mnaſeas, and from the tenor of their reſpective hiſtories: their character therefore of infernal deities muſt in ſome manner be connected with their character of diluvian or arkite deities; in other words, the fabulous Hades muſt have ſome relation to the rites of the Ark. This train of reaſoning may be thrown into a different ſhape. Oſiris and Bacchus are each the ſcriptural Noah; Bacchus is the ſame as Pluto, therefore Pluto is Noah; but Pluto is the great god of the infernal regions, therefore Noah is the great god of the infernal regions: in a ſimilar manner, Ceres or Proſerpine is the lunar Ark; but Ceres or Proſerpine is the great goddeſs of the infernal regions; therefore the lunar Ark is the great goddeſs of the infernal regions.

Since then Bacchus, Oſiris, Adonis, and Hercules, are all equally the patriarch Noah, they are likewiſe all equally feigned to have deſcended into hell, by which nothing more is meant, than that they were all inveloped in the darkneſs of the diluvian chaos, and that they all entered into the gloomy interior of the Ark. The place, where Bacchus was ſuppoſed to have deſcended, was Lerna [p]; the fa-

[p] Pauſ. Corinth. p. 200. Strab Geog lib. viii. p 371.

bulous

bulous hiſtory of which will form no improper introduction to a diſſertation on the *Hades* of the Myſteries.

Lerna I apprehend to be a contraction of El-Aran-Ai, *the land of the Ark-god,* and it was ſo called in alluſion to the entrance of Noah into the Ark. It was ſituated near the ſea; and was at once the ſcene both of the metamorphoſis of Io into the ſymbolical heifer [q], and of the mythological rape of Proſerpine. Hence we are informed by Pauſanias, that myſteries were celebrated there, in honour of the Lernèan or arkite Ceres [r]. In theſe myſteries we find her connected with a perſon ſtyled *Aras,* who was reported to have been the firſt of men, and to have flouriſhed in the neighbourhood of Sicyon and Phliun. He was an *autochthon,* or *gegenes*; and was

[q] Ευθυς δε μορφη και φρενες διαστροφοι
Ησαν, κερας·ις δ', ὡς ὁρατ', οξυςομῳ
Μυωπι χρισθεισ', εμμανει σκιρτηματι
Ηισσον προς ευποτον τε Κερχνειας ρεος
Λερνης ακρην τε· βουκολος δε γηγενης
Ακρατος οργην Αργος ὡμαρτει ——
Æſch Prom Vinc. ver. 674.

[r] Περιβολος εςι λιθων· και τον Πλουτωνα αρπασαντα, ὡς λεγεται, κορην την Δημητρος, καταβηναι ταυτῃ φασιν ες την ὑπογεων νομιζομενην αρχην· ἡ δε Λερνα εςιν, ὡς και τα προτερα εχει μοι του λογου, προς θαλασσῃ, και τελετην Λερναια αγουσιν ενταυθα Δημητρι. Pauſ. Corinth. p. 198.

con-

contemporary with Aſopus the ſon of Neptune, and with Prometheus the ſon of Iapetus. Aras is merely Ares, *the ſolar Noah*, and Ceres is a perſonification of the Ark; whence Aras and his children, or, in other words, Noah and his family, were always invoked previous to the celebration of the myſteries of Ceres [s]. This ancient perſonage beſtowed his name upon the country, in which he was ſuppoſed to have lived; but it was afterwards called *Phliaſia*, from Phlias, the ſon of Bacchus, who was one of the Argonauts [t]: whence we find, that the Phliaſians, being connected with the hiſtory of the deluge on the one hand, and with the ſolar ſuperſtition

[s] Εν τῃ γῃ ταυτῃ γενεσθαι πρωτον Αραντα φασιν, ανδρα αυτοχθονα· και πολιν τε ωκισε περι τον βωνον τουτον, ὁς Αραντινος ετι καλειται, και ες ἡμας —και απ᾽ αυτου το αρχαιον ἡ γη και ἡ πολις Αραντια εκληθησαν. Τουτῳ βασιλευοντι Ασωπος Κηγλουσης ειναι λεγομενος και Ποσειδωνος εξευρε του ποταμου το ὑδωρ, ὁντινα οἱ νυν απο του εὑροντος καλουσιν Ασωπον. Pauſ. Corinth p 138. Aſopus is As-Op, *the ſolar ſerpent*. Προ της τελετης εν τῳ Δημητρος ᾳδουσιν Αραντα, και τους παιδας καλουσιν επι τας σπονδας. Ibid p 139 Φλιασιοι γαρ Προμηθει γενεσθαι τῳ Ιαπετου κατα τον αυτον χρονον φασιν Αραντα Ibid p. 143.

[t] Διονυσου δε οιδα καλουμενον (ſcil. Φλιαντα), και των πλευσαντων επι της Αργους και τουτον γενεσθαι λεγομενον. Ὁμολογει δε μοι και του Ῥοδιου ποιητου τα επη·

Φλιας αυτ᾽ επι τοισιν Αραιθυρεηθεν ἱκανεν,
Ενθ᾽ αφνειος εναιε Διωνυσοιο ἑκητι
Πατρος ἑου πηγῃσιν εφεστιος Ασωποιο.

Pauſ. Corin. p. 139.

on

on the other, particularly venerated Juno, *the arkite dove*, and her ſon Mars, or M'Ares, *the great Noëtic Sun* [u].

As Lerna was thus peculiarly devoted to the diluvian Myſteries, we ſhall ſee the propriety with which Lycophron repreſents Io or Iſis to have been carried off from that place by the Phenicians of Carnè [x]:

Ολοιντο ναυται πρωτα Καρνιται κυνες,
Οἱ την βοωπιν ταυροπαρθενον κορην,
Λερνης ανηρειψαντο φορτηγοι λυκοι,
Πλατιν πορευσαι κηρα Μεμφιτη προμῳ [y].

In return for which act of violence, the Curetes, as I have mentioned above, ſtole away Europa.

Conſidered as the land of the arkite God,

[u] Ωλην δε εκ Ἡρας εστιν ὑμνῳ πεποιημενα, τραφηναι την Ἡραν ὑπο των Ὡρων, ειναι δε οἱ παιδας Αρην τε και Ἡβην. Παρα δε Φλιασιοις τη θεῳ ταυτη και αλλαι τιμαι, και μεγιστον το ες τους οικετας εστι· δεδωκασι γαρ δη αδειαν ενταυθα ἱκετευουσιν· λυθεντες δε οἱ δεσμωται τας πεδας προς τα εν τῳ αλσει δενδρα αναθεισιν Pauſ. Corinth. p. 140. This deliverance of the ſlaves in honour of Juno may poſſibly relate to the deliverance from the confinement of the Ark. The hiſtory of the Argonauts, as alluſive to the helio-arkite worſhip, ſhall be conſidered hereafter Vide infra chap. viii.

[x] Car-Ain-Ai, *the land of the fountain of light*.

[y] Lycoph Caſſan. ver 1291. The title *Boopis* here applied to Io, is the ſame as that, which Homer continually beſtows upon Juno It is uſually tranſlated *ox-eyed*, but it appears in reality to be compounded of Bo and Op, *an ox* and *a ſerpent*, the emblems of the two great ſuperſtitions.

Lerna

Lerna was naturally dedicated to Neptune, the ruler of the Ocean. It was ſituated moreover in Argolis, or *the country of the Ark*; and was originally called *Amymomè*, from one of the daughters of Danaus, who was the concubine of Neptune[z].

> Teſtis Amymome, latices cum ferret in arvis,
> Compreſſa, et Lerne pulſa tridente palus[a].

This Amymomè, according to Hyginus, was the mother of the Argonaut Nauplius[b]; but the ſcholiaſt upon Apollonius repreſents him as only a remote deſcendant of Amymomè through the line of her ſon Archèus[c]. The whole however of his genealogy is a mere ſeries of repetitions; and all the various perſons, who occur in it, are equally the patriarch Noah. Thus, Danaus is Da-Nau; Archèus is Arechi; Nauplius and Naubolus are each equally Nau-Bal; and Lernus is El-Aran-

[z] Λερνη κρηνη του Αργους ἱερη Ποσειδωνος Schol. in Apoll Argon lib. iii. ver. 1240. Αμυμωμη δε τουτῳ (Ποσειδωνι) συνευναζεται· και αυτῃ Ποσειδων τας εν Λερνῃ πηγας εμηνυσε Apollod Bibl. lib. ii cap. 1

[a] Propert. lib. ii. ver 20.

[b] Nauplius Neptuni et Amymomes Danai filiæ filius Argivus. Hyg Fab. 14.

[c] Ναυπλιος απογονος του Αρχαιου του Ποσειδωνος ὑιου, και Αμυμωνης της Δαναου. Schol. in Apoll Argon. lib. i. ver. 136.

Nus.

Nus [d]. It is worthy of notice, that Nonnus makes Amymomè to be the ſame as the Phenician Beroè, whom I ſhall hereafter ſhew to be the *Beruth* of Sanchoniatho, and the *Berith* or *covenant* mentioned in Holy Scripture [e].

Tradition aſſerted, that Danaus ſailed from Egypt in the ſhip Argo [f], and that he firſt landed in Argolis upon the coaſt of Lerna, where he built a temple to Neptune the generator [g], and conſecrated a ſhrine to the arkite Minerva. In the ſacred grove were the ſtatues of Bacchus and Ceres, or Noah and the Ark; and in another temple the images of Bacchus the preſerver, and Venus floating upon the ſea, that Venus, who, no

[d] Apoll Argon lib. i ver 133. This genealogy muſt neceſſarily be mythological, for, ſince the Argo is ſaid to have been the ſhip in which Danaus made his eſcape from Egypt, ſo remote a deſcendant from him as Nauplius could never have been engaged in the Colchian expedition, and that in the *very ſame* veſſel, if the voyages of Danaus and Jaſon be taken as genuine hiſtorical facts

[e] Vid infra chap. ix.

[f] Schol. in ibid. ver. 4. The hiſtory of the Argo, or Ark, will be conſidered at large hereafter.

[g] Εςι δε εκ Λερνης και ἑτερα παρ᾽ αυτην ὁδος την θαλασσαν επι χωριον, ὁ Γενεσιον ονομαζουσι. Προς θαλασσῃ δε του Γενεσιου Ποσειδωνος ιερον εςιν ου μεγα—γης δε ενταυθα πρωτον της Αργολιδος Δαναον συν τοις παισιν αποβηναι λεγουσι. Pauſ. Corin p 201.

less

leſs than Ceres, was a perſonification of the veſſel, in which the great patriarch made his eſcape. The inſtitutor of the Lernèan myſteries is ſaid to have been Philammon; and they were the ſame as thoſe of Ceres at Eleuſis[h].

Laſtly, it was at Lerna alſo, that Hercules ſlew the famous water-ſerpent[i]; as he had contended in Crete with the bull, at Nemèa with the lion, and in Arcadia with the boar.

Herculis antiſtare autem ſi facta putabis,
Longius a vera multo ratione ferere.
Quid Nemæus enim nobis nunc magnus hiatus
Ille leonis obeſſet, et horrens Arcadius ſus?

[h] Εντος δε τε άλσες, αγαλματα εϛι μεν Δημητρος Προσυμνης, εϛι δε Διονυσε και Δημητρος καθημενον αγαλμα ου μεγα.—Ἑτερῳ δε ναῳ Διονυσες Σαωτης καθημενον ξοανον, και Αφροδιτης αγαλμα επι θαλασση λιθου· ανωθειναι δε αυτο τας θυγατερας λεγουσι του Δαναου· Δαναον δε αυτο το ἱερον επι Ποντιῳ ποιησαι της Αθηνας· καταϛησασθαι δε των Λερναιων την τελετην Φιλαμμωνα φασι. Ibid. p. 198. Eſchylus and his Scholiaſt make Danaus the fifth in deſcent from Io, and the immediate ſon of Belus. Prom. Vinct. ver. 352. This genealogy is entirely fabulous, but it ſerves to ſhew the connection between Io and Danaus, the Ark and the god of the Ark.

[i] It is not unworthy of notice, that, according to ſome of the ancient mythologiſts, Cadmus was the perſon who ſlew the hydra of Lerna. Palæph. de incred. Hiſt. c. 6. The fact is, that Cadmus and Hercules were one and the ſame perſon, Noah worſhipped in conjunction with the Sun. More will be ſaid reſpecting Cadmus hereafter. Vide infra chap. vii.

Denique

Denique quid Cretæ taurus, Lernæaque peſtis
Hydra venenatis poſſet vallata colubris [k].

All theſe different monſters however, which make ſo prominent a figure in ancient poetry, were merely the ſymbols of the helio-arkite worſhip [l]: while Hercules himſelf, like the infernal Bacchus, was Erech-El-Es, or, as the Phenicians called him, Arcles, *the ſolar god of the Ark*. Hence Nonnus addreſſes him as the Sun:

Αςροχιτων Ἡρακλες, αναξ πυρος, ορχαμε κοσμυ,
Ἡελιε, βροτεοιο βιυ δολιχοσκιε ποιμην [m].

All-hail, thou brilliant orb of heavenly fire,
Majeſtic in thy ſtar-beſpangled robe,
The world's dread ſovereign, mighty Hercules.

while Apollodorus deſcribes him, as ſailing over the vaſt Ocean in a golden cup, which

[k] Lucret. de Rer. de Nat lib. v. ver 22. Apollodorus ſpeaks of the Hydra having nine heads, eight of which were mortal, and the laſt immortal. Ειχε δε ἡ Ὑδρα υπερμεγεθες σωμα, κεφαλας εχον εννεα, τας μεν οκτω θνητας, την δε μεσην αθανατον. Apollod. Bibl. lib. ii. cap. 4. I know not what this tradition can mean, unleſs it allude to the mortality of the arkite ogdoad as individuals, and to their immortality in the continued ſtream of their poſterity.

[l] Hence the Cretan bull is ſaid to have been that which carried off Europa. Apollod. Bibl lib. ii. cap 4.

[m] Dionyſ lib xl. p. 683.

had been presented to him by Apollo[n], and which Macrobius pronounces to be nothing more than a ship[o].

Hercules then, being the solar Noah, was naturally esteemed one of the Idèi Dactyli, or Cabiri, and as such was joined with the great infernal or arkite goddesses Ceres and Proserpine;

[n] Ὁ δε (Ἡλιος) την ανδρειαν αυτου (Ἡρακλεους) θαυμασας, χρυσεον εδωκε δεπας, εν ᾧ την Ωκεανον διεπερασε—Ἡρακλης ενθεμενος τας βοας εις το δεπας, και διαπλευσας εις Ταρτησσον, Ἡλιῳ παλιν απεδωκε το δεπας. Apollod. Bibl. lib. ii. cap. 5. See also Athen. Deipnos. lib. xi. p. 470. Tartessus, where Hercules was supposed to have restored his cup to the Sun, was a Phenician colony; and it seems to have derived its name from Tar, or Tor, *a bull*. Stephanus of Byzantium says, that it was so called from the river *Tartessus*, which flows from the mountain *Argyrus*. If we suppose these to be Phenician appellations, which is certainly the most probable, Argyrus, or Arg-Ar, will be equivalent to *the mountain of the Ark*; but, if it be a Greek word, it will signify *silver*. I am aware, that both gold, silver, and tin, abounded formerly in Spain, which by a singular fatality was the *Peru* both of Tyre and Carthage; (Pomp. Mel. de Situ Orb. lib. ii. cap. 6.) the title *Argyrus* therefore may undoubtedly relate to that circumstance: but concerning this let the reader form his own judgment. A variety of Punic names however certainly occur in ancient Spain, whatever may be the most proper explanation of *Argyrus*. Pomponius Mela in a single sentence mentions the city of Tarracon or Tara-Chon, *the priest of the heifer*; of Eluro or El-Ur, *the burning god*; of Betullo or Beth-El, *the house of god*; of Barcino or P'Arca-No, *the Ark of Noah*; and of Telobi or Tel-Ob, *the solar serpent*. Pomp. Mel. lib. ii. cap. 6.

[o] Saturn. lib. v. cap. 21.

Proserpine; the latter of whom was honoured by the Arcadians, under the title of *the Saviour*[p] Hence he was feigned to have descended into hell, and upon his return to have been initiated into the mysteries of the Eleusinian Ceres[q], whose peculiar emblem, like that of Isis, was a boat or ship. Accordingly in a curious picture of the mystic infernal regions, mentioned by Pausanius, we find two figures introduced, the one of a man named *Tellis*, and the other of a female denominated *Cleobœa*, who was reported to have first brought the rites of Ceres to Thasus. She was painted, holding upon her knees a boat, like those, which, Pausanias observes, were usually consecrated to Ceres[r]. Tellis is

p Αἱ δε εισιν αἱ μεγαλαι θεαι Δημητηρ και Κορη—την Κορην δε Σωτειραν καλουσιν οἱ Αρκαδες—Εστι δε και Ἡρακλης παρα τη Δημητρι μεγεθος μαλιστα πηχυν τουτον τον Ἡρακλην ειναι των Ιδαιων καλουμενων Δακτυλων, Ονομακριτος φησιν εν τοις επεσι. Pauf. Arcad. p 664.

q Μεμυη, τῳ Ἡρακλει· διοτι εμυηθη εν Ελευσινι τα δι' αυτον λεγομενα μικρα μυστηρια. Tzet. in Lycoph ver. 1328. It is remarkable, that Hercules is sometimes said to have been the son of Iapetus and Thornax. Pauf. Arcad. p. 658. The paternal side of this genealogy is evidently a precise inversion, for Iapetus was the son, not the father, of Noah, but the maternal side, if considered mythologically, is perfectly accurate, Thornax being Tor-Nach, *the tauric Ark of Noah*.

r Τελλις μεν ἡλικιαν εφηβου γεγονως φαινοιτ' αν, Κλεοβοια δ' ετι παρθενος· εχει δε εν τοις γονασι κιβωτον, ὁποιας ποιεισθαι νομιζουσιν Δημητρι. —Κλεοβοιαν

Tel-Es, *the Noetic Sun*; and Cleobèa, whose name signifies *the illustrious heifer*, seems, like Ceres, to be merely the Ark personified under the character of a woman.

From these general remarks on the mythological history of Lerna, as connected with the descent of Bacchus and Hercules, the mysteries of Ceres, the rape of Io, the landing of Danaus, and the worship of the diluvian Neptune, I shall proceed to examine the grotesque machinery, which the ancient fabulists have introduced into their imaginary Hell.

Justin Martyr, Eusebius, and Clemens Alexandrinus, have preserved a very ancient hymn ascribed to Orpheus, which Bishop Warburton, and I think very justly, supposes to have been chanted by the mystagogue for the instruction of those, who were about to be initiated. This hymn is addressed to a person denominated *Musèus*[s], who is styled *the offspring of the resplendent Moon*; and it contains a formal declaration of the unity of the godhead, in opposition, as I apprehend, to the arkite Cabiri.

—Κλεοβοιαν ες Θασον τα οργια της Δημητρος ενεγκειν πρωτην εκ Παρυ φασιν. Pauf. Phoc. p. 866.

[s] To this Musèus the Orphic Argonautics are likewise addressed.

Φθεγξομαι

Φθεγξομαι οἱς θεμις εϛι, θυρας δ' επιθεσθε βεβηλοις
Πασιν ὁμως· συ δ' ακȣε, φαεσφορȣ εκγονε μηνης,
Μȣσαι', εξερεω γαρ αληθεα· μηδε σε τα πριν
Εν ϛηθεσσι φανεντα φιλης αιωνος αμερσῃ·
Εις δε λογον θειον βλεψας, τȣτῳ προσεδρευε,
Ιθυνων κραδιης νοερον κυτος· ευ δ' επιβαινε
Ατραπετȣ, μȣνον δ' εσορα κοσμοιο ανακτα.
Εἱς δ' εϛ' αυτογενης, ἑνος εκγονα παντα τετευκ]α
Εν δ' αυτοις αυτος περινισσεται· ȣδε τις αυτον
Εισορᾳα θνητων, αυτος δε γε παντας ορᾳται [t].

Musèus, I doubt not, is the ſame as Noah. The title itſelf ſignifies *a perſon in the midſt of water*, from the Coptic Mu or Mo, *water* [u]; whence the cognate name of *Moſes* was beſtowed upon the Jewiſh legiſlator, in memory of his expoſure upon the Nile. This Musèus is celebrated as the ſon of Mena, or the Moon; the cauſe of which was ſimply the joint adoration of the Moon and the Ark. Hence, when he is denominated *the ſon of the Moon*, nothing more is meant than that he was the allegorical ſon of the Ark. It is worthy of obſervation, that in the war of Jupiter with the Titanic giants, which relates, I apprehend, to the cataſtrophè of the deluge, a perſon, named *Musèus*, is ſaid to have vo-

[t] Orph. apud Div. Leg. b. ii. ſect. 4. p. 154.

[u] Μω, το ὑδωρ. Heſych

luntarily quitted the caufe of his rebellious brethren, and in return to have received from the gods proportionable honours[x].

As the *Musèus* of the Epoptæ was the patriarch Noah, fo, as I have already obferved, the myftic Hades was merely the vaft central abyfs, from which iffued thofe mighty ftreams, that reduced the earth to its original chaos. Hence Virgil, with ftrict propriety, opens his defcription of the infernal regions by an invocation of Chaos and Phlegethon.

> Dî, quibus imperium eft animarum, umbræque
> filentes;
> Et Chaos, et Phlegethon, loca nocte filentia latè,
> Sit mihi fas audita loqui: fit numine veftro
> Pandere res alta terra et caligine merfas[y].

In a fimilar manner the author of the Orphic Argonautics joins together the overthrow of the giants or diluvians by Bacchus and Apollo, the dire neceffity of the archèan or arkite Chaos, Cronus or Noah, the wanderings of Cybelè or the Ark, and the illuftrious orgies of the Cabiri.

> ——Βακχοιο και Απολλωνος ανακτος
> Κεντρῳ ελαυνομενος, φρικωδεα κηλ' επιφασκον,

[x] Diod. Bibl. lib. v. p. 338.

[y] Æneid. lib. vi. ver. 263.

Θνητοις

Θνητοις ανθρωποισιν αχη· μετα δ' ὁρκια μυςαις·
Αρχαιυ μεν πρωτα Χαυς αμεγαρτον αναγκην,
Και Κρονον,——
———— ηδ' εργ' αιδηλα
Γηγενεων,————
————ορεσσιδρομυ τε λατρειαν
Μητρος,————
———— ηδ' αγλαα δωρα Καβειρων[z].

Epiphanius in ſhort plainly informs us, that Chaos was the very ſame as the vaſt abyſs. Χαος δε και Βυθος τινι υκ αν σαφες ειη, ὡς το ὁμωνυμον κεκτηται[a];

Cloſely connected with the diluvian Chaos were the Stygian pool, the rivers of Hades, and the mighty Ocean, from which the waters of Styx were ſuppoſed to iſſue. Theſe waters, I apprehend, were no other than the waters of the deluge, as will ſufficiently appear from an attentive examination of their mythological hiſtory.

The Ocean, which is introduced ſo very conſpicuouſly into the genealogies of the hero-gods, and which was ſuppoſed to have been the origin of all things, obviouſly derived

[z] Orph Argon. ver. 9.

[a] Epiph adv. Hær vol. i p. 164. This was true at the time of the deluge, becauſe the waters of the abyſs were then no longer confined to the central cavity of the earth, but overflowed the whole habitable globe.

its name from the radical *Oc*, *Og*, *Aug*, *Ag*, *Onc*, *Ong*; for it is indifferently written in all theſe various, though kindred, forms. The primary ſignification of *Oc* is undoubtedly *the Ocean*, of which word it accordingly compoſes the firſt ſyllable; and, in conſequence of ſuch ſignification, it involves alſo the idea of *antiquity*[b]. Hence Heſychius informs us, that Ogen is *the Ocean*; Ogenidæ, *the daughters of the Ocean*; Oganon, *a ſtream of water*; Ogenion, *any thing ancient*[c]: while Suidas mentions Ogenus, *an ancient* or *archèan god*; Ogyris, *a lake*; Ogè, *a mound*, or *dam*; Ogygion, *any thing very ancient*, from Ogyges the firſt reputed king of Thebah[d], or *the Ark*, in whoſe time, according to Varro[e], a great deluge happened. *Ogyges*, or *Ogygiſan*, as we learn from Pſeudo-Beroſus[f], was a title of Noah. It ſeems to have been beſtowed upon him deſcriptively, for Ogygi-San is equivalent

[b] Thus the Greek words *Archè* and *Archèus*, which ſignify *the beginning*, and *old*, ſeem to be derived from Archa, *the Ark*.

[c] Ωγην, ωκεανος—Ωγενιδαι, ωκεανιδαι—Ωγενιον, παλαιον—Ωγανον, αμαρη.

[d] Ωγενος, αρχαιος θεος, ὁθεν Ωγενιδαι και Ωγενιοι αρχαιοι—Ωγυρις, λιμνη—Ωγυγιον, αρχαιον, δια το Ωγυγον πρωτον αρξαι των Θηβων—Ωγη, διαφραξις.

[e] Varr. de Re Ruſt. lib. iii. cap. 1.

[f] Beroſ. Ant. lib. ii. fol. 13.

to

to *the solar-diluvian god*: whence also Bacchus, who was at once the patriarch and the Sun, was styled *Ogygius*[g]. With a similar reference to Og, *the Ocean*, Thasus, celebrated for the mysteries of Ceres or *the Ark*, bore the additional name of *Ogygia*[h]. The island of Calypso was also called *Ogygia*[i]. This nymph is said by Apollodorus to have been the daughter of Nereus and Doris, children of the Ocean[k]; and she is styled by Ovid *the maritime goddess*[l]: but Homer makes her the offspring of Atlas.

Ωγυγιη τις νησος αποπροθεν ειν ἁλι κειται,
Ενθα μεν Ατλαντος θυγατηρ, δολοεσσα Καλυψω,
Ναιει ευπλοκαμος, δεινη θεος[m].——

Calypso I take to be Cal-Hippasa, *the hollow Hippa or Ark*; whence she is sometimes represented as the daughter of the sea-god Nereus, and sometimes of the astronomer Atlas, whom we have already seen to be the solar Noah[n]. The same title of *Ogygia* was given

[g] Ovid. Epist. x. ver. 48.

[h] Ωγυγιη τι Θασος Δημητερος ακτη· εξ αρχης γαρ την Δημητραν μεγαλας ετιμων. Etym. Magn.

[i] Ωγυγιη, ονομα της νησου Καλυψους. Hesych.

[k] Apoll Bibl. lib. i. cap. 2.

[l] Ovid. Epist. ex Pont. lib. iv. Epist. x. ver. 14.

[m] Odyss lib. vii. ver 244.

[n] Homer accordingly describes her father Atlas, as being well ac-

by the Egyptians, from whom the Greeks borrowed the principal part of their theology, to the far-famed city of Thebah, the prototype of the capital of Beotia, and devoted like it to the myſtic rites of the Ark.

Των μετα καλλιρροιο κατερχεται ὑδατα Νειλε.
Και την μεν πολλοι τε και ολβιοι ανδρες εχεσιν·
Η μεν ὁσοι Θηβων ερικυδεα ναιεταεσι,
Θηβην Ωγυγιην εκατομπυλον[o]. ———

As Thebes bore the name of *Ogygia*, ſo Minerva, or the divine wiſdom by which the Ark was preſerved, was worſhipped there under the title of Ogga or Onga, *the marine goddeſs*[p]. Hence ſhe is ſaid to have been the

acquainted with all the depths of the ſea; and repreſents Calypſo herſelf as dwelling in an iſland, which was the *Omphalus* or *navel* of the Ocean. This inſular *Omphalus*, like that near the Egyptian Buto, was nothing more than an arkite Om-Phi-Al, or *an oracle of the helio-diluvian god*.

———Ὁθι τ' ομφαλος εςι θαλασσης,
Νησος δενδρηεσσα· θεα δ' εν δωμασι ναιει
Ατλαντος θυγατηρ ολοοφρονος, ὁςε θαλασσης
Πασης βενθεα οιδεν.——— Odyſſ. lib. i. ver. 50.

[o] Dionyſ. Perieg. ver. 246.

[p] Ογγα, Αθηνα εν Θηβαις. Heſych. The Scholiaſt upon Eſchylus ſays, that *Onca* was a Phenician name of Minerva, introduced by Cadmus: (Schol. in Sept. adv. Theb. ver. 169.) and Tzetzes informs us, that Thebes itſelf was called *Onca*, from the worſhip of Onca. Εςι και Ογκαι κωμη Θηβων, ὁ Καδμος Αθηνας αγαλμα ἱδρυσατο. Tzet. in Lycoph. ver. 1225.

daugh-

daughter of the diluvian Neptune, and the lake Tritonis; and to have placed herself under the protection of Jupiter, in order that she might be preserved from the wrath of her father[q]: and hence the city of Thebah, or *the Ark*, was esteemed sacred to her, and denominated *Tritonian*[r].

> Εστι γαρ πλοος αλλος, ὁν αθανατων ἱερηες
> Πεφραδον, οἱ Θηβης Τριτωνιδος εκγεγαασιν[s].

We learn from Lycophron, that Ceres, or the Ark, was styled *Oncæa*[t]; and from Pausanias, that Apollo, or the solar Noah, was called *Onceates*[u]. The author of *the Etymologicon Magnum* mentions an ancient personage named *Oncus*, or *Ogcus*, from whom some towns in Arcadia, or *the land of the Ark*, received their appellations[x]. Stephanus of Byzantium makes him a king of Arcadia[y], and that with perfect propriety, for he seems to have been no other than the great diluvian patriarch. He

[q] Herod. lib. iv. cap 180.

[r] This Minerva, along with her father Neptune, is said to have instituted chariot races at Barcè. See Hesych. vox Βαρκαιοις οχοις. Barcè seems to be P'Arc-Ai *the land of the Ark*.

[s] Apoll. Argon lib iv. ver. 259.

[t] Cassan. ver. 1225. See Tzet. in loc.

[u] Arcad. p. 651

[x] Ογκαι, πολεις εν Αρκαδια απο Ογκου τινος ονομασθεισαι.

[y] Steph. de Urb. p. 602.

was

was the ſame, I apprehend, as *Ogoa*, the marine god of the Carians, under whoſe temple the ſea was artificially conducted[z]; and as the arkite Hercules, who was intitled by the ancient Gauls *Ogmius*, or *the deity of the Ocean*. We have already ſeen this hero traverſing the ſea in a golden cup, and deſcending into the infernal regions; but the Gauls aſcribed to him thoſe attributes, which claſſical writers uſually give to Mercury. He was repreſented drawing after him a number of men by ſmall golden chains, faſtened at one end to their ears, and at the other to his own tongue. The men however do not follow him reluctantly, but with evident pleaſure, for the chains are deſcribed as being ſlack[a]. From ſuch a mode of repreſentation, it is clear, that the Gauls conſidered him as the god of eloquence, like *the Mercury* of the Greeks and Romans. He was in fact the very ſame as Mercury, who like him was ſuppoſed to be an infernal deity, and who like him was no other than the patriarch Noah. The Gauls beſtowed alſo upon Hercules the name of

[z] Θαλασσης δε αναφαινεσθαι κυμα εν τῳ ἱερῳ τουτῳ (ſcil. Ποσειδωνος) λογος εςιν αρχαιος· εοικοτα δε και Αθηναιοι λεγουσιν ες το κυμα το εν ακροπολει· και Καρων οἱ Μυλασα εχοντες, ες του θεου το ἱερον, ὁν φωνη τη επιχωριᾳ καλουσιν Ογωα. Pauſ. Arcad. p. 619.

[a] Lucian apud Ban. Mythol. vol. iii. book vi. chap. 6.

Macuſan,

Macusan, as appears from a medal ſtruck in the reign of the Emperor Commodus. This word, which is nearly of the ſame import as *Ogmius*, is compounded of M'Ogu-San, *the great helio-diluvian*: accordingly we find Hercules-Macuſan depicted, holding a dolphin in his right hand, and in his left a two-grained ſceptre; on one ſide of him is a blazing altar, and on the other a ſmall ſea-monſter [b]. Olaus Rudbeck derives the appellative *Ogmius* from the Celtic *Oggur*, which ſignifies *powerful by ſea* [c]; but the word *Oggur* itſelf is ultimately deducible from the primitive radical *Og* [d].

[b] Keiſler Ant. Celt. p. 200. apud Ban. Mythol. vol. iii. book vi. chap. 6.

[c] Ol Rudb. Att. c. 53 apud Ban. vol iv book iii. chap. 6.

[d] I am aware, that Col. Vallancey ſuppoſes the Celtic Hercules to have been denominated *Ogmius* from *Ogham*, or *Oghma*, by which name the Iriſh expreſſed a particular mode of writing that prevailed among them. This was frequently, though I believe not always, diſpoſed in the form of a circle. He informs us, that *Ogh* ſignifies *a circle*, and, in conſequence of the circle being thus uſed to convey knowledge, that its derivative *Eag* ſignifies *wiſdom* (Vindication of the Ancient Hiſt. of Ireland, Collect de Reb Hibern vol. v. p. 82.) Hence, I apprehend, according to this etymology *Ogmius* will be equivalent to *the wiſe one*. Granting the propriety of theſe remarks, I may ſtill be allowed to aſk, whether the primitive of *Ogh* or *Ogham* be not Og, *the Ocean*. Every perſon, in the leaſt degree acquainted with the genius of the oriental languages, knows that they are almoſt entirely ideal · that is, in the formation of derivatives from primitives, certain leading ideas run through the

This maritime Hercules was the ſame as Palemon[c], whom Ovid deſcribes as the ſon of Athamas king of Thebes. Palemon and his mother Ino are reported to have been terrified with ſerpents by the goddeſs Juno, to ſuch a degree, that they plunged into the Ocean.

the ſeveral ramifications of the original word. The primitive *Og* ſignifies *the Ocean*. From the circular appearance of the ſea when land is out of ſight ſprings Ogh, *a circle*. All poſtdiluvian knowledge of antediluvian events has been conveyed to us through the medium of the Ogenidæ, or oceanic Noachidæ: hence Minerva was ſtyled *Ogga*, partly as a marine goddeſs, and partly as the goddeſs of wiſdom; and hence the Chaldèans affirmed, that they owed all their knowledge of the creation to the amphibious Oannes. For the ſame reaſon the Greek word Nus, *intelligence*, and the correſponding words in Greek, Latin, and Engliſh, *Gnoö* or *Ginoſco*, *Noſco*, and to *know*, may all be traced to the name of the patriarch Noah. It is remarkable, that the Iriſh arrive at their word *Eag*, *wiſdom*, by following a ſomewhat different chain of ideas. Ogh is *a circle*; but their literature was diſpoſed in the form of a circle; therefore Eag is *wiſdom*, or *mental application*. That the preceding remarks may not be eſteemed too fanciful, I ſhall trace the ramification of two Hebrew radicals. Gal ſignifies *to roll*; Galiun, *a book*, that is *a roll* or *volume*; Gali, *waves* of the ſea from their being rolled round; Gal, *a ſpring of water*; Galah, *the bowl of a candleſtick*, from its rotundity; Gal, *to exult*, i. e. to teſtify joy by dancing round; Gal, *a round heap of ſtones*; Agal, *a drop*; Magal, *a ſickle*; Gelilim, *rings* or *bracelets*; Gelilah, *a boundary*; Galal, *dung*; Galgal, *a wheel*; Galgalath, *the ſkull*. Aleph ſignifies *to lead*; Aleph, *a chieftain*; Aleph, *a thouſand*; Aleph, *an ox*; Aleph, *to teach*.

[c] Παλαιμων, ὁ Ἡρακλης. Heſych. Palemon is Bal-Am-On, *Baal the burning Sun*.

Nep-

Neptune however, interposing, saved them from destruction; and afterwards, at the request of Venus, enrolled them among the dieties of the sea [f]. The name of Palemon, prior to his apotheosis, was *Melicerta*. This is evidently the same title as *Melicarthus*, or *the king of the city* [g], under which appellation the

[f] Ovid Metam lib. iv. ver. 478. et infra.

[g] Melicarthus is מלך קרית Melech Kirjath, *rex urbis*, Athamas is Ath-Am-As, *the blazing Sun*, and Ino is the same as Io, Isis, or the Ark. Ino was feigned to be the nurse of Bacchus, the scriptural Noah, and, during the continuance of the sacred mania sent upon her by that deity, she was supposed to have rambled wildly through the forests of mount Parnassus. Hyg. Fab 4 This celebrated hill was a high place of P'Arn-As, *the fiery god of the Ark*, and was accordingly dedicated to Apollo, *the solar Noah*. Hence we find, that Deucalion and his wife Pyrrha were thought to have landed, after their escape from the deluge, upon mount Parnassus Apollod Bibl lib. i. cap. 7. Deucalion is Du-Cal-Ionah, *the god of the arkite dove*, and Pyrrha seems to have derived her name from the worship of P'Ur, *the Sun*. For the same reason the Hindoo Menu, who was saved from the waters of a flood with seven other holy persons, was styled *Vivaswata*, or *the offspring of the Sun* Asiat Res. vol ii. p. 117. According to Hellanicus, Parnassus was so called from the hero Parnassus; but Andron with greater propriety asserts, that it was originally denominated *Larnassus*, on account of the Larnax, or *Ark*, of Deucalion having landed there, and that its name was afterwards changed to *Parnassus* Schol in Apoll. Argon. lib. ii ver. 713. The inhabitants of Delphi, celebrated for being the seat of the principal oracle of Apollo, were sometimes called *Lycoreans*, from Lycoreus, an imaginary son of that deity. Lycoreus however, no less than

his

Tyrians worſhipped Hercules. Sanchoniatho makes him the ſon of Demaroön; but, as I have already obſerved, both he, and his imaginary father, are equally the ſcriptural Noah. Hence we find that Hercules, or *the arkite god*, is ſaid to have been ſwallowed by a Cetus, or whale [h]. The Cetus however was nothing more than the Ark, repreſented under its uſual ſymbol of a fiſh; and accordingly we are informed by Heſychius, that its derivative *Cetenè* is *a large ſhip* [i]. In alluſion to the Noëtic ogdoad, Hercules is ſaid by Pindar to have had eight children by his wife Megara [k]; and, with a reference to the triple

his father, is Luc-Or, *the fiery Sun*. Athamas, after the ſuppoſed death of Palemon, adopted Coronus and Haliartus, who became the founders of the two Beotian cities, called after their reſpective names. Pauſ. Bœot. p. 779. Coronus is Cor-On, *the Sun*; and Haliartus is *the marine deity*.

[h] Στας ωπλισμενος (ὁ Ἡρακλης) περι το στομιον, ὡς κεχηνος επηει το κητος, αθροως τῳ τουτου εμπεπηδηκε στοματι· τρισι δε ἡμεραις ενδοθεν κατακοπτων αυτος, εξηλθεν αποβεβληκως και την της ἑαυτου κεφαλης τριχωσιν. Tzet. in Lycoph. ver. 34. This exploit of Hercules was performed, when he delivered Heſionè, upon which occaſion he was attended by Telamon, or Tel-Am-On, *the burning Sun*. The ſtory is a mere repetition of that of Perſeus and Andromeda.

[i] Κητηνη, πλοιον μεγα ὡς κητος. From the ſame root comes the Engliſh word Cat, *a kind of ſhip*. Johnſon's Dictionary.

[k] Ὁ δε Πινδαρος οκτω λεγει παιδας Μεγαρας και Ἡρακλεους. Tzet. in Lycoph. ver. 38.

off-

offspring of the patriarch, Herodotus describes him as becoming the father of three sons by a monster compounded of a woman and a serpent[1]. This last affair happened in Scythia; consequently the person, mentioned by the Greek historian, must be *the Hercules Ogmius* of the Celts. From the same root *Oc*, or *Og*, I am inclined to think, that we may derive the numeral Octo or Ogdoas, *eight*. In this case, the literal signification of Oc-Toi will be *the gods of the Ocean*, that is, the *eight* persons

[1] Herod. lib iv. cap 9. Hercules left with this woman, at his departure, a bow, and a belt with a cup suspended to it; and gave directions, that the son, who could bend the bow, should have the belt, and along with it the sovereignty of the whole country. The cup here mentioned was a model of the golden cup, in which Hercules sailed over the Ocean, in other words, of the Ark. Parthenius says, that the name of this paramour of Hercules was *Celtinè*, and that of her father, *Britannus*. Parth. Nic. Erot. cap. 30. Celtinè is Cal-Tinin, *the arkite sea-monster*, and I think it by no means improbable, that the original form of this goddess was compounded, like the image of Derceto, of a woman and a fish, while Britannus may perhaps be Brit-Tan-Nus, *the fish-god Noah the covenanter*. Should this etymology be allowable, our own island will be Brit-Tan-Nu-Aia: it may be proper however to mention, that Bochart gives a different derivation of *Britannia*. According to another tradition, the great ancestor of the Goths was not Hercules, but Targitaus, who yet, like Hercules, was the father of three sons. Herod. lib. iv. cap. 5. I am much inclined to think, that Targitaus is a corruption of Atar-Gat, as Atar-Gat is of Adar-Dag, *the illustrious fish-god*.

 pre-

preſerved in the Ark. If written hieroglyphically, it would probably be expreſſed by the ſymbol of *eight men ſailing together in a boat on the ſea.* Accordingly, the character, by which the Chineſe deſignate *a ſhip*, conſiſts of *a boat, a mouth, and the number eight.* Two of theſe characters, *the eight*, and *the mouth*, added to that by which water is deſignated, preſents to their minds the idea of *a proſperous voyage* [m]. The radical *Onc* appears to enter alſo into the language of China, no leſs than into thoſe of Greece, Italy, and Gaul. Thus the allegorical Puoncu, who is ſaid to have ſprung from the mundane egg, is perhaps a compound of Pu-Oncu, *the oceanic god* [n]. The ſame radical, in its kindred form of *Ag*, or *Aug*, occurs likewiſe in the *Hebrew* word, Agam, *a pool of ſtanding water* [o]: and, in the Chaldaic coſmogony, the chaotic maſs previous to its reduction into order and regu-

[m] Bryant's Anal. vol. iii. p. 9. *The mouth*, which makes a part of this hieroglyphic, ſeems to mean *an oracular mouth*. Thus *Phi* ſignifies either *a mouth*, or *an oracle*. The Argo, or Ark, was always ſuppoſed to be an oracular veſſel. Erat. Cataſt. cap. 35—Calliſtrat. Stat. cap. 10—Val. Flac. Argon. lib. i.

[n] Martin. Hiſt. Sin. lib. i. p. 13.

[o] אגם *Stagnum*—R. Sal. ſcribit, אגם eſt collectio aquarum non ſcaturentium neque fluentium, ſed ſtantium in uno loco. Buxt. Heb. Lex.

larity,

larity, is called *Omoroca*; a term, which ſeems to be compounded of Om-Or-Oc, *a confuſed mixture of fire and water*, whence Syncellus informs us, that it ſignifies *the ſea* [p].

The Ocean then of the Grecian mythology, from which all the hero-gods derived their origin, and which was ſuppoſed to have been the parent of Styx, is the vaſt maſs of waters, whether ſupernal or infernal, which conſtitutes ſo large a portion of our planet. Plato accordingly fixes Tartarus, and the four rivers of hell, in the centre of the earth, cloſely connecting them with the Ocean; the mighty ſtreams of which, as we learn from the inſpired hiſtorian, iſſuing from the great central abyſs, principally occaſioned the cataſtrophè of the deluge [q].

As the Ocean, to adopt the ſcriptural expreſſion, is *the gathering together of the waters*, ſo his allegorical daughter Styx ſeems to be a perſonification of the flood [r]. Hence we find,

[p] Ομορωκα· ειναι δε τετο Χαλδαιςι μεν θαλατθ, Ἑλληνιςι δε μεθερμηνευεται θαλασσα Syncel Chronog. p. 29.

[q] Phæd Sect 60, 61, 62.

[r] Accordingly the Scholiaſt upon Heſiod declares, that Styx was the water, which proceeded from the loweſt parts of the earth, and occaſioned the phenomenon of the rainbow. Στυγα νυν λεγει τους ςαλαγμες των ὑδατων, και τας ψεκαδας τας απο των κατω τοπων αναδιδομενας,—και ποιεσας ιριδα. Schol. in Heſ. Theog. ver 776.

 that

that ſhe makes a vary conſpicuous figure in the hiſtory of the Titans. We are informed by Apollodorus, that Jupiter ordained every oath taken by Styx the daughter of Oceanus to be inviolable; becauſe he wiſhed to pay her the higheſt honour, on account of her having aſſiſted him, with all her children, in his war againſt the Titans[s]. In a ſimilar manner Lycophron repreſents Jupiter as making a libation of the waters of Styx, and ſwearing a tremendous oath, when about to attack the Titans, and the giants.

Στυγος κελαινης νασμον, ενθα τερμιευς
Ορκωμοτȣς ετευξεν αφθιτοις ἑδρας,
Λοιβας τ᾽ αφυσσων χρυσεαις πελλαις γανος
Μελλων γιγαντας, κἀπι Τιτηνας περαν[t].

[s] Το δε της Στυγος ὑδωρ, εκ πετρας εν ἁδου ῥεον, Ζευς εποιησεν ὁρκον, ταυτην αυτῃ τιμην διδȣς, ανθ᾽ ὡν αυτȣ κατα Τιτανων μετα των παιδων συνεμαχησεν. Apollod. Bibl. lib. i. cap. 2. The children of the diluvian Styx are evidently the rivers and fountains; accordingly theſe are, with perfect propriety, enumerated by Hyginus in his liſt of the offspring of Styx and Pallas. Hyg. Fab. p. 8.

[t] Caſſan. ver. 706. Tzetzes applies this to the war of Jupiter with the other gods, which however is in fact the very ſame as the Titanic conteſt. Schol in loc. The arkite ogdoad being the great gods of the Gentiles, theſe gods are almoſt univerſally ſaid to be deſcended from the Ocean; and to this very cauſe Ariſtotle, in a remarkable paſſage, aſcribes the oath by the waters of Styx. Εισι δε τινες, οἱ και παμπαλαιȣς, και πολυ προ της νυν γενεσεως, και πρωτους θεολογησαντας, ούτω οιονται περι της

Φυσεως

Theſe Titans ſeem to have been the whole race of mankind living at the era of the deluge, both thoſe who periſhed beneath its waves, and thoſe who were preſerved in the Ark [u]. Accordingly, they are ſometimes deſcribed as warring againſt the majeſty of heaven, but overpowered by the waters of Styx or hatred, thoſe waters by which the Almighty teſtified in ſo eminent a manner his hatred of ſin; and at other times, as being ſeven in number, the children of Cronus or Noah, and the ſame as the Cabiri. In this laſt caſe one of them is ſaid to have been called *Iapetus* If then the Titans be the diluvians, the Styx muſt be the deluge, and conſequently the inviolable oath of Jupiter muſt refer to the oath of God, that he would no more drown the world; for which reaſon, Iris the rainbow, the daughter of Thaumas, is repreſented by Heſiod as hovering over the broad ſurface of the Ocean, when this oath of Jupiter was taken [x]. Now that ſuch a pheno-

φυσεως διαλαβειν. Ωκεανον τε γαρ και Τηθυν εποιησαν της γενεσεως πατερας, και τον ορκον των θεων υδωρ, την καλυμενην υπ' αυτων Στυγα των ποιητων. Τιμιωτατον μεν γαρ το πρεσβυτατον· ορκος δε και τιμιωτατον εστιν Ariſt. apud Cudworth's Intell. Syſt p 120

[u] This ſubject will be reſumed hereafter, when the Titanic war is diſcuſſed. Vide infra chap ix.

[x] Theog ver. 779

menon appeared immediately after the deluge, we are expresſly informed by Moſes; and it is obſervable moreover, that it was made a ſpecial ſign of God's oath to Noah [y]. Thaumas may poſſibly have derived his name from Thaum, *the abyſs*. He ſeems to be the ſame as the ſcriptural Thammuz, under which title Adonis, or the great diluvian patriarch, was worſhipped in Paleſtine. It is remarkable, that Thaumas is ſuppoſed by Ptolemy Hepheſtion to have had another daughter called *Arca*, who aſſiſted the Titans, during their tremendous conflict with Jupiter [z]. The explanation of this fable is perfectly obvious. The Ark, in the uſual ſtrain of oriental allegory, is ſaid to be the daughter of Noah, and the ſiſter of the rainbow; while the Titans, whom ſhe is feigned to have aſſiſted, are evidently, not the impious, but the Noëtic Titans.

In conſequence of Styx being a perſonification of the deluge, Parthenius the Phocenſian aſſigns to her the epithet *Ogenia*, and connects her with the marine deity *Tethys* [a]; while, to perpetuate the memory of that aw-

[y] Gen. ix. 13.

[z] Ἡ δε Αρκη Θαυμαντος ην θυγατηρ, ἧς ἡ αδελφη Ιρις. Ptol. Heph. Nov. Hiſt. lib. vi.

[a] Parth. apud Steph. Byzant. de Urb. p. 766.

ful

ful event, the title of *Styx* was conferred upon a fountain in Arcadia, or *the land of the divine Ark*[b]. Pausanias informs us, that Styx flowed from a lofty crag near the ruins of Nonacris; a small town, which was so called from the wife of Lycaon[c]. This prince is said by Ovid to have been king of Arcadia immediately before the flood; and his presumptuous impiety towards Jupiter was one principal cause of that catastrophè[d]. As the Arcadian Styx then received its appellation in memory of the diluvian waters of hatred, so its branch Titaresius evidently derived its name from Tit, *the colluvies of the flood*[e].

> Οἱ τ' αμφ' ἱμερτον Τιταρησιον εργ' ενεμοντο,
> Ὁς ῥ' ες Πηνειον προιει καλλιρροον ὑδωρ,
> Ουδ' ὁγε Πηνειῳ συμμισγεται αργυροδινῃ,
> Αλλα τε μιν καθυπερθεν επιρρεει, ηυτ' ελαιον·
> Ὁρκȣ γαρ δεινȣ Στυγος ὑδατος εστιν απορρωξ[f].

Or where the pleasing Titaresius glides,

[b] Περι τε εν Αρκαδιᾳ Στυγος ὑδατος ὑτω φασιν. Ptol. Hephæst. Nov. Hist lib. iii. See also Stob. Eclog. Phys. lib. i. p. 130.

[c] Το μεν δη αρχαιον Νωνακρις πολισμα ην Αρκαδων, και απο της Λυκαονος γυναικος το ονομα ειληφει· τα δε εφ' ἡμων ερειπια ην—Των δε ερειπιων ȣ πορρω κρημνος εστιν ὑψηλος—και ὑδωρ κατα τȣ κρημνȣ σταζει καλȣσιν δ' Ἑλληνες αυτο ὑδωρ Στυγος. Pauf. Arcad. p. 634.

[d] Metam lib. i. ver 165.

[e] Whence also *Titan*.

[f] Iliad. lib. ii. ver. 751.

 And

And into Peneus rolls his easy tides;
Yet o'er the silver surface pure they flow,
The sacred stream unmix'd with streams below,
Sacred and awful! from the dark abodes
Styx pours them forth, the dreadful oath of gods.

Pope.

Styx at length empties itself into the river *Crathis*[g], near which is also a mountain denominated *Crathis*. Here we find a temple of Diana Pyronia, from which the Argives were wont, in old times, to bring fire for the mysteries of Lerna[h]. Diana, as we have seen, is the same as Isis, or Ceres; and her name *Pyronia* relates to the worship of P'Ur-On, *the blazing Sun*: while Crathis was so called in honour of Car-Ath, *the solar heat*.

It has been stated, that Bacchus was worshipped by the Arabs under the title of Dus-Ares, *the divine Sun*; and it may now be observed, that, as he was the *Noah* of scripture, so we meet with a river Styx also in Arabia[i]. Tradition asserted, that, when Bacchus was

[g] Pauf. Arcad. p. 635.

[h] ——επι το ορος αγουσης την Κραθιν· εν τουτῳ τῳ ορει του ποταμου της Κραθιδος εισιν αἱ πηγαι —απο τουτου δε καλειται του Κραθιδος και εν Ιταλιᾳ ποταμος εν τῃ Βρεττιων. Εν δε τῃ Κραθιδι τῳ ορει, Πυρωνιας ἱερον εστιν Αρτεμιδος· και τα ετι αρχαιοτερα παρα της θεου ταυτης απηγοντο Αργειοι πυρ ες τα Λερναια. Pauf. Arcad. p. 632.

[i] Της Αραβιας και το Στυγαιον ὑδωρ κατειβομενον απεδημησεν εις τα Βοστρα. Damaf. Vit. Ifid. apud Phot. Bibl. p. 1060.

furi-

furiously pursued by Lycurgus, he plunged for safety into the Erythrèan sea [k]. It is probable, that Lycaon and Lycurgus are merely different names of the same person, or rather indeed persons, for they seem to represent all the diluvians, considered as one great body [l]. Both these appellations are derived from Luc, *the Sun*, the grand object of the primitive antediluvian superstition.

According to Hesiod, Styx was the wife of Pallas; but, according to Empedocles, she espoused Piras, and by him became the mother of the serpent Echidna [m]. The purport of both these fables is exactly the same; for, as Pallas is P'Al-As, *the god of fire*, so Piras is P'Ares, *the solar deity*. The allegorical nuptials therefore of Styx and Piras, and the birth of their daughter Echidna, allude only to the union of the two superstitions, and to the emblematical serpent of the Sun. We learn from Hyginus, that the mythological children

[k] Nonni Dionys. lib. xx. p. 361.

[l] The history of Bacchus plunging into the Erythrèan sea will be resumed hereafter. Vide infra chap. ix

[m] Ειναι δε την Στυγα Ἡσιοδος μεν εν Θεογονιᾳ εποιησεν — πεποιημενα μεν ουν εστιν ενταυθα Ωκεανου θυγατερα την Στυγα, γυναικα δε αυτην ειναι Παλλαντος — Εμπεδολλης δε ὁ Κρης ειναι μεν και ουτος θυγατερα Ωκεανου την Στυγα εποιησε, συνοικειν δε αυτην ου Παλλαντι, αλλα εκ Πειραντος Εχιδναν τεκειν, ὁστις δε ὁ Πειρας εστιν. Pauf. Arcad. p. 634.

of

of Styx and the giant Pallas were Strength, Jealousy, Power, Victory, Fountains and Lakes[n]; and that the offspring of Echidna and Typhon[o] were Gorgon, Cerberus, Scylla, Chimera, the dragon which guarded the golden fleece, the Theban Sphinx, the Hydra of Lerna, and the serpent of the Hesperides[p]. In this singular assemblage we repeatedly behold the combination of the emblematical snake of the Sun with the waters of the diluvian Ocean; and, what is worthy of our particular attention, we perceive moreover, that these various monsters are all connected with each other, though placed by the poets in widely separated countries. The snaky locks of Gorgon[q] and the Colchian dragon, equally

[n] Ex Pallante gigante et Styge, [Scylla,] Vis, Invidia, Potestas, Victoria, Fontes, Lacus. Fab. p. 8. Scylla seems to have crept erroneously into the text, for she is shortly after by the same author said to be the daughter of Typhon and Echidna.

[o] Or the Ocean.

[p] Ex Typhone et Echidna, Gorgon, Cerberus, Draco, qui pellem auream arietis Colchis servabat: Scylla quæ superiorem partem fœminæ, inferiorem canis habuit, quam Hercules interemit: Chimæra, Sphinx, quæ fuit in Bœotia: Hydra serpens, quæ novem capita habuit, quam Hercules interemit: et draco Hesperidum. Ibid. p. 12.

[q] Strangely as the Greeks have corrupted the history of Gorgon, we are plainly told by Palephatus, that she was the same as Minerva, or the divine wisdom which preserved the Ark. He

relate to the solar superstition [r]; while the terrific Scylla, like the arkite Derceto of Palestine, was represented as terminating in the tail of a fish, and was supposed to occupy a cave near the dreadful whirlpool of Charybdis. However the history of Scylla may have been corrupted, I suspect, that she was originally the same as Isis, Venus, Derceto, or the Ark, and that the title of *Charybdis* was bestowed upon the Sicilian whirlpool from its resemblance to the agitated waves of the deluge. The word Scylla is accordingly derived from Saul, *the infernal regions*; and *Charybdis* from Chor-Obdan, *the pit of destruction* [s]. Some relics of the primitive tradition appear to have reached even the days of Virgil. That poet describes Helenus as enjoining his hero

He adds, that her father was called Phorcyn. Palæph. de Incred. Hist. cap. 32. Hence I conjecture, that Gorgon derived her name from G'Orga, *the illustrious Ark*, and that she was decorated with snakes for the very same reason that Hecatè and Ceres were. Apoll. Argon lib. iii. ver. 1214—Pauf. Arcad. p. 686. As for her supposed father Phorcyn, he seems to be no other than Ph'Orc-Chen, *the priest of the Ark*.

[r] This will plainly appear, when the history of the Argonautic expedition is considered.

[s] Scylla is שאולה, and Charybdis חור-אובדן. See Boch. Canaan, lib i. cap. 28 Bochart chooses rather to derive Scylla from סקול, *destruction*, but I prefer the other etymology.

to pray, in an eſpecial manner, to Juno, the propitious dove, when paſſing through the tremendous ſtraits.

Dextrum Scylla latus, lævum implacata Charybdis
Obſidet: atque imo barathri ter gurgite vaſtos
Sorbet in abruptum fluctus, rurſuſque ſub auras
Erigit alternos, et ſidera verberat unda.
At Scyllam cæcis cohibet ſpelunca latebris,
Ora exertantem, et naves in ſaxa trahentem.
Prima hominis facies, et pulchro pectore virgo
Pube tenus: poſtrema immani corpore priſtis,
Delphinum caudas utero commiſſa luporum[t].

- - - - - - - - - - - - - -

Unum illud tibi, nate dea, præque omnibus unum
Prædicam, et repetens iterumque iterumque monebo.
Junonis magnæ primum prece numen adora:
Junoni cane vota libens, dominamque potentem
Supplicibus ſupera donis[u].———

Far on the right her dogs foul Scylla hides:
Charybdis roaring on the left preſides;
And in her greedy whirlpool ſucks the tides:
Then ſpouts them from below; with fury driven

[t] Compare with this Lucian's deſcription of Derceto. Δερκετους δε ειδος εν Φοινικη εθηησαμην, θεημα ξενον· ἡμισεη μεν γυνη· το δε ὁκοσον εκ μηρων ες ακρους ποδας, ιχθυος ουρη αποτεινεται. Luc. de Dea Syra.

[u] Æneid, lib. iii. ver. 420.

The

The waves mount up and wafh the face of heaven.
But Scylla from her den with open jaws,
The finking veffel in her eddy draws;
Then dafhes on the rocks: a human face,
And virgin bofom, hides her tail's difgrace.
Her parts obfcene below the waves defcend,
With dogs inclos'd, and in a dolphin end.
Do not this precept of your friend forget,
Which therefore more than once I muft repeat.
Above the reft great Juno's name adore:
Pay vows to Juno; Juno's aid implore.

Dryden.

The hiftory of Bellerophon and the Chimera, who is defcribed as the fifter of Scylla, is entirely founded upon the union of the two fuperftitions. The Chimera was compounded of a lion, a goat, and a ferpent; and fhe is faid to have been encountered by Bellerophon riding upon the winged horfe Pegafus, which fprung from the blood of Gorgon [x]. The confideration of this legend however muft be referved for a future page; at prefent therefore, fince I have been obliged to touch upon it, on account of its connection with the Chimera, and confequently with her allegorical father Typhon, I fhall merely obferve, that

[x] Fulgen. Mythol. lib iii. cap. 1.

Bel-

Bellerophon or Bellerophontes is a title of Noah, compounded of Bel-Ur-Oph-Phont[y], *the prieſt of Bel the bright ſolar ſerpent*, while the horſe Pegaſus is no other than the ſymbolical arkite Hippa.

Nearly related to the Chimera was the Theban or *arkite* Sphinx. This monſter had the face of a virgin, the feet of a lion, and the wings of a ſeraph, or flying ſerpent; and ſhe is ſaid by Lycus to have been ſent into Beotia by Dionuſus, the *Noah* of Scripture[z]. Palephatus informs us, that the Sphinx was the wife of Cadmus, the founder of Thebah, and the ſlayer of the dragon; and he further adds, that ſhe was an Amazon[a]: ſhe is cloſely connected therefore with Harmonia, who is alſo deſcribed as the wife of Cadmus, and the mother of the Amazons[b]. She ſeems in fact to have been nothing more than an hieroglyphical repreſentation of the two united ſuperſtitions, by means of their ſym-

[y] *Phont* in the Coptic is *a prieſt*. Jablonſk. Panth. Ægypt. Pars I. p. 139.

[z] Schol. in Heſiod. Theog. p. 261.

[a] Καδμος εχων γυναικα Αμαζονιδα, ἡ ονομα Σφιγξ, ηλθεν εις Θηβας, και αποκτεινας τον δρακοντα, την τουτου βασιλειαν παρελαβε. Palæph. de Incred. Hiſt. cap. 7.

[b] Schol. in Apoll. Argon. lib. ii. ver. 992. The hiſtory of Cadmus and Harmonia ſhall be reſumed hereafter. Vide infra chap. 7.

bols,

bols, the woman, the lion, and the ſerpent: hence Palephatus, with great propriety, ſtyles her an *Argive*, or *arkite*[c], as well as an *Amazon*, or *worſhipper of the Sun*[d]. The whole fable was moſt probably ingrafted upon the emblematical theology of the Cuthites, whom the Greeks denominated *Ethiopians*: accordingly we learn from Piſander, that the Sphinx was ſent by Juno out of Ethiopia, for the puniſhment of Laius and the Thebans[e].

As for the ſtory of the ſerpent of the Heſperides, ſome traditional remembrance of Paradiſe and the fall ſeems to have been ſuperadded to the prevailing ſolar ſuperſtition. Such were the mythological deſcendants of Styx, of Piras, of Echidna, and of Typhon.

It is obſervable, that *Styx* was alſo the name of an ill-omened bird of night, into which Polyphontè was metamorphoſed. She is ſaid to have been the offspring of Thraſſa, the daughter of Mars by Terina: but Mars, as we have ſeen, was the Sun; and Terina, who was the reputed child of the river Strymon, ſeems to be Tora-Nah, *the arkite heifer of Noah*. A ſtrange ſtory is told by Antoninus

[c] Σφιγξ—η Αργεια. Palæph de Incred. Hiſt. cap. 7.

[d] The Amazons received their name from the worſhip of Am-Azon, *the burning Sun*.

[e] Schol in Eurip Phœniſſ. ver. 1789.

Libe-

Liberalis respecting this Polyphontè. Venus, offended at her neglect, inspired her with an unnatural passion for a bear; and she was afterwards changed by Diana into the bird Styx[f]. The whole of this legend is built upon a perversion of the primitive diluvian tradition. The word *Polyphontè* is Bol-Oph-Phonta *the priestess of Baal the solar serpent*; and the Greek term for *a bear* happens to be *Arctos*: hence that ingenious people, whose attachment to the marvellous is well known, converted the union of the solar and arkite worship into the fable of a nymph falling in love with a bear. Some traces of the primitive signification of *Arctos* may still be found in the circumstance of its being also the name of a fish[g]; and I apprehend, that it was with a similar allusion to the Ark, that Rhea was venerated in a mountain denominated *Arcton*[h].

I have mentioned, that the Cabiri were sometimes called *Telchines*, or *priests of the Sun*[i]; as such, they were of course connected

[f] Anton. Liber. Metam. cap. 21.

[g] Arist. apud Scap. Lex.

[h] Και τοτε μεν δαιτ' αμφι θεας θεσαν ερεσιν Αρκτων,
Μελποντες Ῥειην πολυποτνιαν ——
Apollon. Argon. lib. i. ver. 1150.

[i] Telchin is Tel-Chen, a contraction of Ait-El-Chen, *a priest of the burning deity.*

with

with Styx, or *the deluge*. Strabo accordingly informs us, that they were magicians, who ſprinkled the Stygian waves with ſulphur, in order that they might bring deſtruction both upon animals and vegetables[k]. Now, ſince the Cabiri are the Noëtic family, and ſince Styx is the deluge, this deſtruction muſt evidently relate to the deſtruction of the primitive world; while the ſulphur, here mentioned by Strabo, may perhaps allude to thoſe deſolating balls of fire, which, according to Cedrenus, were the prelude to that cataſtrophè[l].

With regard to the four infernal rivers, they are each, in reality, the ſame as the diluvian Styx. Phlegethon, which from a miſinterpretation of its title the Greeks repreſented as a ſtream of liquid fire, is Peleg-Eth-On, *the ocean of the ſolar Noah*; Lethè, and

[k] Οἱ μεν βασκανȣς φασι και γοητας (ſcil Τελχινας) θειῳ καταῤῥαινοντας το της Στυγος ὑδωρ, ζωων τε και φυτων ολεθρȣ χαριν. Strab. Geog. lib. XIV. p. 654.

[l] Cedren. Hiſt. Comp. p. 10 Upon the ſuppoſition of a comet's having been the natural cauſe of the deluge, I am almoſt led to conjecture, that the tradition of theſe balls of fire took its riſe from the too near approach of one of thoſe bodies in a ſtate of high ignition. Perhaps alſo the poetical account of the overthrow of Typhon, or the diluvian ocean, in the midſt of flames, thunder, and lightning, may have originated from the ſame circumſtance.

Cocy-

Cocytus, derive their refpective names from the oblivion of death, and from the loud lamentations of defpair, which were heard during the increafe of the waters; and Acheron is Ac-Aron, *the ocean of the Ark.* Hence Suidas very properly defcribes Acheron, as the great central abyfs, the refervoir of rivers and fountains [m]; and hence he is faid by fome to have been the fon of Ceres, or the Ark, and by others the offspring of Titan and the Earth [n]. The original *Palus Acherufia* was in Egypt [o]; and it feems to have received its appellation, like the Arcadian Styx, in memory of the deluge. For the fame reafon I apprehend we find fo many different lakes and rivers all equally bearing the name of *Acherufis* or *Acheron*. Thus, there was a lake *Acherufis* and a river *Acheron* in Epirus [p]; a river

[m] Αχερων, τοπος τις μεσος του παντος, εν ῳ αναμισις εστιν ὑδατων και καταποσις. I cannot believe with Mr Bryant, that the infernal river Acheron is nothing more than the fly-god Accaron, or Achor, whom Ahaziah confulted during his laft illnefs. The *river* Acheron, which both Plato and Suidas place in the centre of the earth, and the *Phenician god* Accaron, or Baal-Zebub, feem to me to be two entirely diftinct and different characters. For Mr. Bryant's remarks on this fubject, fee his *Obfervations on the Plagues of Egypt*, p. 72.

[n] Clafenii Theol. Gent p 243.—Ban. Mythol. book iv. chap. vii

[o] Diod. Sic. Bibl lib i p 86.

[p] Plin Nat. Hift. lib. iv. cap. 1.

Ache-

Acheron in Italy [q]; and a ſuppoſed place of deſcent into hell denominated *Acheruſia*, at Tenarus in Laconia [r]. There was an *Acheron* moreover in the land of the Mariandyni, and another ſuppoſed place of deſcent into the infernal regions.

> Γην Μαριανδυνων επικελσετε νεϛησαντες·
> Ενθα μεν εις ᾽Αἰδαο καταιβατις εϛι κελευθος·
> Ακτη τε προβλης Αχερȣσιας ὑψοθι τεινει·
> Δινηεις τ᾽ Αχερων αυτην δια νειοθι τεμνων
> Ακρης εκ μεγαλης προχοας ἱησι φαραγγας [s].

Andron mentions an ancient king of that country named *Acheron*, whoſe daughter Dardanis was feigned to be the concubine of the arkite Hercules [t]. Dardanis is Dar-Da-Nah, *the illuſtrious Noëtic Ark*; and is a word of the ſame origin as Dardanus, whoſe hiſtory ſhall be conſidered hereafter.

I ſhall next proceed to analyſe the mythological character of Charon [u]. The waters

[q] Liv. Hiſt lib. viii. cap. 24.

[r] Tzet. in Lycoph. ver. 90.

[s] Apoll. Argon lib. ii. ver. 352.

[t] Schol in ibid. ver 354.

[u] Bp. Warburton obſerves, that Charon "was a ſubſtantial "Egyptian, fairly exiſting in this world" This may be perfectly true without invalidating the preſent hypotheſis; for as the Myſteries were a ſcenical repreſentation of the events of the

 deluge,

of Styx, or hatred, as we have ſeen, are the waters of the deluge; hence, as we learn from Virgil, the golden branch, ſacred to the infernal Juno, grew upon its banks.

——Latet arbore opaca
Aureus et foliis et lento vimine ramus,
Junoni infernæ dictus ſacer. [x]——

——In the neighbouring grove
There ſtands a tree; the queen of Stygian Jove
Claims it her own; thick woods, and gloomy night,
Conceal the happy plant from human ſight.
One bough it bears; but, wondrous to behold;
The ductile rind, and leaves, of radiant gold.
Dryden.

This branch, thus dedicated to Juno *the arkite dove*, and flouriſhing in the vicinity of the retiring deluge, is evidently the olive-branch, by means of which Noah learned, that the waters had abated [y]. Accordingly Eneas, the hero of the myſteries celebrated by Virgil, is led to it by the propitious doves of his ſuppoſed mother Venus, or the Ark.

deluge, ſo doubtleſs thoſe, who perſonated Oſiris, Iſis, Charon, and Typhon, were all living characters.

[x] Æneid. lib. vi. ver. 136.

[y] The olive has ever ſince been the emblem of peace and reconciliation.

Vix

Vix ea fatus erat, geminæ cum fortè columbæ
Ipſa ſub ora viri cœlo venere volantes,
Et viridi ſedere ſolo: tum maximus heros
Maternas agnoſcit aves——
Inde ubi venere ad fauces graveolentis Averni,
Tollunt ſe celeres, liquidumque per aera lapſæ,
Sedibus optatis gemina ſuper arbore ſidunt,
Diſcolor unde auri per ramos aura refulſit [z].

Scarce had he ſaid, when full before his ſight
Two doves, deſcending from their airy flight,
Secure upon the graſſy plain alight.
He knew his mother's birds———
————They led him on
To the ſlow lake; whoſe baleful ſtench to ſhun,
They wing'd their flight aloft; then ſtooping low,
Perch'd on the double tree, that bears the golden bough:
Through the green leaves the glittering ſhadows glow. *Dryden.*

The ſtern Charon, who had before refuſed to admit Enèas into his bark, immediately relents at the ſight of the branch, and wafts him over in ſafety to the oppoſite ſhore.

Si te nulla movet tantæ pietatis imago,
At ramum hunc (aperit ramum qui veſte latebat)
Agnoſcas. Tumida ex ira tum corda reſidunt:

[z] Æneid. lib. vi. ver. 190.

 Nec

Nec plura his. Ille admirans venerabile donum
Fatalis virgæ, longo poſt tempore viſum,
Cæruleam advertit puppim, ripæque propinquat [a].

If neither piety, nor heaven's command,
Can gain his paſſage to the Stygian ſtrand,
This fatal preſent ſhall prevail at leaſt,
Then ſhew'd the ſhining bough conceal'd within her veſt.
No more was needful: for the gloomy god
Stood mute with awe, to ſee the golden rod:
Admir'd the deſtin'd offering to his queen;
(A venerable gift ſo rarely ſeen;)
His fury thus appeas'd, he puts to land.

Dryden.

If Styx then be the deluge, the god, who floats upon its ſurface in a ſhip, muſt neceſſarily be the great patriarch; and the crowd of ghoſts, that throng the banks, vainly ſoliciting admiſſion into his veſſel, muſt conſiſt of thoſe, who miſerably periſhed beneath the waves of the flood. Hence we find, that the ſum of money, which Charon extorted from his paſſengers, was, from Da-Nach, or Noah, denominated *Danacè* [b]. As the ſituation of the

[a] Æneid. lib. vi. ver. 405.

[b] Αχερουσια εστι λιμνη εν Αἰδου, ἡν διαπορθμευονται οἱ τελευτωντες, το νομισμα, ὁπερ Δανακη καλειται, τῳ πορθμει διδοντες. Suid.

the Stygian ferryman ſhews him to be the ſecond progenitor of mankind, ſo his name *Car-On* points him out to be that progenitor worſhipped in conjunction with the Sun[c].

Enèas, having croſſed the Stygian lake, forthwith encounters the three-headed dog Cerberus[d], who is ſaid to have been dragged

[c] Antigonus Caryſtius mentions, that thoſe deep natural orifices, which probably are openings into the central abyſs, were called *Charonia*. Και πολλαχȣ δε εοικεν, το, τε των βαραθρων καλȣμενων, και Χαρωνιων ειναι γενος. Ant. Car. Hiſt. Mirab. cap. 135. It is ſomewhat remarkable, that, in the dialect of Macedon, *Charon* ſignified *a lion*. Χαρων, ὁ λεων κατα Μακεδονας. Tzet in Lycoph. ver. 455. This aroſe, I conjecture, from the circumſtance of a lion being a ſymbol of the Sun.

[d] I perfectly agree with Bp. Warburton, that the introduction of the dog Cerberus into the Myſteries is alluded to by Pletho, when he ſpeaks of κυνωδη τινα φασματα, *certain canine phantoms*, riſing from the bowels of the earth, and exhibiting themſelves to the initiated. Theſe infernal dogs are declared, in the Chaldèan oracles, to be not realities, but mere apparitions.

Εκ δ' αρα κολπων γαιης θρωσκȣσι κυνες χθονιοι,
Ουτ' αληθες σημα βροτω δεικνυντες. Orac. Chald. p. 90.

Hence we ſee, with how much propriety they are introduced by Apollonius into the noble deſcription, which he gives, of the appearance of Brimo or Hecatè to Jaſon.

——— ἡ δ' αιȣσα
Κευθμων εξ ὑπατων δεινη θεος αντεβολησεν
Ἱεροις Αισονιδαο, περιξ δε μιν εστεφανωντο
Σμερδαλεοι δρυινοισι μετα πτορθοισι δρακοντες.
Στραπτε δ' απειρεσιον δαιδων σελας· αμφι δε τηνγε
Οξειῃ ὑλακῃ χθονιοι κυνες εφθεγγοντο.

from his infernal den by Hercules, and whoſe tail was an immenſe ſnake, while his back was covered with the heads of ſerpents [e]. Here we behold the principal ſolar emblem, united with the form of a dog, a compound by no means unuſual. Thus the Egyptian Anubis who was the ſame as Cronus [f] or Noah, was depicted with the head of a dog, and with the caduceus, round which two ſnakes were intwined, in his hand [g]. In a ſimilar manner, Diana or Hecatè, the lunar Ark, is deſcribed by the author of the Orphic

Πεισε δ' ετρεμε παντα κατα ςιβον· αἱ δ' ολολυξαν
Νυμφαι ἑλειονομοι ποταμηΐδες αἱ περι κεινην
Φασιδος εἱαμενην Αμαραντιυ εἱλισσονται.
Αισονιδην δ' ητοι μεν ἑλεν δεος.——

Argon. lib. iii. ver. 1211.

It is a curious circumſtance, that a dog was no leſs a tenant of the Gothic, than of the Grecian Hades. See Gray's Deſcent of Odin.

[e] Δωδεκατον αθλον επεταγη, Κερβερον εξ Αἱδυ κομιζειν. Ειχε δε ὗτος τρεις μεν κυνων κεφαλας, την δε ὑραν δρακοντος, κατα δε τυ νωτου παντοιων ειχεν οφεων κεφαλας. Apollod. Bibl. lib. ii. cap. 5.

[f] Ενιοις δοκει Κρονος ὁ Ανυβις ειναι· διο παντα τικτων εξ ἑαυτυ, και κυων εν ἑαυτῳ, την τυ κυνος επικλησιν εσχεν. Plut. de Iſid. p. 368.

[g] There is a print of this deity in *Montfaucon's Antiquity explained*, vol. ii. part ii. p. 197. in which he is repreſented with the head of a dog, and holding the caduceus, round which two ſnakes are twiſted, in his hand. Beneath his feet is a crocodile, under his arm a globe, and by his ſide the head of an ox bearing the Egyptian modius.

Argo-

Argonautics, as having the heads of a dog, a horse, and a lion.

Τρισσοκεφαλος ιδειν, ολοον τερας, ϛτι δαητον
Ταρτεροπαις Εκατη· λαιϛ δ' αρ' επεσσυθεν ωμϛ
Ἱππος χαιτηεις· κατα δεξια δ' ηεν αθρησαι
Λυσσωπις σκυλακη· μεσση δ' εφυ αγριομορφος[h].

As for Cerberus, he is often represented upon medals at the feet of the Egyptian Serapis[i], who was esteemed the same as Osiris[k], Pluto[l], and the Sun[m]. Hence, in allusion to the solar worship, that deity was depicted with a serpent twisted round his body[n]; while, in reference to the arkite superstition, he was not unfrequently represented also with the head of a bull[o], and described as sailing

[h] Orph Argon. ver. 973.

[i] Mont. Ant vol. ii. part ii. p. 189.

[k] Ibid. p. 186.

[l] Plut de Isid. p 361, 362.

[m] Eidem Ægypto adjacens civitas, quæ conditorem Alexandrum Macedonem gloriatur, Sarapin atque Isin cultu pœne attonitæ venerationis observat: omnem tamen illam venerationem Soli se sub illius nomine testatur impendere, vel dum calathum capiti ejus infigunt, vel dum simulacro signum tricipitis animantis adjungunt; quod exprimit medio eodemque maximo capite leonis effigiem; dextera parte caput canis exoritur mansueta specie blandientis; pars vero læva cervicis rapacis lupi capite finitur; easque formas animalium draco connectit volumine suo capite redeunte ad dei dexteram, qua compescitur monstrum. Macrob. Saturn. lib. i. cap. 20.

[n] Mont. Ant Supplem. p. 211.

[o] Ægyptios certè Osiridem seu Solem bovino capite. Kirch. China

in a boat, along with Isis, and some other goddess, who holds in her right hand a cornucopia, and in her left a rudder [p]. He was sometimes joined with Isis, Apollo, and Cerberus; and sometimes with Isis, and Minerva, while Cerberus reclines at his feet [q]. All these, as I have repeatedly observed, are helio-arkite deities; and even Cerberus himself is a mere hieroglyphic of the Sun, from which circumstance indeed his name *Cerberus* or Cer-Abor-As, *the illustrious solar orb*, is apparently derived. Nor let this interpretation be deemed fanciful: Porphyry, who was deeply versed in the mythology of the pagans, makes the very same assertion. "Cerberus," says he, "is described with three heads, in "reference to the rising, the meridian alti-"tude, and the setting of the Sun [r]."

China Illust. p 143. Montfaucon has given us two very curious delineations of the union of the bull, the lion, and the serpent. The first, which I have already noticed as an hieroglyphic of the solar Noah, consists of a bull's head joined to the body of a serpent, the second, which has the same relation to the solar deity, consists of a lion's head surrounded with rays of glory, and connected, like the former, with the symbolical serpent Mont Ant vol ii part ii p 204.

[p] Mont. Ant. Suppl p 215.

[q] Ibid.

[r] Ὁ δε Κερβερος τρικεφαλος, ὁτι τρεις αἱ ανω χωραι Ἡλιου, ανατολη, μεσημβρια, δυσις. Porph apud Euseb. Præp. Evan. lib. iii. p. 113. See also Macrob. Saturn. lib. i. cap. 20. It is remark-

As the office of Charon was to convey the ſouls of the deceaſed over the Stygian pool, ſo that of Mercury was to conduct them from the ſupernal to the infernal world. This deity, like moſt of the principal gods of the heathens, is the ſolar Noah; whence he was intitled *M'Erech-Ur*, or *the great burning divinity of the Ark*. He was the ſame as Arcas, Boötes, Butes, Buddha, Budſdo, Fohi, Odin, Wudd, Hermes[s], and Taut; and we ſhall invariably find his hiſtory connected with ſome tradition of the deluge.

I have obſerved, that the ſphere is replete with conſtellations alluſive to this event, one

markable, that Cerberus was ſometimes, like Pluto, denominated *Orcus*. Illatrat jejunis faucibus Orcus. Sil. Ital. lib xiii. ver 845.

[s] *Hermes* ſeems to be a corruption of *Hermon*, or Ar-Mon, *the deity of the lunari-arkite mountain* From the ſame compound radical ſprings *Armenia*, the country where the Ark landed, which is called by Jeremiah *Minni*, and by the Chaldee Paraphraſt *Ar-Minni*, (Jerem. li 27.) Harmonia, the ſuppoſed wife of Cadmus, is another word of ſimilar ſignification, and Cadmus himſelf is declared by Tzetzes to be no other than Hermes or Mercury. (Tzet. in Lycoph ver. 219.) Cadmus was worſhipped by the Phenicians ſometimes under the title of Cadm-On, *the oriental Sun*, and ſometimes under that of Baal-Hermon, *the lord of the lunari-arkite mountain* Hence the author of *the Book of Judges* mentions a hill ſacred to Baal-Hermon, in the country of the Hivites or Ophites, near mount Lebanon, which in a ſimilar manner derived its appellation from Lebanah (לבנה), *the arkite creſcent*. Judg. iii. 3.

of

of the moſt remarkable of which is that of Arctos, or the great bear. Lycaon, whoſe wickedneſs was fabled to have haſtened the deſtruction of the old world, was the father of Calliſto. Her charms engaged the affections of Jupiter, and ſhe became by him the mother of Arcas; but his jealous conſort, having diſcovered the amour, changed her into a bear, in which ſhape ſhe was placed by her immortal lover in the ſphere. Juno however yet remained implacable, and prevailed upon her nurſe Tethys, the wife of Oceanus, to withhold from the new cataſteriſm the privilege of ſetting beneath the waters of the ſea [t]. Cloſe to this conſtellation is that of Boötes or Arctophylax, who is deſcribed as the guardian of the bear [u], and who was generally ſuppoſed to be Arcas, the ſon of Calliſto [x].

[t] Hyg Fab 176, 177.

[u] Hyg. Poet. Aſtron. lib iii. cap 2, 3.

[x] Hyg. Poet. Aſtron. lib. ii. cap. 1. Nonnus however aſſerts, that Bootes was Icarius

Ικαριον δε γεροντα συνηλυδα γειτονι κερη
Εις πολον αϛεροφοιτον αγων ονομηνε Βοωτην.

Dionyſ. lib. xlvii. p. 802.

and yet, in another paſſage, he makes Arcas to be the conſtellation Bootes:

——— Αρκαδιην πολιν Αρκαδος' ὁν ποτε μητηρ
Καλλιϛω Δii τικτε' πατηρ δε μιν εις πολον αϛρων

Στηριξας

This ſtory is founded upon the ſame perverſion of the word *Arctos* as the preceding fable of Polyphontè. Calliſto, the Arcadian princeſs, is a perſonification of the Ark: hence ſhe is called *Cal-Eſto*, or *the Ark of the ſolar Noah*; and hence ſhe is feigned to have been metamorphoſed by the dove Juno into *Arctos*, which the Greeks rendered a *bear*. The circumſtance of the Ark floating upon the ſurface of the waters, and never ſinking beneath them, is aſtronomically deſcribed under the allegory of Tethys refuſing to ſuffer the bear to ſet in the Ocean; while her ſon Boötes, or Arcas, is the principal deity of the Ark ſymbolized by a bull [y].

Στηριξας εκαλεσσε χαλαζηεντα Βοωτην.

Dionyſ. lib. xiii. p. 240.

This difference is more apparent than real, for, as Arcas is Arc-As, *the ſolar god of the Ark*, ſo Icarius is only a variation of Car, *the Sun*, from which radical it is formed in the ſame manner as Inachus is from Nach.

[y] Boötes is the ſame mythological character as Beotus, or Boiotus, who was ſuppoſed to have given his name to Beotia, and who is ſaid by Hyginus to be the ſon of the diluvian Neptune Hyg Fab 157, 186. The word *Boötes*, whether pronounced *Beotus*, *Butes*, *Buddha*, *Budo*, *Buto*, or *Budſdo*, is compounded of Bu-Deo, or Bu-Deva, *the god of the arkite heifer*. From the ſame root *Bu*, Hercules was called *Buzuges*. Βουζυγης, ὁ Ἡρακλης. Suid. He was likewiſe entitled *Buphagus*, and was reported to have been diſmiſſed by the Argonauts from their crew on account of his voracity. Ban. Mythol vol iv. p 120. Buzuges is Bu-Z'Og, *the great arkite diluvian*; and Bu-

Arcas then, being the grandſon of the antediluvian Lycaon, and the ſon of Calliſto or the Ark, muſt neceſſarily be the patriarch Noah, by whoſe inſtrumentality the ancients ſuppoſed the arts and ſciences of the old world to have been introduced into the new. Hence Arcas is repreſented as having learned the art of weaving from Adriſta, or Adar-Eſta, *the illuſtrious Veſta*, and that of making bread from Triptolemus the favourite of Ceres, who is ſaid by Apollodorus, in alluſion to the worſhip of the Sun, to have rode in a chariot drawn by winged dragons[z].

The wife of Arcas was the Naiad Erato, by whom, like Noah, he had three children, Azan, Aphidas, and Elatus, among whom, at his death, he divided his dominions[a]. The

Buphagus, upon which term the Greeks founded the preceding ridiculous ſtory, is Bu-Ph'Ag, *the arkite diluvian*

[z] Apollod Bibl. lib. i. cap. 5.

[a] Μετα δε Νυκτιμον αποθανοντα Αρκας εξεδεξατο ὁ Καλλιϛους την αρχην. Και τον τε ἡμερον καρπον εσηγαγετο ὑτος παρα Τριπτολεμου, και την ποιησιν εδιδαξε τυ αρτυ, και εσθητα ὑφαινεσθαι, και αλλα τα ες ταλασιαν, μαθων παρ᾽ Αδριϛα. Απο τυτυ δε βασιλευσαντος Αρκαδια τε αντι Πελασγιας ἡ χωρα, και αντι Πελασγων Αρκαδες εκληθησαν οἱ ανθρωποι. Συνοικησαι δε υ θνητη γυναικι αυτον, αλλα νυμφη Δρυαδι ελεγον. Δρυαδας γαρ δη και Επιμηλιαδας τας ἑαυτων εκαλυν Ναιδας —Την δε νυμφην ταυτην καλυσιν Ερατω, και εκ ταυτης φασιν Αρκαδι Αζανα και Αφειδαντα γενεσθαι και Ελατον —Τοις δε παισιν ὡς ηυξηθησαν διενειμεν Αρκας τριχη την χωραν Pauſ Arcad p. 604.

names

names of these sons all relate to the solar worship: Azan is As-Ain, *the fountain of fire*; Aphidas is Aph-Ad-As, *the one fire God*[b]; and Elatus is El-Ait, *the burning deity*. Arcas himself was reported to have been buried near the altar of Juno, the dove, at Mantinèa[c].

Boötes, or Butes, seems to be the same as the *Buddha* of Hindostan. Buddha was the ninth incarnation of Vishnou, who had previously appeared in the form of a man, issuing from the mouth of a fish; and he is represented as a mild and beneficent prince, averse from bloodshed and violence. He is also said to have espoused Ila, whose father had been preserved in an ark from the waters of an universal deluge[d]. Ila is evidently the mythological daughter of Ilus, the name assigned by Sanchoniatho to Cronus. The Hindoo tradition indeed appears, at the first point of view, to make Buddha the son of Noah, rather than Noah himself; but this I apprehend is not really the case. I have already observed, that most of the pagan goddesses are

[b] An inscription upon a gem of Serapis is mentioned by Montfaucon, (Ant. vol ii. p. 188) which nearly resembles this. Εἰς Ζευς Σαραπις, *One Jupiter Sarapis*.

[c] Προς δε της Ἡρας τῳ βωμῳ και Αρκαδος ταφος τυ Καλλιϛυ: ε-ι. Pauf. Arcad p. 616.

[d] Asiat. Research. vol. ii. p. 376.

per-

perſonifications either of the Earth emerging from the waves of the flood, of the Ark, of the Dove, or of the divine preſerving Wiſdom. Agreeably to this notion, Ila was ſuppoſed to be the daughter of Cronus, becauſe the Ark was built by Noah; and Buddha was the reputed huſband of Ila, on account of his connection with the Ark [e].

The ſame deity was worſhipped in Japan under the name of *Budſdo*, or, as the word was pronounced with ſome variation of the breathing, *Fotokè* [f]. "I have ſtrong reaſons "to believe," ſays Kæmpfer, "both from the "affinity of the name, and the very nature of "this religion, that its author and founder is "the very ſame perſon, whom the Brachmins "call *Buddha*, and believe to be an eſſential "part of Wiſthnou, or their deity, who made "his ninth appearance in the world, under "the name, and in the ſhape of this man [g]."

Buddha is alſo the *Fohi* of the Chineſe [h].

[e] The Ark, as I have ſtated in *the preliminary obſervations*, was indifferently reckoned the wife, the mother, or the daughter of the great patriarch.

[f] Kæmpfer's Japan, book iii. chap. vi. p. 241.

[g] Ibid.

[h] "The *Buddha* of the Hindus is unqueſtionably the *Foe* of "China; but the great progenitor of the Chineſe is alſo named "by them *Fo-hi*, where the ſecond monoſyllable ſignifies, it "ſeems, *a victim*." Sir Wm. Jones's Diſcourſe on the Chineſe;

This prince was their firſt emperor, and he is ſaid never to have had any father; but as his mother was walking on the bank of a lake, ſhe was ſuddenly encompaſſed by a rainbow, and having conceived in conſequence of it, ſhe brought forth Fohi [i]. The Chineſe moreover relate, that Fohi bred ſeven different kinds of animals for the purpoſe of ſacrifice [k]; and that he was born in the province of Xenſi, or Shenſi, which, excepting Sifan, is the moſt weſterly, and conſequently the neareſt to mount Ararat, of all the diſtricts of China [l]. In this fable, the mother of Fohi, ſurrounded as ſhe was by the rainbow, is evidently an allegorical parent, and ſignifies nothing more than the Ark; and the ſeven claſſes of pure animals forcibly remind us of the clean beaſts and birds, which Noah was directed to take into the Ark along with him by ſevens [m].

neſe; Aſiat. Reſ. vol. ii. p. 375. Perhaps the epithet *victim*, joined with the name *Fo*, may allude to the Noetic ſacrifice immediately after the deluge.

[i] Mart Hiſt Sin. lib i p 21.

[k] Le Compte's Mem. of China, p. 313.

[l] Mart. Hiſt. Sin. lib. i. p. 21.

[m] Couplet mentions, that Fohi had the body of a ſerpent, and his ſon Shin Nungh the head of an ox; on which account he eſteems them fabulous perſonages, and omits them in his catalogue of the Chineſe kings. Coup. Præf. ad Tab. Chron. p. 3.

It is more than probable, that Odin or Woden, the great God of the northern nations, was another variation of Buddha[n]. The Goths certainly followed their predeceſſors the Celts from thoſe parts of Aſia, which border upon Perſia and Hindoſtan[o]: hence Odin and his children are conſtantly ſtyled *Aſæ* or *Aſiatics*[p]. Our anceſtors ſpeak of a deluge in the days of the giant Ymer, who is deſcribed as a monſter of wickedneſs[q]; and affirm, that in it all the families of the giants periſhed, one only excepted, who eſcaped in his bark. At this era was produced a vaſt cow, and from

p. 3. The ſerpent however and the ox are merely the uſual emblems of the ſolar and arkite worſhip, and, as Fohi is Noah, ſo I apprehend his imaginary ſon to be the very ſame patriarch, Shin Nungh being Sen-Nuh, *Noah the Sun*.

n "The Scythian and Hyperborean doctrines and mythology may alſo be traced in every part of theſe eaſtern regions; nor can we doubt, that Wod or Odin, whoſe religion, as the northern hiſtorians admit, was introduced into Scandinavia by a foreign race, was the ſame with Buddh, whoſe rites were probably imported into India nearly at the ſame time, though received much later by the Chineſe, who ſoften his name into *Fo*." Sir Wm. Jones' third Anniv. Diſc. Aſiat. Reſ. vol. i. p. 425.

o Herodotus mentions a Scythian tribe, who were called *Budini*, moſt probably from their worſhip of Buddha or Odin. Herod. lib iv. cap. 108.

p Edda in Procem.

q Edda, Fab. 2, 4.

her

her was born Bure, the father of Bore, who begot three ſons, Odin, Vile[r], and Ve[s].

The cow of the Gothic mythology is plainly the ſacred heifer of Egypt, the conſtant emblem of the Ark; and the allegorical children aſſigned to her are Noah and his triple offſpring. The ſcriptural hiſtory is indeed corrupted in this tradition, much in the ſame manner as it is in the fable of Saturn and his three ſons; and Odin, like Pluto, is made the ſon of Noah, inſtead of being repreſented as the patriarch himſelf: but the cauſe, which has been already aſſigned for the one perverſion, will equally ſerve to point out the origin of the other[t].

The wife of Odin is ſaid to have been Frea, or Venus. Frea is evidently the ſame as the *Rhea*, or *Cybelè*, of Phrygia. She ſeems alſo to be the ſame as another Gothic goddeſs denominated *Freya*; who was deſcribed as the daughter of Niord, the ruler of the winds and waves, who dwelt in a place called *Noatun*. Freya married Oder, and by him became the mother of Noſſa. Oder however left her, and travelled into remote countries; ſince which

[r] Vile, or Vilus, is probably a mere variation of Ilus, and both Bure and Bore ſeem to ſpring from the radical Bu, *an ox*.

[s] Edda, Fab. 3.

[t] Vide ſupra p 15.

 time

time Freya has wandered over the whole world in queſt of him. Hence ſhe had a great variety of names, each people, among whom ſhe came, giving her a different one [w].

The whole of this fable appears to me preciſely the ſame as that of Ceres and Iſis. Freya, the daughter of the Gothic Neptune, is no other than the Ark; and, accordingly, ſhe is ſaid to have been born at Noatun, or *the city of Noah* [x]. Her mythological huſband Oder is the Egyptian Oſir, or Oſiris; and the wanderings of Freya, in queſt of the former of theſe deities, are equivalent to thoſe of Iſis, in queſt of the latter. Hence *the many-named Freya* is *the Iſis myrionymos* [y]; while her daughter *Noſſa* ſeems to be the ſame as *Nuſa*, or the Ark, the ſuppoſed nurſe of Bacchus.

As the claſſical Mercury was at once the reputed inventor of letters, and one of the Cabiric or infernal deities; ſo we find the diſcovery of the Runic characters aſcribed to

[w] Edda, Fab. 12, 13, 18.

[x] *Tun* is the old Saxon mode of writing *Town*; thus the modern name of *Townley* was anciently ſpelt *Tunlay*. Whitaker's Hiſt. of Whalley, p. 321.

[y] It is obſervable, that one of the names of Freya was *Syra, the Syrian Goddeſs*. Edda, Fab. 18. Lat. Verſ. Snor. Sturl.

Odin,

Odin [z], and his deſcent into hell celebrated with all the wild ſolemnity of the northern muſe.

Uproſe the king of men with ſpeed,
And ſaddled ſtraight his coal black ſteed;
Down the yawning ſteep he rode,
Which leads to Hela's drear abode.
Him the dog of darkneſs ſpied,
His ſhaggy throat he open'd wide,
While from his jaws, with carnage fill'd,
Foam and human gore diſtill'd [a].

In alluſion to the ſolar devotion, Odin is ſaid to have been the father of Balder, or Bal-Ader, *the illuſtrious Baal*, whoſe eyes were ſo piercing, that they ſeemed to dart forth rays of light [b]. He is alſo deſcribed as the father of Thor, concerning whom a variety of wild fables are recited in the Edda, which render it extremely probable, that the ancient idolaters had preſerved ſome remembrance of the fall of man, the garden of Eden, and the promiſe that the ſeed of the woman ſhould bruiſe the head of the ſerpent. Theſe circumſtances however they ſeem almoſt invariably to have confounded with their tradi-

[z] Mallet's North. Ant. vol. 1. p. 371.
[a] Gray's Deſcent of Odin.
[b] Edda, Fab. 12.

tions of the deluge, and their superstitious veneration for the solar orb [c]. Hence I conceive that Thor, perverted as his history may be, was originally no other than the Tauric Noah.

That Odin, and Buddha, were likewise the *Mercury* of the Greeks and Romans, appears from the circumstance of the very same day of the week being uniformly designated by their several names. Thus the Gothic *Wednesday*, or *Wodin's day*, was called by the Latins *dies Mercurii*, and by the Hindoos *Bhood-War* [d]. Hence Tacitus, speaking of Odin the great god of the Goths, very justly styles him *Mercury* [e].

The genealogy of Mercury, like that of Minerva, is variously stated, which gave rise to the notion of there being four different Mercuries, though they are all in reality one and the same person. Sometimes he was esteemed the son of Jupiter and Maia, and sometimes of Bacchus and Proserpine; while at other times he was supposed to be the

[c] Some of these traditions I have noticed in a former publication: see Horæ Mosaicæ, vol. i. p. 73. et infra.

[d] Maurice's Hist. of Hind. vol. ii. p. 481.

[e] Deorum maximè Mercurium colunt. Tac. de Mor. Germ. cap. 9.

off-

offspring of Uranus and Hemera [f], of Cronus and Maia, of Jupiter and Cyllenè, or of Valens and Phoronis [g].

With regard to his hiſtory, he was, like Adonis, Bacchus, and Pluto, the lover of Proſerpine. He was moreover the grandſon of Atlas, the conductor of ghoſts into the infernal regions, and the ſlayer of Argus [g]. This Argus was an ancient king of Arcadia, who was fabled to have had his body entirely covered with eyes [h]. He is ſaid to have encountered a tremendous bull, and the ſerpent

[f] Ang. *the heaven* and *the day*.

[g] Corvilius quatuor Mercurios eſſe ſcribit; unum Jovis et Maiæ filium; alterum cœli et diei; tertium Liberi et Proſerpinæ; quartum Jovis et Cyllenes, a quo Argus occiſus eſt. Quem ipſum ob hanc cauſam Græci profugum dicunt, Ægyptiis autem literas demonſtraſſe. Ergo Liberi et Proſerpinæ filium dicunt animas evocare. Schol in Stat Theb. lib. iii. ver. 483. Alter Valentis et Phoronidis filius, is, qui ſub terris habetur, idem Trophonius. Cic. de Nat. Deor. lib. iii. cap. 22. Nonnulli quatuor Mercurios tradunt, unum cœli et diei filium, amatorem Proſerpinæ, alterum Liberi patris et Proſerpinæ filium; tertium Jovis et Maiæ; quartum Cyllenii filium, cujus mater non proditura arcu clam occiſa eſt Serv. in Æn lib iv. ver. 577. Theſe laſt words are corrupted, and ſhould moſt probably be read, cujus mater non proditur, a quo Argus clam occiſus eſt. Mercurii quatuor; primus cœli et diei filius, ſecundus Jovis et Croniæ filius, vel Proſerpinæ; tertius Croni filius et Maiæ, qui eſt inventor Lyræ. Quartus Quilleni filius Ampel cap 9.

[h] Eſchylus makes him a *gegenes*. Prom Vinct. ver. 678.

Echidna; and to have ſlain them both. He afterwards wore the hide of the bull as a trophy. He was likewiſe the guardian of Io or Iſis, who, as we have ſeen, was the daughter of Inachus, though Heſiod and Acuſilaus make Piren to be her father; and in that capacity he was killed by Mercury, who thence acquired the title of *Argiphontes*[i].

Mercury then, as we have juſt ſeen, was ſometimes ſuppoſed to be the ſon of Bacchus and Proſerpine. As ſuch he had the office beſtowed upon him of conducting the dead into Hades; or, in other words, of conſigning his impious contemporaries to a watery grave. Accordingly, while Mnaſeas aſſerts that the Cabiri were the infernal deities Pluto, Proſerpine, and Ceres, he adds Mercury to them as a fourth, under the name of *Caſmilus*[k]. In a ſimilar manner Tzetzes mentions, that *Cadmilus* was the Beotic title of Mercury[l]; and Macrobius informs us, that the Tuſcans worſhipped that deity under the cognate appellation of *Camillus*[m]. The ſame aſſertion is

[i] Apoll. Bibl. lib. ii. cap. 1.

[k] Schol. in Apoll. Argon. lib. i. ver. 917.

[l] Καδμιλος ὁ Ἑρμης Βοιωτικως. Schol. in Lycoph. ver. 162. This Cadmilus was the ſame perſon as the Phenician Cadmus. Ibid. ver. 219.

[m] Statius Tullianus de vocabulis rerum libro primo ait, dixiſſe

made by Servius; and he further obſerves, that the prieſts and prieſteſſes of the great gods were named from them *Camilli* and *Camillæ*, as the prieſts of the Cabiri were themſelves called *Cabiri*[n]. Thus likewiſe Dionyſius of Halicarnaſſus remarks, that, as, among the Tuſcans and Pelaſgi, thoſe, who were initiated into the myſteries of the Curetes and Dii Magni, were ſtyled *Cadoli*; ſo, among the Romans, they were denominated *Camilli*[o].

dixiſſe Callimachum Tuſcos *Camillum* appellare Mercurium; quo vocabulo ſignificant *præminiſtrum deorum*; unde Virgilius ait, Metabum *Camillam* appellaſſe filiam, Dianæ ſcilicet præminiſtram. Nam et Pacuvius, cum de Medea loqueretur, *Cœlitum Camilla exſpectata adveni, ſalve hoſpita.* Romani quoque pueros et puellas nobiles et inveſtes *Camillos* et *Camillas* appellant. Macrob. Saturn. lib. iii cap 8.

[n] Unde et *Camilla* dicta eſt, licet ſupra et a matre dixerit eſſe nominatam. Sed illud poetice dictum eſt. nam Camilla quaſi miniſtra dicta eſt: miniſtros enim et miniſtras impuberes *Camillos* et *Camillas* in ſacris vocabant. Hinc et Camilla dicta. Unde et Mercurius Hetruſca lingua *Camillus* dicitur, quaſi miniſter deorum. Serv. in Æneid. lib. xi. p 650.

[o] Ὁσα δε παρα Τυρρηνοις, και ετι προτερον παρα Πελασγοις ετελουν επι τε Κουρητων και Μεγαλων Θεων οργιασμοις οἱ καλουμενοι προς αυτων Καδωλοι, ταυτα κατα τον αυτον τροπον ὑπηρετουν τοις ἱερευσιν οἱ λεγομενοι παρα Ῥωμαιων Καμιλλοι. Dion. Halic. Ant. Rom. lib. ii. cap. 12.

Varro ſpeaks, as follows, of the word *Camillus:* Dicitur in nuptiis *Caſmillus*, qui Cummerum fert, in quo quid ſit in miniſterio plerique extrinſecus nectunt, hinc *Caſmillus* nominatur in

Mercury was ſometimes alſo eſteemed the ſon of Valens and Phoronis. This deſcent is virtually the ſame as the preceding one, for Valens, no leſs than Bacchus, is Bal-Ain, *Baal the fountain of light* [p], while Phoronis is Ph'Aron, *the Ark*.

He was alſo ſuppoſed to be the offspring of Jupiter and Cyllenè. Here likewiſe he, and his imaginary father, are equally the ſolar Noah; while Cyllenè, like Phoronis, is Cula-Nah, *the Noëtic Ark*.

With the ſame double alluſion to the two great ſuperſtitions, we ſometimes find him repreſented as the grandſon of Atlas, and the ſon of Cronus or Jupiter by Maia. Atlas, the allegorical aſtronomer, is At-El-As, *the ſolar god*; and Maia, who was feigned to be one of his ſeven daughters [q], borrowed her name from the ancient word Maia, *a mother* [r]. If we recur to the Brahminical theology, we

in Samothraces myſteriis Dius quidam adminiſter Diis Magnis. Varro de Lin. Lat. lib. vi. p. 72. It is remarkable, that the prieſt or Mercury of the Iriſh great gods was called *Cadmaol* or *Caſmaol*. See Vallancey's Vindication apud Collect. de Reb. Hib. vol. v. p. 494.

[p] It is almoſt ſuperfluous to mention the convertibility of the two letters *V* and *B*.

[q] Theſe ſeven daughters were the ſame as the ſeven Cabiræ or Titanides. Vide infra chap. vi.

[r] Μαια, πατρος και μητρος μητηρ. Heſych.

ſhall

ſhall learn, that the mother of Buddha, the Hindoo Mercury, was called *Maha-Maya.* She was feigned to be the wife of the rajah Sootah Dannah; but this rajah nevertheleſs was not the father of Buddha, who was eſteemed on the contrary to be an incarnation of the god Viſhnou [s]. Maha-Maya is literally *the great mother*; and ſhe was no doubt the ſame mythological character as Cybelè, or the Ark, the *magna mater* of claſſical antiquity. Her huſband Dannah I take to be the Grecian Danaus, or Da-Nau, and conſequently, like Buddha, the great diluvian patriarch: for Noah, as I have already intimated, is indifferently deſcribed, as the father, the ſon, or the huſband, of the veſſel which he conſtructed; the father, as having built the Ark, the ſon, as having iſſued from it, and the huſband, as being cloſely connected with it. As the allegorical parent of Mercury was denominated *Maia,* and that of Buddha *Maha-Maya,* ſo the mother of the Chineſe Fohi was called *Moye,* or *Maia* [t]; a circumſtance, which completely eſtabliſhes the identity of theſe different deities. Ratramnus mentions, that the Brahmins believed Buddha to have been born

[s] Maurice's Hiſt of Hind. vol ii. p 485.

[t] Aſiat. Ref. vol. ii. p. 125.

of

of a virgin[u]. This is merely the counterpart of the Chinese tradition, that Fohi was born without a father, and of the Greek legend, that a virgin was the mother of Perseus[x]. Perseus, like Buddha and Fohi, was the patriarch Noah; and the virgin, in all these several cases, was simply the Ark. Hence Buddha was supposed to have remained in his mother's womb ten months and ten days[y], which was the precise duration of Noah's confinement in the Ark, provided we calculate by the ancient year of ten months, instead of the more modern one of twelve[z]. This Hin-

[u] An certe Bragmanorum sequemur opinionem, ut, quemadmodum illi sectæ suæ auctorem Bubdam per virginis latus narrant exortum, ita nos Christum fuisse prædicemus? Ratramn. de Nat. Christi, cap. 3. For *Bubdam*, we ought undoubtedly to read *Buddam*.

[x] Just. Mart. Dial. cum Tryph. p. 297.

[y] Maur. Hist. of Hind. vol. ii. p. 485, 486.

[z] "In the six hundredth year of Noah's life, *in the second* "*month*, on *the seventeenth day* of the month,—in the self-same "day entered Noah—into the Ark." Gen. vii. 11, 13. "*In* "*the second month, on the seven and twentieth day of the month*— "Noah went forth with his sons." Gen. viii. 14, 18. I must not however suffer myself to be so far led away by the love of hypothesis, as to dissemble the assertion of Calmet, that the Jewish year *always* consisted of twelve months. Whether the Hindoo year was ever confined to ten, I am not sufficiently master of Sanscrit literature to be able to determine; if it were, it is evident that the preceding supposition will hold equally good, whatever number of months the Jewish year might contain.

doo deity is further ſaid to have been attacked by the Aſſoors, the *Titans* of the Brahminical theology, and in his diſtreſs to have invoked the aſſiſtance of the earth. She immediately attended to his ſummons, and poured forth ſuch an inundation, as compelled the Aſſoors to make a precipitate retreat [a]. It is obſervable, that, in the third Avatar, which is generally thought to relate to the deluge, theſe Aſſoors, whom I conjecture to be, like the Titans, the impious antediluvians, are introduced churning the waters of the troubled ſea with a huge mountain.

From the genealogy of Mercury, as connected with that of Buddha and Fohi, I ſhall proceed to conſider ſome particulars of his fabulous hiſtory. Whether the heifer Io, of whom Argus was ſuppoſed to be the guardian,

tain. The ancient Roman year certainly conſiſted of only ten months:

> Tempora digereret cum conditor urbis, in anno
> Conſtituit menſes quinque bis eſſe ſuo.
>
> Ovid. Faſt. lib. i. ver. 27.

and from the very great apparent reſemblance between the mythologies of Greece, Italy, and Hindoſtan, it is poſſible, that ſuch alſo might be the diviſion of the Hindoo year. See Sir Wm. Jones' Diſſert. on the Gods of Greece, Italy, and Hindoſtan; Aſiat. Reſ. vol. i.

[a] Maur. Hiſt. of Hind. vol. ii. p. 488.

[b] Ibid. vol. i. p. 581.

be

be esteemed the daughter of Inachus, or of Piren, she will still be equally a personification of the Ark; for Inachus is Noah, and Piren or Pirenus is P'Aron-Nus, *the arkite Noah*. In a similar manner her keeper Argus also, who was feigned to be a king of Arcadia, is *the god of the Ark*; and his combat with the bull and the serpent relates only to the violent union of the two religions, of which those animals were the constant symbols: but it does not appear, at the first glimpse, quite so evident, why he should be fabled to have been killed by Mercury; especially since Argus, Arcas, Mercury, and Boötes, were all one and the same mythological character. The whole of this tradition however is a mere perversion of a sacred title of the arkite deity. He was called Arga-Phont, *the priest of the Ark*, which the Greeks changed into Argiphontes, *the slayer of Argus*, and thence concluded, that Mercury had killed some prince of the name of *Argus*.

There is a story related by Antoninus Liberalis concerning a person denominated *Battus*, which induces me to think, that he exhibits to us another variation of the term *Boötes*, *Buto*, or *Buddha*. Argus, the son of Phrixus by Perimela daughter of Admetus, begot Magnes, who was the father of Hymenèus.

Apollo

Apollo was greatly attached to this youth; insomuch that he left the oxen, which he was feeding, in his pastoral capacity, that he might enjoy the pleasure of his society. Mercury thereupon, watching his opportunity, stole the cattle, and drove them away. In the course of his journey he met with Battus, and bribed him to secrecy. Wishing however to prove his fidelity, he returned in disguise; and offered him a reward, provided he would discover the thief, and point out the course which he had taken. Battus immediately assented; and Mercury, to punish his treachery, changed him into a stone[c].

This fable has originated partly from a perversion of the history of the two superstitions, and partly from a misconception of a well-known symbol of Mercury. Argus is *the god of the Ark:* and he is the same person as his supposed father Phrixus, or Ph'Erech-Zeus, *the arkite Jupiter*; his grandfather Admetus, or Ad-Am-Ait, *the solar deity*; his son Magnes, Manes, or Menes, *the great Noah*; and his grandson Hymenèus or Ham-On-Nus, *the burning Noëtic Sun*. Phrixus is said to have crossed the Hellespont upon a ram[d],

[c] Anton Liber. Metam. cap 22.

[d] Hyg. Fab. 3.

which

which was one of the ſymbols of the Ark: accordingly the ſcholiaſt upon Apollonius informs us, that this ram was merely a ſhip[e]. Its golden fleece afterwards occaſioned the Argonautic expedition, which has been moſt ably ſhewn by Mr. Bryant to relate to the Ark and the deluge, and which, in its proper place, I ſhall attempt to prove to be no leſs connected with the worſhip of the Sun. The mother of Phrixus, like the mother of the fabulous Centaur, was ſuppoſed, in alluſion to the allegorical birth of Noah amidſt rain and fogs, to be Nephelè or Nebula, *a cloud*[f], his father was Athamas; and his brother was

[e] Ενιοι δε φασιν αυτον επι κριοπρωρου σκαφους πλευσαι. Schol. in Argon. lib. i. ver. 256. It is not impoſſible, that the introduction of this particular ſymbol into the mythology of the Greeks might have been occaſioned by the following coincidence. They had heard of the principal arkite deity being ſaved in an Aran, or *ark*; and hence they feigned, that Phrixus eſcaped on the back of a lamb, in the Greek *Arnos*. It is almoſt ſuperfluous to obſerve, that from the Greek Αρς, *a lamb*, the Latin Aries, *a ram*, is evidently derived. The Arcadian tradition reſpecting the fountain of Arnè may be accounted for in a ſimilar manner. When Rhea, the great arkite mother of the gods, had brought forth Neptune, ſhe is ſaid to have placed him in the midſt of a flock of lambs, which were feeding near a fountain; and from that circumſtance the fountain acquired the name of *Arnè*. Pauſ. Arcad. p. 613. This fable, like moſt of the other fables of Arcadia, aroſe merely from the connection of Rhea and Neptune with Aran, *the Ark*.

[f] Hyg. Fab. 3.

Orcho-

Orchomenus or Orca-Menu, *the arkite Noah*[g]. This Phrixus was commiſſioned by Athamus to put to death Ino, and her ſon Melicerta or Hercules, whoſe hiſtory has been noticed above; but Bacchus ſurrounded him with a thick miſt, and delivered his nurſe Ino from the danger[h]. The four ſons of Phrixus were Argus, Phrontis, Melas, and Cylindrus or Cutorus; the whole however of his genealogy, as the reader will have already perceived, is a mere ſeries of repetitions[i]. Phrontis is Ph' Aron-Dus, *the god of the Ark*; Melas is M' El-As, *the great god of fire*; Cylindrus is Cula-Nah-Ador, *the illuſtrious arkite Noah*; and Cutorus is compounded of the name of the patriarch *Cuſh* or *Cuth*, and Or, *light:* while Apollo, or the Sun, who is introduced into the preceding fable as tending the oxen of Admetus, is the ſolar Noah united with the ſymbolical arkite heifer.

The only part of the legendary hiſtory of Battus, which now remains to be accounted for, is that which repreſents him to have been

[g] Hyg. Fab 1.

[h] Ibid Fab. 2.

[i] Filii ejus (Phrixi) Argus, Phrontis, Melas, Cylindrus. Hyg. Fab. 3. Εγενοντο δε εκ Χαλκιοπης της Αιητου τεσσαρες Φριξω παιδες, Αργος, Μελας, Φροντις, Κυτωρος. Apollod. Bibl. lib. i. cap. 9.

metamorphoſed into a ſtone; a tradition, which ſeems to have originated from the circumſtance of the god Mercury being uſually worſhipped under that form. Pauſanias notices ſeveral different inſtances of this peculiar ſuperſtition. On the gateway of Ithomè, which led to Arcadia, was fixed a ſquare ſtone ſtatue of Mercury, of Attic workmanſhip [k]; and in the gymnaſium of Ptolemy at Athens were placed a number of ſimilar ſtones. The Athenians called them *Hermæ*, and pretended to have been the firſt inventors of this mode of imagery [l]. The *Hermæ* were uſed as landmarks, and accordingly we find them erected at the territorial boundaries of the Lacedemonians, the Argives, and the Tegeatæ [m]. Mercury however was not the only deity repre-

[k] Ιοντι δε απ᾽ Αρκαδιας ες Μεγαλην πολιν, εϛιν εν ταις πυλαις Ἑρμης, τεχνη της Αττικης. Αθηναιων γαρ το σχημα το τετραγωνον εϛιν επι ταις Ἑρμαις, και παρα τουτων μεμαθηκασιν οἱ αλλοι. Pauſ. Meſſen. p. 361.

[l] Εν δε τῳ γυμνασιῳ της αγορας απεχοντι ου πολυ, Πτολεμαιου δε απο του κατεσκευασμενου καλουμενῳ, λιθοι τε εισιν Ἑρμαι, θεας αξιοι. Pauſ. Att. p. 39. Πρωτοι μεν γαρ Αθηναν επωνομασαν Εργανην, πρωτοι δ᾽ ακωλους Ἑρμας. Ibid. p. 56.

[m] Ανατεινει δε ὑπερ τας κωμας ορος, παρ᾽ ὁ και Λακεδαιμονιων επ᾽ αυτου προς Αργειους ὁροι, και Τεγεατας εισιν· ἑϛηκασι δε επι τοις ὁροις Ἑρμαι λιθου, και του χωριου το ονομα· εϛι δε απ᾽ αυτων ποταμος καλουμενος Τανος· εἱς γαρ δη ὑτος εκ του Παρνωνος κατεισι ῥεων δια της Αργειας. Pauſ. Corin. p. 202. The Parnon here mentioned was ſo called from P'Arn-On, *the ſolar god of the Ark*.

ſented

ſented in this manner; Apollo, being in fact the ſame mythological character, was ſometimes alſo worſhipped under the ſame ſymbol of a ſquare ſtone, as were likewiſe Minerva, Neptune, and Hercules; a remarkable inſtance of which occurs in the temple of the great goddeſſes, or Cabiræ, at Megalopolis in Arcadia [n]. A large black ſtone was alſo the emblem of the Hindoo Buddha [o], and a ſquare ſtone of the Arabian Manah, or Venus [p]; for, conſidered as the Ark, Venus was of courſe connected with Buddha or Noah, whoſe rites were not unknown to the Arabs, and who by them was denominated

[n] Εςι δε εντος τȣ περιϐολȣ των μεγαλων θεων και Αφροδιτης ἱερον· προ μεν δη της εξοδȣ, ξοανα εςιν αρχαια, Ἡρα και Απολλων τε και Μȣσαι—την δε επικλησιν τῃ θεῳ (ſcil. Αφροδιτῃ) Μηχανιτιν εθεντο— Ἑςηκασι δε και ανδριαντες εν οικηματι, Καλλιγνωτȣ τε και Μεντα, και Σωσιγενȣς τε και Πωλȣ. Καταςησασθαι δε ȣτοι Μεγαλοπολιταις λεγονται πρωτον των μεγαλων θεων την τελετην, και τα δρωμενα των εν Ελευσινι εςι μιμηματα. Κειται δε εντος τȣ περιϐολȣ θεων τοσαδε αγαλματα αλλων, το τετραγωνον παρεχομενα σχημα, Ἑρμης τε επικλησιν Αγητωρ, και Απολλων, και Αθηνα τε και Ποσειδων· ετι δε Ἡλιος επωνυμιαν εχων σωτηρ δε ειναι, και Ἡρακλης. Ωκοδομηται δε και σφισιν ἱερον μεγεθει μεγα, και αγȣσιν ενταυθα την τελετην ταις θεαις. Pauſ. Arcad. p. 665 In this ſtriking aſſemblage of Cabiri or arkite Gods, we have Venus the Mechanic, in alluſion to the building of the Ark, Juno, the dove; Mercury, ſurnamed Agetor, or Ag-Ait-Or, *the fiery god of the ocean*, Apollo, Minerva, Neptune, the Sun, Hercules, Ceres, and Proſerpine

[o] Maur. Hiſt. of Hind. vol ii p. 481.

[p] Seld. de Dis Syr. Proleg cap. iii. p. 52.—Sale's Preſim. Diſc. to Koran, ſect. i. p. 17

Wudd or *Wodin*[q]. Manah is Menah, *the Noëtic Ark*[r]; and the ſtone, by which ſhe was ſymbolized, was at length demoliſhed by Saad in the eighth year of the Hejira[s]. In a ſimilar manner Theus-Ares, or Dus-Ares, the Arabic Bacchus, was worſhipped under the ſame form of a ſquare ſtone[t]; and, if we direct our attention to the North, we ſhall find, that a cube was no leſs the emblem of the Gothic Odin[u]. The whole of this peculiar ſymbolical adoration moſt probably took its riſe from the Betulia, or ſtone pillars, mentioned by Sanchoniatho, the firſt of which, after the deluge, was the altar erected by Noah; and I am much inclined to ſuſpect, that the tra-

[q] "The adoration of ſtones, and the name of the idol *Wudd*, "may lead us indeed to ſuſpect, that ſome of the Hindoo ſu-"perſtitions had found their way into Arabia." Sir W. Jones on the Arabs; Aſiat. Reſ. vol. ii. p. 8.

[r] Hence the Arabs, before the time of Mahomet, very naturally invoked the arkite Monah, when they wiſhed to procure rain. Monah idolum venerabantur Arabes eo conſilio, ut pluvias opportunas impetrarent. Pocock. Specim. Hiſt. Arab. p. 92.

[s] Sale's Prelim. Diſc. to Koran, p. 18.

[t] Suid. Lex. vox Θευς-Αρης.

[u] "A cube was the ſymbol of Mercury." Borlaſe's Cornwall, p. 108. "Thorſtein upon his arrival entered into the "temple. In it was a ſtone, which he had been accuſtomed to "worſhip; he proſtrated himſelf before it, and prayed to it." Bartholin. lib. iii. cap. 11. apud Mallet.

dition

dition of Deucalion and Pyrrha throwing ſtones behind them, after their eſcape from the perils of the deluge, originated from the ſame ſource [x].

The laſt particular, which I ſhall mention reſpecting the claſſical Mercury, is one which completely proves his identity with Cronus, Sydyk, and Noah. He is celebrated by Nonnus, as the father of the ſeven Corybantes, or Cabiri, by the nymph Combè [y].

With regard to Taut, or Taautus, the Egyptian Mercury, he is uſually deſcribed, like his claſſical counterpart, as the inventor of letters; and, in alluſion perhaps to the triple offspring of Noah, he was adored under the title of *Triſmegiſtus*. Sanchoniatho, as I have already obſerved, erroneouſly repreſents him as the ſon of Miſor or Mizraim; but he is neverthelefs ſaid by that author to have exerciſed a ſort of authority over the Cabiri, commanding them to write thoſe memoirs, from which the Phenician mythologiſt profeſſes to have copied his narrative [z].

[x] It is poſſible however that this fable may have ariſen from another cauſe The legend of the converſion of the ſtones into men and women may have been founded upon a miſtake of the word Abenim, *ſtones*, for Benim, *children*.

[y] Nonni Dionyſ. lib xiii p. 233.

[z] This Taautus or Thoth was worſhipped by the Iriſh under

At the entrance into Hades, Virgil places the centaurs, the gorgons, and the harpies;

the name of *Tat* or *Tath*. Hence, as the firſt month of the Egyptians, which commenced on the calends of Auguſt, was called *Thoth* in honour of Taautus, ſo the firſt day of Auguſt was called by the Iriſh *la Tat*. (Vallancey apud Collect. de Reb. Hib. vol. iv. p. 469.) This Tat, Toth, or Tot, ſeems to be the ſame as Tit, or Titan, *the diluvian*; a name, by which the Sun was ſometimes called, in conſequence of his being worſhipped along with the great diluvian Noah. Accordingly in the Iriſh, Tath is *a lion*, becauſe a lion was ſymbolical of the Sun; Teith, *heat*; Tethin, *the Sun*; Taithneadh, *to thaw*, or *melt*; and Taith, *the course of the Sun*. Vallan. Ibid. p. 471. The Iriſh ſometimes ſtyled their god Tath, *Coll*; (Vallancey's Vindication apud Collect. de Reb. Hib. vol. v. p. 82.) by which they meant nothing more, than that he was a diluvian. (Vide infra chap. vii.) For the ſame reaſon Mercury was denominated by the Chaldèans *Culis*; (Plantavit. Heb. Lex. apud Vallancey ut ſupra;) and Hercules, by the old Spaniards, *Goles*. (De Laſtonoſa ibid. p. 291.)

It is almoſt ſuperfluous to obſerve at the cloſe of this lengthened analyſis of the hiſtory of Mercury, that I can in no wiſe adopt the opinion of the very learned Huetius, that this deity was Moſes, that the Myſteries of Samothrace were a corrupted tranſcript of the Levitical law, and that the Cabiric iſland Imbrus derived its name from Amram. That great man clearly ſaw the undoubted truth, that Mercury, Adonis, Thammuz, Oſiris, Bacchus, Apis, Serapis, Horus, Anubis, Vulcan, Zoroaſter, Pan, Eſculapius, Prometheus, Minos, Proteus, Perſeus, Ariſtèus, Muſèus, Orpheus, Linus, Amphion, Eumolpus, Janus, and the principal god of the Penates and Lares, were all one and the ſame perſon: but he unfortunately ſuppoſed that perſon to be the Jewiſh lawgiver, inſtead of Noah; while, in direct oppoſition to the unanimous voice of antiquity, he ſeparated Hercules from the preceding deities, and conjectured that he

and joins them with Scylla, Briareus, Geryon, the Chimera, and the Hydra of Lerna. Some of theſe fabulous monſters, ſuch as Meduſa, Scylla, the Chimera, and the Hydra, have already been conſidered as only various modifications of the ſolar and arkite emblems: the hundred-armed giant Briareus ſeems to be a perſonification of all the impious antediluvians, whoſe hiſtory is more particularly detailed in the legend of the Titans waging war againſt Jupiter: and Chiron, who was

he was Joſhua. This mode of interpretation, which has been adopted by other writers as well as Huetius, ſeems principally to have ariſen from the circumſtance of both Noah and Moſes having been incloſed within an ark; there appear to me however to be inſuperable objections to it. I can neither believe, that the lawgiver of a deſpiſed and deteſted nation ſhould have been erected into the great god of Egypt, nor can I comprehend how it is probable, not to ſay poſſible, that Moſes, or Mercury according to Huetius, ſhould have been venerated from China and Hindoſtan to Britain and Gaul, from Egypt and Phenicia to Greece, Germany, and Scandinavia. See Huet. Demon. Evan.

For ſomewhat ſimilar reaſons I can as little adopt the opinion of Bochart, that Mercury was Canaan. (Boch. Phal. lib. i. cap. 2) If ſuch be the caſe, Canaan will likewiſe be the ſame as Bacchus, Oſiris, and all the above-mentioned deities, for each of them is ſeverally the ſame as Mercury. in other words, Canaan will be the great god of the whole world from north to ſouth, and from eaſt to weſt, of that god, who is uſually deſcribed as having been incloſed within an ark The whole of this appears to me utterly incredible.

 feigned

feigned to have conſtructed a ſphere for the Argonauts, and to have been the offspring of a cloud, is one of the many gentile deities, under whoſe names the patriarch Noah was worſhipped; hence his title *centaur* is compounded of Chen-Tor, *the prieſt of the arkite ox*[a]. As for the three-headed Geryon, he appears, as far as concerns his figure, to be an oriental repreſentation of the principal arkite god united with his three ſons.

Qualis Atlantiaco memoratur littore quondam
Monſtrum Geryones immane tricorporis iræ,
Cui tres in pugna dextræ varia arma gerebant
Una ignes ſævos, aſt altera pone ſagittas
Fundebat, validam torquebat tertia cornum
Atque uno diverſa dabat tria vulnera niſu[b].

Thus on the coaſt, from hoary Atlas nam'd,
Stood triple Geryon: in his three right hands
Three weapons fierce he brandiſh'd, vengeful fire,
Unerring arrows, and a ponderous lance.

Nearly ſuch is the form of the great triple deity of the Hindoos, the vaſt buſt of Brahma, Viſhnou, and Seeva; a triad, which is

[a] The hiſtory of Chiron ſhall be reſumed hereafter. Vide infra chap. viii.

[b] Sil. Ital. Bell. Pun. lib. xiii. ver. 200.

ſaid

ſaid to have been produced from a fourth yet ſuperior god, named Brahmè [c]. Brahmè may poſſibly be Bu-Rama, *the lofty divinity of the arkite heifer*; his ſon Brahma (whoſe name nearly reſembles that of his father, much in the ſame manner as the ſon of the Phenician Cronus was alſo denominated *Cronus*,) is ſtyled *Narayen*, or *he that moves on the ſurface of the water* [d]; Viſhnou is immediately connected with the deluge, and is the ſame as the *Dagon* of Paleſtine; while the peculiar emblems of Seeva, like thoſe of the Egyptian Oſiris, are a ſerpent and a bull [e]. This triad in ſhort is compoſed of Shem, Ham, and Japhet, the three great gods, whoſe hiſtory is more or leſs preſerved in the annals of every nation; and yet, like the *Jupiter*, *Neptune*, and *Pluto* of the weſtern world, Brahma, Viſhnou, and Seeva, when taken ſeparately, are each the patriarch Noah worſhipped in conjunction with the Sun [f]. Accordingly, while the tri-

[c] Inſtit. of Menu, cap. 1.—Aſiat. Reſ. vol. i. p. 242.

[d] Inſtit. of Menu, cap. 1.

[e] See Sir Wm Jones on the gods of Greece, &c. Aſiat. Reſ. vol. i. p 250 and the Print prefixed to Maurice's Indian Antiquities, vol. i. in which Seeva is depicted holding a ſerpent in his hand.

[f] The lotus, from its well-known quality of always floating above the ſurface of the water, ſeems to have been adopted very generally as a ſymbol of the Ark. Hence we find, that the

ple buſt of the Hindoo deity exhibits to us,

the diluvian god Brahma was repreſented ſitting upon one of theſe plants; and hence we may obſerve, that in the third Indian Avatar a ſmall figure is introduced in preciſely the ſame attitude, and deſcribed as looking towards a rainbow. (See the Prints of the firſt and third Avatar in Maur. Hiſt. of Hind. vol. i.) If from Hindoſtan we paſs to Egypt, we ſhall learn from Jamblichus, that a man ſitting upon the lotus, ſurrounded with mud, was an emblem of the Sun; (Jamb. de Myſt. ſect. vii.) and from Plutarch, that the Sun was repreſented under the ſymbol of an infant ſitting upon this ſame plant. (Plut. de Iſid. p. 555.) It is manifeſt, notwithſtanding the phyſical refinements of Jamblichus and Plutarch upon theſe hieroglyphics, that ſomething more muſt be meant by them than merely the natural Sun; and I apprehend, that, in both caſes, the perſon, who ſits upon the lotus, is the great ſolar patriarch, and that, in the latter, he was repreſented as a child, in alluſion to his myſtical ſecond birth. The ſame ſymbol of the lotus occurs alſo in the mythology of Japan. Kæmpfer has given us a curious repreſentation of the goddeſs Quanwon ſitting upon this aquatic plant. In one part of his work he deſcribes her, as having *eight* little children placed round her head, ſix of whom formed a ſort of crown, while the two others were larger than the reſt; (Kæmpfer's Japan, p. 595.) and in another part of the ſame work, ſpeaking of a different ſtatue of the ſame goddeſs, he obſerves, that "*ſeven* ſmaller idols "adorned her head, like a crown or garland, whereby is de-"noted, that ſhe was *the happy mother of many a deified hero:* "nay, *the Japaneſe look upon this idol, as an emblematical repre-*"*ſentation of the birth of the gods in general.*" (Kæmpfer's Japan. p. 542.) From theſe remarks of Kæmpfer it is ſufficiently evident, that the goddeſs Quanwon is the Magna Mater of the weſtern world, and the very ſame perſon as Iſis or Atargatis, whom Simplicius deſcribes as the receptacle of the gods. (Vide ſupra p. 141.) The eight children, two of whom

are

in one compound figure, Noah and his off-

are delineated larger than the reſt, are the Noetic family; and the ſeven, which are annexed to the other ſtatue of the goddeſs, are the ſeven Cabiri. The reader will hereafter find, (Vide infra chap. viii.) that Quanwon is alſo the ſame as the Hindoo Sita; and that the circumſtance of her being an emblematical repreſentation of the birth of the gods is preciſely equivalent to the burſting aſunder of Sita, and to the egreſs of the hero-gods from her womb.

Theſe remarks will prepare us for what I conceive to be the proper explanation of the famous Siberian medal, now depoſited in the imperial cabinet at Peterſburg. On one ſide of this medal is repreſented a deity with three heads, and ſix arms. He ſits croſs-legged, not ſurely upon what Dr Parſons calls *a low ſopha*, but, as will evidently appear to any perſon who examines the fac-ſimile, upon the ſymbolical lotus. On the reverſe of the medal is an inſcription, which Col. Grant, with what juſtice I will not pretend to ſay, aſſerts to be ancient Iriſh or Celtic, and of which he gives the following tranſlation "The ſacred image of God in three images by theſe "collect the holy will of God from them love him." The medal itſelf was in all probability brought either from the empire of the Dalai-Lama, or from Hindoſtan, in both which countries a notion of three gods cloſely connected together has immemorially prevailed Hence I think we may reaſonably conclude, that the deity repreſented upon it is the ſame as that revered throughout the Lama dominions, as the triple god of Japan deſcribed by Kircher, (ſee his China) and as the *Brahma-Viſhnou Seeva* of Hindoſtan. Col Grant and Dr Parſons both conceive, that the deity in queſtion is deſcriptive of the Trinity; (See Parſons' Remains of Japhet, chap. 7.) and the very ingenious Mr. Maurice embraces their ſuppoſition, conjecturing at the ſame time, that not only this triad, but that the triad of Brahma, Viſhnou, and Seeva, and in ſhort all the other triads of the Gentile world, are corruptions of the catho-

lic

ſpring, it is at the ſame time, like Cerberus,

lic doctrine of the Chriſtian church. I had once adopted the ſame opinion, (ſee Horæ Moſaicæ, vol. i. p. 44, 48, 57, 60.) but a more attentive ſurvey of Pagan mythology has obliged me, however unwillingly, to relinquiſh it; and I cannot help ſuſpecting, that the various triads of the Gentiles, diſcuſſed at large by Dr. Cudworth and Mr. Maurice, may be ultimately traced to the triple offspring of the great patriarch. The ſame remark will of courſe apply to the elaborate, and ingenious, though fanciful Treatiſe of Mr. Hutchinſon on *the Names and Attributes of the Trinity of the Gentiles*; and to the fifth Section of Von Strahlenberg's *Introduction to his Deſcription of Siberia*. If Brahma, Viſhnou, and Seeva relate to the Trinity, it will not be eaſy to aſſign a reaſon, why they ſhould be repreſented as ſpringing from a fourth yet ſuperior god; and if Viſhnou be the *Dagon* of Paleſtine, he certainly cannot, *as ſuch*, have any connection with God the Son. Mr. Maurice preſents his readers with three very curious repreſentations of Viſhnou encompaſſed with the volumes of a ſerpent, the head of which is placed beneath the heel of the deity. Agreeably to the ſyſtem, which he has adopted, he conjectures, that this mode of deſcribing Viſhnou originated from the firſt-recorded prophecy, that the ſeed of the woman ſhould bruiſe the head of the ſerpent, but that it ſhould bruiſe his heel. I much doubt however, whether the framers of this celebrated hieroglyphic had even the moſt remote idea of our bleſſed Saviour impreſſed upon their minds, at the time that they conſtructed it. Viſhnou, in his human capacity, is the great fiſh-god of ancient mythology, or in other words the patriarch Noah; while, in his divine character, he is the Sun. Hence we may naturally expect to find him connected with the ſymbolical ſerpent; and hence, for preciſely the ſame reaſon, the helio-Noëtic Oſiris was repreſented preciſely in the ſame manner. (See the Plate in Montfaucon's Supplem. to Antiq. p. 211.) Such alſo was the mode of deſignating the Perſian Mithras; (Ban. Mythol.

an hieroglyphic, of the solar god. " At night,

thol. vol ii p. 104.) and, as the head of the serpent is placed under the heel of Vishnou, so Macrobius, having first informed us, that a dragon was emblematical of the Sun, adds, that upon this account it was placed at the *feet* of Esculapius. (Macrob. Saturn. lib i cap. 20) With regard to the belief of the Hindoos, that Vishnou was saved amidst a promiscuous slaughter of infants, that certainly cannot have originated from patriarchal tradition, but is evidently built upon the history of Herod's barbarity, which was most probably brought into the East by the Christians of St. Thomas.

Before I entirely dismiss this subject, I shall notice a single legend, which Mr Maurice adduces in support of his system. It relates to a triple god compounded of *Sree Mun Narrin*, a beautiful woman named *Maha Letchimy*, and *a serpent* "These " persons are by the Hindoos supposed to be wholly indivisible; " the one is three, and the three are one." (Ind Ant vol iv. p 750.) *Sree* appears, like *Surya*, to be the usual solar title *Sur*; *Mun* is the abbreviated form of *Munah* or *Menu*, and *Narrin* or *Narayen*, a title of Brahma, signifies *moving on the waters*. consequently *Sree Mun-Narrin* is equivalent to *the solar Noah moving on the waters* In a former work, *Horæ Mosaicæ*, I supposed the epithet *Narayen* to relate to the incubation of the Spirit during the process of reducing the primeval chaos to form and order, and I still think, that there is some allusion to the creation in the beginning of *the Institutes of Menu* · but I am now persuaded, that most of the ancient cosmogonies are confounded, in a greater or less degree, with traditions of the deluge. *Maha Letchimy*, the beautiful woman, is merely the *Venus*, *Isis*, *Cybelè*, *Derceto*, or *Latona*, of the western nations, in other words, the Ark, and *the serpent* is the usual solar emblem. As for the indivisibility and unity of these deities, it relates, as in the case of the immense bust of Brahma, Vishnou, and Seeva to the *mode* of representing the idol, not to his *nature* It may be proper to observe, that Brahma

" and in the weſt, the Sun is Viſhnou ; he is " Brahma in the eaſt, and in the morning ; " from noon to evening he is Seeva[g]." Hence, in alluſion to the ſolar worſhip, Brahma is ſaid to be armed with fiery ſhafts[h]; while, in reference to the arkite ſuperſtition, Viſhnou, in the form of a fiſh, guards the ark of Menu[i], and deſcends, like Bacchus, Oſiris, Adonis, and Hercules, into the infernal regions of Sheſhanaga, king of ſerpents[k]. The genealogy of Geryon connects him with both the ancient ſuperſtitions. From Neptune, and Meduſa, ſprung Chryſaor, and the horſe Pegaſus ; and from Chryſaor, and Callirhoè daughter of Oceanus, was born the monſter Geryon[l]. *Chryſaor* is a title of the Sun, compounded of Chryſos, *gold*, and Or, *light*, whence it is con-

Brahma is ſometimes deſcribed as the god of creation, but *that* I apprehend is merely in the ſame manner as what the claſſical Jupiter is.

[g] Aſiat. Reſ. vol. v. p. 254. " They confeſs unanimouſly, " that the Sun is an emblem or image of their three great dei- " ties, jointly and individually, that is of Brahm, or the ſu- " preme one, who alone exiſts really and abſolutely, the three " male divinities themſelves being only Maya, or illuſion." Aſiat. Reſ. vol. iii. p. 144.

[h] Ibid. vol. i. p. 248.

[i] Ibid. p. 233.

[k] Ibid. p. 249.

[l] Apoll. Bibl. lib. ii. cap. 4.

tinually

tinually beſtowed by Homer upon Apollo; the horſe Pegaſus is the Hippa-P'Aga, or *diluvian Ark*; and, in alluſion to the ſymbolical heifer, Geryon is ſaid to have been famed for his breed of oxen, which Hercules at length drove away from him, notwithſtanding they were guarded both by the giant himſelf, and his two-headed dog. The name of this animal, according to Apollodorus, was *Orthrus*; and he was born of the diluvian Typhon, and the ſerpent Echidna [m], who were likewiſe the parents of the dragon of the Heſperides [n]: but Julius Pollux calls him *Gargittius*, and ſays, that he was the brother of Cerberus [o]. Orthrus is Or-Athr, *the illuſtrious Sun*; and Gargittius is G'Arg-Ait, *the great burning god of the Ark*. Hercules is ſaid by Conon to have carried off the oxen into Italy [p], or Ait-Al-Aia, *the land of the blazing Sun* [q]; and Ptolemy Hepheſtion introduces Juno, *the dove*,

[m] Apoll. Bibl. lib ii. cap. 5.

[n] Ibid

[o] Ὁ δε Γηρυονȣ κυων, ὁ τας βȣς φυλαττων, αδελφος ην τȣ Κερβερου, ανῃρεθη δε ὑφ' Ἡρακλεȣς. Το δε ονομα αυτȣ Γαργιττιος. Onomaſt. lib. v. cap. 5.

[p] Conon Narrat. cap. 3.

[q] The hiſtory of Italy, as connected with Minos and the worſhip of the ſolar orb, will be reſumed hereafter.

aſſiſt-

aſſiſting Geryon in his combat with that hero [r]. As for the name of Geryon, it is variouſly written *Geryon*, *Geryones*, and *Geryoneus* [s]; and it ſeems to be a compound of G'Aron-Nus, *the illuſtrious arkite Noah*.

If we next turn our attention to the fabulous fates and furies, we ſhall find, that they alſo, being introduced into the infernal regions, are connected with the Myſteries of the Ark. The furies were by the Greeks called *Erinnues*, a word derived from Aron-Nus, *the Ark of Noah*; whence the Cabiric Ceres, or the Ark, is ſaid to have changed herſelf into an Erinnus, in the neighbourhood of Styx or the deluge, and in that form to have received the embraces of the Hippian Neptune [t]. The fates were denominated *Parcæ*, a title ſimilarly derived from P'Arca,

[r] Juno is perpetually introduced into the hiſtory of Hercules, though ſhe is generally repreſented as hoſtile to him; but Ptolemy Hepheſtion has preſerved a curious tradition, in which Hercules Nilus is ſaid to have delivered her from the attack of two giants. Νειλος ὁ Ἡρακλης απο γενεσεως φασιν εκαλειτο· επει δ' Ἡραν εσωσεν, επερχομενον αυτῃ ανελων τον Ανωνυμον και Πυριπνοον γιγαντα, εκειθεν δια το απαλαλκειν της Ἡρας τον πολεμον, μετεβαλε την κλησιν. Ptol. Heph. lib. ii.

[s] Λεγεται δε και Γηρυων, και Γηρυονης, και Γηρυονευς. Euſtath. in Dionyſ. Perieg. ver. 561.

[t] Apoll. Bibl. lib. iii. cap. 6.

the

the Ark; accordingly, they were ſuppoſed to be the ſiſters of Venus, and the Erinnues, and the children of Cronus or Noah [u].

With regard to the three judges of Hell, Minos, Rhadamanthus, and Eacus, they ſeem, if taken conjointly, to be the three ſons of the patriarch; if ſeparately, each will be diſcovered to be the patriarch himſelf. Minos, the imaginary king of Crete, is the *Menu*, of Hindoſtan, and the *Menes* of Egypt; his brother [x] Rhadamanthus is Rada-Man-Thus, *the god of the lordly Ark*; and Eacus, or, according to the Greek pronunciation, Aiacus, the mythological ſon of Jupiter and Egina, ſeems to have borrowed his name from Ai-Ac, *the coaſt of the Ocean* [y]. Hence we find, that Eacus, like Noah, was ſuppoſed to have had three ſons, Telamon and Peleus by the daughter of the centaur Chiron, and Phocus by the daughter of Nereus [z]. Telamon, Peleus, and Phocus, appear, in fact, to be the ſame as the

[u] Schol. in Œdip Colon ver 42.

[x] Plut. in Vit. Theſ

[y] Æacus Æginam genetricis nomine dixit.

Ovid Metam. lib vii. ver 474

See alſo Apollod. Bibl. lib. iii. cap. 11.

[z] Apoll. Bibl. lib. iii. cap. 11. The firſt of theſe fabulous heroes accompanied Hercules in his adventure with the Cetus on the coaſt of Troy.

Corybantes, or Cabiri. Accordingly, as one of theſe is ſaid by Clemens Alexandrinus to have been killed by his two brothers[a], ſo, in a ſimilar manner, Phocus was ſuppoſed to have been ſlain by Peleus and Telamon[b]. Telamon, after the murder of his brother, fled to Salamis, the ſovereignty of which was conferred upon him at the death of his predeceſſor Cychreus, who was the ſon of Neptune by Salamis daughter of Aſopus. This Cychreus was reported to have ſlain an immenſe ſerpent, which committed depredations on his kingdom[c]. The ſerpent however is merely the uſual ſolar emblem; and hence we find, that the imaginary grandfather of Cychreus was called *Aſopus*, or As-Op, *the fiery dragon.*

From Peleus the brother of Telamon, and the ſea-goddeſs Thetis, was born the celebrated Achilles, who is feigned to have been plunged beneath the waters of the diluvian Styx, and thence rendered invulnerable. I ſtrongly ſuſpect, that Achilles is a mere mythological character; and that his name is a compound of Ac-El-Es, *the burning god of the Ocean.* He was alſo called *Pyriſſoüs,* from

[a] Cohort. ad Gent. p. 15.
[b] Apollod. Bibl. lib. iii. cap. 11.
[c] Ibid.

the

the circumſtance, as we learn from Ptolemy Hepheſtion, of his having been ſaved from the fire, into which he had been caſt by his mother[d]. The ſame fable is mentioned by Lycophron, who adds to it, that Thetis bore ſeven ſons to Peleus, and caſt them all into a fire, from which Achilles alone was preſerved.

> Πελασγικον Τυφωνα γεννᾳται πατηρ,
> Αφ᾽ ἑπτα παιδων φεψαλῳ σποδȣμενων,
> Μȣνον φλεγȣσαν εξαλυξαντα σποδον[e].

I am much inclined to think, that this was originally the ſame legend, as that noticed by Herodotus of Seſoſtris and his wife burning their children[f]; and that they both equally allude to the dreadful human ſacrifices, which were offered to the Sun. The ſeven children of Peleus and Thetis ſeem in ſhort to have been no other than the ſeven Cabiri, Corybantes, or Titans; hence we find, that ſome writers ſuppoſed Thetis to be the daughter of Chiron[g], or Noah.

As the oceanic Achilles was dipped in the diluvian waters of Styx, ſo his fabulous rival

[d] Ptol. Heph. Nov. Hiſt. lib. vii.
[e] Caſſan ver. 177.
[f] Herod. lib. ii. cap. 107
[g] Schol. in Apoll. Argon. lib. i. ver. 558.

 Aga-

Agamemnon, as we are plainly told by Tzetzes, was no real perſon, but the very ſame deity as the Ercèan, or arkite Jupiter; that Jupiter, before whoſe altar Danaè, the mother of Perſeus, was brought by Acriſius[h]. In a ſimilar manner, Athenagoras obſerves, that Helen, Hector, Jupiter-Agamemnon, and Erechtheus, were all adored as gods along with the marine deity Neptune[i]. What may ſerve to confirm the propriety of theſe remarks, Peleus and his brethren are deſcribed as being contemporaries of the Dioſcori or Cabiri. Perhaps it may be too bold, with Mr. Bryant, abſolutely to deny the exiſtence of *any* ſiege of Troy; but I cannot but be perſuaded, that the poem of Homer at leaſt is a mere mythos[k], which very probably however is ingrafted upon the hiſtory of ſome predatory war between the Greeks and the Ilienſes[l].

[h] —αμφι τυμβῳ και ναῳ τυ Αγαμεμνονος Διος, ητοι τυ Ερκειου Διος, δαμασθεις— Tzet. in Lycoph. ver. 335. Agamemnon ſeems to ſignify *the diluvian*, from Agam, *a pool*.

[i] Athen. Legat. p. 1.

[k] Some further remarks upon this ſubject will be made hereafter. Vide infra chap. viii.

[l] It is remarkable, that the ſcholiaſt upon Heſiod cloſely connects the war of the Titans or diluvians with that of Troy. Δεκα δε ετη εμαχοντο (οἱ Τιτηνες)— δio και τοσαυτα ετη περι Ἑλενην της ὑλης τα εναντια Τρωες και Ἑλληνες εμαχοντο. Schol. in Heſ. Theog. ver. 629.

After

After all that has been written upon the ſubject, we can never build with any confidence upon a ſeries of facts, which are ſaid to have happened, *as all allow*, in the fabulous or uncertain age. The truth, in this, like moſt other controverſies, ſeems to lie ſomewhere in the middle: hence, while we admit the probability of *ſome* Trojan war having really happened, credulity itſelf can ſcarcely believe, that the Iliad contains any thing like a true account of it.

In the very loweſt region of hell, ſurrounded by the Tartarean Phlegethon, Virgil places the impious race of the diluvian Titans, thoſe, who by a long repetition of the moſt enormous crimes called forth at length the vengeance of offended heaven. This loweſt region however, as we have ſeen from Plato, was ſimply the centre of the earth, from which proceeded the mighty waters that occaſioned the deluge.

Here likewiſe along with the Titans, the poet ſtations the huge monſter Tityus. This giant was the ſon of Jupiter by Elara daughter of Orchomenus, and was born in the centre of the earth, Jupiter having there concealed his mother through fear of Juno. At length he emerged from his dark confinement, and immediately attempted to raviſh

Latona[m]. Tityus derives his name from the ſame root as Titan, and is, like Typhon, nothing more than a perſonification of the deluge. Hence he is ſaid to iſſue from the great central abyſs, and to attempt the chaſtity of Latona, or the Ark[n]. His fictitious anceſtor Orchomenus is Orca-Menu, *the arkite Noah.* The reader will remember, that this Orchomenus was an ancient king of Arcadia, ſon of Pelaſgus, and brother of Lycaon, in whoſe days happened the deluge; that he gave his name to the city Orchomenus, which was reported to have been ſwallowed up by a flood; and that one of his brothers was called *Titanas.* He was moreover the father of Minyas, and through him connected with the Argonautic expedition[o].

Here alſo in the depths of Hades Virgil places Phlegyas, and deſcribes him as exhorting all men to reverence the gods, and to adhere to the paths of rectitude and virtue. Now, were this man literally in hell, it would be abſurd in the poet to repreſent him as inculcating juſtice, becauſe his audience would be compoſed of the damned alone, who could

[m] Apollod. Bibl. lib. i. cap. 4.

[n] Tityus was ſometimes feigned to be the father of Europa, or the Ark. Vide ſupra p. 179.

[o] Anton. Liber. Metam. cap. 10.

not

not have any motive to induce them to repent; whence we may conclude, that Phlegyas was no other than a well-known character in the Myſteries, whoſe office was to perſonate one of the wicked antediluvians, and in that capacity ſolemnly to admoniſh the initiated[p]. Phlegyas ſeems to have been ſo called from Peleg, *the Ocean*[q]; and his children the Phlegyæ were ſaid to have come from the land of Minyas[r], and in the pride of their heart to have quitted the city of the Orchomenians, or arkites[s]. This defection from the Minyæ, or Noachidæ, proved the cauſe of their deſtruction, for it was in reality the ſeparation of the antediluvian giants, or Titans, from the family of Noah. They refuſed to imitate the piety of that patriarch, and were conſequently excluded from the Ark by their own wickedneſs. Accordingly

[p] This argument is uſed by Bp. Warburton to prove, that the ſixth book of the Eneid related to the myſteries of Eleuſis. Though I cannot adopt his explanation of the Myſteries, yet, whatever their import may be, the argument, ſo far as it concerns the intention of Virgil in writing that part of his poem, will hold equally good.

[q] Phlegyas is ſaid to have been the father of Coronis, who was the concubine of Apollo, and the mother of Eſculapius. Vide ſupra p. 101.

[r] Pauſ. Bœot. p. 728.

[s] Ibid p. 782.

Nonnus repreſents them as being overwhelmed by Neptune with the waters of the Ocean.

Και Φλεγυας ὁτε παντας ανερριζωσε θαλασσῃ
Νησον ὁλην τριοδοντι διαρρηξας Ενοσιχθων[t].

From its deep rooted baſe the Phlegyan iſle
Stern Neptune ſhook, and plung'd beneath the waves
Its impious inhabitants.

It is not unworthy of notice, that the very crimes, which, as we learn from Ovid, diſgraced the iron age, and eventually produced the cataſtrophè of the deluge, are thoſe, which Virgil ſuppoſes the damned to have been guilty of.

——————— Tartarus ipſe
Bis patet in præceps tantum, tenditque ſub umbras,
Quantus ad ætherium cœli ſuſpectus Olympum.
Hic genus antiquum terræ, Titania pubes,
Fulmine dejecti, fundo volvuntur in imo.
- - - - - - - - - - - - -
Nec non et Tityon, Terræ omniparentis alumnum
Cernere erat; per tota novem cui jugera corpus
Porrigitur; roſtroque immanis vultur obunco
Immortale jecur tondens, fecundaque pœnis

[t] Nonni Dionyſ. lib. xviii. p. 319.

Viſ-

Viſcera, rimaturque epulis, habitatque ſub alto
Pectore; nec fibris requies datur ulla renatis.
- - - - - - - - - - - - - - - -
Hic, quibus inviſi fratres, dum vita manebat;
Pulſatuſve parens, aut fraus innexa clienti;
Aut qui divitiis ſoli incubuere repertis,
Nec partem poſuere ſuis, quæ maxima turba eſt;
Quique ob adulterium cæſi, quique arma ſecuti
Impia, nec veriti dominorum fallere dextras:
Incluſi pœnam exſpectant——
——— Phlegyaſque miſerrimus omnes
Admonet, et magna teſtatur voce per umbras:
" Diſcite juſtitiam moniti, et non temnere di-
" vos[u]."
Vendidit hic auro patriam, dominumque poten-
tem
Impoſuit; fixit leges pretio, atque refixit.
Hic thalamum invaſit natæ, vetitoſque hyme-
næos.
Auſi omnes immane nefas, auſoque potiti[x].

The gaping gulph low to the centre lies;

[u] It is not improper to obſerve, that Bp. Warburton ſuppoſes Theſeus, and not Phlegyas, to have pronounced this ſolemn exhortation, making *Phlegyas* the accuſative caſe plural from *Phlegyæ*, inſtead of the proper name of a man. The interpretation however, which I have given of this part of the Myſteries, will remain equally unaffected, whether the Biſhop's mode of rendering the paſſage be adopted, or whether the common tranſlation be preferred.

[x] Æneid. lib. vi. ver. 576

And

And twice as deep as earth is diſtant from the
ſkies.
The rivals of the gods, the Titan race,
Here ſing'd with lightning, roll within the unfathom'd ſpace.

- - - - - - - - - - - - - - -

There Tityus was to ſee, who took his birth
From heaven, his nurſing from the foodful earth.
Here his gigantic limbs, with large embrace,
Infold nine acres of infernal ſpace.
A ravenous vulture in his open'd ſide
Her crooked beak and cruel talons tried:
Still for the growing liver dug his breaſt;
The growing liver ſtill ſupplied the feaſt.

- - - - - - - - - - - - - -

Then they, who brothers' better claim diſown,
Expel their parents, and uſurp the throne;
Defraud their clients, and to lucre ſold
Sit brooding on unprofitable gold:
Who dare not give, and ev'n refuſe to lend
To their poor kindred, or a wanting friend:
Vaſt is the throng of theſe; nor leſs the train
Of luſtful youths, for foul adultery ſlain.
Hoſts of deſerters, who their honour ſold,
And baſely broke their faith for bribes of gold:
All theſe within the dungeon's depth remain,
Deſpairing pardon, and expecting pain.

- - - - - - - - - - - - - -

——— Phlegyas warns the world with cries;
(Could warning make the world more juſt or
wiſe,)

"Learn

"Learn righteousness, and dread the avenging
"deities."

To tyrants others have their country sold,
Imposing foreign lords, for foreign gold.
Some have old laws repeal'd, new statutes made;
Not as the people pleas'd, but as they paid.
With incest some their daughters' bed prophan'd;
All dar'd the worst of ills, and what they dar'd,
attain'd. *Dryden.*

Emerging from the deep gloom of Tartarus, Eneas and the Sibyl next enter into the Elysian plains, which afford a wonderful contrast to the terrific scenes they had last beheld. From darkness they pass into light, from danger to safety, and from the regions of death to the land of life. This passage, as exhibited in the Eleusinian orgies, is thus described by Themistius.

"Entering now into the mystic dome, the "aspirant is filled with horror and amaze"ment. He is seized with solicitude, and a "total perplexity. He is unable to move a "step forward, or how to begin right the road, "that is to lead him to the place he aspires "to, till the prophet or conductor lays open "the vestibule of the temple. Being tho"roughly purified, he now discloses to the "initiated a region all over illuminated, and "shining with a divine splendor. The cloud

"and

" and thick darkneſs are diſperſed; and the " mind emerges, as it were, into day, full of " light and chearfulneſs, as before, of diſcon- " ſolate obſcurity."

After citing this curious deſcription, Bp. Warburton obſerves, that ſuch a " ſucceſſion " from Tartarus to Elyſium, makes Ariſtides " call theſe rites *moſt horrible, and moſt raviſh-* " *ingly pleaſant.*" All the ancient writers indeed, who treat of the Myſteries, unanimouſly aſſert, that they began in ſorrow, and ended in joy.

The paſſage then from Tartarus to Elyſium was only another mode of deſcribing the death and revivification of Bacchus, Oſiris, or Adonis. It repreſented the egreſs of the Noachidæ from the gloom of the Ark, ſurrounded as they had long been with clouds and darkneſs, to the chearful light of heaven.

From what has been ſaid we may now ſee the reaſon, why the Cabiri were eſteemed infernal deities; why they were ſometimes ſtyled *Manes* and *Lares*, words uſually ſuppoſed to ſignify *the ſouls of the deceaſed*; and why their mythological mother was called *Mania*[y]. *Manes* is derived from *Menes*, or *Manes*, the name of the diluvian patriarch,

[y] Vide ſupra p. 41.

and,

and, when ufed plurally, is equivalent to *Noachidæ*; *Lar* is a contraction of El-Ar, *the god of light*; and *Mania*, or Manah, is *the Noëtic Ark*.

CHAP.

CHAP. VI.

CONCERNING THE VARIOUS COUNTRIES, WHICH WERE DEVOTED TO THE CABIRIC SUPERSTITION; PARTICULARLY ITALY, CRETE, SAMOTHRACE, AND TROAS.

SINCE the Myfteries of the Cabiri relate entirely to the helio-arkite fuperftition, we fhall not be furprifed to find them introduced into a variety of different countries; while the deities, in whofe honour they were celebrated, were known by the feveral names of *Corybantes*, *Curetes*, *Idæi Dactyli*, *Cabiri*, or *Telchines*. As fome remembrance of the flood feems to have been preferved by all the pofterity of Noah, though it was frequently reprefented as partial and confined to a particular diftrict, inftead of being univerfal and unbounded; fo the Cabiri, notwithftanding their being the general anceftors of all mankind, were continually viewed in the light of mere local and appropriated deities. Thus, while Sanchoniatho places them in Phenicia [a]; Herodotus makes them the fons of the Egyp-

[a] Eufeb. Præp. Evan. lib. i. cap. 10.

tian

tian Vulcan by Cabira the daughter of Proteus, and yet aſſerts, that their obſcene rites were communicated by the aboriginal Pelaſgi to the Samothracians and Athenians [b]. Nor are theſe the only variations with reſpect to their country. Strabo mentions, that ſome deduced the origin of the Curetes from Acarnania, ſome from Etolia, ſome from Crete, and others from Eubèa [c]. Pleuronia alſo was inhabited by them, and was thence called *Curetis* [d]; Chalcis was another of their ſettlements [e]; and, under the name of *Idèi Dactyli*, they bore a conſpicuous part in the myſteries of the Phrygian Cybelè [f]. They were likewiſe worſhipped at Lemnos [g]; and from

[b] Herod lib. ii. cap. 51.

[c] Τȣς δε Κȣρητας των μεν Ακαρνασι, των δε Αιτωλοις προσνεμοντων, και των μεν εκ Κρητης, των δ' εξ Ευβοιας το γενος ειναι φασκοντων. Strab. Geog. lib. x. p. 462.

[d] Την Πλευρωνιαν ὑπο Κȣρητων οικȣμενην, και Κȣρητιν προσαγορευομενην. Ibid. p. 465

[e] Αρχεμαχος δ' ὁ Ευβοευς φησι τȣς Κȣρητας εν Χαλκιδι συνοικησαι. Ibid.

[f] Τινας δαιμονας η προσπολȣς θεων τȣς Κȣρητας φασιν· οἱ δε παραδιδοντες τα Κρητικα και τα Φρυγια ἱερȣργιαις τισιν εμπεπλεγμενοι, ταις μεν μυϛικαις, ταις δ' αλλως, περι τε την τȣ Διος παιδοτροφιαν την εν τη Κρητη, και τȣς της μητερος των θεων οργιασμȣς εν τη Φρυγια, και τȣς περι την Ιδην την Τρωικην τοπȣς. Ibid. p 466

[g] Και τα ἱερα τροπον τινα κοινοποιεισθαι, ταυτα τε, και των Σαμοθρακων, και τα εν Λημνῳ, και αλλα πλειω Ibid. The Tyrrhenians, who afterwards colonized Tuſcany in conjunction with the

Samothrace, Crete, and Phrygia, their rites were carried to Rome, the citizens of which were thence denominated *Quirites*, or *Curetes*.

The Hiſtory of this laſt tranſaction is one of the moſt curious portions of ancient mythology, and is cloſely connected with the fabulous hiſtory of Troy. According to Dionyſius of Halicarnaſſus, Atlas was the firſt king of Arcadia; a country, which derived its name from Arcas, ſon of Calliſto, and the ſucceſſor of that Nuctimus [h] during whoſe life a great deluge is ſaid to have happened [i]. Atlas had ſeven daughters, denominated *Pleiades*; one of whom, Electra, was the concubine of Jupiter, and the mother of Dardanus and Iaſus, or, as he was ſometimes called, Iaſion.

the Pelaſgi, and brought along with them the rites of the Cabiri, firſt inhabited Lemnos.—Λημνος. Τυρσηνοι γαρ αυτην πρωτοι ῳκησαν. Schol. in Apoll. Argon. lib. i. ver. 608.

[h] Μετα δε Νυκτιμον αποθανοντα Αρκας εξεδεξατο ὁ Καλλιςυς την αρχην. Pauſ. Arcad. p. 604.

[i] Tzetzes ſuppoſes, that this deluge commenced at Helicè and Bura. Schol. in Lycoph. ver. 72. Helicè received its name from the nymph Helicè, one of the nurſes of Jupiter, who was afterwards placed in the conſtellation of the leſſer bear; (Hyg. Poet. Aſtron. lib. ii. cap. 2.) and in Bura we find the radical Bu, *an ox*, the uſual arkite ſymbol. As for Nuctimus, he is evidently Nuch-Tam, *the perfect man Noah*. See Gen. vi. 9.

Iaſus remained unmarried[k]; but Dardanus took to wife Chryſè, the daughter of Palas, and by her became the father of Idèus, and Dimas, who inherited the kingdom of Arcadia from their great-grandfather Atlas. In their days a flood having inundated the plains, half of the inhabitants fled to the mountains; while the other half migrated to an iſland on the coaſt of Thrace, to which they gave the name of *Samothrace*. After they had remained there a ſhort time, the greateſt part of them croſſed over into Aſia, under the command of Dardanus; and at length Idèus, the ſon of that prince, led his diviſion of the coloniſts into the mountainous country of Ida, where he eſtabliſhed the worſhip and myſteries of the mother of the Gods, which afterwards became famous throughout all Phrygia[l]. It is remarkable, that Dardanus is ſaid by Tzetzes to have left Samothrace, no leſs than Arcadia, on account of a flood[m]; a cir-

[k] Other writers however, as we ſhall preſently ſee, do not agree with Dionyſius in this particular; but ſpeak of Iaſus, as the huſband of Ceres, or Cybelè.

[l] Dionyſ. Halic. Ant. Rom. lib. i. cap. 61

[m] Ηλεκτρας γαρ της Ατλαντος και Διος, Ιασιων και Δαρδανος— Δαρδανος δε κατακλυσμȣ γεγονοτος εκ Σαμοθρακης εις αντιπερα γην περαιουται, και την νυν Τροιαν εμελλεν κτιζειν. Schol in Lycoph. ver. 29.

cumſtance not mentioned by Dionyſius: and it is highly worthy of obſervation, that this flood was the very ſame as that of Deucalion or Noah[n]. Accordingly we find, that the Phrygian Cybelè, or the Ark, whoſe rites he introduced into Troas, was no other than Hecatè, the deity worſhipped in Samothrace[o].

The fabulous conſort of Atlas was Pleionè, the daughter of the Ocean, or, according to Dictys Cretenſis, of Danaus[p]. The purport however of both theſe genealogies is preciſely the ſame; for Danaus, as I have repeatedly obſerved, is merely the compound title Da-Nau.

With regard to the ſeven daughters of Atlas and Pleionè, they are ſaid to have been purſued by Orion, during the ſpace of five whole years, through the country of Beotia. At length, having invoked the aſſiſtance of the gods, they were changed into doves; and Jupiter, pitying their calamity, placed them

[n] —Δαρδανȣ, ὃς ποτε επι τȣ κατακλυσμȣ,—διαπερασας επι την Ιλιον, καταλειψας το κατοικητηριον των Κορυβαντων. Τȣτο δε εποιησε ποτε, ὁτε κατεκλυσε πασαν την γην ὁ Ζευς επι τȣ Δευκαλιωνος. Schol. in Lycoph. ver. 69.

[o] Το Θρακικον καταλιπων σπηλαιον της Ῥεας, η της Ἑκατης, ὁ Δαρδανος. Ibid. ver. 77.

[p] Ex Pleione, Danai filia, et Atlante, Electram natam, quam ex Jove gravidam Dardanum genuiſſe. Dict. Cret. de Bello Troj. lib. i. cap. 9.

among

among the conſtellations, under the name of *the Pleiades*[q].

Atlas himſelf, according to Sanchoniatho, was the brother of Cronus, and Dagon; or, according to the ſcholiaſt upon Aratus, the brother of Prometheus and Epimetheus, and the ſon of Uranus by Clymenè, daughter of Oceanus[r]. He was in ſhort, as I have already ſtated, the great ſolar patriarch, and the ſame mythological character as his brethren Cronus, Dagon, Prometheus, and Epimetheus. Hence he was the reputed ſon of Clymenè, or Cula-Menah, the Noëtic Ark; and hence Clymenè herſelf was ſuppoſed to be the offſpring of the Ocean[s].

Since Atlas then is the patriarch Noah, and the ſame as Cronus or Sydyk, his ſeven daughters muſt neceſſarily be the ſame as the ſeven Cabiræ, or the ſeven Titanides; and the hiſtory of their being changed into doves in the land of Beotia, or *the arkite heifer*, muſt re-

[q] Φασι δε οἱ μυθοι περι των Πλειαδων, ὁτι απο Ατλαντος εγεννηθησαν, και Πλειοινης, της τȣ Ωκεανȣ θυγατρος—Γεννηθεισαι δε ȣτως απο τȣ Ατλαντος και της Πλειονης εδιωκοντο πεντε ὁλȣς ενιαυτȣς κατα Βοιωτιαν ὑπο τȣ Ωριωνος,—και τοις θεοις ευξαμεναι, προς πελειαδας ημειφθησαν· ειτα οικτειρας αυτας ὁ Ζευς της κακοπαθειας, εν τῳ ȣρανῳ κατηστερισεν. Schol. in Arat. Phœn p. 35.

[r] Schol. in Arat. Phœn. p. 35.

[s] For a more particular account of the genealogy of Atlas, vide ſupra p. 113.

late entirely to the Noëtic dove and the Ark. Accordingly the name of their ſuppoſed mother *Pleionè*, or *Peleionè*, is compounded of Belah-Ionah, *the lordly dove*; while their own appellation *Pleiades* is evidently a contraction of *Peleiades*[t].

I am inclined to think, that the fable of their being purſued by Orion points out to us the particular era, when the violent union of the two great ſuperſtitions was accompliſhed. We are informed by Cedrenus, that Orion is the mighty hunter Nimrod[u]; who, as we learn from Scripture, firſt attempted to eſtabliſh an univerſal empire, and to build a lofty tower in honour of the hoſt of heaven[x]. Hence he is univerſally ſuppoſed to have been the principal introducer of idolatry, the grand author of poſtdiluvian apoſtaſy. Eratoſthenes teaches us from Heſiod, that he was the ſon of Neptune by Euryalè the daughter of Minos; that he poſſeſſed the faculty of walking upon the ſea, as if it were dry land; and that he was a mighty hunter of wild beaſts in the

[t] Gr. Πελειαδες.

[u] Τον Νεβρωδ αποθεωσαντες οἱ Ασσυριοι, εν τοις αϛροις του ουρανου εταξαν, και καλουσιν Ωριωνα. Cedr. Hiſt. Comp. fol. 14.

[x] See this ſubject diſcuſſed at large in Horæ Moſaicæ, vol. i. p. 207. and for a deſcription of the tower ſee Herod. lib. i. cap. 181.

iſland

iſland of Crete [y]. Suppoſing Minos to be the ſcriptural Noah, Orion will hold nearly the ſame place in the poſtdiluvian genealogy, that Nimrod does; and as for the power of walking ſecure upon the waves, it ſeems to have been erroneouſly aſcribed to him, in conſequence of his devotion to the arkite worſhip. I have obſerved, that the union of the two ſuperſtitions is frequently repreſented under the image of a rape; in conſequence of this we find, that Orion is ſaid to have been ſlain by Diana in the iſle of Delos, on account of his offering violence to Opis, one of the Hyperborean virgins, whoſe hiſtory has been already conſidered [z].

Atlas moreover was the father of Hyas, and

[y] Τουτον (Ωριωνα) Ἡσιοδος φησιν Ευρυαλης της Μινωος, και Ποσειδωνος ειναι· δοθηναι δε αυτῳ δωρεαν, ὡστε επι των κυματων πορευεσθαι, καθαπερ επι της γης—απηλθεν εις Κρητην, και περι τας θηρας διηγε κυνηγετων Erat. Cataſt. Ωριων—Schol. in Arat. Phœn. p. 43.—Apollod. Bibl. lib i. cap 4

[z] Ωριωνος δ' Ηως ερασθεισα ἡρπασε, και εκομισεν εις Δηλον—(εκει) βιαζομενος Ωπιν, μιαν των Ὑπερβορεων παραγενομενων παρθενων, ὑπ' Αρτεμιδος ετοξευθη. Apollod Bibl. lib. i. cap 4 Non deſunt, qui Oriona ex Jove, Neptuno, et Mercurio, prognatum eſſe narrant In corium ſcilicet tauri, quem Hercules immolaverat, minxerunt dii, et in terram obruerunt, unde natus eſt Orion Vide Hyg. Fab. 195. In hac fabula præcipuè eſt notanda pellis bovina, ſymbolum nempe archæum, hiſtoria vero ad Noachum omnino, non ad Nebrodum, pertinet. De generatione hac bovina mox diſſerendum eſt. Vide infra chap. x.

the Hyades[a]; which, in the ſphere, are placed upon the forehead of the bull[b], as the Pleiades are in his neck[c]. The Hyades were ſeven in number, and were ſuppoſed to have been the nurſes of Bacchus, who accordingly takes his ſtation near them under the title of *Hyas*[d]. They were the ſame mythological characters as the ſeven Cabiræ, the ſeven Pleiades, and the ſeven Titanides. It is remarkable, that although the ſcholiaſt upon Aratus repreſents the Hyades as the offspring of Atlas, yet, according to Euripides, they were the daughters of Erechtheus[e]. There is no real diſcrepancy however between theſe two genealogies, for as Atlas is *the ſolar Noah*, ſo Erechtheus is *the god of the Ark*; hence Hyginus, with perfect propriety, aſſerts, that Beotia was the mother of the Hyades[f].

[a] Εκ τουτου δε του Ατλαντος φασιν οἱ μυθοι και τας Ὑαδας γενεσθαι, και τον υἱον Ὑαντα — Ζευς δε αστερας αυτας πεποιηκε, τας καλουμενας Ὑαδας. Schol. in Arat. Phœn. p. 35.

[b] This bull, as I have already obſerved, was the bull of Europa.

[c] Του δε Ταυρου το μετωπον συν τῳ προσωπῳ αἱ Ὑαδες καλουμεναι περιεχουσι, προς δε τῃ αποτομῃ της ῥαχεως, ἡ πλειας εστιν, αστερας εχουσα ἑπτα. Erat. Cataſ. Ταυρος.

[d] Ὑης δε ὁ Διονυσος. Schol. in Arat. Phœn. p. 25. Has autem (Hyadas) Pherecydes Athenienſis Liberi nutrices eſſe demonſtrat, numero ſeptem. Hyg. Poet. Aſtron. lib. ii. cap. 21.

[e] Schol. in Arat. Phœn. p. 25.

[f] Hyg. Poet. Aſtron. lib. ii. cap. 21.

I juſt

I juſt obſerved, that Electra, the parent of Jaſion and Dardanus, was a Pleiad. In conſequence of this circumſtance, we find her connected with the city of Thebah, or *the Ark*, one of the ſeven gates of which received its name from her [g]. Another of the Pleiads was Maia, the mother of Mercury [h]. Thus it appears, that the hiſtory of Hermes, Bootes, Buddha, or Fohi, is very nearly related to that of the Pleiads [i] and Dardanus. This prince

[g] The ſeven gates of Thebes were called *Electra,* from El-Oc-Tora, *the divine oceanic heifer*, *Ogygia,* from Og, *the Ocean*; *Pretis,* from Berith, *the covenant*, *Oncais,* from Onc, *the Ocean*; *Hypſiſta,* from Hip-Z'Eſta, *the great ſolar Ark*, *Crenis,* from Car-Ain, *the fountain of light*; and *Homolois,* from Ham-El, *the burning god.* Apoll. Bibl. lib. iii. cap 6. Theſe derivations appear to be allowable, becauſe we learn from the ſcholiaſt upon Eſchylus, that Cadmus uſed the Egyptian dialect in the ſacred rites, which he eſtabliſhed at Thebes, and that the names of the gates were to be ſought for in that language. Ηλθεν εις Θηϐας, ωλισθεν ἡ βȣς, και ὁ Καδμος εκει ῳκισε, και εθυσε την βουν Αθηνᾳ, και τῃ Αιγυπτιᾳ φωνῃ ταυτην ετιμησεν εκει, ὁθεν ȣτως και αἱ πυλαι ωνομασθησαν. Schol in Sept. cont. Thebas, ver. 492.

[h] Apollod. Bibl lib. iii. cap. 10.

[i] It is worthy of obſervation, that at preſent the conſtellation of the Pleiads conſiſts of only ſix ſtars, which Hyginus accounts for in the following manner. Electra, the ſeventh Pleiad, wild with grief at the deſtruction of Troy, ſtarted from her appointed ſtation, and rambling with diſhevelled hair through the Arctic circle, was changed into a comet. Poet. Aſtron. lib. ii. cap 21. From this fable we evidently learn, that at the time, when the conſtellation of the Pleiads was firſt

 noted,

in ſhort, who quitted the land of the Cabiri on account of a flood, and who was ſtyled by the Samothracians, in the ancient language of the Myſteries, *Polyarches*, or Bol-Arca, *the lord of the Ark*[k], like perhaps every fabulous founder of a primitive monarchy, is ſimply Dar-da-Nus, *the illuſtrious Noah*[l]. Accordingly, his mythological wife was called *Ariſba* or *Batea*[m]; the firſt of which titles is Ares-Ba, *the heifer of the ſolar god*, and the ſecond Bu-Dea, *the divine heifer*.

With regard to the poſterity of Dardanus, it is certainly a mere ſeries of genealogical repetitions. Dardanus is ſaid to have been the father of Ilus, and Erichthonius; Erichthonius, of Tros; and Tros, of Ilus the younger, and Aſſaracus[n]. All theſe apparently different perſons are in fact one and the ſame

noted, a comet appeared in its vicinity, which was then too haſtily reckoned the ſeventh Pleiad.

[k] —Δαρδανον, ὁν και Πολυαρχη φασι λεγεσθαι ὑπο των εγχωριων. Schol. in Apoll. Argon. lib. i. ver. 916. The language of the Samothracians, as we learn from Diodorus, was not Greek; conſequently the etymology of the word *Polyarches* muſt be ſought for in the ſacred dialect of the Myſteries. See Diod. Bibl. lib. v. p. 322.

[l] Dar-da-Nus is the contracted form of Adar-da-Nus, as Derceto is of Ader-Ceto, or Atargatis.

[m] Lycoph. Caſſ. ver. 1308. and Tzet. in loc.

[n] Apollod. Bibl. lib. iii. cap. 11.

mytho-

mythological character. Erichthonius, like the imaginary Athenian sovereign of that name, is the deity of the Ark, worshipped equally at Troy, and at Athens; Tros is Toros, *the Noëtic bull*; Assaracus is As-Arach, *the helio-arkite god*, who was adored by the Babylonians under the appellation of *Nisroch* or *Asarach* [o]; and Ilus, as we are plainly informed by Sanchoniatho [p], is the same as Cronus [q], whence, in the theology of Hindostan, Ila, the daughter of Satyavrata or Noah, is feigned to be the wife of Buddha [r]. What decidedly confirms the propriety of this supposition is, that the story of the founding of Thebes by Cadmus is repeated without any variation in the narrative of the building of

[o] Vide supra p. 123

[p] Euseb. Præp. Evan lib. i. cap. 10.

[q] M Court de Gebelin observes very justly, that this Ilus was the same as the Phenician Ilus or Saturn; but I cannot assent to his supposition, that the whole history of the founding of Troy is a mere agricultural allegory. (Monde Primitie, tom. i. p 166, 419) The whole of his work indeed is founded upon the erroneous principle of converting the mythology of the pagans into a series of physical allegories This mode of interpretation was doubtless adopted by Jamblichus, Porphyry, and the later heathens, when pressed by the arguments and ridicule of the Christians; but we have no reason to think, that it was the original idea of paganism

[r] It is almost superfluous to observe, that from *Ilus* is derived *Ilium*.

Troy

Troy by Ilus. This prince was commanded by an oracle to follow a ſpotted heifer, and whereſoever it ſhould lie down, there to found his intended city. The divine injunction was implicitly obeyed; and, in purſuance of it, Ilium was built upon the hill of the Phrygian Atè[s]. The ſacred Palladium, or image of Minerva, was now miraculouſly ſent down from heaven[t]; of that Minerva in fine, whom Lycophron denominates *the Phenician Goddeſs*, and whom Sanchoniatho deſcribes as the daughter of Ilus or Saturn. The Palladium, I apprehend, was nothing more than a perſonification of the divine wiſdom, which preſerved the Ark: whence it was ſuppoſed to have a peculiar influence over the deſtiny of Troy.

As the city of Ilium was founded by Ilus,

[s] —Δοντος αυτῳ (τῳ Ιλῳ) τȣ βασιλεως κατα χρησμον και βȣν ποικιλην· και φρασαντος εν ῳ ὑπερ αν αυτη κλιθη τοπῳ, πολιν κτιζειν, εἱπετο τῃ βοΐ. Ἡ δε αφικομενη επι τον λεγομενον της Φρυγιας Ατης λοφον, κλινεται. Ενθα πολιν κτισας Ιλος, ταυτην μεν Ιλιον εκαλεσε. Apollod. Bibl. lib. iii. cap. 11. In alluſion to this circumſtance, Lycophron ſtyles the hills, upon which Troy was built, *buplanoctiſti*.

Ατης απ' ακρων βȣπλανοκτιςων λοφων,
Τοιων δ' απ' αρχης ηρχ' Αλεξανδρα λογων.

Lycoph. Caſſ. ver. 29.

The ſame ſtory of the heifer is related by his ſcholiaſt Tzetzes without any variation. Tzet. in loc.

[t] Apollod. Bibl. lib. iii. cap. 11.

ſo

ſo its walls are feigned to have been built by Neptune and Apollo, or Noah conſidered in his twofold character of a diluvian and a ſolar god; while the Cetus, ſent by the former of theſe deities, and conquered by Hercules, when engaged with Telamon in the Argonautic expedition, was merely a ſymbol of the Ark: hence Hercules is ſaid by Hyginus to have given the kingdom of Troy to Podarces, or Bud-Arc, *the tauriform god of the Ark*, who was afterwards called Priam [u]. The early hiſtory indeed of the Ilienſes, like that of perhaps all other aboriginal nations, is ſimply a fabulous detail of the events of the deluge. Accordingly we are informed by Apollodorus, that Ilus or Cronus, the ſuppoſed ſon of Dardanus, eſpouſed Eurydicè the daughter of Adraſtus; and that ſhe bore to him Laomedon, the father of Podarces or Priam, and Tithonus, the paramour of Aurora [x]. This Tithonus however, the imaginary brother of Priam, Apollodorus afterwards aſſerts to have been, not the lover of Aurora, but her ſon by Cephalus; and he adds, that he was the father of Phaëthon, and the anceſtor of Adonis or Noah [y]. It is ſufficiently evident therefore,

[u] Hyg. Fab. 89

[x] Apollod Bibl. lib iii. cap 11.

[y] Ibid. cap. 13.

that

that Tithonus is purely a mythological character. He is in fact Tithon-Nus, *the Titanic Noah:* while Eurydicè is Ura-Daga, *the fish sacred to the Sun*; and Adrastus, Adar-As-Theus, *the illustrious deity of fire.* The very name of Tróy itself alludes to the arkite superstition, Troia being a contraction of Tor-Aia, *the land of the bull*: and, with a similar allusion to the solar devotion, its citadel seems to have been called *Pergamus*, in honour of P'Ur-Cham, *the blazing Sun*; and the country, in which it was situated, *Phrygia*, as being Ph'Ur-G'Aia, *the land of the illustrious fire* [z].

The early history of Troy then being thus entirely mythological, we shall not wonder to find a curious legend preserved among the Ilienses, which precisely resembles those of Perseus, Telephus, Anius, and Bacchus. We learn from Conon, that Tennes and Hemithea were the children of Cycnus king of Troas. This prince, having lost his first wife, espoused a second, who conceived an adulterous passion for her son-in-law. Tennes however refused to comply with her desires; upon which the

[z] Hence the following kindred words have all a relation to fire or dryness. Φρυγανα, ὑλη λεπτη και ξηρα—Φρυγια, ἡ φρυγεσα—Φρυγιον, ξυλον ξηρον—Φρυκτα, ξηρα—Φρυκτορια, πυρκαϊα πυρσεια. λαμπας. καυσις. Hesych.

enraged

enraged queen accuſed him to her huſband of the very crime, of which ſhe herſelf had been guilty. Cycnus immediately apprehended his ſon, and incloſed him within an ark, along with his ſiſter Hemithea, who had too unguardedly expreſſed her ſorrow at the misfortunes of her brother. The ark was caſt into the ſea, and at length drifted on ſhore upon an iſland, which from Tennes, or Ten-Nus, *the fiſh-god Noah*, was afterwards called *Tenedos* [a].

I ſhall now return to Iaſus or Jaſion, the brother of Dardanus. This prince is ſaid by ſome to have been ſtruck with lightning for attempting the chaſtity of Ceres [b]; but others ſuppoſe him to have been beloved by that goddeſs [c], who bore him a ſon named *Plutus* [d]. Plutus or Pluto [e] was one of the Cabiri, and

[a] Conon Narrat. 29.

[b] Ιασιων μεν Δημητρος εϱασθεις κεϱαυνουται. Tzet. in Lycoph. ver. 29

[c] Επι δε Ιασωνι Δημητρι. Clem. Alex. Cohort. ad Gent. p. 28. Και βροτον Ιασιωνα ποσιν προσπτυξατο Δηω. Nonni Dionyſ. lib. v. p. 108. See likewiſe Athen. Deipnoſ. lib xiii. p. 566.

[d] Πλυτον δε γενεσθαι φασιν εν Τριποδῳ της Κρητης εκ Δημητρος και Ιασιωνος. Diod. Sic. Bibl. lib. v. p. 343. See alſo Schol in Theoc. Idyll. x. ver. 19.

[e] That Plutus was the ſame as Pluto appears from the united teſtimony of Cicero, Fulgentius, and Julius Firmicus.

Cic.

the ſame perſon in fact as his imaginary father, whom I apprehend, like his brother Dardanus, to be no other than the great patriarch. Jaſion is alſo the ſame as Triptolemus, or Tor-Ip-Tol-Am, *the ſolar deity of the Ark*; whence they are both ſaid to have been favourites of Ceres, and both to have firſt ſowed the earth with grain [f]. He ſeems moreover to be nearly allied to the fabulous leader of the celebrated Argonautic expedition; whence he is even called *Jaſon*, both by Conon [g], and by Clemens Alexandrinus [h]. The name, however varied and corrupted, is compounded of As-On, *the blazing Sun* [i].

It is remarkable, that Io or Iſis, though generally eſteemed the daughter of Inachus, is alſo deſcribed as the offspring of a perſon de-

Cic. de Nat. Deor. lib. ii. cap. 26.—Fulg. Mythol. lib. i. cap. 4.—Jul. Firm. de Err. Prof Rel. p. 17.

[f] Φασι την γην σπαρεισαν ὑπο Ιασιωνος. Diod. Sic. Bibl. lib. v. p. 343.

[g] Δαρδανος και Ιασων παιδες ησην Διος εξ Ηλεκτρας της Ατλαντιδος, ωκεν Σαμοθρακην την νησον. Con. Narrat. 21.

[h] Επι δε Ιασωνι Δημητρ. Clem. Alex. Cohort. ad Gent. p. 28.

[i] This point will be diſcuſſed more fully hereafter. Vide infra chap. viii. Jaſion was alſo called *Eetion*, which is a word of the very ſame import; Ait-On being only the Chaldaic form of As On.

nomi-

nominated *Iasus*, who was the son of Triops. The father of this Triops was Phorbas; Phorbas and Pirasus were the children of Argus; Argus was the grandson of Phoroneus; and Phoroneus was the son of Inachus[k] The whole of the preceding genealogy is entirely mythological. Inachus, Phoroneus, and Argus, are all equally *the patriarch Noah*; Pirasus is P'Ares, *the Sun*; Phorbas is Ph'Or-Ob-As, *the burning solar serpent*; Triops is Tor-Op, *the ophite god of the tauric Ark*; Agenor is Ag-Ain-Or, *the solar deity of the ocean*; and lastly Io, or Isis, is *the Ark*[l].

Diodorus Siculus informs us, that Jasion espoused Cybelè, who is the same as Ceres, and by her became the father of Corybas and the Corybantes. After his translation into heaven, his brother Dardanus, Cybelè, and Corybas, brought the Samothracian mysteries into Phrygia[m]. It appears then, that Jasion

[k] Φορωνεα εν τῃ γῃ ταυτῃ (scil. Αργολιδι) γενεσθαι πρωτον· Ιναχον δε ουκ ανδρα, αλλα τον ποταμον, πατερα ειναι Φορωνει—Αργος δε Φορωνεως θυγατριδους, βασιλευσας μετα Φορωνεα, ωνομασεν αφ' αὑτου την χωραν. Αργου δε Πειρασος γινεται και Φορβας· Φορβαντος δε Τριοπας· Τριοπα δε Ιασος και Αγηνωρ. Ιω μεν ουν Ιασου θυγατηρ. Pauf Corinth p. 144, 145.

[l] Hence, in the progress of genealogical repetition, she is said to have been the daughter of Argia and Inachus. Hyg. Fab. 145. Argia however and Io are equally the Noetic Ark.

[m] Φασι δε τον Ιασιωνα γημαντα Κυβελην γεννησαι Κορυβαντας.

Ιασιωνος

is the father of the Cabiri, and consequently the *Sydyk* or *Noah* of Sanchoniatho. Hence we find, that his supposed son Corybas is fabled to have espoused Thebah, or *the Ark*, the daughter of Cilix; and to have given the title of *Corybantes* to the priests of his mother Cybelè [n]. From Jasion or Jasus, the bay of Prienè, celebrated for the mythological voyage of the Phenician statue, received its name of *Jasus* [o].

Ιασιωνος δε εις θεους μεταςαντος, Δαρδανον και Κυβελην και Κορυβαντα μετακομισαι εις την Ασιαν τα της μητρος των θεων ἱερα, και συναπαραι εις Φρυγιαν. Diod. Sic. Bibl. lib. v. p. 323. See also Strab. Geog. lib. vii p. 331.

[n] Τον δε Κορυβαντα τους επι τοις της μητρος ἱεροις ενθουσιασαντας αφ᾽ ἑαυτου Κορυβαντας προσαγορευσαι· γημαι δε Θηβην την Κιλικος θυγατερα. Diod Sic. Bibl. lib. v. p. 323. This Cilix was the son of the Phenician Agenor, and the brother of Cadmus, and Europa. He was supposed to have given his name to Cilicia. Apollod. Bibl. lib. iii. cap 1. Hence we plainly see the reason, why Thebah was feigned to be his daughter; and why the inhabitants of Cilicia asserted, that the fabulous monster Typhon was produced from a cave in their country. Typhon, as we have repeatedly observed, was merely the diluvian ocean.

Τον γηγενη τε Κιλικιων οικητορα
Αντρων ιδων ωκτειρα, δαιον τερας
Ἑκατονταχαρηνον προς βιαν χειρουμενον
Τυφωνα θουρον, πασιν ὁς αντεςη θεοις,
Σμερδναισι γαμφηλαισι συριζων φονον.

Æschyl. Prom. Vinc. ver. 351.

[o] Vide supra p. 108.

As

As for Samothrace, the land of Jasion, Dardanus, and the Cabiri, it was anciently called *Samos* [p], and was inhabited by a primitive race of men [q]. These had a peculiar language of their own, which prevailed in their sacred rites [r]: whence originated the injunction of the Magian oracle, not to change barbarous names [s]; and the declaration of Plato, that the Greeks borrowed many words from the barbarians, the etymology of which would be vainly sought for in their own tongue [t]. The Samothracians, in the time of Diodorus, had faithfully preserved an account of the deluge, which overflowed their country, and obliged Dardanus to migrate into Troas [u]. This circumstance is mentioned by Nonnus, but, like Tzetzes, he esteems the Samothracian flood the third which had happened; a mistake

[p] Samos was so denominated in honour of Sames, (שמש) *the Sun*. It was esteemed peculiarly sacred to Juno, or the dove Apoll Argon lib. i. ver. 187.

[q] Ταυτην (Σαμοθρακην) την νησον ενιοι μεν φασι το παλαιον Σαμον ονομασθηναι—ῴκησαν δε αυτην αυτοχθονες ανθρωποι. Diod. Bibl lib. v. p. 321.

[r] Εσχηκασι δε παλαιαν ιδιαν διαλεκτον οἱ αυτοχθονες, ἧς πολλα εν ταις θυσιαις μεχρι τε νυν τηρειται. Ibid. p. 322

[s] Vide supra p 116.

[t] Vide supra p 117.

[u] Οἱ δε Σαμοθρᾳκες ἱσορεσι, προ των παρα τοις αλλοις γενομενων κατακλυσμων, ἑτερον ενει μεγαν γενεσθαι. Diod Bibl lib v. p 322.

eaſily accounted for, when we recollect, that moſt nations have changed the primitive tradition of an univerſal deluge, into a belief of one, that was only partial and appropriate.

Γλωτῳ κληρον ελειπεν εχειν και σκηπτρα Καβειρων
Δαρδανος,———
——— ὁτε τριτατȣ χυσις ομβρȣ
Κυμασι πυργωθεισα κατεκλυσεν ἑδρανα κοσμȣ[x].

Jaſion moreover was not only connected with Dardanus, but, as we are expreſsly informed by Pauſanias, was one of the Idèi Dactyli, Curetes, or Cabiri, and the brother of Hercules, Peonius, Epimedes, and Idas[y]. Hence he is ſaid by Apollodorus to have eſpouſed Clymenè, or Cula-Menah, *the Noëtic Ark*; who was ſuppoſed to be the daughter of Minyas, or Menu, the anceſtor of the Minyæ[z]. By her he became the father of the huntreſs Atalanta[a].

x Nonni Dionyſ lib. iii. p 59.

y Διος δε τεχθεντος επιτρεψαι Ρεαν τε παιδος την φρȣραν τοις Ιδαιοις Δακτυλοις, καλȣμενοις δε τοις αυτοις τȣτοις και Κȣρησιν· αφικεσθαι δε αυτȣς εξ Ιδης της Κρητικης, Ηρακλεα, και Παιωνιον, και Επιμηδην, Ιασιον τε, και Ιδαν. Pauſ 1 Eliac p 391.

z Apollod. Bibl. lib iii cap 9

a Her hiſtory muſt be reſerved, till the radical *Hiph* is taken into conſideration. Clymenè, as we have ſeen, was alſo the reputed mother of Atlas, and the daughter of Oceanus. There

——— Ἀταλαντην
Κȣρην Ιασιοιο συοκτονον Αρκασιδαο [b].

He is likewiſe feigned to be the ſon of Argus, and the brother of Piranthus, or P'Aran-Thus, *the god of the Ark*; while Io, whom we have already conſidered, both as his daughter, and as the daughter of Inachus, is further ſaid by Heſiod and Acuſilaus to be the offspring of Piren [c]. Theſe varying accounts can only be reconciled upon the ſuppoſition, that ſuch ancient genealogies are in reality mere fables. Io, being the Ark, is indifferently deſcribed as the child of Inachus, or Noah; of Jaſion, or the patriarch worſhipped in conjunction with the Sun; and of Pirenus, or the arkite Noah. She is uniformly however ſaid to be the daughter of a king of Argos [d], and the prieſteſs of Juno, *the dove*; by whom ſhe was changed into a heifer, or, according to Eſchy-

There is no real diſcrepancy however between the two accounts.

[b] Callim Hymn in Dian ver 215.

[c] Apollod Bibl. lib ii. cap 1.

[d] Ιω βασιλεως των Αργειων ην θυγατηρ. Palæph in Incred Hiſt cap. 43. The name *Io* ſeems to be a contraction of Ionah, *the dove*; whence alſo Ionia, which Apollodorus ſays was ſo called from Io. Bibl lib. ii. cap 1. I have already noticed the intercommunion of the heathen goddeſſes.

 lus,

lus, into a monſter compounded of a woman and a heifer.

> Βροτοι δ' οἱ γας τοτ' ησαν εννομοι,
> Χλωρῳ δειματι θυμον
> Παλλοντ', οψιν αηθη,
> Βοτον εσορωντες δυσχερες μιξομβροτον,
> Ταν μεν βοος,
> Ταν δ' αυ γυναικος· τερας δ' εθαμβουν [e].

This compound figure is an hieroglyphic of the ſame import and nature, as that of Derceto: the only difference between them is, that, in one caſe, the ſymbolical ox, and, in the other, the ſymbolical fiſh, is joined to the woman. In this ſhape Io rambled through Ionia, and ſeveral other countries both of Europe and Aſia. At length, in Egypt, ſhe recovered her priſtine form; and became the mother of Epaphus, and the wife of Telegonus [f]. The weariſome journey, to which ſhe was compelled by the divine impulſe of Juno [g],

[e] Supplic. ver. 574.

[f] Apollod Bibl lib ii. cap. 1. According to Strabo however, ſhe became a mother in Eubèa. Strab Geog lib x. p. 445.

[g] Ἡρα δε τη βοι οιστρον εμβαλλει. Apollod. Bibl. lib. ii cap. 1 Eſchylus introduces Io, bewailing, in a very ſtriking manner, the fatal impulſe, which compelled her to wander

> Α α, εα εα·
> Χριει τις αυ με ταλαιναν οιστρος,
> Ειδωλον Αργου γηγενους αλευ ω δα,

Φοβουμαι

relates, I apprehend, only to the voyage of the Ark; and her marriage with Telegonus, or Tel-Og-On, *the solar god of the ocean*, is merely the allegorical nuptials of the Ark and the arkite deity.

Such is the history of the mythological founders of Troy; a history connected at once with the Argonautic expedition, and with the Hellenic fables respecting the princes of Argolis and Arcadia. Let us next proceed to trace the introduction of the Cabiric mysteries into Italy, by the Pelasgi, the Lydians, the Cretans, the Iliensians, and the Argonauts[h].

I have observed, that Pelasgus, the reputed father of the Pelasgi, was the patriarch Noah[i];

Φοβοιμαι τον μυριωπον εισορωσα βουταν.
Ὁ δε πορευεται δολιον ομμ᾽ εχων,
Ὁν ουδε κατθανοντα γαια κευθει.
Αλλα με ταν ταλαιναν εξ ανερων περων
Κυνηγετει, πλανᾳ τε νηστιν ανα ταν παραλιαν
Ψαμμον, ὑπο δε κηροπλαστος οττοβει δοναξ
Αχετας ὑπνοδοταν νομον ιω ιω, ποι ποι,
Πω, πω, πω, πη μ᾽ αγουσι τηλεπλαγκτοι πλανοι.

Prom Vinc ver. 568 See also v. 700. 785.

[h] I do not mean to say, that the Argonauts ever literally sailed to Italy, for the whole of their voyage seems to be purely fabulous, but the very early introduction of the Cabiric mysteries into that country appears from the fiction of the Argonauts having touched upon it. For an account of this famous voyage, vide infra chap. viii.

[i] Vide supra p 93.

and I conjecture, that, in allusion to the deluge, he derived his name from Pelagim, *streams of water*. With regard to his supposed descendants, the Pelasgi, all ancient writers, as we learn from Strabo, unanimously allow, that they formerly spread themselves over the whole of Greece, and particularly over that district of Thessaly, which was possessed by the Eolians. Ephorus thinks, that they were originally Arcadians[k]; and that they adopted a military, in preference to a pastoral life. They sent colonies into Crete; and all that part of Thessaly, which lies between the river Peneus and Thermopylæ, as far as the mountainous country in the neighbourhood of Pindus, bore the appellation of *Pelasgic Argos*, on account of the empire which they had there established[l]. Homer represents them, as seated at Larissa[m], or Lares-Ai, *the land of the La-*

[k] That is, *worshippers of the Ark.*

[l] Τȣς δε Πελασγȣς, ότι μεν αρχαιον το φυλον κατα την Ἑλλαδα παρ-πεπολασε, και μαλιςα παρα τοις Αιολευσι τοις κατα Θετταλιαν, ὁμολογȣσιν ἁπαντες σχεδοι τι Νομιζειν δε φησιν Εφορος, το ανεκαθεν Αρκαδας οντας ἑλεσθαι ςρατιωτικον βιον—Της Κρητης εποικοι γεγονασιν—Και το Πελασγικον Αργος, ἡ Θετταλια λεγεται, το μεταξυ των εμβολων του Πηνειου, και των Θερμοπυλων, ἑως της ορεινης της κατα Πινδον, δια το επαρξαι των τοπων τȣτων Πελασγοις. Strab. Geog. lib v. p 220.

[m] Ἱπποθοος δ' αγε φυλα Πελασγων εγχεσιμωρων,
Των οἱ Λαρισσαν εριβωλακα ναιεταασκον. Iliad. ii. 840.

res,

res or *ſolar Cabiri*[n]; Eſchylus affirms, that they came originally from Argos in the neighbourhood of Mycenæ; Ephorus mentions, that Peloponneſus was alſo denominated *Pelaſgia*; Euripides ſays, that the Pelaſgi received their more modern title of *Danai* from Danaus, who migrated from Egypt to Argos; and Anticlides relates, that they firſt inhabited Lemnos and Imbrus, whence ſome of them ſailed into Italy along with Tyrrhenus the ſon of Atys[o]. According to Strabo, they were the moſt ancient people of Greece; from which aſſertion we are led to conclude, that they were the aboriginal inhabitants of that peninſula, being ſeated there long before the arrival of the Egyptian coloniſts[q]. This

[n] Lar is El-Ar, *the Solar God.*

[o] Αισχυλος δ' εκ του περι Μυκηνας Αργυς φησιν εν Ικετισιν η Δαναϊσι το γενος αυτων. Και την Πελοποννησον δε, Πελασγιαν φησιν Εφορος κληθηναι· και Ευριπιδης δ' εν Αρχελαω φησιν, ὁτι

Δαναος, ὁ πεντηκοντα θυγατερων πατηρ,
Ελθων ες Αργος, ῳκισεν Ιναχυ πολιν.
Πελασγιατας δ' ωνομασμενους το πριν,
Δαναους καλεισθαι νομον εθηκεν.

Αντικλειδης δε πρωτους φησιν αυτους τα περι Λιμνον και Ιμβρον κτισαι· καὶ δη τουτον τινας, και μετα Τυρρηνου του Ατυος εις Ιταλιαν συναραι. Strab. lib v p. 221.

[p] Οἱ δε Πελασγοι των περι την Ἑλλαδα δυναςευσαντων αρχαιοτατοι λεγονται. Strab. lib. vii. p. 327. The whole indeed of Greece was formerly called *Pelaſgia*—της νυν Ἑλλαδος, προτερον δε Πελασγιης καλουμενης της αυτης ταυτης —Herod. lib. ii. cap. 56.

ſuppoſition is confirmed by the expreſs declaration of Herodotus, that they ſpoke a totally different language from the Hellenes [q]. Hence I conceive the ancient Pelaſgi to have been the children of Japhet, by whom the iſles of the Gentiles were peopled [r]; while the Hellenes, as it appears from the unanimous conſent of Hiſtorians [s], came from Egypt, and muſt therefore be eſteemed the progeny of Ham [t].

[q] Herod. lib i cap. 57

[r] I cannot aſſent to Mr. Bryant's ſuppoſition, that the Pelaſgi were an Ammonian race.

[s] Diod Bibl. lib. i p. 25 et lib. v. p. 329 —Herod. lib. ii. cap. 91. et lib. vi. cap. 54 —Pauſ. Att p 95, 106.— Tzet. Chil. v Hiſt. xviii. p. 91 —Syncel. Chronog p. 158.

[t] The very learned and ingenious Col. Vallancey ſuppoſes on the one hand, that the Pelaſgi penetrated, along with the deſcendants of the Dodanim, into Ireland, and on the other hand, that they were the ſame race as the ſcriptural Philiſtines; while the no leſs ingenious Capt. Wilford conjectures, that the Philiſtines were a colony of the Indian Palli. Theſe ſeveral opinions will be found perfectly compatible with the ſyſtem, which I have adopted reſpecting the Pelaſgi. I apprehend this people to be a Celtic or Japhetic tribe, and the aboriginal inhabitants of Greece. Accordingly, as they were termed *Pelagim*, or *Pelagians*, partly from their devotion to the arkite Myſteries, and partly from their planting the iſles of the Gentiles; ſo the Celtæ, Galli, or Galatæ, derived their name either from Cal, *the Ark*, or from Galim, *the waves of the ſea*. (The radical Cal or Cul will be diſcuſſed at large hereafter. Vide infra chap vii) With regard to the Palli, I conceive them to have been a branch of the Celto-Scythians, for they are

The Pelaſgi are ſaid to have been joined, in their expedition to Italy, by the Tyrrheni, or Lydians; whence the two nations naturally became connected with each other, and were

are evidently conſidered as a diſtinct race from the Hindoos. Such alſo was the caſe with the Philiſtines. Hence the LXX. well knowing, that they were of a different line from the Canaanites the deſcendants of Ham, invariably denominate them *Allophyli*, or *men of another tribe*, that is to ſay, of another tribe than thoſe of the Canaanites, Perizzites, or Hivites Thus far I have the happineſs of agreeing with Col Vallancey; but I doubt whether the Danai were the ſame as the Iriſh Dadanas, or ſcriptural Dodanim; for, if there be any truth in hiſtory, the Danai came from Egypt, not from Chaldèa. It is proper for me to obſerve, that Col Vallancey derives the word *Pelaſgi* from the Iriſh or Celtic Felaſge, *a wanderer*. Such an appellation certainly deſcribes their character very accurately; the reader therefore will judge for himſelf, whether he prefers this etymology, or the former one. It is poſſible, that the Phallus received its name from the Palli, Pelaſgi, or Paleſtini. How much the Pelaſgi were addicted to the phallic worſhip, the reader will ſhortly be informed. Miphletzeph, the idol of Maachah, (1 Kings xv 13) ſeems to be Ma-Phallaſath, *the great phallic goddeſs*. I think, that ſhe was rather Venus or Mylitta, than Priapus, as Selden ſuppoſes. (See Seld. de Diis Syris, Synt. ii. cap. 5.) Perhaps however we ought to derive *Palli, Pelaſgi, Paleſtini*, neither from *Peleg* nor *Felaſge*; but to deduce theſe ſeveral appellations from *Phallus*, rather than, what I juſt obſerved, vice verſa. It certainly is not improbable, that thoſe nations were ſo called from their worſhip of the Phallus, ſince the Hindoos aſſure us, that the Ionians or Yonijas received their name from their devotion to the myſteries of the Yoni.

ſome-

ſometimes, as we learn from Dionyſius of Halicarnaſſus, even conſidered as one and the ſame people [u]. Sophocles accordingly, in a fragment of *the tragedy of Inachus*, mentions them as ſuch.

Ιναχε γεννατωρ, παι κρηνων
Πατρος Ωκεανȣ, μεγα πρεσβευων
Αργȣς τε γυαις, Ἡρας τε παγοις,
Και Τυῤῥηνοισι Πελασγοις [x].

Hail Inachus, thou ſon of hoary Ocean!
Great is thy name throughout Junonian Argos,
And dear to the Tyrrhenian Pelaſgi.

In Italy, they ſeated themſelves upon the banks of the lake Cotylè, the floating iſland of which I have already conjectured to be of the ſame nature as that in the vicinity of the Egyptian Buto [y]. Here, during the prevalence of a famine with which their new ſettlements were afflicted, they vowed tenths to Jupiter, Apollo, and the Cabiri.

The leader of the Pelaſgi and the Lydians, in this expedition, was Tyrrhenus or Tyrſenus, who was ſuppoſed by ſome to have been

[u] Εκαλȣντο δε ὑπο των αλλων ανθρωπων, της τε χωρας επικλησει αφ' ἧς εξανεςησαν, και του παλαιου γενȣς μνημῃ, οἱ αυτοι Τυῤῥηνοι και Πελασγοι. Dion Halic Ant Rom. lib. i. cap. 25.

[x] Soph. apud Dion. Halic. Ant. lib. i. cap. 25.

[y] Vide ſupra p. 61, 65.

the

the ſon of Atys or Attis king of Lydia [z]; by others, of Hercules [a]; and by others of Telephus, who, as we have ſeen, was born of Hercules and Augè, and was expoſed along with his mother in an ark. The ſecond ſon of Telephus was Tarchon [b].

With regard to theſe varying genealogies it may be obſerved, that Hercules, Attis, and Telephus, are in fact one and the ſame perſon, being all equally the patriarch Noah: accordingly we find, that Attis is repreſented as the paramour of Cybelè, the great arkite mother of the hero-gods. Attis in ſhort was no other than Bacchus [c]; and the ſhameleſs rites, attached to his ſervice, appear to have originated, partly perhaps from a tradition of the crime committed by Ham againſt his father, but principally from a notion, that the Ark was the conſort of Noah. The ancient mythologiſts conſidered this veſſel in the light of an univerſal mother to the renovated human ſpecies, and the patriarch in that of a

[z] Τυρσηνος, και Λυδος, Ατυος παιδες ησαν, του Λυδων βασιλεως. Tzet. in Lycoph. ver 1351

[a] Tyrrhenus Herculis filius. Hyg Fab. 274.

[b] Τυρσηνια δε ἡ Ιταλια, απο Τυρσηνου του Τηλεφου υἱου—Ἡρακλεους και Αυγης της θυγατρος Αλεου, παις Τηλεφος· Τηλεφου και Ἱερας, Ταρχων και Τυρσηνος. Tzet. in Lycoph. ver 1237, 1242.

[c] Τον Διονυσον τινες Αττιν προσαγορευεσθαι θελουσιν, αιδοιων εστερημενον. Clem. Alex. Cohort ad Gent p 16.

fa-

father: whence they were adored in the Mysteries under symbols, by which, not only genuine religion, but even common decency, was most scandalously outraged [d].

[d] De origine superstitionis phallicæ, a famoso quodam libello, non minus impio quod ad fidem Christianam, quam spurco et impudico quod ad bonos mores attinet, prorsus dissentio. In hoc scilicet libello, phalli mysteria ad universæ naturæ vim genialem passim referuntur: mihi vero contra ad diluvium omnino pertinere videntur; sicut enim Arcæ vulva, ita Noaci phallus erat symbolum Inter Tyrrhenos igitur sive Lydos, Pelasgorum socios, necnon inter Indos, Hierapolitanos, atque Corybanticos, invaluere quædam fabulæ, unde apertè liquet mysteria phallica eadem esse quæ mysteria Cabirica sive archica.

"Apud Timotheum non ignobilem theologorum virum," verba sunt Arnobii, "necnon apud alios æque doctos, super "magna deorum matre, superque sacris ejus, origo hæc sita "est, ex reconditis antiquitatum libris et ex intimis eruta, "quemadmodum ipse scribit, insinuatque mysteriis. In Phry-"giæ finibus inauditæ per omnia vastitatis petra, inquit, est "quædam, cui nomen est *Agdus*, regionis ejus ab indigenis sic "vocata · ex ea lapides sumptos, sicut Themis mandaverat "præcinens, in orbem mortalibus vacuum Deucalion jactavit "et Pyrrha . ex quibus cum cæteris et hæc, *Magna* quæ di-"citur, informata est *Mater*, atque animata divinitus."—Reliqua pars fabulæ minimè patet, donec infortunium Agdestidis narrat Arnobius. "Fit, ut insolita re (nempe vino) victus, "Agdestis soporem in altissimum deprimatur. Adest ad insi-"dias Liber, ex setis scientissimè complicatis unum plantæ in-"jicit laqueum, parte altera proles cum ipsis genitalibus occu-"pat: exhalata ille vi meri corripit se impetu, et adducente "nexus planta, suis ipse se viribus, eo, quo fuerat, privat sexu" (Arnob. adv Gent. lib v. p. 157.) In hac fabula quanquam in-

The Pelasgi are said by Herodotus to have

interesse quoddam Agdestidi Liber videtur, nihilominus Agdestis iste *deviratus* procul dubio est Attis sive Bacchus. Hinc rectè Clemens· Τον Διονυσον τινες Αττιν προσαγορευεσθαι θελουσιν, ΑΙΔΟΙΩΝ ΕΣΤΕΡΗΜΕΝΟΝ. (Cohort. ad Gent p. 16) Hinc etiam Ovidius:

> Deque viro fias *nec fœmina, nec vir*, ut Attys,
> Et quatias molli tympana rauca manu
>
> Ibis, ver. 455.

Hinc idem Clemens. Ταυτα οἱ Φρυγες τελεσκουσιν Αττιδι, και Κυβελη, και Κορυβασιν (Cohort. p. 13) Sicut igitur Agdestis sive Attis Noacus, ita Cybelè magna mater sive Arca. Vocula autem *Agdestis* vel *Agdus* est Ag-Dus, *deus Oceani*, lapisque Agdus, nihil aliud quam cubus archæi Mercurii.

Valent etiam apud Indos eadem mysteria phallico-archica. Inter diluvium scilicet το Yoni, sive vulva, formam navis Arghæ, (hoc est Arcæ Noeticæ,) fertur induisse, Lingam interea sive Phallo mali officium sibi vindicante. (Asiat Res vol. vi p. 523.) Notandum est Phallum Maha-Devæ, qui Osiris vel Noacus solaris procul dubio est, sacrum in primis haberi; (Maur. Ind Ant. vol ii p 158, 166) unde in sacello speluncæ Elephanticæ apud Bombaiam symbolum hoc impurum adhuc videre licet. (Ibid. p. 156) Hinc evenit, ut Maha-Deva Noeticus, in tabellis Indicis, media nave Argha haud raro sese erigat, vicesque mali aut ithyphalli ipse gerat. (Asiat. Res vol vi p. 523)

Eadem necnon mysteria apud Hierapolitanos invaluere; famaque crebra pervulgata fuit, quod quidem animadversione est præcipuè dignum, a Baccho seu Noaco fuisse instituta in perpetuam Deucalionis diluvii memoriam. Τα δε προπυλαια του ἱρου, ες ανεμον Βορεην αποκεκρινται, μεγεθος ὁσον τε ἑκατον οργυιεων. Εν τουτοισι τοις προπυλαιοισι και οἱ φαλλοι ἑςασι, τους Διονυσος εςησατο, ἡλικιην και οἱδε τριηκοσιων οργυιεων — Ες τουτεων τον ἑνα φαλλον ανηρ ἑκαςου ετεος δις ανερχεται, οικεει τε εν ακρῳ τῳ φαλλῳ χρονον ἑπτα ἡμερεων. Tot nempe dies inter singulos ex arca columbæ volatus inter-

formerly occupied Samothrace, and to have

interfuerunt —Αλλοισι δε δοκεει και ταδε Δευκαλιωνος εινεκα ποιεισθαι, εκεινης ξυμφορης μνηματα, όκοτε οἱ ανθρωποι ες τα ουρεα και ες τα περιμηκεα των δενδρεων ηεισαν, το πολλον ὑδωρ ορρωδεοντες. (Luc. de Dea Syra, sect 28) In Hierapoli ædes fuit celeberrima Deæ Syræ, a Lydo Attide Rheæ dicata; Attis scilicet orgia Phrygibus, Lydis, et Samothracibus, tradidit alii vero se persuasos habuerunt a Semiramide conditum fuisse templum, matrique Dercēto dicatum. (Ibid sect. 14, 15) Hæc autem Derceto sive Rhea, sicuti jam antea monstravimus, Venus est marina, id est Arca Noetica, Semiramisque, columba. Bene ergo docet Hesychius, Σεμιραμις, περιϛερα ορειος.

Quoniam igitur phallica superstitio a diluvio originem duxit, apud mystas veneratione habita est maxima arca quædam, veretrum Bacchi continens, haud aliter quam navis Argha phallum Maha-Devæ. Hanc nefandam idololatriam secum in Hetruriam tulerunt sacerdotes Corybantici Καβειρους δε τους Κορυβαντας καλουντες, και τελετην Καβειρικην καταγγελλουσιν· αυτω γαρ δη τουτω τω αδελφοκτονω, την κιϛην ανελομενω, εν ᾗ το του Διονυσου αιδοιον απεκειτο, εις Τυρρηνιαν κατηγαγον, ευκλεους εμποροι φορτιου· κανταυθα διετριβετην, φυγαδε οντε, την πολυτιμητον ευσεβειας διδασκαλιαν, αιδοια και κιϛην, θρησκευειν παραθεμενω Τυρρηνοις. (Clem. Alex. Cohort. ad Gent. p. 16.)

Hæc Phalli mysteria, teste Herodoto, primum apud Graios instituit Melampus, Bacchi sive Noaci honoris causa ipso nempe Melampo a Cadmo, Phœnicibusque, initiato. Orgia autem phallico-Cabirica prius nota erant Pelasgis, quam in Græciam sese contulerunt Ægyptiaci Hellenes. Ἑλλησι γαρ δη Μελαμπους εϛιν ὁ εξηγησαμενος του Διονυσου τουνομα, και την θυσιην, και την πομπην του φαλλου —πυθεσθαι δε μοι δοκεει μαλιϛα Μελαμπους τα περι τον Διονυσον παρα Καδμου τε του Τυριου, και των συν αυτῳ εκ Φοινικης απικομενων ες την νυν Βοιωτιαν καλεομενην χωραν —Του δε Ἑρμεω τα αγαλματα ορθα εχειν τα αιδοια ποιευντες, ουκ απ' Αιγυπτιων μεμαθηκασι, αλλα απο Πελασγων, πρωτοι μεν Ἑλληνων ἁπαντων Αθηναιοι παραλαβοντες, παρα δε τουτων ωλλοι. Αθηναιοισι γαρ δη τηι-

there eſtabliſhed the myſteries, which they

τηνικαυτα ες Ἑλληνας τελεουσι Πελασγοι. συνοικοι εγενοντο εν τη χωρῃ· ὁθεν περ και Ἑλληνες ηρξαντο νομισθηναι· ὁστις δε τα Καβειρων οργια μεμυηται, τα Σαμοθρηικες επιτελεουσι λαβοντες παρα Πελασγων, ὁυτος ωνηρ οιδε τα λεγω. Την γαρ Σαμοθρηικην οικεον προτερον Πελασγοι ὁυτοι, τοι περ Αθηναιοισι συνοικοι εγενοντο, και παρα τουτων Σαμοθρηΐκες τα οργια παραλαμβανουσι. Ορθα ων εχειν τα αιδοια ταγαλματα του Ἑρμεω, Αθηναιοι πρωτοι Ἑλληνων παρα Πελασγων μαθοντες, εποιησαντο. Οἱ δε Πελασγοι ἱρον τινα λογον περι αυτου ελεξαν, τα εν τοισι εν Σαμοθρηικη μυστηριοισι δεδηλωται. (Herod. lib ii. cap. 49, 51.) Mercurius iſte ithyphallicus, ab Herodoto memoratus, idem eſt qui Maha-deva, Oſiris, Bacchus, Attis, Priapus, Baal-Peor, et Baal-Berith; unde τε Baal-Berith, ſive *domini fœderis*, (ſcilicet Noetici,) non minus quam aliorum numinum Cabiræorum, ſymbolum fuit phallus. (Talm. Hier. fol xi col. 4.)

In ipſa etiam Anglia adhuc ſuperſunt quædam phallicæ Hyperboreorum ſuperſtitionis veſtigia Primo ſcilicet die Maii, per vicos Britanniæ haud paucos, circa perticam terræ infixam, quam Græci φαλλον nuncupant, tripudiare ſolent puellæ, juveneſque ruſtici, vulgi interim hilari circumſtante corona. Ab Indis autem, Ægyptiis, et Druidibus, hic ipſe dies myſteriis phalli helio-archicis æque fuit dicatus tunc enim temporis Sol conſtellationem ſubit Tauri, qui divo Arcæ magno, ſive *Jupiter*, ſive *Maha-Deva*, ſive *Bacchus*, ſive *Oſiris* ſit nuncupatus, ubique ſacer habitus eſt, intereſque mythologi, qui aſtronomiam idololatriæ nunquam non miſcebant, in medio cœlo taurum archæum lucentemque Solem una conjunctos viderunt. (Maur. Ind Ant. vol vi p 87. et infra)

Denique, quoniam Cabiri ſunt dii architæ, quoniamque myſteria phallica myſteriis Cabiricis per omnem terrarum orbem ſunt conjuncti; quoniam inſuper Bacchi, Oſiridis, ſive Noaci, honoris cauſa inſtituta fuit phallophoria; quoniamque tandem, cum apud Phrygas, Corybantas, et Tyrrhenos, tum præcipuè apud Indos, et Hierapolitanos, ad Noacum atque Arcam Phallum et vulvam pertinere omnino liquet: myſteria certè

afterwards, in conjunction with the Tyrrheni, carried into Italy [e]. Hence the term *Casmilus*, the Samothracian title of Mercury, was well known to the ancient Etrurians; hence also we have every reason to suppose, that the names of those, who conducted the expedition of the Pelasgi and the Lydians into Italy, would be fragments of the old sacred dialect of Samothrace; and hence we shall have no reason to be surprized, if we find the whole country replete with appellations allusive to the united worship of the Sun and the Ark. Accordingly Tyrsenus is Tor-San-Nus, *the helio-tauric Noah* [f]; Tarchon is Tor-Chon, *the priest of the bull*; Attis is At-Es, *the burning Sun*; Telephus is Tel-Oph, *the solar serpent*; Augè is Auga, *the oceanic Ark*; and her imaginary mother Neèra, who was descended from Arcas [g], is Nera, *the marine Ark* [h]. In a similar manner, the Etrurian city Perusia [i] is P'Eres-

certè antiqua phallica sive Bacchi, sive Osiridis, sive Attidis, sive Maha-Devæ, sive Cabirorum, ad diluvium, ut videtur, jure sunt referenda.

e Herod. lib ii cap. 51.

f Hence Jupiter or the Sun is called *Zan*; Ζαν, Ζευς. Hesych. Our own word *Sun* is the same ancient term. Zan or San appears to be a contraction of As On, *the solar orb*.

g Apollod Bibl. lib. iii. cap. 9

h From the same radical *Nei* we may also deduce *Nereus*.

i Strab. Geog lib. v. p 226.

Aia,

Aia, *the land of the Sun*; while the Italian river Ciris [k]; and the Italian city Siris, in the neighbourhood of which a colony of the Ionians, or *worſhippers of the dove*, fixed their reſidence [l], derived their reſpective names from Car, or Sir, *the Sun*. Italy itſelf, according to Tzetzes, was originally called *Argeſſa*, or *the land of the Ark*. It was afterwards denominated *Saturnia*, from Saturn or Noah; *Auſonia*, from Auſon, or As-On, *the ſolar fire*; *Tyrſenia*, from Tor-San, *the helio-tauric god*; and laſtly *Italia*, from Italus, or Taurus, *the helio-Noëtic bull* [m]. This Italus, as we ſhall

[k] Κιρις και Κυλισαρνος, ποταμοι εισι Ιταλικς. Tzet. in Lycoph. ver. 946.

[l] Σιρις και Λευταρνια πολεις Ιταλιας. Ibid. ver. 978. Ιωνες, ηγουν Αθηναιοι, προ των Τρωικων ελθοντες εις Ιταλιαν, ῳκησαν περι Σιριν. Ibid. ver. 987.

[m] —Ιταλιαν, ἡ πριν Αργεσσα εκαλειτο· ειτα Σατουρνια, απο του Κρονου·—ειτα απο τινος Αυσονος, Αυσονια· ειτα Τυρσηνια· ειτα απ᾽ Ιταλου, η αφ᾽ ἑνος ταυρου—Ιταλια ἡ χωρα εκληθη. Ibid. ver 1232. Italus is Ait-Al or Tal, *the Sun*, and in conſequence of the ſolar deity being worſhipped along with the Tauric Noah, the word *Italus*, in the ancient Etruſcan dialect, ſignified *a bull* Τυῤῥηνοι γαρ Ιταλον τον ταυρον εκαλεσαν. Apollod. Bibl. lib. ii. cap. 5. It had the ſame meaning alſo in the old language of Greece. Græcia antiqua, ut ſcribit Timæus, tauros vocabat Ιταλους Varro de Re Ruſt lib ii. cap. 5. And yet Heſychius aſſures us, that Talus is *the Sun* Ταλος, ὁ ἡλιος Italy was likewiſe called *Janicula* from Janus-Oenotrius, and *Cameſina* from Cameſes, or Cam-Es-Es, *the intenſely burning god* Italia complura a diis et ducibus ſortita fuit nomina, a Jano quidem

hereafter ſee, was the ſame mythological character as the Cretan Talus or Italotus; in other words, the tauric Noah worſhipped in conjunction with the Sun. We find alſo evident veſtiges of the introduction of the diluvian ſuperſtition in the fabulous hiſtory of the foundation of Mantua. This city is ſaid to have been built by Ocnus the ſon of Manto, who was a reputed propheteſs, and was feigned to have fled from Thebes into Italy: hence Mantua was always conſidered as a Theban colony [n]. The circumſtance of this colony

Janicula, quem quidam *Oenotrium* dictum exiſtimant, quia invenit vinum et far: *Cameſena* a Cameſe, et a Saturno *Saturnia*, *Salumbrona* quoque a gentilibus. M. Caton. Fragm. de Orig. fol. 165. Cameſes et Saturnus rate Thuſcum venerunt in amnem ad eundem Janum, uti Beroſus, Trallianus, Hyginus, et Macrobius in primo Saturnalium, et Ovidius in primo de Faſtis aſſerunt. Ann. Viterb. Comment. in Caton. Fragm. fol. 166. It is remarkable, that Janus-Oenotrius is ſaid by Myrſilus to have been an Arcadian, or arkite, and by his commentator Annius, to have been the ſon of Jaſius, the brother of Dardanus. (Myrſ. de Bello Pelaſg. fol. 146.) Pſeudo-Beroſus however plainly aſſerts, that Janus was no other than Noah; (Beroſ. Ant. lib. iii. fol. 25.) a circumſtance, which greatly corroborates the preceding remarks on the mythological hiſtory of Troy. Cato mentions a town in Italy ſuppoſed to have been founded by this Janus, and thence called *Arin-Janus*. (Cat. Fragm. fol. 162.) This name is evidently Aron-Jain, *the Ark of the wine god*. I was miſtaken in a former etymology which I gave of Janus. See Horæ Moſaicæ, vol. i. p. 167.

[n] Ocnus Mantuam dicitur condidiſſe, quam a matris nomine

having come from Thebes or Thebah ſuffici-ently points out the import of the tradition: accordingly Ocnus is Oc-Nus, *the oceanic Noah*; and Manto is Man-To, *the divine Ark*. The ſame helio-diluvian worſhip ſeems likewiſe to have been carried into ſeveral of the Italian iſlands. Hence Elian ſpeaks of a terrific dragon, which was adored in Malta [o]; hence Corſica was called by the Greeks *Cur-nus*, from Cur-Nus, *the ſolar Noah*; and hence Sardinia received its appellation of Sar-Adon-Aia, or *the land of the lord Sun*. In the laſt of theſe iſlands was a city built by the Carthaginians, and denominated *Carnalis*, in honour of Car-Ain-Al, *the ſolar fountain of fire* [p].

I ſhall now proceed to conſider the mytho-

ne appellavit nam fuit filius Tyberis et Mantûs Thyreſiæ Thebani vatis filiæ, quæ poſt patris interitum ad Italiam venit. Serv. in Æneid lib. x. p. 587 Thebani ab Ocno miſſi. M Caton. Fragm. de Orig. fol. 188 Mantua ſuo conditore Ocno illuſtris. Ibid fol. 172 Servius however informs us alſo, that *Mantus* was a title of Pluto Mantuam autem ideo nominatam, quod Etruſca lingua *Mantum* Ditem patrem appellant, cui etiam cum cæteris urbibus et hanc conſecravit The reaſon of this is obvious; Pluto is Noah, and, as Manto is the Ark, ſo Mantus is Man-Thus, *the god of the Ark*

o Ælian. de Anim lib. xi. cap 17. In the apocryphal ſtory of Bel and the Dragon we find the ſolar god Baal accompanied by his uſual emblem the ſerpent.

p Pauſ. Phoc. p. 838.

logy of Crete, which was one of the principal ſettlements of the Cabiric prieſts, and from which a colony was ſuppoſed to have migrated into Italy, under the command of Cleolaus the ſon of Minos [q].

In Crete then we find the Cabiri worſhipped under the title of *Curetes, Idèi Dactyli*, or *Telchines*; the import of which laſt word is *prieſts of the Sun* [r], the prieſts frequently bearing the names of the gods, whom they ſerved. Theſe Telchines are ſaid by Nonnus, in alluſion to the deluge, to be the ſons of Neptune [s]: Diodorus however varies, in ſome ſlight meaſure, from the poet of the Dionyſiacs, though, according to his account alſo, they were allied to the ocean. They firſt, he informs us, inhabited Rhodes, and were reported to be the children of the ſea. Neptune was committed to their care when an infant by his mother Rhea; and they brought him up, in conjunction with Caphira, or Cabira, the daughter of Oceanus [t].

[q] Solin. Polyhiſt. cap. 2.

[r] Tal-Chon is a contraction of Ait-Al-Chon, as Italia is of Ait-Al-Aia.

[s] *Σωματα Τελχινων τυμβευσατε γειτονι ποντῳ,*
Πατρι Ποσειδαωνι μεμηλοτα.—
Dionyſ. lib. xxvii. p. 463.

[t] Caphira is evidently a mere variation of Cabira, *the great god-*

They were celebrated for many useful inventions[u]: and several ancient statues of the gods were ascribed to their workmanship; such as the Telchinian Apollo of Lindus, Juno and the Telchinian nymphs of Jalisus, and Juno Telchinia of Camira[x]. They were also reckoned magicians, who could produce clouds and rain at pleasure[y]; and are even said to have foretold a deluge[z]. When this catastrophè took place, a few persons only escaped, among whom were the sons of Jupiter[a]. As for the Telchines, they were dispersed; and one of them went into Lycia, where he built a temple to Apollo upon the river Xanthus,

goddess, and, like Venus, or Isis, she was a personification of the Ark.

[u] Την δε νησον ονομαζομενην Ῥοδον πρωτοι κατῳκησαν οἱ προσαγορευομενοι Τελχινες· ὑτοι δ' ησαν υἱοι μεν θαλασσης, ὡς ὁ μυθος παραδεδωκε· μυθολογυνται δε μετα Καφειρας της Ωκεανου θυγατρος εκθρεψαι Ποσειδωνα, Ῥεας αυτοις παρακαταθεμενης το βρεφος. Γενεσθαι δ' αυτους και τεχνων τινων εὑρετας, και αλλων των εις τον βιον χρησιμων τοις ανθρωποις εισηγησασθαι. Diod. Sic. Bibl. lib. v. p. 326.

[x] Παρα μεν γαρ Λινδιοις Απολλωνα Τελχινιον προσαγορευθηναι, παρα δε Ιαλισιοις Ἡραν και νυμφας Τελχινιας, παρα δε Καμειρευσι Ἡραν Τελχινιαν. Ibid

[y] Λεγονται δε ὑτοι και γοητες γεγονεναι, και παραγειν ὁτε βυλοιντο νεφη τε και ομβρυς και χαλαζας Ibid.

[z] Χρονῳ δε ὑϛερον προαισθομενους τυς Τελχινας τον μελλοντα γινεσθαι κατακλυσμον, εκλιπειν την νησον, και διασπαρηναι. Ibid. p. 327.

[a] Ibid.

ſo called from Zan-Thus, or Zan-Dus, *the ſolar deity*[b].

The Telchines are further ſaid to have had a ſiſter, denominated *Halia*. She was the concubine of Neptune; and bore to him ſix ſons, and one daughter, from whom the iſland Rhodos or Rhodes was ſuppoſed to have received its name[c]. This happened at the period of the Titanic or diluvian war; whence we find a prevailing tradition, that there were giants at that time in the iſle of Rhodes. Theſe giants were, in fact, the ſame as the impious race of the Titans, who periſhed beneath the waves[d]. They are accordingly ſaid to have been ſubdued by Jupiter, who afterwards eſpouſed the nymph Imalia, and by her became the father of Spartèus, Cronius, and Cutus[e].

[b] Diod. Bibl. lib. v. p. 327.

[c] Ποσειδωνα δε ανδρωθεντα ερασθηναι της των Τελχινων αδελφης Ἁλιας, και μιχθεντα ταυτῃ γεννησαι παιδας, ἑξ μεν αρρενας, μιαν δε θυγατερα Ῥοδον, αφ' ἡς την νησον ονομασθαι. Diod. Sic. Bibl. lib. v. p. 327.

[d] Vide infra chap. ix.

[e] Γενεσθαι δε κατα τον καιρον τουτον, εν τοις προς Ἑω μερεσι της νησου τες κληθεντας γιγαντας· ὁτε δη και Ζευς καταπεπολεμηκως Τιτανας, ερασθηναι μιας των νυμφων Ιμαλιας ονομαζομενης, και τρεις εξ αυτης τεκνωσαι παιδας, Σπαρταιον, Κρονιον, Κυτον. Diod. Sic. Bibl. lib. v. p. 327.

In

In the poſterity of Neptune by Halia, we may again obſerve the number *ſeven* occur; the number equally of the Titans, the Corybantes, and the Cabiri; the number in ſhort of the perſons preſerved in the Ark, excluſive of the head of their family: while in the three ſons of Jupiter we recognize the triple offſpring of Noah, excepting only that Cuſh, or Cuth, is erroneouſly introduced among them [f].

With regard to Rhodos, the daughter of Neptune, ſhe is ſaid to have been beloved by the ſolar deity, and to have borne him ſeven ſons and a daughter, who were ſtyled *Heliadæ*. Theſe ſeven Heliadæ, for the number *ſeven* here again makes its appearance, are the ſame as the ſeven Titans, Cabiri, or Corybantes; and their father is the great patriarch worſhipped in conjunction with the Sun. Hence their names are all ſignificant. Ochimus is derived from Oc, *the Ocean*; Cercaphus from Cer-Oc-Aph, *the ſolar god of the Ocean*; and Macar from Ma-Car, *the great Sun* [g]. Actis ſignifies *a*

[f] This circumſtance aroſe from the confuſion among the heathen deities, which I have noticed above. Jupiter was ſometimes Noah, and ſometimes Ham; hence, while a triple offſpring is aſſigned to him, Cutus or Cuth is mentioned as one of that offſpring.

[g] Car or Macar was alſo the name of the ſon of Phoroneus, the founder of Megara. Pauſ Attic. p. 95.

ſolar ray; Genages is Chen-Ag, *a prieſt of the Ocean*; Triopas is Tor-Op, *the bull-ſerpent*; Candalus is Chan-Tal, *a prieſt of the Sun*[h]; and laſtly, the virgin Electryonè, who is joined with her ſeven brothers, is El-Oc-Tor-Ionah, *the divine tauric dove of the Ocean*[i].

I have obſerved, that one of the Corybantes was ſuppoſed to have been ſlain by his two brothers[k]. This imaginary murder I apprehend to be the very ſame circumſtance as the death of Bacchus, Oſiris, or Adonis; in other words, it was nothing more than the allegorical death of Noah, his entrance into the Ark. A ſimilar tradition occurs alſo in the hiſtory of the Telchines. Apis, of the line of Inachus, is ſaid by Apollodorus to have been killed by Thelxion and Telchin[l]; and yet, with a variation not unuſual among the ancient mythologiſts, Apis is alſo made the ſon of Telchin, the grandſon of Europs, and the

[h] Chan-Tal is the ſame as Tel-Chin; the radicals being merely inverted.

[i] Ἡλιον δε κατα μεν τον μυθον ερασθεντα της Ῥοδε,—και γενεσθαι τους κληθεντας απ' αυτε Ἡλιαδας ἑπτα τον αριθμον.—Ειναι δε τους ἑπτα υἱας, Οχιμον, Κερκαφον, Μακαρα, Ακτινα, Γεναγην, Τριοπαν, και Κανδαλον· θυγατερα δε μιαν, Ἡλεκτρυωνην. Diod. Sic. Bibl. lib. v. p. 327.

[k] Vide ſupra p. 131.

[l] Apollod. Bibl. lib. ii. cap. 1

great

great grandſon of Egialeus, who was reckoned by the Sicyonians an *autochthon*, or *aboriginal*[m]. This Egialeus, the fabulous founder of Sicyon, is ſuppoſed by Clemens Alexandrinus to have flouriſhed at the era of the flood of Ogyges; and to have been contemporary with Phoroneus the ſon of Inachus, and with Cres the firſt king of Crete[n]. It is very remarkable, that, while Apis is fabled on the one hand to be the ſon of Telchin, or the deſcendant of Inachus, he is deſcribed on the other as the ſon of Jaſon the Argonaut[o]; and yet is further declared to be the ſame as the Egyptian Serapis[p]. Hence it appears, that three ſeveral genealogies are aſcribed to Apis: he is deſcended from Inachus; from Telchin, and Europs; and from Jaſon. This apparent diſcrepancy can only be accounted for, upon the ſyſtem, adopted throughout the whole of the

[m] Αιγιαλεως δε Ευρωπα γενεσθαι φασιν, Ευρωπος δε Τελχινα, Τελχινος δε Απιν Pauſ Corin p 123

[n] Ην δε κατα την Ἑλλαδα, κατα μεν Φορωνεα τον μετ' Ιναχον, ὁ επ' Ωγυγε κατακλυσμος, και ἡ εν Σικυωνι βασιλεια, πρωτου μεν Αιγιαλεως, ειτα Ευρωπος, ειτα Τελχινος· και ἡ Κρηλος εν Κρητῃ. Ακεσιλαος γαρ Φορωνεα πρωτον ανθρωπον γενεσθαι λεγει· ὁθεν και ὁ της Φορωνιδος ποιητης, ειναι αυτον εφη πατερα θνητων ανθρωπων Clem. Alex. Strom. lib. 1 p 380

[o] Απιν τον Ιασονος. Pauſ i Eliac. p. 376

[p] Απις—νομισθεις θεος εκληθη Σαραπις Apollod. Bibl. lib ii. cap. 1

pre-

preſent work. The genealogies, and the perſons contained in them, are equally fabulous, relating on the one hand to the events of the deluge, and on the other, to the introduction of the ſolar ſuperſtition. Thus, while Apis is ſuppoſed to be the deſcendant of Inachus, Phoroneus, or Jaſon; he is likewiſe the great god of the Egyptians, and the offspring of Telchin, *the prieſt of the Sun*, and Europs, *the fiery ſerpent*[q].

Strabo informs us, that the Telchines were originally ſettled in Crete; whence they migrated, firſt into Cyprus, and afterwards into Rhodes. He mentions likewiſe, that they were excellent artificers in braſs and iron, and that they made the ſickle of Cronus[r]. In

[q] This Egyptian tauriform god Apis was worſhipped alſo in Italy. Duravit Saturnia nomen totidem ferme annis quot ante aurea ætas uſque ad Apim, deorum Italiæ ultimum, ut Antiochus Syracuſanus ſcribit, a quo Apenina, quam Tauricam idem interpretatur. M. Caton. Fragm. de Orig. fol. 166. Oſiris, being the ſame as Saturn or Janus, is likewiſe ſaid to have come into Italy, and there to have conquered the giants. Oſiris depreſſit gigantes, qui jam tyrannidem cœperant—Oſiris tota Italia potitus, decem annos illam tenuit, et a ſe nominavit in triumphum. Beroſ. Ant. lib. v. fol. 65, 66.

[r] Ελθειν δ' εκ Κρητης (τους Τελχινας) εις Κυπρον πρωτον, ειτ' εις Ροδον· πρωτους δ' εργασασθαι σιδηρον τε και χαλκον· και δη και την αρπην τῳ Κρονῳ δημιουργησαι. Strab. Geog. lib. xiv. p. 654. We have already ſeen, from the ſame author, the connection of theſe Telchines with the river Styx, or the deluge; in alluſion

confequence however of the wide diffufion of the helio-arkite fuperftition, many different places, and thofe in many different countries, were called after the name of the Telchines, and the folar god Tel or Tal. Thus *Telchis* was a city in Ethiopia; and *Telchinia* was the ancient title both of Crete and Sicyon[s]. In a fimilar manner, *Telamon* was a town in Tyrfenia; *Telanè* was the oldeft city of Syria, being founded by Ninus[t]; *Telmera* and *Telmiffa* were cities of Caria; and *Telphuffa* was a city of Arcadia[u]. One of the colonies of the Telchines is faid by Paufanias to have come from Cyprus into Beotia, *the land of the arkite bull*, and there to have built a temple to Minerva Telchinia[x]. Rhodes was from

fion to which event they were fuppofed to have forged the trident of Neptune.

—— Μεγας θεος ερεα θεινων
Αορι τριγλωχινι, το οἱ Τελχινες ετευξαν.

Callim Hymn. ad Del. ver. 30.

From this circumftance of the Cabiri or Abiri being efteemed artificers, while they were at the fame time thought to be the fons of Vulcan, I fufpect that the Latins termed all artificers in general *Fabri*, which feems to be Ph'Abiri, and contractedly Ph'Abri.

[s] Steph. Byzan. de Urb. p. 702.

[t] Ibid. p 701.

[u] Ibid p. 702.

[x] Καὶ Αθηνας εν Τελμησσῳ Τελχινιας εστιν ἱερον, αγαλμα ουκ εχον. Ες δε την επικλησιν αυτης εστιν εικαζειν, ὡς των εν Κυπρῳ ποτε οικησαντων

them called *Telchinis*; and before their time, it bore the name of *Ophiusa*, on account of the serpent worship which had been established in it[y]. We find a people denominated *Talares* in Thessaly[z], and in Caria we meet with a soothsayer, intitled *Telmisius*, or *a priest of the Sun*[a]. Another of these Cabiric priests was called *Telondes*; and he flourished at the time, when Pelargè was fabled to have restored the Cabiric worship, which had been interrupted by a Theban war[b]. Pelargè I take to be Bela-Arga, *the lordly Ark*; and the war was probably that, which preceded the union of the two superstitions, and which the Greeks had translated into their own country.

The Telchines then being thus seated in Crete, we shall find also, in the same country, the Curetes, and the Idèi Dactyli. The first of these, when they quitted the island, are

των Τελχινων αφικομενη μοιρα ες Βοιωτας, ἱερον ἱδρυσατο Αθηνας Τελχινιας. Pauf. Bœot. p. 746.

[y] Εκαλειτο δ' ἡ Ῥοδος προτερον Οφιεσα και Σταδια, ειτα Τελχινις απο των οικησαντων Τελχινων την νησον. Strab. Geog. lib. xiv. p. 653.

[z] Ταλαρες Θεσσαλων. Ibid. lib. ix. p. 434.

[a] Τελμισσον εν Καρια. Clem. Alex. Strom. lib. i. p. 400.

[b] Τηλωνδης δε, και όσοι γενους Καβειριτων ελειποντων, κατελθουσιν αυθις εις την Καβειριαιαν. Πελαργην μεν δη κατα μαντευμα εκ Δωδωνης και αλλα εμελλεν ες τιμην καταστησεσθαι, και οἱ θυσια φερον εν τη γαστρι ἱερειον. Pauf. Bœot. p. 759.

said

ſaid to have ſettled in Caria [c]. Much about the ſame time, Inachus was buſied in ſearching for his daughter Io, in which ſervice he employed Curnus; who, at length deſpairing of ſucceſs, took up his abode in Caria, where he built a city of his own name [d]. A variety indeed of countries, as well as a variety of genealogies, is aſſigned to the Curetes, or Cabiri; and the chronological order of their migrations is equally confuſed. The fact is, each particular nation, from a vain deſire of acquiring the reputation of ſuperior antiquity, pretended, that the Cabiri had firſt reſided among them; and had afterwards proceeded to other parts of the world: accordingly we find, that they are ſometimes ſaid to have come from Crete to Rhodes, and ſometimes from Rhodes to Crete. With ſimilar inconſiſtency, the author of *the Phoronis* mentions, that the Curetes were Phrygian muſicians;

[c] Λεγεται πεντε Κȣρητας εκ Κρητης—πλευσαντας εις την χερρονησον τȣς μεν κατοικȣντας αυτην Καρας εκβαλειν Diod Sic. Bibl. lib. v p 331. Hence, as I have juſt obſerved, a *Carian* prieſt was called *Telmiſus*

[d] Ου πολυ δε τȣτων κατοπιν, Ιναχον τον Αργειων βασιλεα, αφανισθεισης της θυγατρος Ιȣς εξαποςειλαι Κυρνον ἑνα των ἡγεμονων ανδρων—Ὁ δε Κυρνος επι πολλα της οικȣμενης μερη πλανηθεις, και μη δυναμενος εὑρειν ταυτην, κατεπλευσε της Καριας εις την προειρημενην χερρονησον—Πολιν εκτισεν ὁμωνυμον ἑαυτω Κυρνον. Ibid. Curnus is Cur-Nus, *Noah the Sun*.

and yet immediately after declares, that the Corybantes were Phrygians, and the Curetes, Cretans. He aſſerts moreover, that they firſt invented brazen weapons in Eubèa; but others ſuppoſed, that they originally came from Bactriana, and that they were given by the Titans to Rhea, as her ſervants. Some were of opinion, that they were *gegenis*, or *perſons ſprung from the earth*; and ſome believed them to be Colchians. In *the Cretici Logi*, they are ſaid to be the guardians of Jupiter, and to have accompanied Rhea from Phrygia into Crete; while many very juſtly maintained the identity of the Curetes, and Telchines[e].

We have already ſeen, that Crete was not only denominated *Telchinis*, but alſo *Curetis*, and thence contractedly *Crete*. It was ſo called from the worſhip of Cur-Ait, *the ſolar orb:* accordingly, the moſt ancient king of the iſland was ſuppoſed to have been named

[e] Ὁ δε την Φορωνιδα γραψας, αυλητας και Φρυγας τους Κουρητας λεγει· αλλοι δε γηγενεις, και χαλκασπιδας. Ὁ δ' ου τους Κουρητας λεγει, αλλα τους Κορυβαντας Φρυγας, εκεινους δε Κρητας· περιθεσθαι δ' οπλα χαλκα πρωτους εν Ευβοιᾳ· διο και Καλχιδιας αυτους κληθηναι· οἱ δ' ὑπο Τιτανων Ῥεᾳ δοθηναι προσπολους ενοπλους τους Κορυβαντας εκ της Βακτριανης αφιγμενους· οἱ δ' εκ Κολχων φασιν. Εν δε τοις Κρητικοις λογοις οἱ Κουρητες Διος τροφεις λεγονται, και φυλακες, ες Κρητην εκ Φρυγιας μεταπεμφθεντες ὑπο της Ῥεας· οἱ δε Τελχινων εν Ῥοδῳ εννεα οντων, τους Ῥεᾳ συνακολουθησαντας εις Κρητην, και τον Δια κουροτροφησαντας, Κουρητας ονομασθηναι. Strab. Geog. lib. x. p. 472.

Cres;

Cres; and the firſt inhabitants were from him denominated *Eteo-Cretes*[f]. Theſe are undoubtedly the ſame as the Idèi Dactyli, who, conſidered in the light of prieſts to the gods from whom they borrowed their name, were generally eſteemed the aborigines of Crete. Sometimes however, as it has been obſerved, they were placed in Phrygia; from which country, as we are informed by Ephorus, they

[f] Οἱ μεν γαρ την Κρητην κατοικουντες φασιν αρχαιοτατους παρ᾽ αυτοις γενεσθαι τους ονομαζομενους Ετεο-Κρητας αυτοχθονας· ὡν των μεν βασιλεα Κρητα καλουμενον, πλειστα και μεγιστα κατα την νησον ευρειν τα δυναμενα τον κοινον των ανθρωπων βιον ωφελησαι. Diod. Sic Bibl. lib v. p. 333. Both Cres and the Eteo-Cretes were *autochthones*, a name generally applied to all the diluvians: hence, while Diodorus, as we have juſt ſeen, terms the Eteo-Cretes *autochthones*, Marcianus Heracleotes beſtows, in a ſimilar manner, the title of *autochthon* upon their imaginary monarch Cres.

—— Εφορος φησι τε
Επωνυμον την νησον απο Κρητος τινος,
Του δη γενομενου βασιλεως αυτοχθονος.

Mar. Herac. Perieg. p 23

Crete was alſo called *Aeria*, as well as *Curetis*, from Aur-Aia, *the land of the Sun*. Solin. Polyhiſt. cap 11. The ſame appellation was likewiſe beſtowed upon Egypt, and for the ſame reaſon. Steph. Byzan de Urb p 38 When the two ſuperſtitions were united, words expreſſive of the arkite worſhip were naturally introduced. Hence we find in Crete the hill *Arginus*, (Schol. in Apoll Argon. lib ii ver 299) and the city *Arcades*; (Steph de Urb p 166) while in Phenicia we meet with a town denominated *Arce* (Ibid p. 167.) There was likewiſe an *Arcadia* in Egypt, (Ibid.) and an iſland called *Arconeſus* on the coaſt of Caria. Ibid. p 168

ac-

accompanied Minos into Europe. They were reckoned magicians, and inventors of the Myſteries; and, during their abode at Samothrace, they are ſaid to have greatly terrified the natives by their incantations[g]. In Crete they diſcovered the uſe of fire, and the art of metallurgy[h]; and one of them bore the name of *Hercules*[i]. They were occaſionally ſuppoſed to be ten in number, from ſome imaginary connection with the fingers of Cybelè[k], the word *Dactylus* happening in the Greek language to ſignify *a finger*; and they were afterwards increaſed to an hundred, which is the ſquare of ten[l]. The name *Dactylus* how-

[g] Πρωτοι τοινυν των εις μνημην παραδεδομενων ῳκησαν της Κρητης περι την Ιδην οἱ προσαγορευθεντες Ιδαιοι Δακτυλοι.—Ενιοι δ᾽ ἱϛορουσιν, ὧν εϛι και Εφορος, τους Ιδαιους Δακτυλους γενεσθαι μεν κατα την Ιδην την εν Φρυγιᾳ, διαβηναι δε μετα Μινωος εις την Ευρωπην· ὑπαρξαντας δε γοητας, επιτηδευσαι τας τε επῳδας και τελετας και μυστηρια, και περι Σαμοθρᾳκην διατριψαντας, ου μετριως εν τουτοις εκπληττειν τους εγχωριους. Diod. Sic. Bibl. lib. v. p. 333.

[h] Οἱ δ᾽ ουν κατα την Κρητην Ιδαιοι Δακτυλοι παραδεδονται την τε του πυρος χρησιν, και την του χαλκου και σιδηρου φυσιν εξευρειν. Diod. Sic. Bibl. lib. v. p. 333.

[i] Ἱϛορουσι δ᾽ αυτων ἑνα μεν προσαγορευθηναι Ἡρακλεα. Ibid. The ſame is aſſerted by Pauſ. Bœot. p. 747. and by Strab. Geog. lib. viii. p. 355. and lib. x. p. 473.

[k] Οἱ δε φασιν, ὁτι Ιδαιοι Δακτυλοι εκληθησαν, ὁτι εντος Ιδης εντυχοντες τῃ Ῥεᾳ, εδεξιωσαντο την θεον, και των δακτυλων αυτης ηψαντο. Schol. in Apollon. Argon. lib. i. ver. 1129.

[l] Diod. Sic. Bibl. lib. v. p. 333.

ever,

ever, as applied to the Cabiri, has not the ſlighteſt reference to the human finger; but is one of the many inſtances of the ſtrange confuſion, which the Greeks have introduced, by perverting the terms of ancient mythology into words of a ſimilar ſound in their own dialect. Dactylus is Dag-Tal, *the ſolar fiſh-god*; a compound of the very ſame ſignification as Dag-On, the idol of the Philiſtines. Theſe both equally allude to the worſhip of Noah, united as it was with the Sabian idolatry. Accordingly we find, that the Idèi Dactyli are ſometimes ſaid to have been the children of Dactylus and Ida, and to have borrowed their title from the name of their father[m]. As Dactylus then is Dag-Tal, ſo their imaginary mother Ida ſeems to be nothing more than Aida[n], the thick *vapour* or *fog*, in which the Ark was inveloped during the prevalence of the diluvian waters. For a ſimilar reaſon, the Centaur, or *the tauric prieſt Noah*, was ſuppoſed to be the offspring of Nephelè, or *a cloud*.

[m] Ὡς δε Μνασεας εν πρωτῳ περι Ασιας, Ιδαιοι Δακτυλοι λεγονται, απο τȣ πατρος Δακτυλȣ και της μητρος Ιδης. Schol. in Apollon. Argon. lib. i ver. 1129. It may be proper to obſerve, that the Idèi are not always deſcribed as being ten: their number varies very conſiderably. See Schol. ut ſup.

[n] Heb. אידה.

Notwithſtanding the identity of the Idèi Dactyli, and the Curetes, with an inconſiſtency by no means unuſual in the pagan records, the latter are repreſented by Diodorus as being poſterior in point of time to the former. All knowledge of the truth however was not abſolutely loſt; for, while ſome ſuppoſed the Curetes to be the children of the Idèi Dactyli, others with more propriety aſſerted them to have been *gegenis*, or *aboriginals*[o].

In the time of the Curetes flouriſhed the Titans, who are ſaid by the author of the works aſcribed to Orpheus, to have conſiſted of ſeven brothers, and ſeven ſiſters[p]. Theſe, as we have ſeen, were generally ſuppoſed to be the children of Cronus: ſome however deduced their origin from Heaven, and Earth; while others believed them to be the offspring of Titèa, and one of the Curetes[q]. They

[o] Μετα δε τες Ιδαιες Δακτυλες ἱςορεσι γενεσθαι Κερητας εννεα. Τετους δ' οἱ μεν μυθολογεσι γεγονεναι γηγενεις, οἱ δ' απογονους των Ιδαιων Δακτυλων. Diod. Sic. Bibl. lib. v. p. 333.

[p] Orph. apud Proc. in Tim. lib. v. p. 295.

[q] Μυθολογεσι γαρ οἱ Κρητες γενεσθαι κατα την των Κερητων ἡλικιαν τες καλουμενους Τιτανας· ὑπαρξαι δε τον αριθμον ἑξ μεν ανδρας, πεντε δε γυναικας, ὡς μεν τινες μυθολογεσιν, Ουρανου και Γης ονλας· ὡς δε τινες φασιν, εκ τινος των Κερητων, και μητρος Τιταιας, αφ' ἡς αυλους ταυτης τετυχηκεναι της προσηγοριας. Αρσενας μεν ουν γενεσθαι τον τε Κρονον και Ὑπεριωνα και Κοιον, ετι δε Ιαπετον και Κριον, και το τελευταιον Ωκεανον· αδελφας δε τουτων την τε Ῥεαν και Θεμιν και Μνημο-

were, in fact, as I have before obſerved, the ſame as the Corybantes, the Cabiri, or the Curetes; in other words, they were the arkite navigators, excluſive of the illuſtrious head of their family.

In conſequence of the identity of the Titans, and the Idèi Dactyli, Apollonius calls one of the latter of theſe deities, *Titias*, and repreſents him as the brother of *Cyllenus*.

—— Αμφι δε φυλλοις
Στεψαμενοι δρυινοισι θυηπολιης εμελοντο,
Μητερα Δινδυμιην πολυποτνιαν εγκαλεοντες,
Ενναετιν Φρυγιης, Τιτιην θ᾽ ἁμα, Κυλληνον τε·
Οἱ μȣνοι πολεων μοιρηγεται, ηδε παρεδροι
Μητερος Ιδαιης κεκληαται, ὁσσοι εασι
Δακτυλοι Ιδαιοι Κρηταεες· ὃς ποτε νυμφη
Αγχιαλη Δικταιον ανα σπεος, αμφοτερῃσιν
Δραξαμενη γαιης Οιαξιδος εβλαστησε [r].

They rear an altar next on riſing ground,
Of ſtones that readieſt lay, and wide around
Diſpoſe the branches of the ſacred oak,
And Dindymus's deity invoke,
The guardian power of Phrygia's hills and woods,
The venerable mother of the gods.
On Titias and Cyllenus too they call,
Of all her prieſts moſt lov'd, and honour'd moſt
of all.

Μνημοσυνην, ετι δε Φοιβην και Τηθυν. Diod Sic. Bibl. lib. v. p. 334.

[r] Apoll. Argon. lib. 1 ver 1123

For

For ſkill prophetic they alone are fam'd;
Idèan Dactyli theſe prieſts are nam'd;
Both whom Anchiala in Dictè's cave
Brought forth, where chill Oaxis rolls his wave.
Fawkes.

Titias is a word of the ſame import as *Titan*, for they both equally ſignify *a diluvian*; and Cyllenus is Cula-Nus, *the arkite Noah*. This Cyllenus is evidently the ſame perſon as Mercury Cyllenius [s], who was worſhipped along with the other Cabiri by the name of *Caſmilus*; and who, as I have ſhewn in a former page, was the great oceanic patriarch [t]. Hence, under the title of *Socus*, or Z'Ocus, *the mighty god of the Ocean* [u], he is celebrated by Non-

[s] Apollod. Bibl. lib. iii. cap. 10.—Virg. Æneid. lib. viii. ver. 138.

[t] Vide ſupra p. 283. et infra.

[u] *Socus* was an ancient appellation of Mercury. Σωκος, ὁ Ἑρμης. Suid. Lex. Σωκος εριουνιος Ἑρμης. Hom. Iliad. lib. xx. ver. 72. Though the primary ſignification of *Socus* is *the great diluvian*, yet we find that the title was likewiſe applied to the crocodile; for *Socus* ſeems to be the ſame term as *Suchus* or *Souchus*, which, as Damaſcius informs us, was a name of that animal. (Damaſ. Vit. Iſid. apud Phot. Bibl. p. 1048.) This ſuppoſed identity of the two words *Socus* and *Suchus* will appear in a ſufficiently ſtriking point of view, if we call to our recollection, that Anubis or the Egyptian Mercury was repreſented ſtanding upon a crocodile: (ſee the Print of this deity in Mont. Ant. Exp. vol. ii. part ii. p. 197.) a mode of repreſentation adopted, no doubt, becauſe the crocodile was one of the

nus as being the father of the ſeven Corybantes, or Cabiri, by the nymph Combè.

> Ευβοεων δε Φαλαγγας εκοσμεον ασπιδιωται
> Παιδοκομοι Κορυβαντες αεξομενου Διονυσου.
> \- - - - - - - - - - -
> Οἱ τοτε παντες ικανον αειδομενης απο νησου·
> Πρυμνευς, ειλιποδης τε Μιμας, και οριδρομος Ακμων,
> Δαμνευς τ', Ωκυθοος τε σακεσπαλος· οἱς ἁμα βαινων
> Συνδρομος Ιδαιῳ κορυθαιολος ηλθε Μελισσευς·
> Οὑς ποτε δυσσεβιης κεκορυθμενος αφρονι κεντρῳ
> Σωκος αλιζωνοιο πατηρ νοσφισσατο πατρης,
> Κομβης ἑπτατοκου μετα μητερος· οἱ δε φυγοντες
> Κνωσσιον ουδας ἱκοντο· και εμπαλιν ησαν αληται
> Ες Φρυγιην Κρητηθεν, απο Φρυγιης ες Αθηνας,
> Αλλοδαποι ναετηρες ὁμεστιοι· εισοκε Κεκροψ
> Σωκον απηλοιησε δικης ποινητορι χαλκῳ·

the many ſymbols of the Ark, as is evident from the circumſtance of the Egyptians denominating it *Campſa*, (Herod. lib II cap 69) which Heſychius aſſures us ſignifies *an ark* or *cheſt*. Καμψα, θηκη.

Whether Mr. Bryant's very curious remarks upon the allegory of Cupid and Pſuchè reſt upon any ſolid foundation, I will not venture to determine, but I cannot forbear adding to them a conjecture, which will hold equally good, whatever opinion may be entertained reſpecting his interpretation of that allegory. As the arkite crocodile, which ſaved the life of Menes, Menu, or Noah, (ſee Diod. Bibl. lib. I. p. 80.) was called *Suchus*; ſo it is poſſible, that the Greek term *Pſuchè*, which ſignifies *life* or *ſoul*, may be nothing more than the feminine of *Suchus*, or, with a ſlight variety of pronunciation, *Pſuchus*.

Και χθονα καλλειψαντες αλικλυςου Μαραθωνος,
Νοςιμον ιχνος εκαμψαν ες ἱερον ουδας Αβαντων,
Κουρητων προτερων χθονιον γενος [x].——

The Corybantes, guards of youthful Bacchus,
Led on the hardy troops of fam'd Eubèa;
Brave Primneus, Mimas, and undaunted Acmon,
Ocythoüs, Damneus, and with waving plume
Meliſſeus, and Idèus ſtern in fight.
Theſe from their ſea-girt country their dread ſire
Socus once baniſh'd far; nor did he ſpare
The partner of his bed, the beauteous Combè,
But with her ſons the exil'd mother fled.
Crete firſt receiv'd the wanderers, Phrygia next,
Then Athens; till at length the pitying Cecrops
Socus compell'd his children to reſtore,
Safe to their home, Abantian Eubèa.

From this citation it appears, that the Corybantes were ſuppoſed to have migrated from Eubèa to Crete, from Crete to Phrygia, from Phrygia to Athens, and from Athens back again to Eubèa; a ſeries of journeys completely imaginary, and relating only to the eſtabliſhment of the Cabiric ſuperſtition in theſe different countries.

With regard to the Abantes, whom Nonnus places in Eubèa, they are ſaid to have come originally from Thrace, and to have derived their name from Abas, an ancient

[x] Nonni Dionyſ. lib. xiii. p. 233.

king

king of Argos, the ſon of Neptune and Arethuſa [v]. Hence Acriſius, the father of Danaè, and the grandfather of Perſeus, was ſtyled *Abantiades* [z]. The ſame appellation was alſo given to Perſeus [a]; and Argos itſelf was denominated *Abantèan* [b]. From the Abantes moreover the iſland Eubèa was called *Abantis*; though it ſometimes alſo bore the title of *Macris* [c]. The ſuperſtition of the Abantes then, being thus connected with Perſeus, Danaè, and Argos, muſt neceſſarily be likewiſe connected with that of the Cabiri, and conſequently muſt relate to the ſame events. Accordingly Abas is Ab-As, *the father fire*,

[v] Apollodorus makes Abas the ſon of Hypermneſtra by Lynceus the ſucceſſor of Danaus in the kingdom of Argos. Apollod. Bibl. lib. ii. cap. 2. More will be ſaid reſpecting this Abas hereafter Vide infra chap. vii.

[z] Ovid Metam. lib. iv. ver 606

[a] Ibid. ver 672.

[b] Ibid. lib. xv. ver. 164.

[c] Αβαντις, ἡ Ευβοια Suid. Αβαντιας επλετο Μακρις Dionyſ. Perieg. ver. 520. Upon which Euſtathius, Και την μεν Μακριν, ὁ εςι την Ευβοιαν, Αβαντιαδα λεγει, απο του εν αυτη εθνους των Αβαντων· Θρακιου εθνους, ὡς φησιν Αρριανος, κληθεντος ούτως απο τινος Αργειου του Ποσειδωνος Αβαντος. See alſo Hyg. Fab 157. Ovid mentions, that Perſeus was worſhipped in India; (Metam. lib iv ver. 604.) and his accuracy is perfectly eſtabliſhed by the inquiries of modern Europeans The conſtellation of Perſeus and Andromeda is yet called by the Hindoos *Paraſica* and *Antarmada*. See Aſiat Reſ. vol iii p. 222.

 and

and he is reported to have been an Argive, or arkite [d]; Macris is derived from Ma-Car, *the great solar deity* [e]; and Eubèa received its name in honour of the sacred symbolical heifer. Thus, we are informed by Strabo, that it was so called, because Epaphus, the son of the heifer Io, was born there [f].

It is observable, that two of the appellations, which are given by Nonnus to the Corybantes, namely *Damnameneus* and *Acmon*, are applied by the author of *the Phoronis* to the Idèi Dactyli. To these he adds a third, whom he calls *Celmis*; and represents them as being magicians, the servants of Adrastia [g],

[d] *Abas* being a solar title, we shall not be surprised to find a city Abanta, near Parnassus, in which was a temple of Apollo. Hesych. vox Αϐαντα.

[e] The title *Macrobii*, which is applied by Dionysius to the Ethiopians, and which the Greeks have made to signify *long-lived*, is another word formed from the same root. Ma Car-Ob is *the great solar serpent*; and Ethiop is Aith-Op, *the burning serpent*. Dion. Perieg. ver. 560. This mode of derivation will account for the remark of Strabo, that a people upon the borders of Pharnacia and Chaldèa, called *Sanni*, were once denominated *Macrones*. (Strab. Geog. lib. xii. p. 548.) *Sanni* and *Macrones* are in fact synonyms, the import of both being equally *worshippers of the Sun*. The Sanni assumed their name in honour of San, Son, or Azon; and the Macrones, in honour of Ma-Car-On.

[f] Strab. Geog. lib. x. p. 445.

[g] Adrastia is Adar-Asta, *the illustrious goddess of fire*.

and

and the inventors of the art of working iron.

——— Ενθα γοητες,
Ιδαιοι Φρυγες ανδρες ορεςεροι οικι' εναιον,
Κελμις, Δαμναμενευς τε μεγας, και ὑπερϐιος
Ακμων,
Ευπαλαμοι θεραποντες ορειης Αδρηςειης,
Οἱ πρωτοι τεχνην πολυμητιος Ἡφαιςοιο
Εὑρον εν ȣρειησι ναπαις, ιοεντα σιδηρον,
Ες πυρ τ' ηνεγκαν, και αριπρεπες εργον εδειξαν[h].

Celmis however is called *Telmis* by Eufebius, and Delas fupplies the place of Acmòn; fo that the three Idèi Dactyli of this laft author are Telmis, Damnameneus, and Delas[i]. I am inclined to think, that fuch is the more proper reading, on account of the connection of the Idèi Dactyli and the Telchines. Telmis and Delas are both derived from Tal, *the Sun*; the former being Tel-Am-Es, *the burning Sun*; the latter, Tel-As, *the folar fire*[k].

[h] Phoron. apud Schol. in Apoll. Argon. lib. i. ver. 1129.

[i] Τελμις τε και Δαμναμενευς οἱ των Ιδαιων Δακτυλοι, πρωτοι εν Κυπρῳ σιδηρον εὑρον· Δελας δε αλλος Ιδαιος εὑρε χαλκου κρασιν. Eufeb. Præp Evan. lib. x cap. 6.

[k] Virgil calls one of the three Cyclopes, *Pyracmon*. Thefe, like the Egyptian Cabiri, were the fons of Vulcan; and moft probably are nearly connected with thofe difcoverers of metallurgy, the Telchines. Æneid lib. viii ver. 424. The Cyclopes feem to have received their name from Za-Cul-Op, *the great white ferpent*: hence the fcholiaft upon Efchylus makes the

The circumſtance of the Telchines being ſeated in Crete will enable us at once to account for the ſingular fable of Talus, and for the name of *Italia*. Talus is deſcribed, in the wild language of fiction, as being a brazen man, and as having only a ſingle vein, which reached from his neck to his heel. He was the ſervant of Minos, and ran thrice each day round the whole iſland. He was likewiſe called *Taurus*, or *the bull*, and *Aſterius*, or As-Tor, *the ſolar bull*[l]; and he is ſaid to have oppoſed the landing of the Argonauts on the ſhore of Crete. Apollodorus repreſents him as being a preſent from Vulcan to Minos[m]; but Apollonius affirms, that he was given by

the names of the Cyclopes to be *Brontes*, *Steropes*, and *Argus*; and deſcribes them as aſſiſting Jupiter in his war with the Titans or antediluvians. Schol. in Prom. Vinct. ver. 351. Hence alſo Hyginus, and the ſcholiaſt upon Aratus, agree in maintaining, that the altar, upon which Jupiter ſwore an oath previous to his attacking the Titans, was the workmanſhip of the Cyclopes. Hyg. Poet. Aſtron. lib. ii. cap. 39.—Schol. in Arat. Phænom. p. 52.

[l] Tzet. in Lycoph. ver. 1301.

[m] Κωλυονται (οἱ Αργοναυται) Κρητῃ προσισχειν ὑπο Ταλω. Τουτον, οἱ μεν, του Χαλκου γενους ειναι λεγουσιν· οἱ δε, ὑπο Ἡφαιστου Μινῳ δοθηναι· ὁς ην χαλκεος ανηρ· οἱ δε, Ταυρον αυτον λεγουσιν· ειχε δε φλεβα μιαν απο αυχενος κατατεινουσαν αχρι σφυρων· κατα δε το δερμα της φλεβος ἡλος διηρειστο χαλκους. Οὑτος ὁ Ταλως τρις ἑκαστης ἡμερας την νησον περιτροχαζων ἐτηρει. Apollod. Bibl. lib. i. cap. 9. See alſo Plat. Minos, p. 568.

Jupi-

Jupiter to Europa, in order that he might perform the office of a guard to the iſland[n]. With regard to his genealogy, Rhadamanthus, according to Cinethon, was the ſon of Vulcan, Vulcan of Talus, and Talus of Cres[o]; while, according to Ion, Talus was the offſpring of Oinopion, and accompanied his father from Crete to the iſle of Chios[p]. By Agatharchides he is called *Italotus*[q], inſtead of *Talus*; and that with perfect propriety, for Talus is the contracted form of Ait-Al, *the god of fire*: whence, as we have ſeen, *Talus* is ſaid by Heſychius to ſignify *the Sun*. The whole tradition in ſhort is founded upon the union of the two ſuperſtitions: in one point of view, Talus is the bright luminary of day performing his accuſtomed revolutions through the wide expanſe of heaven; and in another, he is the Noëtic bull of Europa. Hence Nonnus, celebrating him under the cognate name of *Tulus*, feigns, that he taſted death, and afterwards experienced a wonder-

[n] Apollon. Argon lib. iv. ver. 1643

[o] Κιναιθων δε εν τοις επεσιν εποιησεν, ὡς Ῥαδαμανθος μεν Ἡφαιστου, Ἡφαιστος δ' ειη Ταλω, Ταλων δε Κρητος παιδα. Pauſ. Arcad. p. 707.

[p] Οινοπιωνα ες την Χιον καταραι ναυσιν εκ Κρητης, αφικεσθαι δε οι τους παιδας Ταλον κ. τ. λ Pauſ Achaic p. 532.

[q] Agath apud Phot Bibl p. 1328.

ful

ful revivification, during the time that Cybelè was in labour[r]. This death and revivification of Tulus are the very ſame as the death and revivification of Oſiris, Bacchus, and Adonis; in other words, the entrance of Noah into the Ark, and his ſubſequent egreſs: accordingly the miracle is ſaid to have taken place during the time that Cybelè, or the Ark, was in the pangs of her allegorical parturition.

I have mentioned, upon the authority of Tzetzes, that Italy received its name from a perſon called *Italus* or *Taurus*[s]. This perſon is evidently no other than the *Talus, Italotus,* or *Taurus* of Crete; whence it will follow, that the word *Italia* is compounded of Ital-Aia, or Ait-Al-Aia, *the land of Italus* or *Talus, the ſolar bull.* In a ſimilar manner *Talium* or *Italium,* in the territory of the Samnites[t], and *Italica,* in the iſland of Eubèa[u], the country of

[r] Nonni Dionyſ. lib. xxv. p. 439. et infra.

[s] Vide ſupra p. 369.

[t] Diod. Sic. Bibl. lib. xx. p. 764.

[u] Εν τῃ Ευβοιᾳ δε, κατα την Ιταλικην, την συνοριζουσαν τῃ Χαλκιδι, δυο ποταμοι, Κερων και Νηλευς. Antigoni Caryſt. Hiſt. Mirab. cap. 84. According to Lycophron and Eſchylus, the Ionian gulph received its name from the heifer Io; but others derived it from Iaon an Italian. It is remarkable, that the ſea between Gaza and Egypt was likewiſe called *Ionian,* and Gaza itſelf Ionah. See Schol. Euſt. in Dionyſ. Perieg. ver. 92. Iaon the Italian was no other than the tauric or arkite dove.

the Corybantes, both equally derived their reſpective appellations from the worſhip of *Talus*. The ſame remark may be applied to the Teleboæ, the ancient inhabitants of the iſle of Taphos. Theſe are ſaid by the ſcholiaſt upon Apollonius to have originally inhabited Acarnania; and he deſcribes them as coming to Argos, and fighting with Electryon, the father of Alcmenè, for his oxen. Electryon was the ſon of Perſeus and Andromeda; from Hippothoè, the daughter of his brother Meſtor, and Neptune, ſprung Pterelas; and from Pterelas, Taphius, and Teleboas the father of the Teleboæ [x]. Alcmenè afterwards married Amphitryon, and at length became the mother of Hercules by Jupiter [y]. All theſe names are ſignificant. Teleboas is compounded of

[x] Apollodorus and Johannes Diaconus repreſent Taphius as the ſon, not of Pterelas, but of Neptune. This variation however is of little conſequence, for his whole genealogy is purely fabulous. Johannes Diaconus ſuppoſes, after the manner of the Greeks, that the Teleboæ were ſo called, becauſe Taphius τηλε εϐα, never conſidering, that a perſon, named *Teleboas*, was their reputed anceſtor. Apollod. Bibl lib. ii cap 4—Johan. Diac in Heſ Scut. Herc ver. 11. Homer aſſigns the appellation of *Mentes* to the chief of the Taphians Odyſſ lib 1. ver 105. This I apprehend to be a ſacred mythological title, the ſame as the Egyptian *Mendes*, or *Pan* Herod. lib ii. cap. 46 Mentes or Mendes is Men-Deva, *the divine Noah*.

[y] Schol in Apoll. Argon lib. i ver 747.

Tel-

Tel-Ob-Bou, *the helio-tauric ſerpent*; and Electryon is derived from El-Oc-Tor-Ion, *the divine tauric dove of the ocean.* In a ſimilar manner, Alcmenè is Al-Oc-Mena, *the lunar deity of the ſea*; Amphitryon is Am-Phi-Tor-Ion, *the oracular god of the bull and the dove*; Meſtor is M'Es-Tor, *the great ſolar bull*; Pterelas is P'Tor-El-As, *the bull the god of fire*; and Hippothoè, the concubine of Neptune, is Hippo-Thea, *the divine Hippian Ark.* The conteſt in ſhort was between the votaries of the two great ſuperſtitions, and was that which preceded their final union. A colony of theſe Teleboæ, according to Virgil, formerly inhabited Capreæ in the bay of Naples; and he mentions one of their ancient ſovereigns named *Telon,* who was the father of Oebalus.

> Nec tu carminibus noſtris indictus abibis
> Oebale, quem generâſſe Telon Sebethide nympha
> Fertur: Teleboum Capreas cum regna teneret
> Jam ſenior.——[z].

Telon or Tel-On is *the Sun*; and his ſuppoſed offspring Oebalus is Ob-Al, *the ſerpent deity.*

I have obſerved, that a Cretan colony was led into Italy by Cleolaus, the ſon of Minos.

[z] Æneid. lib. vii. ver. 733.

The

The name, which they aſſumed in their new ſettlement, was that of *Daunii*[a]; a title, which ſeems to be of the ſame origin as the word *Danaus,* and I apprehend, that it is preciſely equivalent to *Noachidæ,* or *deſcendants of Noah.* Minos therefore, the father of Cleolaus, will be the ſame as the *Menu* of Hindoſtan[b], or the *Menes* of Egypt, in other words, the great patriarch; and accordingly he is feigned to have been very powerful at ſea[c]. Hence, from the knowledge which all nations muſt have had of their common progenitor, we find ſo many places called *Minoa.* Thus Megara, the citadel of Argos, bore the additional name of *Minoa*[d]. Thus alſo there was a *Minoa* in Crete[e]; and a promontory, denominated *Minoa,* between Megara and Attica, which formed the port Niſèa[f]. This country was

[a] A Cleolao Minois filio Daunios. Solin. Polyhiſt cap 2.

[b] Hence Sir Wm Jones very happily conjectures, that the Inſtitutes of Menu may poſſibly be no other than the far celebrated, though long loſt, Laws of Minos Pref. to Inſtit. of Menu, p 9

[c] Ἡ τε Μινω θαλαττοκρατια θρυλλειται. Strab. Geog. lib. i. p. 48

[d] Μινωα Φρουριον, ὁμωνυμος και αυτη τῃ Μεγαρικῃ. Ibid. lib. viii. p. 368.

[e] Ibid. lib. x. p. 475.

[f] Μετα δε τας Σκειρωνιδας πετρας, ακρα προκειται Μινωα, ποιουσα τον εν τῃ Νισαιᾳ λιμενα. Ibid lib. ix p 391.

for-

formerly poſſeſſed by the Ionians, or *worſhippers of the dove* [g]. There was alſo a *Minoa* in the iſland of Amorgus; a *Minoa*, which was otherwiſe called *Heraclia*, in Sicily; and a *Minoa*, in Siphnus [h], where likewiſe was the fountain *Minoa*. Gaza was once called *Minoa*; there was a *Minoa* moreover in Arabia; and an iſland of the ſame name not far from Megara. The ancient appellation of Paros [i] was *Minoa* [k]; and laſtly, what is ſomewhat remarkable, *Minoa* was a particular ſpecies of vine [l].

Minos then being the ſcriptural Noah, he is very properly repreſented by the poets as the ſon of the tauric Jupiter and the arkite Europa [m]. He is further ſaid to have eſpouſed Paſiphaè, the ſiſter of Persèis and Circè. Persèis

[g] Το παλαιον μεν ουν Ιωνες ειχον την χωραν ταυτην. Strab. Geog. lib. ix. p. 392.

[h] Siphnus ſeems to have been ſo called from Siph-Nus, *the arkite Noah*.

[i] Paros itſelf is derived from P'Ares, *the Sun*.

[k] Μινωα πολις εν Αμοργω τη νησω, μια των Κυκλαδων· δευτερα πολις Σικελιας· τριτη εν Σιφνω, μια Κυκλαδων· εχει δε Μινωαν καλουμενην κρηνην· εκαλειτο και ἡ Γαζα Μινωα· εςι και Αραβιας· εςι και Κρητης· εςι και αλλη νησος, ου πορρω Μεγαρων· και ἡ Παρος Μινωα. Steph. Byzan. de Urb. p. 562. Prius tamen Minoia quam Paros dicta. Solin. Polyhiſt. cap. 11. Ἡρακλεια πολις περι Σικελιαν ἡ λεγομενη Μινωα. Suid.

[l] Μινωα ειδος αμπελου. Heſych.

[m] Vide ſupra p. 178.

seìs was the concubine [n] of the Sun; and ſhe bore to him Eëtes, who was the king of Colchi, and the father of Medèa. Theſe therefore were all contemporary with the Argonauts; and likewiſe with Phrixus, who is feigned to have croſſed the Hellespont on the back of the ram, ſo much celebrated in Epic poetry for his golden fleece. This fleece he brought to the court of Eëtes, and there eſpouſed his daughter Chalciopè; by whom he became the father of Argus, Melas, Phrontis, and Cutorus [o]. Phrixus I apprehend to be Ph'Erech-Zeus, *the ſolar god of the Ark*; and as for the ram, which he employed in croſſing the Helleſpont, it was one of the ſeveral animals, under which the Ark was typified [p].

[n] Notwithſtanding Persèis is ſaid to have been the concubine of the Sun, and the *ſiſter* of Circè and Paſiphaè; yet both Circè and Paſiphaè were themſelves ſuppoſed to be *daughters* of the Sun

Proxima Circææ raduntur littora terræ;
Dives inacceſſos ubi Solis filia lucos
Aſſiduo reſonat cantu.——

Æneid lib. vii. ver. 10.

Hyginus ſomewhat varies from Apollodorus, and thereby makes the genealogy more conſiſtent. According to him, Perſa was the wife of the Sun, and Eetes, Persèis, Circè, and Paſiphaè, their children. Hyg. Fab. in Præf.

[o] Apollod. Bibl lib. i cap. 9.

[p] Ενιοι δε φασιν αυτον (ſcil. Φριξον) επι κριοπρωρου σκαφους πλευσαι. Schol. in Apoll. Argon. lib. i. ver. 256.

Hence we find, that Phrixus was supposed to be the son of Nebula, or *a cloud*, and the brother of Hercules-Melicerta[q], whose history has already been considered[r].

With regard to Pasiphaè, the wife of Minos, she is said, in the language of fable, to have entertained an unnatural passion for a bull, and in consequence of it to have produced the monster denominated *Minotaur*[s]. This bull however, the imaginary paramour of Pasiphaè, was not of the ordinary race of those animals, but was miraculously sent by Neptune from the abyss of the sea[t]. When therefore we recollect, that Pasiphaè was the daughter of the Sun, that a bull was the most common emblem of Noah, and that the union of the two superstitions was very frequently represented under the image either of a rape or of a marriage; we shall find no difficulty in understanding the true import of this fiction, but shall immediately perceive, that the Minotaur is simply Menu-Tor, *the bull Noah*. Additional light moreover will be thrown upon it by recurring to the history of Europa, the parent of Minos, whom I have already

[q] Hyg. Fab. 1.

[r] Vide supra p. 254, 304.

[s] Herac. de Incred. Hist. cap. 2.— Palæph. de Incred. Hist. cap. 2.

[t] Apollod. Bibl. lib. iii. cap. 1.

shewn

ſhewn to be the ſame as Iſis or the Ark[u]. Agenor, the father of that fabulous heroine, was the ſon of Neptune, and her mother was Telephaſſa. The latter accompanied her ſon Cadmus, and Thaſus another of the children of Neptune, in their ſearch for Europa, and at length arrived along with them in Thrace, on the coaſt of which lies Samothrace, the iſland of the Cabiri[x]. Meanwhile Rhadamanthus, the mythological brother of Minos, and who was afterwards conſtituted one of the infernal judges, fled to Beotia, where he eſpouſed Alcmenè, the mother of Hercules[y]. Now it is remarkable, that the Cretan bull, which Hercules ſubdued in his ſeventh labour, is ſaid by Acuſilaus to be the very ſame as that, which carried Europa from Phenicia; while other writers have ſuppoſed it to be the bull of Paſiphaè, which Neptune ſent from the depths of the ocean[z]. Upon the whole therefore I conclude, that all theſe are mere variations of one tradition, built upon the principal arkite ſymbol: and that Italus, Italotus, and Talus; the Cretan bull, the bull of Europa, and the bull of Paſiphaè; the Mi-

[u] Vide ſupra p 178.

[x] Apollod. Bibl lib iii. cap 1

[y] Ibid

[z] Ibid. lib ii cap 4.

 notaur,

notaur, Afterius[a], and even Jupiter himfelf[b]; are all one and the fame mythological character, the great tauric patriarch worfhipped in conjunction with the Sun.

The Cabiric fuperftition appears in the early ages to have been attended with circumftances of very great cruelty. Hence originated the fable that Minos compelled the Athenians to fend feven youths, and feven virgins, to be yearly devoured by the Minotaur[c]. This, as we have repeatedly feen, was the precife number of the Corybantes, the Titans, and the Cabiri; in other words, the

[a] Tzetzes plainly tells us, that Talus or Afterius was the Minotaur. Ὁ Αϛεριος ὗτος εϛιν ὁ και Μινοταυρος· ειχε δε, ὡς φασι, ταυρου προσωπον. Tzet. in Lycoph. ver. 1301. This Afterius, Talus, or Minotaur, was the fuppofed fon of Anac, concerning whom more will be faid hereafter. Pauf. Attic. p. 87.—Pauf. Achaic. p. 524. Talus or Taurus was likewife the fame perfon as Eryx, who is faid to have been the fon of the arkite Venus by Butes, (Hyg. Fab. 260.) or, according to fome writers, by Neptune. (Apoll. Bibl. lib. ii. cap. 5.—Serv. in Æneid. lib. v. p. 356.—Tzet. in Lycoph. ver. 866.) Hence Eryx, who is no other than Erechi, *the god of the Ark*, as his imaginary father is Bu-Dus, *the tauriform deity*, is ftyled by Lycophron *Taurus*.

Ἥξει δε Ταυρου γυμναδας κακοξενους
Παλης κονιϛρας.—— Caffan. ver. 866.

Upon which Tzetzes obferves, Ταυρον δε τον Ερυκα φησι.

[b] Ὁ Λυκοφρων τον Αϛεριον Δια λεγει πατερα ειναι του Σαρπηδονος, Μινωος, και Ῥαδαμανθυος. Tzet. in Lycoph. ver. 1301.

[c] Apollod. Bibl. lib. iii. cap. 14.

com-

complement of the Ark, exclusive of Noah: and the story of their being devoured relates, I doubt not, to the horrid human sacrifices, with which the idolatry of the early ages was polluted. The seven sacella, in which victims were offered up to the bull Moloch; were constructed with a similar allusion to the number of the Cabiri, and the number of the planets; while Moloch himself was evidently the same deity as the Minotaur [d].

Before the mythology of the Cretans be dismissed, it will be proper to notice a remarkable personage, who was highly venerated by them, under the name of *Britomartis*, or *Dictynna*. Britomartis is represented by Apuleius as being the same goddess as Diana, Rhea, or Venus [e]; and she is said by Nonnus to have been the daughter of the Ocean [f]: but Pausanias makes her the offspring of Jupiter by Carmè the daughter of Eubulus. This Eubulus was supposed by the Cretans to be the son of Carmanor, who purified Apollo after the slaughter of the serpent

[d] Vide supra p 190.

[e] Apul. Metam. lib. xi. Vide supra p 147.

[f] Οφρα νεη Βριτομαρτις εγω φυγοδεμνος ακουσω,
Ἡν ποτε Ποντος ετικτε.
Nonni Dionys. lib. xxxiii. p. 551.

Python[g]: but, according to Cicero, he was one of the Diofcori or Cabiri, and the fon of Jupiter, and Proferpine[h]; or, according to the Orphic poet[i], and Diodorus Siculus[k], of Ceres. Hence the connection between the Cabiri, and Britomartis, is fufficiently evident. But the fulleft account of her is given by Antoninus Liberalis. This writer informs us, that Carmè, her mother, was the daughter of Phenix, the fon of Agenor king of Tyre; and that her father was Jupiter. She was born in Phenicia, whence fhe came to Argos. She next proceeded to Cephallenia, where fhe was worfhipped under the title of *Laphria*; and afterwards went into Crete. Here fhe was purfued by Minos, whofe affections fhe had gained; and, in order to efcape him, fhe hid herfelf among the nets of

[g] Φασι δε οἱ Κρητες Καρμανορος του καθηραντος Απολλωνα επι φονῳ του Πυθωνος, παιδα Ευβουλον ειναι· Διος δε και Καρμης της Ευβουλου Βριτομαρτιν γενεσθαι. Pauf. Corin. p. 180.

[h] Διοσκουροι etiam apud Graios multis modis nominantur. Primi tres, qui appellantur Anactes, Athenis ex Jove rege antiquiffimo et Proferpina nati, Tritopatreus, Eubuleus, Dionyfius. Cic. de Nat. Deor. lib. iii. cap. 21.

[i] Orph. Hymn. 40.

[k] Βριτομαρτιν δε, την προσαγορευομενην Δικτυνναν, μυθολογουσι γενεσθαι μεν εν Καινοι της Κρητης εκ Διος και Καρμης της Ευβουλου, του γεννηθεντος εκ Δημητρος. Diod. Sic. Bibl. lib. v. p. 342.

fome

fome fishermen: a circumftance, which procured her the name of *Dictynna.* At length fhe fled to Egina, and was no more feen by mortal eyes. The inhabitants of the ifland erected a fhrine to her in the temple of Diana, and beftowed upon her the appellation of *Aphaè*[l].

Britomartis, being the fame mythological character as Diana, Venus, or Rhea, muft evidently, like them, be a perfonification of the Ark worfhipped in conjunction with the Moon. Hence her wanderings, like thofe of Venus in queft of Adonis, of Ifis in queft of Ofiris, and of Ceres in queft of Proferpine, will relate to the erratic ftate of the Ark upon the furface of the waters. Accordingly fhe is fometimes reprefented as the daughter of the Ocean, and fometimes as the daughter of Jupiter or the tauric Noah; and is feigned, in the courfe of her travels, to have arrived at Argos, or *the city of the Ark.* Solinus informs us, that her title *Britomartis* fignified, in the Cretan language, *the fweet virgin*[m]; and the name feems to have been beftowed upon her in confequence of the fame allegorical mode

[l] Anton Lib Metam. cap. 40.

[m] Cretes Dianam religiofiffime venerantur, Βριτομαρτιν gentiliter nominantes, quod fermone noftro fonat *virginem dulcem* Sol. Polyhift. cap 17.

 of

of fabulizing, as that which ſuppoſes a virgin to have been the mother of Fohi, Buddha, and Perſeus. With regard to her other appellation *Dictynna,* which the Greeks, agreeably to their uſual cuſtom, derived from a word in their own language [n], it is compounded of Dag-Tinin, *a ſea-monſter*; one of the moſt uſual ſymbols of the Ark, as we have repeatedly ſeen, being a huge fiſh. Conſidered then as the Ark, Britomartis is deſcribed as being beloved by Minos, or Menus, *the patriarch Noah*; and as being deſcended from Agenor the father of Europa, and from the Cabiric deities Eubulus, Jupiter, Ceres, and Proſerpine: while, conſidered as the waning Moon, ſhe is celebrated under the title of *Aphaè,* and is ſuppoſed to have concealed herſelf from the ſight of men.

We have now ſeen the introduction of the Cabiric rites into Italy by the Pelaſgi, the Lydians, and the Cretans; it will next be proper to notice Enèas, and the Ilienſians. This hero, after his departure from Troy, is ſaid by Livy to have firſt landed in Macedon; whence he proceeded to Sicily,

[n] It may be obſerved by the way, that Dictys, *a net,* from which the Greeks derived Dictynna, probably ſprings from the ſame Hebrew root Dag, *a fiſh.*

and

and afterwards took up his final abode in Italy [o]. Along with him he brought the Cabiric Penates, or, as Virgil ſtyles them, the Great Gods. Of theſe deities Dionyſius of Halicarnaſſus has given us a very particular account. He informs us, that the Penates were called in the Greek language, *Patroï, Genethlii, Cteſii, Muchii* [p], or *Ercii* [q]; and he deſcribes the Trojan Gods, as being very ancient ſtatues of two young men, holding ſpears in their hands, and inſcribed with the word *Denas* [r]; which he conceives to be equivalent

[o] Liv. Hiſt. lib. i cap. 1.

[p] The import of *Muchius* ſeems to be *the great diluvian*. Hence we find that Hercules was denominated *Machius*; (Orph. Argon. ver. 24) and that the great god both of the Iriſh and the Perſians was called *Much*, and Ireland itſelf *Mucinis*, or Much-Innis, *the iſland of Much*. (See Collect. de Reb. Hiber. vol. iv. p. 77. Pref.) A ſmall iſland upon the coaſt of Scotland is likewiſe called *Muck*, moſt probably from the ſame god *Much*; whoſe name appears to enter alſo into the compoſition of *Mucenæ*, a town uſually celebrated in conjunction with Argos.

[q] Τους δε θεους τουτους Ῥωμαιοι μεν Πενατας καλουσιν· οἱ δε εξερμηνευοντες εις την Ἑλλαδα γλωσσαν τουνομα, οἱ μεν Πατρωους αποφαινουσιν, οἱ δε Γενεθλιους· εισι δ' οἱ Κτησιους, αλλοι δε Μυχιους, οἱ δε Ἑρκιους. Dion Hal. Ant Rom. lib i. cap. 67. *Ercius* is derived from Erech, *the Ark*; and *Patrous*, from Patar (פטר), *to diſmiſs, to open*, or *to let out*, in alluſion to the egreſs from the Ark For ſome further obſervations upon this word, vide infra chap. viii.

[r] Denas ſeems to be Da-Noas.

to

to *Penas*, the found of the letter *P* not having been then difcovered. For a further account of them he refers to Calliftratus, who compiled a hiftory of Samothrace; to Satyrus, an old mythological writer; and to the poet Aratinus, from whofe works he has extracted the following particulars.

Chrysè, the daughter of Palas, having efpoufed Dardanus, brought him as a marriage portion the Palladia, and the Myfteries of the Great Gods. Thefe Myfteries, when the Arcadians left Peloponnefus on account of a deluge [s], Dardanus eftablifhed in Samothrace, enjoining at the fame time the ftricteft fecrecy refpecting the names of the deities, to whofe honour they were devoted [t]. Afterwards he carried the greateft part of the people with him into Afia; leaving however the Myfteries in poffeffion of the iflanders, while he conveyed away the Palladia, and the ftatues of the Gods. In procefs of time, his pofterity founded Ilium, and removed to it the rites of the fame Great Gods. Thefe they preferved with the utmoft care, building for them a temple in their citadel, and confidering them in the light of their peculiar guar-

[s] Vide fupra p. 337.

[t] Dionyfius mentions, that thefe rites ftill continued even in his time to be celebrated by the Samothracians.

dians.

dians. When at length the city was taken by the Greeks, Enèas carried off the Myſteries of the Great Gods, and the remaining Palladium into Italy, the other having been ſtolen by Ulyſſes and Diomede.

Such is the account given by thoſe ancient mythologiſts: and, upon their authority, Dionyſius pronounces the ſtatues of the Cabiri, which were ſeen by himſelf, to be the ſame as thoſe worſhipped in Samothrace, and aſſerts, that the Palladium was ſtill religiouſly preſerved in the temple of Veſta [u].

The figures of the two young men are undoubtedly thoſe of the Dioſcori, of whom more ſhall be ſaid, when I come to treat of the Argonautic expedition; and with regard to the Palladium, the reader will recollect, that, according to Lycophron, it came originally from Phenicia.

Several different opinions however were entertained reſpecting the Trojan Penates. Nigidius, and Cornelius Labeo, ſeem to think, that they were Apollo and Neptune, by whom the walls of Ilium were built; Macrobius is inclined to believe them to be Jupiter, Juno, and Minerva, who were worſhipped in the capitol, in one and the ſame temple, firſt built

[u] Dion. Halic. Ant. Rom lib. i cap. 67, 68, 69

by

by Tarquinius Priſcus, a prince deeply converſant in the Samothracian myſteries; and Caſſius Hemina ſcruples not to aſſert the identity of the Penates, and the Gods of Samothrace[x]. Servius maintains, that the Great Gods, who were worſhipped at Rome, and whom Enèas brought with him from Samothrace, were Jupiter, Minerva, and Mercury[y]; Tertullian deſcribes the Samothracian Cabiri, as being three in number, though he does not mention their names[z]; and Dionyſius of Halicarnaſſus obſerves, that many were of opinion, that the Cabiric rites of Troy and Samothrace were preſerved in the temple of Veſta, during the reign of Numa[a]. Accord-

[x] Macrob. Saturn. lib. iii. cap. 4. ſee alſo Arnob. adv. Gent. lib. iii. p. 123.

[y] Dii Magni ſunt Jupiter, Minerva, Mercurius, qui Romæ colebantur. Serv. in Æneid. lib. iii. p. 274. Ut Magnos Deos accipias Jovem, Minervam, Mercurium, quos Æneas de Samothracia ſuſtulit. Ibid. lib. viii. p. 532.

[z] Tres aræ trinis diis parent, magnis, potentibus. Eoſdem Samothracas exiſtimant. Tertull. de Spectac. cap. 8.

[a] Οἱ μεν, εκ των εν Σαμοθρακῃ λεγοντες ἱερων μοιραν ειναι τῳ Αινειᾳ φυλαττομενην την ενθαδε· Δαρδανου μεν εις την ὑφ᾽ ἑαυτȣ κτισθεισαν πολιν εκ της νησȣ τα ἱερα μετενεγκαμενου· Αινειου δε, ὁτε εφυγεν εκ της Τρωαδος, ἁμα τοις αλλοις και ταυτα κομισαντος εις Ιταλιαν. Οἱ δε το διοπετες Παλλαδιον αποφαινοντες ειναι το παρα Ιλιευσι γενομενον. Ant. Rom. lib. ii. cap. 66. This circumſtance induces me to think, that the Arician foreſt, in which Numa held his nocturnal conferences with the nymph Egeria, was ſo denominated by ſome of the Pelaſgic or Cretan ſettlers from Arech, *the Ark*.

Ex-

ing to Mnaſeas, the Cabiri of Samothrace were called *Axieros*, *Axiocerſa*, and *Axiocerſus*. Axieros was Ceres; Axiocerſa, Proſerpine; and Axiocerſus, Pluto. To theſe a fourth was added, by the name of *Caſmilus*, or *Mercury*. Some however ſuppoſed, that there were originally only two Cabiri; the elder being Jupiter, and the younger, Bacchus [b].

There will be no great difficulty in reconciling theſe various opinions, when we call to mind the obſervations, which have been already made reſpecting the polyonymy of the

Extinctum Latiæque nurus, populuſque, patreſque,
Deflevere Numam; nam conjux urbe relicta
Vallis Aricinæ denſis latet abdita ſylvis.

Ovid. Metam. lib xv. ver. 486.

Dionyſius ſpeaks likewiſe of a temple of Venus at Actium, near which was another temple, dedicated to the Great Gods, and ſaid to have been built by the followers of Eneas, in the courſe of their voyage to Italy. Εν Ακτιῳ μεν Αφροδιτης Αινιαδος ἱερον, και πλησιον αυτου θεων μεγαλων, ἁ και εις εμε ην. Ant Rom. lib. i cap. 50. The word *Actium* ſeems to have derived its name from Ac, *the Ocean*.

[b] Μυουνται δε εν τη Σαμοθρακη τοις Καβειροις, ὡν Μνασεας φησι και τα ονοματα. Τεσσαρες δ' εισι τον αριθμον· Αξιερος, Αξιοκερσα, Αξιοκερσος. Αξιερος μεν ουν εστιν ἡ Δημητηρ· Αξιοκερσα δε, ἡ Περσεφονη· Αξιοκερσος δε, ὁ Αιδης. Ὁ δε προστιθεμενος τεταρτος Κασμιλος, ὁ Ἑρμης εστιν, ὡς ἱστορει Διονυσοδωρος — Καβειροι δε δοκουσι προσαγορευεσθαι απο Καβειρων των κατα Φρυγιαν ορων, επει εντευθεν μετηνεχθησαν. Οἱ δε δυο ειναι τους Καβειρους φασι προτερον· πρεσβυτερον μεν Δια, νεωτερον δε Διονυσον. Schol in Apoll. Argon lib. i. ver 917.

ſolar

solar deity, and the intimate connection, which subsists between the apparently different goddesses of heathen mythology. The rites of the Cabiri are in fact a symbolical history of the union of the arkite and solar superstitions; and hence we shall not be surprized to see the Dove, the Ark, the Ocean, and the divine Wisdom, worshipped in conjunction with the bright luminaries of heaven.

In consequence of the Iliensian Mysteries being thus early imported into Italy, we shall find, in the account of the ancient kings of Latium, several Trojan, or, to speak more properly, Phenician names. Thus Ascanius, the son of Enèas, is As-Chan, *the priest of fire*; and his other appellation, *Ilus* [c], is the very same as that by which the Phenicians designated their god Cronus [d]. In a similar manner, the mother of Romulus and Remus, the fabulous concubine of Mars or M'Ares, *the great Sun*, is indifferently denominated *Ilia*, and *Rhea Sylvia* [e]; and one of their ancestors

[c] At puer Ascanius, cui nunc cognomen Iulo
Additur (Ilus erat, dum res stetit Ilia regno.)
Æneid. lib. i. ver. 271.

[d] Euseb. Præp. Evan. lib. i. cap. 10.

[e] Æneid. lib. i. ver. 278.—Liv. Hist. lib. i. cap. 3.

tors

tors bears the title of *Atys*, which was alſo the name both of Bacchus, and of a king of Lydia, whoſe ſon Tyrſenus led the firſt colony into Etruria[f]. Thus alſo Acca Laɾentia, the nurſe of Romulus, ſeems to have derived the firſt of her names from Ac, *the Ocean*, and the ſecond from El-Aran, *the divine Ark*[g]; while the Palatium, which was fortified by that prince, was probably ſo called from Palas, the father-in-law of Dardanus, as Palas himſelf received his appellation from P'Al-As, *the god of fire*. What Livy ſays upon this ſubject is much to the ſame purpoſe: he deduces the word *Palatium* from *Pallantèus*, a city of Arcadia; and mentions the rites, which were there inſtituted in honour of the Lycèan Pan by Evander's colony of Arcadians[h].

The introduction of the Cabiric rites into Italy will likewiſe account for the tradition, which brings the arkite Hercules into that country, and repreſents him as the gueſt of Evander[i]. To this circumſtance a claſs of prieſts, inſtituted by Numa, and denominated Argèan,

[f] Liv Hiſt. lib i cap 5

[g] Sabinus Maſſurius in primo Memorialium ſecutus quoſdam hiſtoriæ ſcriptores Accam Larentiam Romuli nutricem fuiſſe dicit Aul. Gell. Noct Att lib. vi. cap 7.

[h] Liv Hiſt. lib i cap 5.

[i] Ibid cap 7.

owed

owed their origin [k], being ſo called, according to Varro, from the chieftains, who accompanied the Argive Hercules, and ſettled in Saturnia [l]. The Argèan plain at Rome alſo, as we learn from Fabius Pictor, received its appellation from the Argive Hercules [m]; who is ſaid by Pſeudo-Beroſus to have been the ſon of Oſiris, and to have been ſurnamed *Arnus*, *Lubarnus*, or *Muſarnus* [n]. All theſe titles relate to the arkite worſhip. Arnus is Arn-Nus, *the arkite Noah*; Muſarnus is Mus-Arn-Nus, *the diluvian arkite Noah*; and Lubarnus is Lubar-Nus, *the Noah of the Armenian hill Lubar*. Epiphanius accordingly mentions, that in the high tract of country in Armenia, called *the Gordyèan hills*, where, as we learn from Joſephus, the Ark reſted, one mountain in particular, loftier than the reſt, bore in his days the name of *Lubar*, which, in the Armenian language, ſignifies *the deſcending place* [o].

It is poſſible alſo, that the preceding obſer-

[k] Liv. Hiſt. lib. i. cap. 21.

[l] Varr. de Ling. Lat. lib. iv.

[m] Subſidens ſeptem collibus, campus Argeus dictus eſt ab Argo Evandri hoſpite, et comitibus Argivi Herculis, qui ad Evandrum venerunt, et in Saturnia ſubſederunt. Hinc extrema Argileta dicuntur. Fab. Pictor. de aureo ſæculo. Fol. 130.

[n] Beroſ. Ant. lib. v. fol. 74.

[o] Epiph. adv. Hær. lib. i.—Joſeph. Ant. Jud. lib. i. p. 12.

vations,

vations, may throw ſome light upon the very obſcure hiſtory of the Palici. Theſe are ſaid by Macrobius to have been two in number; and he very highly applauds the poet Virgil, for his accuracy in having recorded them.

Stabat in egregiis Arcentis filius armis,
Pictus acu chlamydem, et ferrugine clarus Ibera,
Inſignis facie; genitor quem miſerat Arcens
Eductum matris luco Symetia circum
Flumina, pinguis ubi et placabilis ara Palici [p].

The ſon of Arcens ſhone amid the reſt,
In glittering armour, and a purple veſt.
Fair was his face, his eyes inſpiring love,
Bred by his father in the Martian grove:
Where the fat altars of Palicus flame,
And ſent in arms to purchaſe early fame.

Dryden.

Of the hiſtory of theſe Palici Macrobius gives us the following particulars. The nymph Thalia, having conceived by Jupiter near the Sicilian river Symetus, beſought the earth to open, in order that ſhe might eſcape the vengeance of Juno. Her prayer was anſwered, and ſhe brought forth her offspring beneath the ſurface of the ground; who, afterwards emerging to open day, acquired the

[p] Æneid. lib ix. ver. 582.

name of *Palici*[q]. Near this place were certain lakes of an immenſe depth, which the inhabitants highly venerated, eſteeming them the brethren of the Palici. The water contained in them was ſtrongly impregnated with ſulphur[r]; and if any perſon ſwore by them, his oath was deemed peculiarly obligatory, inſomuch that they conſtituted a kind of ordeal for the purpoſe of deciding differences[s]. Macrobius adds, that, according to Polemo, the Palici were reckoned *autochthones*, or *aborigines*; and he obſerves, that Eſchylus the Sicilian particularly notices their paſſing from darkneſs into light[t]: Heſychius however main-

[q] Απο τυ παλιν ιεσθαι.

[r] Antigonus Caryſtius mentions, that there was a ſmall building near the Palician lake, in which if any perſon lay down, he immediately died; but if he remained in an upright poſture, he experienced no inconvenience. Της Σικελιας εν Παληκιεις οικοδομηθηναι τοπον· εις ὃν ὁςις αν εισελθῃ, ει μεν κατακλιθειη, αποθνησκει· ει δε περιπατοιη, ωδεν πασχει. Antig. Caryſt. de Hiſt. Mir. cap. 133. This place was evidently of the ſame nature with the famous *grotto del cane*; in both caſes, the ſulphureous vapour roſe only to a certain height, and thus ſuffocated perſons in a reclining poſture, while thoſe, who were erect, remained uninjured. Springs of water were always deemed ſacred by the ancients, but particularly thoſe impregnated with ſulphur; hence the very name of ſulphur, θειον, ſignifies *ſomething divine.*

[s] Macrob. Saturn. lib. v. cap. 19.

[t] Τι δηθει αυτοις ονομα τιθενται βροτοι;
Σεμνους Παλικους Ζευς εφιεται καλειν,

tains,

tains, that the Palici were the children of Adranus [u]. This Adianus I apprehend to be Adar-Nus, *the illustrious Noah*: whence I think it probable, that the Palici were the same as the Dioscori; that the oath by their consecrated lakes, like that by the waters of Styx, alludes to the postdiluvian oath of God; and that their connection with Juno, and their emerging from night into day, relates to the dove on the one hand, and to the passing of the Noëtical family from the obscurity of the Ark, on the other. The consecrated lake was a very usual appendage of Cabiric devotion, as sufficiently appears from those of Buto and Cotylè, and as will hereafter be made yet more evident from a variety of other instances [x].

The very early introduction of the Cabiric Mysteries into Italy further appears from the

Η και Παλικων ευλογως μενει φατις;
Παλιν γαρ ἱκυσ' εκ σκοτους τοδ' ες φαος.

Æschyl. apud Macrob. Ibid.

[u] Παλικοι. Αδρανῳ δυο γεννωνται υἱοι Παλικοι, οἱ νυν της Συρακυσιας εισι κρατηρες οἱ καλουμενοι Παλικοι, οἱ και κατῳκησαντες αυτῃ.

[x] Vide infia chap. x. It is possible, that Palas, Pallas, and the Palici, may have derived their respective titles from the Indian tribe of the Palli; who seem to have given to the holy land its name of *Palestine*, and to have been the original inventors of the history of the Theban Edipus. See a very curious Dissertation on Egypt, &c. by Captain Wilford. Asiat Res. vol. iii.

 fiction

fiction of the Argonautic voyagers having touched there. The miraculous vessel, in which they sailed, is said to have declared with a human voice, that they would find no termination of their troubles till they reached Ausonia. Accordingly, after coasting along the shore of Etruria, they at length arrived at Eëa, where they were purified by Circè[y]. Hence we find an Italian port named *Eëtes*, where the Argo was feigned to have anchored; and near it a place called *Circèum*, and a river denominated *Titon*.

> ——— Αμφι Κιρκαιυ ναπας,
> Αργυς τε κλεινον ὁρμον Αιητην μεγαν,
> Λιμνης τε Φορκης Μαρσιωνιδος ποτα,
> Τιτωνιον τε χευμα[z].———

Upon the banks of Crathis, another Italian river, which was reported to have the peculiar property of changing the hair of those, who bathed in it, into a fiery colour[a], the

[y] Ἡ ναυς φθεγγεται, μη ληξειν την οργην του Διος, ει μη πορευθεντες εις την Αυσονιαν.—οἱ δε—παραμειψαμενοι Τυῤῥηνιαν, ηλθον εις Αιαιαν, ενθα Κιρκη ἱκεται γενομενοι καθαιρονται. Apollod. Bibl. lib. i. cap. 9.

[z] Lycoph. Cassan. ver. 1273. Upon which Tzetzes remarks: Αιητης λιμην εν Ιταλιᾳ—Τιτων ποταμος Ιταλιας, εγγυς Κιρκαιυ, ὁ Κιρκαιον απο της Κιρκης καλειται.

[a] Κραθις, ποταμος Ιταλιας, τῶν λυομενων το ὑδωρ αυλε πυρσαινων τας χαιτας. Tzet. in Lycoph. ver. 1021. This Italian river Crathis received its name from the Arcadian Crathis, into which

Colchians, ſent in purſuit of Media, were feigned to have built cities.

> Κραθις δε γειτων, ηδε Μυλακων ὁροις
> Χωρος συνοικους δεξεται Κολχων Πολαις,
> Μαςηρας ἐς θυγατρος εςειλεν βαρυς
> Αιας, Κερινθου τ' αρχος, Ειδυιας ποσις [b].

We have hitherto traced the introduction of the Cabiric rites into Italy by the Pelaſgi, the Tyrrheni, the Cretans, the Trojans, and the fabulous Argonauts: let us now extend our reſearches into the ancient empire of Hindoſtan.

It has been obſerved, upon the authority of Mnaſeas, that one of the Samothracian Cabiri was Pluto, or Aidoneus, who is ſaid by Fulgentius, Cicero, and Julius Firmicus, to be the ſame as Plutus, the god of riches [c]. In

which the fountain Styx emptied itſelf. Vide ſupra p 264. note h.

[b] Lycoph. Caſſ ver. 1021. Πολαι, πολεις εισιν ηπειρου, ὑπο Κολχων κλισθεισαι.—το δ' εξης ὁυτως· Ὁ Κραθις δε χωρος δεξεται αυτους Σιρινους, ὁ γειτων ταις πολαις των Κολχων, και ταις των Μυλακων ὁροις. Tzet. in loc. In conſequence, I apprehend, of the introduction of the Cabiric worſhip into Italy, a tradition prevailed, that Jaſon buried Medea at Buthrotum, and that their ſon reigned over the Marſi. Medeam ab Jaſone Buthroti ſepultam, filiumque ejus Marſis imperâſſe. Solin. Polyhiſt. cap 2 The Marſi ſeem to have been ſo called from their worſhip of M'Ars, *the great Sun.*

[c] Quartum etiam Plutonem dicunt terrarum præſulem : πλου-

a ſimilar manner, the Hindoo Plutus is denominated *Cuvera*[d], or *Cubera*, which is evidently a mere variation of the word *Cabir*; and he is ſuppoſed moreover, like Cronus, Sydyk, and Mercury[e], to be joined with *ſeven* other genii, though he is, at the ſame time, eſteemed inferior to the three great gods, Brahma, Viſhnou, and Seeva[f].

The moſt ſingular proof however, that the Cabiri were not unknown to the Hindoos, is adduced by Captain Wilford. "In the *Adbuta-Coſa*," ſays he, "we find the following legends, which have an obvious relation to the deities worſhipped in the myſteries of Samothrace.

"In *Patala*, or the infernal regions, reſides the ſovereign queen of the *Nagas*, (large ſnakes or dragons:) ſhe is beautiful, and her

πλουτος enim Græce divitiæ dicuntur, ſolis terris credentes divitias deputari. Fulg. Mythol. lib. i. cap. 4. Thus likewiſe Cicero: Terrena autem vis omnis atque natura Diti patri dedicata eſt: qui Dives, ut apud Græcos Πλȣ́των, quia et recidant omnia in terras, et oriantur e terris. Cic. de Nat. Deor. lib. ii. cap. 26. And Julius Firmicus: Dives ruſticus, cui propter divitias Πλȣ́των fuit nomen. Jul. Firm. de Err. Prof. Rel. p. 17.

[d] Cuvera is the ſame as Cubera, *V* and *B* being letters of the ſame organ.

[e] Vide ſupra p. 389.

[f] Aſiat. Reſ. vol. i. p. 247.

"name

" name is *Aſyoruca*. There, in a cave, ſhe " performed *Tapaſya* with ſuch rigorous au- " ſterity, that fire ſprang from her body, and " formed numerous *agni-tiraths*, (places of " ſacred fire) in *Patala*. Theſe fires, forc- " ing their way through the earth, waters, " and mountains, formed various openings, " or mouths, called from thence *the flaming* " *mouths*, or *juala-much'i*. By *Samudr*, or " Oceanus, a daughter was born unto her " called *Rama-Devi*. She is moſt beautiful; " ſhe is *Lacſhmi*; and her name is *Aſyotcer-* " *ſha* or *Aſyotcriſhta*. Like a jewel ſhe re- " mains concealed in the ocean.

" The *Dharma-Rajah*, or king of juſtice, " has two countenances; one is mild and full " of benevolence: thoſe alone, who abound " with virtue, ſee it. He holds a court of " juſtice, where are many aſſiſtants, among " whom are many juſt and pious kings: *Chi-* " *tragupta* acts as chief ſecretary. Theſe holy " men determine what is juſt or unjuſt. His " *(Dharma-Rajah's)* ſervant is called *Carma-* " *la*: he brings the righteous on celeſtial cars, " which go of themſelves, whenever holy " men are to be brought in, according to the " directions of the *Dharma-Rajah*, who is the " ſovereign of the *Pitris*. This is called his " *divine countenance*, and the righteous alone

" do

" do ſee it. His other countenance or form
" is called *Yama*; this the wicked alone can
" ſee. It has large teeth, and a monſtrous
" body. *Yama* is the lord of *Patala*; there
" he orders ſome to be beaten, ſome to be
" cut to pieces, and ſome to be devoured by
" monſters. His ſervant is called *Caſhmala*,
" who, with ropes round their necks, drags
" the wicked over rugged paths, and throws
" them headlong into hell. He is unmerci-
" ful, and hard is his heart: every body trem-
" bles at the ſight of him.

" According to Mnaſeas, as cited by the
" ſcholiaſt of Apollonius Rhodius, the names
" of the Cabirian gods were *Axieros*, or *Ce-*
" *res*; *Axiocerſa*, or *Proſerpine*; *Axiocerſos*,
" or *Pluto*: to whom they add a fourth
" called *Caſmilus*, the ſame with *the infernal*
" *Mercury*.

" *Axieros* is obviouſly derived from *Aſyo-*
" *ruca*, or rather from *Aſyoru*, or *Aſyorus*;
" for ſuch is the primitive form; which ſig-
" nifies literally, *ſhe whoſe face is moſt beauti-*
" *ful*.

" *Axiocerſa* is derived from *Aſyotcerſa*, a
" word of the ſame import with the former,
" and which was the ſacred name of Proſer-
" pine. This is obviouſly derived from the
" Sanſcrit *Praſarparni*, or *ſhe who is ſurrounded*
" by

" *by large ſnakes and dragons.* Nonnus re-
" preſents her as ſurrounded by two enor-
" mous ſnakes, who conſtantly watched over
" her. She was raviſhed by Jupiter in the
" ſhape of a dragon. She was generally ſup-
" poſed to be his daughter; but the Arcadi-
" ans, according to Pauſanias, inſiſted that
" ſhe was the daughter of Ceres and Nep-
" tune; with whom the ancient mytholo-
" giſts often confound Oceanus.——

" *Axiocerſos,* or in Sanſcrit *Aſyotcerſa,* or
" *Aſyotcerſas,* was Pluto or Dis, and was
" meant for *Viſhnou.* *Viſhnou* is always re-
" preſented as extremely beautiful; but I
" never found *Aſyotcerſa* among any of his
" titles: he is ſometimes called *Atcerſa,* a
" word of the ſame import.

" *Caſhmala* or *Caſhmalas* is obviouſly the
" *Caſmilus* of the weſtern mythologiſts. The
" appellation of *Cabiri,* as a title of theſe
" deities, is unknown to the Hindoos.—The
" *Cuveras* or *Cuberas,* as it is generally pro-
" nounced, are a tribe of inferior deities, poſ-
" ſeſſed of immenſe riches, and who are ac-
" quainted with all places under or above
" ground, abounding with precious metals
" and gems. Their hiſtory, in the *Puranas,*
" begins with the firſt *Menu*; and no men-
" tion is made in it of floods, at leaſt my

" learned friends tell me ſo—Diodorus Sicu-
" lus ſays, that the invention of fire, and the
" working of mines, was attributed to the
" Cabiri: and we find a Cabirus repreſented
" with a hammer in his hand[g]."

In this portion of Hindoo mythology, we may obſerve the very ſame alluſion to the union of the two ſuperſtitions, which pervades the whole claſſical hiſtory of the Cabiri. Aſyoruca is deſcribed as the queen of ſerpents, and the conſort of Oceanus; while her daughter Aſyotcerſha remains concealed like a jewel in the boſom of the ſea. There is likewiſe the ſame reference to the fabulous infernal regions; and the office of the Samothracian *Caſmilus* is accurately aſſigned to the Hindoo *Caſhmala*.

From Hindoſtan I ſhall proceed to Armenia, which is generally allowed to be the country, in which the Ark firſt landed after the cataſtrophè of the deluge; hence, according to Nicolaus Damaſcenus, a tradition had conſtantly prevailed there, that ſome ancient perſonage had been conveyed in an Ark to the ſummit of mount *Baris*[h]. This hill, denominated *Lubar* by Epiphanius, was one

[g] Aſiat. Reſ. vol. v.

[h] Joſeph. Ant. Jud. lib. i. p. 12.

of thoſe, which compoſed the chain of mountains called *Cordyèan,* from Cor-Du, *the ſolar god,* who was there worſhipped in conjunction with the arkite deities, or Cabiri[i]. The ſuperſtition continued to flouriſh even in the days of Strabo; for he mentions a city in Armenia, which bore the name of *Cabira,* and in which was a temple of the arkite Moon, intitled *Pharnacum,* from Ph' Arn-Ac, *the Ark of the ocean.* In alluſion to the poſtdiluvian oath of the Moſt High, an oath by the fortune of the king and the temple *Pharnacum* was, like that by the waters of Styx, deemed peculiarly ſacred and obligatory[k].

We meet with ſome traces of the Cabiri alſo in Pamphylia, the inhabitants of which country had a god, whom they ſtyled *Caber.* He ſeems, like all the other Cabiri, to have been a diluvian, or marine deity; and accordingly his ſacrifices conſiſted of ſmall ſalted fiſh[l].

[i] Joſeph. Ant Jud. lib. i. p. 12.

[k] Εχει δε και το ἱερον Μηνος, Φαρνακυ (leg. Φαρνακου) καλυμενον— Ετιμησαν δ' οἱ βασιλεις το ἱερον τυτο ὁυτως εις ὑπερβολην, ὡςε τον βασιλικον καλουμενον ὁρκον τουτον αποφηναι τυχην βασιλεως, και Μηνα Φαρνακου· εςι δε τουτο της Σεληνης το ἱερον. Strab. Geog. lib. xii. p. 557.

[l] Phaſelitas in Pamphylia legimus, piſciculis ſale conditis placare deos conſueviſſe, in primis vero Cabro Deo ſalſamentis

The territory of Pergamus likewiſe was ſacred to the Cabiri; and its inhabitants preſerved a tradition, that their gods were originally Arcadians, or Arkites, who came into Aſia along with Telephus [m]. This Telephus, as we have already ſeen, was the ſon of Hercules and Augè; and he was feigned to have been expoſed along with his mother in an ark.

tis item divinam rem peregiſſe. Cœl. Rhodig. Lect. Ant. lib. xii. cap. 1.

m Ἡν δε νεμονται οἱ Περγαμηνοι, Καβειρων ἱεραν φασι το αρχαιον. Αὐτοι δε Αρκαδες εθελουσιν ειναι των ὁμȣ Τηλεφῳ διαβαντων ες την Ασιαν. Pauſ. Attic. p. 12.

END OF VOL. I.

CPSIA information can be obtained
at www.ICGtesting.com
Printed in the USA
BVHW040807290119
538866BV00007BB/142/P

9 780342 776